MY LIFE, MY TIMES, MY POEMS

by

John Anthony Banfield

authorHOUSE®

AuthorHouse™ UK Ltd.
500 Avebury Boulevard
Central Milton Keynes, MK9 2BE
www.authorhouse.co.uk
Phone: 08001974150

© *2009 John Anthony Banfield. All rights reserved.*

No part of this book may be reproduced, stored in a retrieval system, or transmitted by any means without the written permission of the author.

First published by AuthorHouse 1/20/2009

ISBN: 978-1-4389-5000-6 (sc)
ISBN: 978-1-4389-4999-4 (hc)

Printed in the United States of America
Bloomington, Indiana

This book is printed on acid-free paper.

I dedicate this book to my wife Pat, son Stuart, and daughter Judy. Without Pat's Patience and encouragement to push me on, my story would not have been told. It was Judy who persuaded me I should write my life story, after listening to some of my stories for the "tenth" time on our many weekend bike rides. I would like to thank Stuart making me the man I am today, a "pauper"! only joking son, and his help in getting my handwritten effort into type has been without question invaluable, and he should be mentioned in dispatches.

Contents

My Evacuation	1
Bournemouth – Hampshire	7
The Jones's	13
Eastbourne Children's Home	19
Dr. Banardoe's Homes	23
Goldie Leigh Hospital	33
White Oak Hospital	40
Return to Paddington	42
Phillip Runs Away	45
The O'donald's	51
Bed and Breakfast Job	52
Museums South Kensington	54
Starting Work	57
Start at Somers & Kirby	61
Joined Samuel Putney	67
Kennings Motors	73
Joined the Royal Engineers	75
The first morning of training	77
Aldershot Field Engineering Course	83
Tidworth Mlitary Hospital	84
School of Military Survey nr Newbury, Berkshire	86
The Brecon Beacons Manoeuvres	94
RE Transit Camp - Chatham – Kent	99
My Weeks Leave	104
Last Weeks of Army Service	106
Finished Army – Mick Levy Greengrocer	108
Start of South Africa	115

The Stowaway	119
Start of new life in Durban	124
Selling Encyclopaedias	152
John Wall the journalist	157
On the Buses	161
Driving my own bus	174
Long Neck comes aboard	182
The Undercover inspectors	185
Tour Bus Driver	187
The Schooner	189
This South Africa	194
The Windsor Castle	205
The "Sprinkler System"	221
Watney Mann	238
Meeting Pat	241
Peter Beesworth	242
"Buying our first home"	251
Goodbye to Liverpool	264
Getting Married	267
Mather and Platt	270
Stuart arrives	272
Judy is born	277
Stoke Mandeville hospital	283
Mary	290
The Service Man	292
Meeting Brian Again	294
Judy in hospital	297
The school building project	301
Started my own business	303
Hemel Hempstead General Hospital	307
Bomb Bunkers High Wycombe	313
Oldham's Press Watford	318
Plymouth Navy Base	324
Kings cross Underground Station	329

Warburgs – Moorgate	338
Skin Cancer	343
Cruise to Norway	345
The Parrot	350
My Metal Detector	354
Table Tennis	356
The Asda interview	358
Ben Nevis	361
Returned to London to work	364
Age Concern	365
Peter Pan's Pipe Confession	368
Who was my Father?	369
My Father's Army Service	372
Observations – Anecdotes – Poems	374

My Evacuation

It all started for me six months before the outbreak of World War II, that's when I was born John Anthony Banfield on the 20/03/1939, at St Mary's Hospital in Paddington, West London. I was brought into the world on that day, also with my twin brother Philip. My mother Josephine had already given birth to my sister Mary a year earlier. My father, Matthew Philip Banfield was still in the Army at this time. It had only been 21 years since World War I finished and yet once again war clouds were gathering and people now feared war could once again start and six months later in September 1939 the war started.

Just before the war started, plans were drawn up to evacuate most children out of large cities and into the safety of the countryside. So this is really where my life story begins with my twin brother Philip. We were both evacuated to a large country house at Henley on Thames, Oxfordshire. Our sister Mary had already been evacuated earlier to the same country house. Like thousands of other London children. We found ourselves taken to small towns and villages scattered all over the southern parts of England.

Poem

Evacuated from London to Henley-on-Thames.
Where I will meet so many childhood friends.
Located by the Thames such a beautiful place.
For 4 1/2 years was to be my base.
My new home is a mansion purchased by the state
With manicured hedges and gardens, some curved some straight
Old father Thames flows by in all its glory.
For such a young child, it's a fairytale story
The Sun is a shining to welcome the day.
Lighting up the sky in an extraordinary way.
Boat trips on the River climbing up the trees.
Watching the dairymaid toiling to make the cheese.
Always playing outside, never mind the weather.
Hoping these wonderful days will last forever.

The country house we were sent to was named Culham Court and was set in 650 acres with rolling countryside to the back of the house and magnificent views, looking down to the River Thames from the front. Culham Court was a Georgian mansion. The government of the day instructed local authorities to hand over old people's homes and care homes etc for the use of thousands of the evacuees. Culham Court housed around 30 children from babies to five-year-olds.

My brother and myself were about six months old when we arrived at Culham Court. What a wonderful place to be sent to and grow up in such a magnificent setting. We had never ending days of summer and being cared for by some lovely nursery nurses, life doesn't get much better than this. All of us children having the freedom to play on well kept lawns and to swim in the Clearwater River Thames, and to be taken to the Henley regatta, watching the very rich people, sitting alongside their luxury cars, picnicking on expensive blankets and guzzling down bottles of very expensive champagne. Even as a tot I realised how lucky we all were to be living in this paradise. Sometimes playing on the lawns, we would look up to the sky and watch in amazement as British and German fighter planes battled it out. These battles were called dogfights, to us kids it was an exciting spectacle. The fighters were making trails across the sky, it was like watching spiders spinning their webs. But we were not to know how serious it was.

Poem

Looking up to the sky dogfights taking place
Those RAF pilots are really giving chase
So young yet spellbound on hearing so much noise
To us it was a game oh such young boys
These brave RAF pilots were victorious in the fight.
Had destroyed the German air force, even at night.
The Battle of Britain had been won in the sky.
But so many pilots on both sides have to die.
Both sides lost so much but that is war
Hoping this is the last one, never any more

The lazy days of summer were endless days of fun and childhood games set in a location that even royalty would be envious of. The rule of the home was that once a child reached the age of five. They had to leave,

Culham Court. My brother and I had one more week before we turned five years old, and even at that age. I was feeling very sad. Knowing that I would have to leave this place, I called home. The week went quickly by and we were then both five! This was the day of our departure, the nurses had packed our belongings, and we were ready to go. But Philip and I had other ideas and planned that we would run into the woods and climb up a tree so that they would not be able to take us away. As time passed, we saw the staff looking for us and calling our names. After searching around we saw them making their way back to the house from the tree. We had a good view of the house and the car that had come to take us away. To our joy, we saw the car disappearing up the drive and out of the grounds. We left it for about an hour before climbing down the tree and making our way back to the house thinking in all our innocence that we would now be able to stay forever.

On entering the house we were surrounded by very angry, but very relieved staff, "where have you been?! We have had the police out looking for you", and with tears streaming down our cheeks. I explained that we had been hiding in the woods, as we didn't want to leave our home. I will never ever forget standing there with uncontrollable bursts of crying and sobbing, saying this is our home. Why should we have to go, leaving all our friends behind in the place we love? Looking up I could see the tears in the nurses eyes, as they must have seen how very upset we both were, I'm sorry boys, rules are rules, and you cannot stay here the matron said, you still must go and we will arrange for you to go tomorrow morning.

The next day came, and they made sure we could not run away. Again from the window I looked as the car pulled up outside the entrance. Once again the tears started to flow, as we were escorted to the waiting car it felt like my heart was being pulled away from my body. Oh the pain and the sorrow. The saddest day of my life. We both have to be picked up fighting and screaming and dragged into the car. The staff must have been as broken-hearted as we were. The car quickly gained speed up the long drive. Looking back I could see the younger children still playing in the grounds that had been my home for 4 and a half years. Goodbye my beloved, Culham Court. Hello to my broken heart.

Poem

I will remember these days and the memories I'll save

Will take them happy years to my grave.

Good times, never last and that's for sure.

Another opening will appear through a new door.

The day had come when we had to go.
In all my young life never felt so low.
With weeping eyes, the tears were flowing
My heart was breaking and it was showing
Had cried my eyes out, there were no more tears.
Have always remembered them days over the years.
It's always so hard to say your goodbyes.
To break the chain and cut the ties
The cutting action of a very sharp knife.

A sorrowful page in that book of life. The car made its way out of the main gates, and then started to build up speed as we headed out into the open countryside, in the car with us was one of the nurses from Culham Court, it must have been heartbreaking for her to have two sobbing children to attend to. We were driving what seemed like hours, not knowing where we were going. All we knew was that we were going to a children's home, with older children.

All of a sudden, we stopped outside a very large house in a small town, with houses all around. It seemed so strange as we had been used to large open spaces. This is your new home boys, the nurse gently, said I will take you inside and you will meet your new house mother. As we approached the front door a large lady was there to greet us, she looked very old to us, but was only probably about 35 years. Hello boys, my name is Jill. I'm your new house mother, I know you will be very happy with us. We said our goodbyes to our nurse, who was returning back to Culham Court. Goodbye boys, she said, I know you will be very happy here, as she stepped into the car. I could see her sobbing, she could not even wave, which upset me a little.

Let me introduce you to all the other children staying here our new house mother said, we have 10 children, now with you two hear six girls and four boys. They were all about 5 years older than us by the time we had met them all the tears disappeared, and we were out exploring our new home, with a huge back garden. The name of our new house was called Bolbeck, and it was situated at Banbury Cross in Oxfordshire, and it was to be my new home for one year. Once again, these were to be the carefree days of childhood. The house was just on the edge of town. So after school and at weekends, we would all go and play in the Meadows and fields. Such happy days, one of the girls who used to hold my hand was named Barbara Allen, such a pretty sweet thing, and of course I fell instantly in love with her. With her curly blonde hair and her pert little nose, she was my very first love. I was 5 ½ years old and she was 7, so I was her little toy boy. It was a very sad day for me when one day she said, I'm leaving today, I have been adopted and I won't be seeing you again. Some people in London are adopting me, and I am going to be brought up by them. That was what happened in them days, if a couple liked you and they wanted a child it was very easy to adopt.

The back of the house overlooked some wonderful views across the countryside. Often we would watch the local hunt in all their splendid red coats, black hats and riding boots. They would ride by on their magnificent horses with the hounds chasing after them. If you had to sum up the countryside in those days this would be it. We used to watch the farmers stack the hay and be fascinated as they proceeded to build a haystack which are never seen these days.

Life was just an endless summer, and how could this ever end, but end it did. I stayed there about a year and once again for reasons I never understood, I was told I was going to another place. My brother Phillip at this time was in hospital so I was on my own on the day of my departure. Just before leaving, Jill, the house mother called me into her office and said, John, I have some bad news for you, your father died this morning...................but as a six year old who had only met him twice before it was with a shrug of shoulders that I took this news. I returned to the large garden and carried on playing with all the children.

Poem

She had to tell me about my father that had departed
Normally hearing news like that you would be broken hearted
But only met him once or maybe it was twice
That's how life is sometimes, the shaking of the dice
When meeting him I was such a young lad
Surely it's a childs right to know their Dad
In life you get your ups and downs, highs and lows
But that's the way things are, that's how it goes.

I once again had to say farewell to all my friends and the wonderful staff who had been so kind with their love and kindness. A car was waiting for me and I stepped into it. So very sad and with all the staff and children waving goodbye, my tears flowed and were uncontrollable. In the car with me was the driver and all my worldly possessions. A small suitcase with very little inside it.

Can you tell me where we are going? I asked the driver, you wouldn't know if I told you he said but if you must know I am taking you to a nice place called Bournemouth on the South coast. He may as well of been talking about the moon as I had never heard of it. It's about a four hour journey, he said, so have a sleep, and hopefully when you wake we should be there. But where will I be staying when I get there? I replied, you are going to a Church of England home for boys and girls.

BOURNEMOUTH — HAMPSHIRE

We finally arrived at my new home. Stopping outside, I was taken back by the sheer beauty of this large Victorian house set in its own grounds. As the driver and myself walked down the long winding path that led to the impressive house, my eyes were drawn to the large fir and oak trees that spread all around the large gardens. On approaching the front door, it opened and there stood the house mother:- Mrs Collins.

"Welcome to your new home John" she said. She seemed a kindly woman with a very friendly smile. "If you come with me, I will introduce you to all the other children. Gather round everybody, I would like you to meet John, he will be staying here with us".

The children's ages ranged from six years to seventeen years and were about equal numbers of boys and girls.

"I will take you around the house and show you your bedroom, the dinning room and parts of the grounds. Now John, I will be known to you as Mrs Collins, and my husband is known as Mr Collins. We have two daughters and a son, and we live in a flat at the end of the house"

As we walked around, we passed a large play area used when it rained, a large dining room and further down the passage a library. Upstairs were all of the bedrooms.

"This will be your room John and you will be sharing it with two others boys"

From my new bedroom window I looked down onto an amazing number of all types of different trees and to the right of them was a tennis court.

"Please Mrs Collins, can I look out of the bedrooms at the other side of the corridors?"

"Of course you can" she said.

On looking out of the back bedrooms it took my breath away. To one side was a very large orchard with every kind of fruit tree you could find. To the side of this was a swimming pool that did look like it had seen better days. Next to the pool, was a large hill that was used for bike riding and four wheel carting. "I'm going to like this place" I thought to myself, and indeed that proved the case.

Poem

I'm now living in Bournemouth by the sea
A happy childhood, I hope it'll be
In a home with children of all different ages
This story of mine will one day make pages
My mind and body are now really shaping
The rest of my life in the making
A sense of humour and sense of fun
Of children's games played in the sun
My life has just started, lets call it the spring
So many battles and hurdles for me to win.

I very quickly got into the routine of the new house. Up for breakfast in the main dining hall, and then set off for school with my bag. It was only 10 minutes walk away, but being only 6 years old, I was escorted to school by the older children.

I started too really like the place, and with so many friends of different ages, it seemed like paradise on earth. At weekends we would climb the large trees. I soon became an excellent climber and was always able to reach the very top of most of them. The other pursuit which we used to get up to, was cycling up the high hill and at full speed race down to the bottom, no helmets of course. With the seaside only 10 minutes walk away we used to spend many hours down by the beach, building sand castles and swimming in the clear blue sea and riding the waves. We would then return back home, to a well prepared evening meal. Life could not get much better.

"John" Mrs Collins said, "I have some good news for you, go into the library and you will get a surprise"

On entering, I could not believe my eyes, it was my brother sitting there. He had been discharged from hospital and had been transferred to join up with me. I was so pleased to see him; it had been six months spent apart.

The staff and children could not believe that twins could be so much alike, we were a carbon copy of each other, but of course later on in life, I was always the better looking one.

Like my brother I soon became unwell and was taken to hospital with a disease quite common at that time. I had ringworm, which had infested my head and required two months in hospital. About four weeks after that I broke my leg falling off my bike at some speed on the hill, this required another six weeks in hospital. Then I seemed to get every illness that was ever invented. I was becoming a very sickly child.

Poem

The journeys of life may be long or short
Many battles and scars will be fought
Illnesses are coming quite rapid and quick
Very often I am poorly and so very sick
My body's immune system is not quite right
But I will learn to fight the good fight.

When I came out of hospital life carried on as usual. Days spent down by the beach, trips to Weymouth, Poole Harbour, all in this beautiful part of Hampshire.

What I did notice upon my return out of hospital, was that two sisters were missing. "Where is Jane and Anne" I asked Mrs Collins.

"Oh they have been adopted by a couple from London"

I was quite sad hearing this as they were very sweet girls, but they had no parents, so it was for the best. Most of the children had couples that came once a week to take them out for the day to see how well they got on with each other. I was in the home for four years and witnessed many children being adopted. It was heartbreaking to see children who you had got to know so very well, being collected by their new parents. Waving their last waves to you with tears streaming down their faces ,but happy to have new parents and a new life, just sad to be saying their last farewells.

Every two weeks my brother Phillip and I would be visited by a middle aged couple who used to take us out to anywhere we wished to go. We had the choice of even going to the beach, or the park or even to the cinema. We used to look forward to these visits, and we started to really get to know them and liked them. The couple were from London, but also owned a large house right on the Bournemouth sea front. Sometimes we would be taken there and used to play games with there daughter. We new the couple as Mr & Mrs Taylor. Mr Taylor owned quite a few dry cleaning shops in London, and he always spoke of his timber yards he owned. All in all they were quite wealthy people. We used to have such wonderful times spent in their company. They used to return us home after every visit, and by such a large car it could have fit all the children from the home in it.

On returning home from one visit with them, our house mother Mrs Collins called us to one side and asked us both, how did we like Mr and Mrs Taylor and how well did we get on with them?

"Yes Mrs Collins, we love them taking us out and visiting different places and we love playing games with their daughter. "Well in that case Phillip and John", she said, "Mr and Mrs Taylor would very much like to adopt you both, they have told me that you all get on so well together, they would like you to be part of their family. So boys, what do you think of that?

"Oh Mrs Collins", I cried, "We would both be so very happy if they could adopt us"

"I am so pleased boys, and I know you will all make a fine family. The next step is to get all the parties to agree on this, that will be your mother and the Bournemouth child care homes. If everyone agrees, you could be living with them quite soon.

We then started to see more of them. Visits used to only be once a week but now they were on Saturdays and Sundays. We found out that their daughter was also adopted as they could not have children of their own, but wanted to be able to give love to children. After about six months of us visiting and them coming to the home our house mother called us into her office.

"Boys I have some bad news for you. Your mother has said no for you to be adopted, so it will now not take place. Mr and Mrs Taylor have been informed and are very upset, but there is nothing anyone can do. I am so sorry boys.

"But why?" I replied, "Our mother has only ever seen us once in our lifetime and Mr and Mrs Taylor are like a mother and father to us"

"I know that boys", she said, "but I can't do anything about it"

We were now eight years old, but that didn't stop us crying our eyes out, with Mrs Collins hugging and sobbing with us, "never mind boys, you still have my love and all the love of the children here". That was the last time we saw Mr and Mrs Taylor, they never even sent us a card, they must have been very upset as we both were.

About two months after Mrs Collins told us we were not to be adopted, she came and found us in the garden to say that a retired couple that lived a mile away from the home would like to take us out for trips and outings. The couple had no children of their own so it was a delight to meet Mr and Mrs Marsh. Of course they seemed very old to us, but we found them to be a very nice and a kind couple. We sometimes would go to their house which was happily situated with breathtaking views. From the back of the house you looked over a small river and to the front were a couple of houses and a very old church whose bells produced the most beautiful chimes. Mrs Marsh, used to help out in the church and Mr Marsh used to ring the bells on Sundays and at weddings. This is how Phillip and I first started to go to church and then went on to sing in the choir. Mr Marsh used to tell us all about his time spent in the Royal Navy as a commander. He had joined the navy as a young lad when the ships were driven by coal. He told us how he rose up to become an officer. We used to be fascinated by his tales and yarns. We had met them for about six months when Phillip was sent away once more to go into hospital again. We got so used to be being apart. Playing out in the garden one day alone, Mrs Collins approached me; I could tell by the look in her eyes that she had news for me.

"John, I'm afraid you will be leaving us next week to go to another home"

As I had been moved from home to home and hospitals all my life I didn't even bother to question why. I was now nine years old and had been at the Suffolk Road home for three years. The day of leaving arrived so quickly. Mrs Collins had lined her own children and all the home children along both sides of the path leading to the front gate. As I stepped out of the house I was overcome with emotion as each child hugged and said their goodbyes. After three years you build up a loving bond and they were like brothers and sisters to me. By the time I got to the main gate I felt that my world had come to an end. As I reached the front gate, I looked back for the last time to see everyone weeping including Mr and Mrs Collins, my wonderful house mother and father who I was leaving behind, a sight and sound that I will never ever forget.

Poem

Climbing, Running and Jumping, Children are playing
Through their games a foundation they are laying
These games will suppress any anger, jealousy or strife
A happy childhood is assured and a rich rewarding life
Children growing up, what a wonderful magical age
The start of the book, that very first page.

The Jones's

A Car was waiting for me just outside the house. Inside was a very mean looking lady who shouted at me to get in the car "and stop that silly crying, boys don't cry. Now driver, get a move on, I want to be back at Bolbeck before darkness sets in". "Yes mam" replied the driver.

As we drove away, I took one more look back at the place that I had called my home. How I never died of a broken heart, I will never know. Once again, after about two hours of driving, I noticed a sign saying Oxfordshire, My heart lifted, maybe I was going back to Culham Court? "Are we going to Culham Court?" "NO WE ARE NOT!" she yelled, "shut up and be quiet".

I had the feeling that things were about to change and I wasn't going to like this lady very much. The car started to slow down and I could make out this quite small house as we approached its drive. As the car came to a standstill, she shouted "get out you snivelling little brat". As we got to the front door, a large, fierce looking man appeared, "come here boy, been crying have we. I don't like cry babies" and with a clip round the head, I had just been introduced to my new house father, Mr Jones. It was his wife who had been with me in the car. "Right boy, get washed and report to me in the dinning room".

On entering the dinning room there was about eight other children eating their supper with their eyes down. They did not look very happy to me. "Right sit there and eat up your supper" cried Mr Jones. In front of me was the worst looking food I had ever seen but as he was prowling around the room I did as I was told. Whether it was the long journey or the food I do not know, but I suddenly felt very sick and within seconds I had vomited into my dinner bowl. There was a roar from the other side of the room, "YOU DON'T LIKE OUR FOOD HERE? If you don't like the food then you can eat up all of your sick"

"I can't and I will not do that", I pleaded. No sooner had I uttered those words, he was undoing his belt from his trousers, "you'll eat it up or you will get my belt"

"I'm not eating it", I cried

"Right come here, bend over........your going to see what happens to children who do not do as they are told". With that he brought down his belt on my buttocks with such force, it knocked me right across the room I had never felt pain like it. He was just to give me another lashing when in walked his wife to see what all the noise was about, what ever she said to him made him calm down. This is the first time I had ever seen an adult in such a rage, and it had really frightened me he could have carried on beating me but I would not have eaten any more. Even at that age, I had a fighting spirit. I was feeling very unwell at this stage as he grabbed me by the hair and pulled me into the kitchen, right boy, you can wash all the dishes up and then wipe them, no one disobeys my orders. What a nasty mean man, I thought, I won't be staying here much longer. With this maniac on the loose. After I had finished all the kitchen duties, he ordered me straight to bed. I shared a bedroom with a boy about six years old. He hardly talked and seemed to be very withdrawn. He must have had dealings with the mad house father. Days went into weeks, I had now started a new school with a very nice lady teacher who took a shine to me her name was Miss Gordon. All my classmates used to shout you're the teacher's pet. She probably felt sorry for me coming from the home.

I had only been living there about six months, and on a Saturday morning we were having breakfast, and I felt quite unwell, because of this I left my breakfast. Mr Jones got very angry and wanted to know why. I told him I felt unwell, and with that the belt was off his trousers. And I was bent over the table in front of all the children and given about six whacks with his leather belt "get upstairs." He cried, and don't come down until I order you to.

Because I was so unhappy with the children's home, and knowing I only had to step out of line. I and all of the other children would be severely dealt with by the mad Mr Jones. Not only did he use his belt, but on one occasion for a slight misdemeanour. He would fill the kitchen sink with water, grabbed hold of my hair, with one hand, and with his other hand, forced my head down into the water. Only pulling my head back up when he thought my punishment had been served. It only lasted seconds but it felt like minutes. This was a terrifying experience. I was sent to bed with no evening meal and with the words "if you ever disobey my orders again sonny Jim. You'll regret it." Laying in my bed that night I was thinking, what other ways, could he punish me after a couple of hours going over in my mind the worst punishments that could be inflicted on me I fell asleep. When I woke in the morning, I couldn't understand why my pyjamas were soaking wet. I then realised I had wet the bed, and with the sheets wringing wet. I was now going to be in big trouble with Mr Jones, as I was not in the mood for a beating or worse, I decided not to say anything, and hoped that it would dry by the time I got back to bed. I went to school that day as usual, and after I returned back to the home I with the other children made my way to the dining room and sat down. Mr Jones came storming in "Banfield, get over here, you disgusting, dirty boy. You wet your bed, and you thought I wouldn't find out, and for that I'm going to punish you. I knew what was coming next, as he took his belt off "get them trousers off" he shouted. "I'll teach you a lesson." And with that, he promptly laid into me with aggressive whacks of his belt. I was bent over facing all the children and I could see the shock on their faces. As the punishment was being inflicted, I noticed Jane, one of the girls with tears streaming down her cheeks after receiving about 10 whacks of the belt he shouted. "This is what happens to bed wetters, now get upstairs, you dirty boy and wait in the bathroom. You won't be sleeping in a bed until you learn to control yourself. I waited in the bathroom for about two hours, and the door opened and Mr Jones shouted "get in that bath that's your new bed from now on. I could hear all the other children making their way to their bedrooms and knowing they would have sheets and blankets but I didn't even have a pillow case! I climbed into the bath, as it started to get dark outside and rested my head on my hands. But I was so cold and uncomfortable I couldn't sleep. I then heard the bathroom door being opened, and I heard a soft voice whisper. "John, you can have my pillow case and blankets for the night and I will get them back in the morning."

I recognized the voice and it was Jane, the girl with the tears on her cheeks watching me getting a beating. I think she had a soft spot for me! What a brave thing to do at such a young age, she risked getting punished herself if she had been caught. As daylight appeared, Jane gently opened the bathroom door and said she must take the pillow case a blanket back and quickly departed.

It was after this incident that I decided to run away. As I knew that I was living in Oxfordshire, and that was where my beloved Culham Court was, I decided that I would make my way to there. I had no money to take with me, and hoped I could slip away when he is in his study. With my door opened, I watched him disappear into his study, as quiet as I could, I crept past his room, opened the front door and went up the path and I was free. Now where do I make for, I asked myself? I know I'll take this left turning, and that will bring me to the Market Square. After walking for about 10 minutes I was in the Market Square and unsure of which way to go. All of a sudden, a very familiar voice shouted "hello John, What are you doing in town by yourself?" "Hello Miss Gordon" I replied. "I have run away from home."

"Why?", she asked in amazement!

"Well miss, the house father has beaten me with his belt twice since I've been there, and I'm not going to take any more." She stood back shocked and looked quite tearful. "You poor child, you should have told me before about this. Putting her protecting arm around me. She softly said, I will make sure it does not happen ever again. I will take you to police constable Wright, who lives in the police house across the street. Taking my hand, she walked me to PC Wright house. She knocked on the door, and there he stood in his uniform. "Hello Miss Gordon, what can I do for you?"

"This boy is a pupil of mine, and I found him in the square. He lives in the local home and he tells me that his house father beat him with his belt and is a very cruel man."

"Okay Miss Gordon thanks for bringing him here, I will take care of all of this."

She thanked PC Wright and gave me a cuddle and left.

As PC Wright led me into his front room, he seemed quite angry. "Now, boy, what's all this about you being beaten?"

"Yes sir." I replied, "My housemaster Mr Jones, has beaten me at least twice and is a very nasty man." With that, he became quite cross. "Mr Jones is a very good friend of mine, and he wouldn't hurt a fly, you're making all this up Sunny Jim, and I am taking you back, and I will find out why you are lying, we will get to the bottom of this; right, come with me lad I'm going to get to the truth ."

"But it is the truth, Sir. I'm not making it up. Please don't make me go back there."

"Just shut up and walk with me," he ordered.

Poem

As a young child grown-up seems so very tall.
Made to do as you're told by one and all
They are always right. They tell you, come what may,
Should be seen and not heard that's what they say.
Such very small feet and young child shoes.
Can I not have an opinion, and some views?
When I grow up, I will remember the beatings I had.

As no one deserves that treatment, especially a young lad.

As we set off I could hear my heart pounding away. It was only a short walk to the home, and as we approached the house, I was imagining all sorts of punishments that were going to be dished out to me. As soon as the policeman knocked on the door it opened immediately, with the housemaster smiling broadly. "Hello Reg what's going on here then? Have you caught this young man stealing someone's apples or something?"

"No" replied police constable Wright. May I have a word with you in private?

"Sit in the dining room boy." Cried Mr Jones. "I'll deal with you later"

I must have been sitting there for a good hour and suddenly the two men came out of the office. They then shook hands and the policeman left without saying a word to me. I thought that quite strange, but then I was only a child. "Right John." He said. "We have some talking to do." I was amazed as this was the first time he had ever said my first name. "Before we start to talk, would you like your house mother to get you some food and drink?"

"No, thank you sir." I replied, I still could not get over how calm and nice he was being towards me.

"Okay John, police constable Wright tells me you told him that I sometimes beat you, and that I go into violent rages with you and all the other children. Let me tell you John, all I ever wanted to do was to instil discipline on you all, and thinking about it now. I think I went about in the wrong manner. Can you forgive me, John and I promise it will never ever happen again."

"Yes sir." I said, "as long as I don't get beaten any more. I'll forgive you."

"Okay John, we will forget what happened in the past, and we will now concentrate on the future. You go out and play with all the other children and we will let bygones be bygones."

Walking out into the garden, I realised that police constable Wright must have warned Mr Jones not to ever hit the children again as he would be in serious trouble. For the first time in ages. I had a happy feeling, and I felt good about life. On the Sunday, the housemaster was laughing and smiling and being so very nice to everyone. The home had that happy feel about it.

Monday came, and once again, I made my way to school. On reaching the playground. I met my teacher Miss Gordon. "Hello John, I was quite worried about you over the weekend, so tell me where the new home is you are staying in?"

"I am not staying in a new home miss; the policeman took me back to the housemaster's home". I have never seen such shock on someone's face. "What! Do you mean to tell me that he took you back to all that again? Well, come with me, John, I'm going to sort this all out ". So off she set with me in tow, we made our way to the headmaster's office. "You wait outside John. I'm going to have a word with the headmaster." It must have been about 20 minutes later, the door opened and I was ushered into the office. "Tell me John, is it all true, what you told Miss Gordon about the living conditions you have been experiencing."

"Yes sir." I replied. "It's all true,"

"That's all I need to know, Miss Gordon please take John back to class, and I will try and deal with all this."

I sat in class for about one hour, when I was once again called back into the headmaster's office. As I entered, I noticed two well-dressed ladies sitting down. The headmaster began talking to these two ladies who were from the children's home welfare unit. "These ladies would like a word with you, John" he said. It was the rather plump lady who started to speak. "Okay, John. We have heard the full story, and you will be pleased to know that you won't have to return to that house or that housemaster ever again. We have arranged for you to be sent to a new home immediately. This new homes in a place called Eastbourne. I was delighted to hear this news and owed it all to Miss Gordon. As I was being escorted down the corridor. Miss Gordon came out of her class with a broad smile on her face and tears in our eyes and gave me a big hug. She wished me well in my new life.

Poem

I was Miss Gordon's pupil, and of course teachers pet.

How can I ever thank her, always in her debt

Sweet Miss Gordon so lovely with love in her heart.

All she wanted for me was a new start

She must have been so happy and yet so sad.

To see me leaving her such a young lad.

Eastbourne Children's Home

So off we set on our way to my new home. I was starting to get used to this new home lark. With the two ladies in tow, one sitting next to me, and the plump one driving, the journey time was about four hours or so. What amused me was that the two ladies talked non-stop for the entire journey. It all went above my head. They hardly stop for breath, my very first time having the experience of chatterboxes. But at least I now felt safe and happy and looking forward to my new home. We had finally arrived turning into a large drive that led us into a village green, which was surrounded by about 10 large houses. The back of all the houses faced on to rolling fields. We pulled up outside what was to be my home for the next two years. The plump lady knocked on the front door of the house and the house mother greeted us. "Hello John, we have been expecting you." She was quite a well rounded lady, and had such a nice smile. I knew from that first meeting that I was going to be happy there. The two ladies who had brought me there said their goodbyes to me and they drove off. "My name is Mrs Watson, you can either call me that or house mother. I have a surprise for you John", as she opened a door that led off to the corridor I could see someone drawing on a board. It was my twin brother Philip. He was as surprised as I was, after all this time we had finally met up. "Well, boys, I will leave you two to get to know each other again." My first words to Philip were "what is it like here?"

"It's great replied Philip, I love it here. I have now been here three months, and Mrs Watson is so nice".

This was music to my ears from hell to heaven, all in one day. The houses formed a circle around the green and the middle of the houses was used as the sick bay and medical centre with two nurses in attendance. They must have been at least 200 children in all the homes. So there was a need for a medical centre to cope with all the scraps children get into. As you came up the path there stood a very well-equipped school with an outside swimming pool in the grounds, with a football field to the back of it. "Am I dreaming?" I thought to myself. After surveying it all. I just could not get over how my life had changed in one day.

Life here in Eastbourne settled down to a steady routine. Making your bed, coming downstairs breakfast, and then walking five minutes to school. It was like being at a public school, with a magnificent cricket pitch next to the football field. I soon made many friends and was taught the rules of cricket and how to bat and bowl. It was not long until I made it into the school team. As one of the masters used to play professional cricket in his younger days, he was able to pass on all his very considerable knowledge to all of us boys. Although Eastbourne is in Sussex, we used to travel as far a field as Hampshire to play our away matches. I became a demon bowler, although I had quite a slight build. My nickname was velocity, and I took many wickets. Oh how I remember those hazy lazy days of summer, with the sounds of the ball hitting the bat with the cries of good bowling, and the fielding side in their whites, running around in never-ending circles trying to get the batsmen out. The motto of the school was all work and no play makes Jack a dull boy. So they made sure all pupils participated in the sports and what made it all that much more enjoyable was a young girl, whose name was Lucky Weeks. She lived in the next house to mine. This house was for girls. She was in the same class as myself and we got on very well together. Lucy was only about eight years old, and she came from Ayr in Scotland. How she ever ended up in Eastbourne I never found out. With her soft Scottish accent, and her beautiful little face, I fell madly in love with this sweet Bonnie Lass. We had a Scottish teacher in the school, who used to teach us Scottish dancing. So I used to end up as a partner to Lucy, I wondered if she ever knew how I felt about her.

I did not see too much of my brother Philip, as he was moved to one of the other houses near my one. I never found out the reason for this. It was just one of those things you just accepted. In the summer after school, and at weekends, some of us would help the local farmer whose farm was at the back of my house. We would help load the tractors with the hay, and then the farmhands would make haystacks out of it. In other fields, magnificent shire horses would be pulling behind them long ploughs, opening up the earth, ready for seeding, chickens were fed and eggs collected, and put into baskets. In one of the fields sheep would be munching grass, and one of treats was going along with the Shepherd and his border collie, to round up all the sheep. Watching the Shepherd and his dog in action was like watching a masterful double act. With the shepherds different tones on his whistle the dog knew exactly which sheep he should be heading for, man and dog, a truly amazing team. What happy and never to be repeated days!! In another one of the farmer's fields was a large orchard, with branches straining under the weight of all the fruit. If we were selected for fruit picking, we would have to pick the apples and then transfer them into the tractor-trailer. This was very hard work for someone so young, but very rewarding as the farmer would pay each child in old money. 05p. we were quite happy with that, as we would have worked for nothing, working all day in the fields there was no such thing as sun lotion, and as for health and safety, them days cigarettes were considered to be cool and health and safety were the pins that held your trousers up.

Poem

Those endless days of summer spent working in the sun
The days never seem to end oh so much fun.
Nature depends on the four season's sun wind and rain.
And another year arrives. It then all repeats itself again,
How did it all happen and what was the source
Did it all not stem from a much higher force?
It's more judgement than luck we have those seasons
Four of them a year, we know he had his reasons.
He created this world of ours with his outreached hand.
Making this United Kingdom of ours, such a promised land

On coming home from school one day, I noticed my brother Philip standing outside my house, I saw him by the front path, and he told me he had been told to report to our house mother. I thought nothing about it, so we both walked in together and was greeted by Mrs Watson, I have good and bad news for you boys, the bad news is you will be leaving us here, however the good news and I know it will be for both of you, is that your returning to your old home Suffolk Road, in Bournemouth. Being so young, you didn't even question why we had to leave, there seemed to be no rhyme or reason. You will both be leaving tomorrow which was a Saturday morning, so Philip you go back to your house and return here at 10pm, john, Mr Watson said, its been a pleasure having you living here with us, and if I had my way, I would keep you here, bit I don't make the decisions. Here we go again I thought to myself, I wonder how many more times this is going to happen, I've lost count how many homes I had been in. Saturday arrived and we collected the few possessions that we owned, we said our farewells to all the staff and children, and it was with a heavy heart that I left, what had been our home for two years, when is this agony ever going to end?

We both jumped into the car, and looking out of the window, we could see that the staff and children had formed a line both sides of the road leading to the main gate. Mrs Watson our house mother was in the car with us, to escort us to Bournemouth. How many more times can my heart be broken? This wonderful place that I have called my home; it seemed so unfair and cruel of them not to consider our feelings. The journey only took about one hour, as it was about thirty miles further south down the coast road.

We got back to Suffolk Road and we were greeted by all our old friends, but after two years, quite a few new children were living there. Over half the children that I had known had been adopted. Things got back to as there were, when I last lived there, going to school, going to the coast swimming and climbing the large trees in the garden. We had both been back there about a month when Philip and I were called in from the garden by Mrs Collins. Boys sit down, I have some news for you, I have here a letter from your mother, requesting that you return to London. This will of course have to be approved by the children's home committee, and if they agree, your mother will have you back. But Mrs Collins I replied, we have only met our mother once before, and that was years ago, why does she want us now, it's not fair. We love it here, and want to stay. Well I will tell the committee how you feel about all this, and let them make up there minds, so in the meantime, just carry on as normal. We only had to wait one more week, when Mrs. Collins got the reply we both didn't want to hear. Very gently Mrs. Collins read out what the committee had decided, that your mother will with immediate effect, shall have her two children returned to her as soon as possible. Within the next two days, we were all packed and ready to leave Suffolk Road for the very last time. Once again, the goodbyes were said, the tears once again started up, and like all the other farewells, a sense of sadness and utter hopelessness, as I knew in my heart that my life would from now on be changed forever.

Poem

I think this will be my last children's home,
Sandy beaches and shore I will no longer roam.
I'm thinking my childhood is about to be taken away,
And in this matter I don't have a say.
What is my future not knowing what's to come.
Just only a child when all is said and done.
And I haven't a clue what lies ahead,
But what will be, will be, that wise man said.

Dr. Banardoe's Homes

Where would I and thousands of other children like me be, if it wasn't for children's homes. It was all mainly due to one man, and his name was Dr.Banardoe. He was born in the Victorian days, and had a very privileged upbringing, and when he reached adulthood he became a very wealthy merchant. He lived in London and walking around the capital he was appalled and horrified at the terrible conditions people were living in. What saddened him the most was the children begging for food, and knowing these children had been abandoned by there parents, who couldn't afford to look after them, and others who had run away from home because of the abuse and beatings given to them. He was a Christian and, was determined that something should be done for these children. Being a wealthy man, he decided to open a children's home for the neediest children, this was opened in about 1870. This proved to be very successful and he opened another one, and went on to open many more. What a truly remarkable man, he could have just ignored the problem and kept his money, but he was a man who cared about mankind, and especially children. Like many before and after me thousands of children have much to thank this great human being, he never got knighted or received any honours for this vital work he carried out.

Philip and I, along with Mr and Mrs Collins, set off on that overcast day, for Bournemouth railway station, it was the first time we had both been on a train. The train was a large steam train, with the back of the engine stacked up with coal, for the journey to London the travel time was about 3 hours to arrive at Waterloo station in London. On the journey, I was feeling very sad and low, not knowing what awaited me.

As the train sped past the open countryside, I wondered how long it would be before I would get to see the green fields and meadows again. The train was now slowing up as we approached the outskirts of south London, and from the window, I could see how ugly and dirty the buildings were, my heart sank to a new low, did people really live in this horrible place? The train slowly made its way into waterloo station and came to a stop just where a large clock was showing the time of one o clock. We all alighted the train. I was feeling very sick and frightened and just wanted to jump straight back on the train and return back to Bournemouth. Come on Mrs Collins cried, we will get to Paddington by the underground. So we all set off to the tube station. Mr Collins purchased four tickets; we then all boarded the tube train. I could not take this all in. Here is a train that runs underground, how could it be? The tube train pulled into Paddington underground station where we all alighted. Stepping onto the moving staircase was quite a strange experience. This was like another world and as we walked out from the station the noise and smell hit me, what am I doing here I thought?

Poem

Now back in London that's where you belong
Don't questions our decisions whether right or wrong
It's not for you to know the reasons why
Dry your eyes young man boys do not cry
You've had a good life for all these years
So just be grateful and wipe away them tears
Bomb damage is everywhere buildings are down
The city took a battering this old London town
I will have to adapt and that's for sure
Because these brave Londoners managed throughout the war.

We need to get to this address, our house mother was saying to the taxi driver. Sorry madam replied the taxi driver, I have no idea where that is, I'll have to go into the post office over there and ask them directions. After about ten minutes he returned, I think I know where it may be but in all my years driving, I have never been to that area of Paddington. So off we set and about ten minutes later we arrived outside the door of 10 Westbury terrace. I could feel my heart pounding against my chest such was the anxiety I was now feeling. As we stepped out Mrs Collins asked the taxi driver to wait until she had handed over her two charges. She gave three loud knocks on the door knocker. There was no reply. Once again, three more loud knocks. Still there was no answer. Looking at her watch she said, the handover was supposed to take place at two o clock and it is now ten past two. Again she knocked, still no reply. By now the time had reached nearly half past two. Well she's definitely not here; I think we should all return back to Bournemouth she snapped. I agree I quickly piped in. By this time the taxi driver was getting quite edgy. I hope you realise you are being charged for me sitting here. Yes, yes driver I do know that. Right that's it, we're not waiting any longer here, all get back in the taxi, and we are going back to Paddington and returning home. Phillip and

I were in that Taxi quicker than a rat up a drainpipe. Just as we were about to pull away, the taxi driver shouted hold on there's a lady walking down the street, it may be her. We all waited in the taxi. As the lady made her way to the taxi, I'm sorry I'm late she said but I was held up at work, we all got out of the taxi and followed her indoors. Please wait, Mrs Collins shouted to the driver, I shouldn't be long. As we entered the hallway it was cold, dark and very uninviting. The lady then unlocked a door to the right of the passageway and we all stepped into a small kitchen come dining room. With three adults and two children you could hardly move in it. Mrs Banfield, can you show me all your other rooms please, asked Mrs Collins, other rooms, snapped the lady! I've only got one other room and it's the bedroom. Opening the dividing door, we all looked into a medium sized bedroom. By now I could see the shock and horror on Mrs Collins face. Do you mean to tell me, Mrs Banfield, you intend to have yourself, your two daughters and two sons living in just two rooms? And all five of you will be sleeping in the same bedroom? I was under the impression you had more rooms than this, if I had known about this I would never have allowed this hand over to take place but it's all been agreed and I cannot stop it now. Right then Mrs Banfield, here are the papers for you to sign. So handing over the papers they both got signed. You could see how sad and upset Mr & Mrs Collins were to be leaving us, with them both knowing the conditions that we will now be living in, as they couldn't control their tears, and with both Phillip and I crying out hearts out, and with a final hug from them both they both departed. It must have been one of the worst days of their lives and must have left a lasting impression on them, as it did with us.

Poem

Up from the countryside to the city called the smoke

Thought I had been dreaming and then suddenly awoke

Rows of terraced houses the chimneys are smoking

With buses and cars the black fog was choking

Back home to London my mother wanted us both back

But her house to me looked just like a shack

But people had nothing and were quite poor

Not long had passed since the ending of war

With myself and two sisters and a twin brother

Also in the house with us was our mother

But you learn to cope you really do suffer

In the end it made you that much tougher.

Right you can both stop that silly crying; your home now, so you might as well get used to it, and you can both start calling me mother or mum. In spite of my tears, I could not help blurting out you're not our mother, we've had house mothers in our homes, how can you be our mother when we have only seen you once before, we loved it in Bournemouth, we do not want to live here. The words kept flowing and I added, we are nine years old, why did you want us both home? Her next words were the words I will never forget, I got you both home for the points, the more points I get the quicker I will be able to get a move from the council, so with four children and one adult, I should go top of the list and as I have only two rooms I will get priority. On hearing this I felt sick. So we had been brought home for points to get a move, not for love. I felt betrayed, and had the view of how unfair it all was, but what could we do, we were only nine years old. Right she said, call me mum or mother both of you. I mumbled something like "um" and Phillip also said something, but it was not the full mum. Right let me tell you both straight away, you will not be getting that posh food you've been used to. I don't have much money and there are five of us now. Where is my sister Mary I demanded to know. Who told you that you had a sister Mary, she shouted. Well I remember Mary pushing me on a swing when I was about four years old, when I was at Culham Court and she stayed the day with us, I replied. She told me she was my sister. Don't you ever mention to anyone about you having a sister, because you haven't got one and that's the end of it. I will bring Mary into the story in another chapter. Just as she finished talking, I heard this noise behind me and opening the kitchen door were two girls. Hello Mum, they said, together. Right girls, these are your two brothers. The two sisters were Irene, 6 years old and Jean who was 3 years old. Irene had quite blonde hair whilst Jean had very dark hair. Irene was the quiet one of the two; she was quite shy, where as Jean was quite bossy and very spoilt. I supposed because she was the youngest, I always thought of her as a right madam. This is the first time I had set eyes on them. Take your sisters on their bikes and look after them. So out in the street we all went. What a shock to the system to be out on the street. So used to playing in fields and a large garden. After about an hour pushing the girls on their bikes, a call came from the house, come in now girls, your supper is ready but you two can stay out till I call you she said. From that moment on, I knew what the pecking order was in the house. Sitting outside the house we were finally let in as it was getting quite dark. Right eat this toast and dripping and get to bed. On entering the bedroom there was a double bed with the girls in it and two single beds. Right she said, that's my bed, next to the girls, you both have to share that one, pointing to a small single bed in the corner of the room, you will have to top and tail, of course this was the first time we ever had to top and tail and if you have never suffered this it is quite an experience. You both had the others persons feet near your head so if you didn't want smelly feet in your face you had to turn the opposite way, an experience most certainly to be missed! At this moment I knew how young Dick Whittingham felt when he first came up to London. My story was beginning to take a similar pattern to his.

No 10 Westbury terrace was a Victorian terraced house, with three flats above and a basement flat which had the use of a very small bricked garden. The house had one toilet for four families. In them days only posh people used toilet paper, we made do with cut up newspaper. In Victorian days these houses would have been owned by one family with the hired help and housekeeper living in the basement. They were about a hundred years old and had seen better days. Because there was a permanent smell of damp throughout the house with no electricity in any of the terraced houses, life was quite hard. The only fire was in the kitchen diner so the bedroom never had any heat in it. The lighting was by gas lamp. This consisted of a pipe bended up in a swan position with a white ball type fitting you switched the tap on the pipe and lit the mantle as it was called. There was one gas mantle in the kitchen and one in the bedroom. Gas was also used for the gas oven; the coal fire in the kitchen was quite small. You ordered your coal from the coal merchant. He would then deliver it into coal chutes that every house had in the basement cellar. If you think the winters used to start in November and go on until early spring and they used to be so very much colder with snow hanging around for eight weeks or so. How everyone survived with no ill effects is amazing. Even the street lights were still lit up by gas and this was right up to the 1960's. They had the same principle as inside gas lights, and just before dusk a man would come round with his pole and ignite the street lamps and just before dawn switch them off. Just across the road from Westbury terrace there was a group of shops in one of these shops, you could buy your fruit and vegetables and in the same shop they sold coal, so if you wanted a bag of coal, they would shovel it into a sack with all the coal dust settling on the fruit and veg. Only the middle classes owned a washing machine so what most people did was put all their dirty washing in a large bag and take it to the bagwash shop which of course was in the fruit and veg coal shop. It was then taken away to be washed and returned two to three days later. It was only washed not ironed; it was quite a cheap and convenient way of getting it done. If today's health and safety man had ever walked into that shop he would have shot himself. Next door to the "you couldn't make it up shop" was a pawn shop. As most people were quite poorly off, this was a haven for families to get paid, spend all their money by Monday and go back into the pawn shop, hand over say a watch for a couple of pounds get paid again, then take the watch out again and so on. The forerunner of all your plastic cards and a lifesaver for many a soul. Next to the pawn shop was the Gregg's house. One of the Gregg's was named Jim, who was to become a very good friend of mine. Behind the Gregg's house was a large school named Edward Wilson School, this school was named after the Arctic Explorer, Edward Wilson who went with Captain Scott to that ill fated expedition to the North Pole. Bourne Terrace led onto the Harrow Road and to the north of it was Wembley Stadium, and to the south was the Edgeware Road, which in turn led to Marble Arch. We had arrived at Westbury Terrace on a Saturday and on the Sunday I had gone out to look at my new surroundings and try to get my bearings. I had only just got into Bourne Terrace when I was surrounded by three mean looking characters. I was just nine at the time and I guess these yobs were about fifteen. Who are you and what are you doing round here? I'm John, I replied, and I live just over there, pointing to my house. No you don't, we know everyone round here, he shouted. Coming from Bournemouth probably didn't help as I must of had a semi-posh accent. The next thing I knew fists were coming at me from all angles. It helped me somewhat as I was backed up against a wall so they could not get me from all sides. Whack, thump, the blows were raining down from all directions, what saved me from further punishment was a rather large lady coming out of a house, shouting and swearing at the yobs, she also had a broomstick in her hands and was ready to lay into them. But I suppose seeing the size of her, they scarppered, leaving me laying on the floor with a bloody nose and a few cuts and bruises. She was truly an angel of mercy. F----g cowards she cried as she picked me up. I was watching from my window when they attacked you she said, but at least you fought back. Thank you very much for stopping the fight I said, that's all right, you go and get yourself cleaned up and with that I made my way home. I now had mixed emotions as this was the only fight I had ever been in, but I felt proud that I had fought back and not let them walk all over me.

On the Monday, we were both due to start our new school as our "mother" had arranged it for us, so on the morning, Phillip and I made our way to the new school. It was only five minutes walk away. As we turned the corner there stood our new school. IT was on the Harrow Road and was an old Victorian school. Paddington was a very run down and rough area, this school was no exception, we both had to see the headmaster before we started class. His first words were, not very encouraging. Right you two, do your work, keep out of trouble and you'll be alright, misbehave and you'll get the cane, right the head boy will show you to your classroom so be off with you. At least Phillip and I were in the same classroom. Walking into the class was quite a frightening experience. The teacher had not arrived in class yet so the head boy showed us where to sit. We were sat in the front of the class, chalk and objects were thrown at us, and to hear words like, hope you can fight, because you're going to get beaten up at break time was not very encouraging. As the teacher entered the classroom they carried on shouting and throwing things until he shouted as loud as he could, then calm took place (when I was in schools in Bournemouth, as the teacher entered the class you all stood up until he told you to sit down). Surely I'm dreaming all this. This just cannot be happening, any minute I will wake up from this nightmare, but it was no nightmare. I was here and I'd better make the best of it, I either sink or swim. The morning break arrived and all the other classes were let out to play in a rather small playground on entering the playground I got my first sight of a huge lad named Peter Groom. New boy he yelled, within seconds he had me around the neck with his long arms, he was only thirteen but over six feet tall. The next thing, I had his belt around my neck. A fire escape went from the top floor of the school to the playground. Picking me up he tied the belt with my neck to the fire escape and left me dangling there. On hearing my yells, a teacher came running out. He knew Peter had strung me up because he was on the floor laughing his head off. Get him down Peter said the teacher. F—k off replied Peter Groom, you f—cing cut him down, because I'm not going to. So the teacher had to get me down. I had only been at the school a couple of hours, this is not a good start I thought to myself. For the next week Phillip and I were in fights nearly every day, mostly it was because we were new there, and also that we were from the country and spoke with a country accent. By now I had enough of all this, so I decided the next one to start a fight with me I would go straight on the attack and get my blows in first. I could see this boy with menace on his face and spoiling for a fight, and I knew his name was Jack Franks and he was one of the school bullies and he was coming towards me. So before he spoke or made a move, I threw a punch as hard as I could straight into his face. He staggered back, more in shock than anything else, I could see that the blow I had given had really hurt him, and he didn't want any more but for good measure I have him a couple more and with that he ran. I felt like a young lion, which had just had his first kill. After that word got round that I would not be pushed round. I never got into a fight again at that school, and as things go in life he became one of my best friends. As I came from a single parent family we were entitled to free school meals. The other way of getting free school meals was to come from a very poor family and there were many of them in Paddington. The school dinner was the most important meal of the day because at home the meals for Phillip and I were very small. Our breakfast consisted of a slice of toast and dripping and the meal in the evening was very basic and small but our two sisters seemed to eat very much better, so we both used to look forward to the school dinners. My two sisters went to other schools so we did not see much of them, only at weekends. In the war, ration books were issued to everyone and these ration books only stopped in about 1950. In these ration books they had different pages in them, one page would have coupons for eggs and the next page would have coupons for meat, and so on with the egg page, you were only allowed 6 eggs a week and with the meat page a roll of beef a week, so you were restricted to what you could buy each week, so a lot of families went hungry unless you had the money, then you could buy goods from "under the counter" as they called it, but not many working class people were able to buy goods this way. Even clothes had to be bought with ration coupons. But the welfare people supplied us with clothes. Both Phillip and I were given a pair of Wellingtons and a pair of short trousers by them, plus a Jacket which proved to be a life saver as we had arrived at Westbury terrace in late September. It was not long before winter started to set in. The winters were much earlier than they are today and much longer going on to late march. By November it was very cold and frosts were quite common and even snow used to fall. We both got into a routine of getting into our "top and tail" bed.

Poem

Topped and tailed meant there were two in a bed

To avoid the smell remember to turn your head

Even facing away from them feet you would still smell

Sleeping all night like this it was just utter hell

No escape from it just had to grin and bare

Must try to find them pockets of fresh air

Don't try this at home not even when drunk

Or your end up smelling like that ugly skunk.

We dressed and washed in cold water, because the only hot water was what was boiled in the kettle. Then having a slice of bread or toast and then off to school. All the pupils at school were given a half pint of milk per day as a lot of children were so undernourished. Our mother insisted we both brought out milk home with us as she needed it. I always thought this was a bit of a liberty as we both needed it ourselves. The girls of course were allowed to drink theirs and were always well fed. World War Two had only just finished five years before we moved to London and looking around bomb damage was everywhere. All around the area bombed houses were still boarded up in some cases whole blocks of houses had been flattened and trees and shrubs and had now grown up in all the waste land. We used to play in these areas. One in particular was so large we called it the lost jungle. Just up from Bourne Terrace was a large piece of land that must have been about two acres. This was hit by one of the first flying bombs called the V2 rocket. The German air force was trying to destroy Paddington Station, a lot of bombs hit the station but a lot went astray. They had cleared the piece of land and had built pre-fabs on the land. These were portable square box bungalow type houses and could be erected in less than a week and you could get many of these bungalows in place quickly so bombed out families were able to move in very quickly. They were only meant to last twenty years but there are still hundreds of these prefabs still being lived in around London to this day. After school we both used to bring out school milk home, have the bare minimum of food and was told to go out and don't come back 'till nine 'o clock at night, so that meant walking the streets for about four hours each night, and with short trousers on and our Wellingtons cutting into our legs it became very painful. This was our first winter now in London and we were very, very cold. We both used to go to Paddington Station just to get out of the cold as this was only about twenty minutes walk from our house. None of these houses had bathrooms in them so each house had a metal tub, so every Saturday night we had to have a bath, there was no hot tap, just a cold tap. Hot water had to be boiled in a kettle. So to fill one of these baths took ages. We used to sit in the bedroom while the girls had their bath together. Once they had bathed, we had to jump into the bath together in the same water, I'm sure we used to come out dirtier than when we went in!

Christmas came around and this one was our first here in London, so we were both looking forward to our presents that we may be getting and of course extra food. As the girls were handed their presents it came as quite a shock when we were handed ours. We both each were given an apple, an orange and a mars bar and that was it. I had never felt so sad in all my life and just thought to myself why is she so cruel to us? I knew we were there to get the extra points on the housing list but to get so little and the sisters to get so much really hurt, but I always had this belief even at ten years old that things will one day get better as they could not get any worse.

Poem

I used to enjoy Xmas in them warm children's homes
Now I'm always chilled down to my bones
Everyone should be happy at this time of year
It's just that time of giving not shedding a tear
But I must be positive and look on the Brightside
That river will change direction a turn of the tide

We had now been at Westbury terrace for a year, Christmas had come and gone and it doesn't matter how bad things are and how awful your situation is you find yourself in, you do get used to it and your body and mind adapt to it. I always had a positive attitude to my plight and knew better times would come around one day. Just a month before Christmas there was a big treat in store for all the pupils at school because every year since the end of the war some of the commonwealth countries would send food parcels to all the schools in London (I don't know if they were sent to the rest of the United Kingdom). These food parcels were made up of mostly tins of fruit, hams, and chocolate bars etc. They realised that people in London and elsewhere in Britain had very little to eat. This was a fantastic gesture by Canada, Australia and New Zealand and even at that time I felt very proud and in some ways quite humbled that these countries should come to the aid of the mother country, and this now as an eleven year old, felt the full benefits of it, and will never forget the kindness shown by these nations. About once a month, the nurse used to visit our school to check on all the pupils making sure all was OK with the children, because of the poor diets and living conditions there was always a danger of diseases breaking out. It was on one of these visits just after Christmas that I and Phillip were being checked out by the nurse she was looking through my head when she cried, how long have you had these spots and scabs in your head and do they itch a lot? I replied No, nurse; I never knew I had scabs and spots in my head. Right she said, you're both coming straight with me to see the doctor and if it's what I think it is you are going to be isolated and sent to hospital. My heart raced on hearing these words. She quickly arranged for us to be examined by the doctor who confirmed her suspicions it was contagious and it was called ringworm and was in quite an advanced stage. Ringworm was quite common at this time. It was caused by bad diet and poor living conditions and a lot of other factors. The doctor was also concerned with both of our appearances as we were both quite thin and looked under nourished. It all happened so quickly after that. The next day we had to report to the local clinic and waiting for us there was a doctor with the words I'm admitting you both to hospital immediately. You will be going to Goldie Leigh Hospital for children in Abbey Wood South London. On hearing these words I felt like crying tears of joy. At last we would have a break from our torment.

GOLDIE LEIGH HOSPITAL

It was arranged that the nurse would pick us both up the following day and she duly arrived at nine that morning. We both couldn't wait to get in her car. The journey only took about one hour as we were only going from North West London to the suburbs of South London and in them days where was not so much traffic around. We were both in a happy state on arriving at the hospital. The hospital was situated between Plumstead and Bexleyheath and near the Woolwich Arsenal, so it was countryside on one side and built up on the other. As we entered the hospital I could see it had large grounds front and back. The hospital was quite a big place and it was filled with children with all different illnesses. We were in the ringworm part. Ringworm was treated by a yellow paste that was put on the head and a bandage covering the head, but their first task was to build up our strength as we were both underweight. Just as with Eastbourne children's home, Goldie Leigh had a circle of houses around a large green. These were used as a convalescent home for the children once their treatment in the main part of the hospital had started to take effect. They were like feeder homes to the hospital. Phillip had exactly the same conditions as myself and was also underweight, but this is no surprise as we were both twins. We stayed in the main hospital for about two months and then were placed into the feeder home. Once again we were put into separate houses. The hospital had a large school it was three schools in one – infant, junior and secondary modern as all the patients were of different ages. It also had its own laundry as with most hospitals they key to better health is good food and Goldie Leigh was no exception. As the food was excellent you were soon able to build up your strength. The illnesses that all the children had, used to take many months sometimes years to heal, because most modern drugs were not available but most of the children in these hospitals were much better off and happier than they were in their own homes. Once again each house had two mothers, one would work for two weeks and have two weeks leave and the other house mother would take her turn. We had both been at the hospital about three months and having regular treatment for our ringworm but the treatment was not working. They tried all different kinds of lotions, ointments but nothing seemed to work. So they decided to transfer us both to St Thomas hospital in London where they thought that we would be able to get specialised treatment. The Hospital was located on the south side of Westminster Bridge right by the Thames. By now, instead of being upset, to us, going to a new hospital was more like an adventure and getting to the hospital only took about forty minutes. On arriving we were told that they did not have a children's ward so we would be going into the men's ward. This proved to be a very good move for us as the men could not do enough for us. We were told that this was the first time that children had been on the ward, even the nursing staff made a big fuss over us. It was fascinating to hear stories from the men about their war time experiences as this was 1951 the war had only been over for six years so it was quite fresh in their memories. Many of these men had been in the forces but quite a few of them who were older had been air raid wardens. As the stories they had to tell were truly amazing. What made this stay, in this hospital different for us, was mixing with grown ups and all our lives we had mixed in the company of children. It was fascinating for us to be with older people. St Thomas Hospital on one side looks out over the Thames with the houses of Parliament on the opposite side and Westminster Bridge to its right hand side. In them days the Thames was a very busy waterway with large barges steaming up and down all day. Westminster Bridge a huge exhibition was being held and this was called "The Festival of Britain" which was to show the world what Britain could manufacture and all things great about Britain. At the Hospital they tried a new treatment for Phillip and me. The new treatment they tried was called Penicillin. These injections had not been out long and they wanted to see if they would make any difference. Within a month there was quite an improvement in our condition so after only about six weeks in St Thomas they decided to transfer us back to Goldie Leigh to carry on the treatment there. It was very sad leaving the men in our ward as we had become quite fond of them all and before we left they put on a small leaving party for us both. We were made to feel like stars and we had brought a bit of Joy into their lives as they had ours and they treated us like stars as they were fascinated in having twins who were so much alike. They were like father figures. We were taken back to Goldie Leigh Hospital in an ambulance which was quite fun, but my request for the bell to be sounded and the blue light to be flashing was politely turned down. On returning back to the hospital things soon got back into the same routine mixing and playing with lots of children, climbing trees and playing in the large grounds of the hospital. It was all so much fun. Our skin complaint was by now healing up quite quickly and because of this we no longer had to wear a bandage around our heads. I knew it wouldn't be long before we would be discharged and my worst fears came true. We were both called into see the doctor. He gave us both an examination and declared that we were now well enough to go home. The words I was dreading to hear we had been at Goldie Leigh for nine months, a better place you could not find to do your growing up in. Once again it was saying the goodbyes that were the hardest. You never got used to saying the dreaded goodbyes to children and staff who have been part of your life and knowing that you will never ever see them again and you feel so sad and angry that this keeps on happening in your life and there is nothing you can do to change things. One of the house mothers escorted us back to Paddington, we were now home again.

Poem

Pack your suitcase again it's time to leave
Dry them eyes you have no time to grieve
Childhood games and fun they'll just have to end
Don't worry about your broken heart it will mend
What do you expect of life affection and joy?
Well life's just not like that you silly boy
Just wanted happiness is that such a crime
Need loving arms around me like that clinging vine.

It was back to Westbury terrace as soon as I stepped inside the damp smell hit me and being in the countryside for so long I noticed it more. Just across the road from us lived a family; they seemed to be middle class. The Mother and Father were church going Christians as were her two boys who were about the same age as Phillip and myself. Not many people went to church around the area so they stood out. After being back about a week the two boys called to see if I would like to go to choir practice with them. At first I said no, but when they told me you get tea and cakes after the practise I couldn't wait to sing (for my supper), as I used to say. After a few weeks I became a choir boy mainly for the grub that was on offer. After the service one of the priests Father Green who was there was a larger than life character. After about two months of being a choir boy he asked if I and three other choir boys would like to go on holiday with him to Romsey in Hampshire and camp in the grounds of Broadlands. The priest had been a master at Eton, in his younger days, and one of his pupils at Eton lived at Broadlands with his parents. Father Green had made friends with the parents and allowed him to take poor London urchins camping on their spacious grounds. Broadlands is an old manor house set in hundreds of acres and at one time was the home of Florence Nightingale. The priest had set up three tents in the beautiful grounds. Father Green made his base in the grounds so our days were spent touring around the countryside and the coast in his 1927 Vauxhall. What a fantastic old car, it had running boards either side of the car and the boot lifted up to expose two extra seats. It had a large hand brake next to the running board. It was old but still could do 100mph. I believe they only made one hundred of these models. At that time there were only five left in the world. One day we all went down to Weymouth on the South Coast and a large American car pulled up along side our car. The driver of the American car had a young lady in the passenger seat and they both got into quite a long conversation with Father Green. As their car pulled away Father Franks, said to us all, well I'll be dammed, would you believe that man   was speaking to was one of my old pupils from Eton, his name was Peter Sellers. That meant nothing to us boys, only in later life did I find out that Peter Sellers was a brilliant comedy actor and film star. At the camp site at night Father Green used to tell us stories about his life and what a fantastic life he led. Some of the ghost stories he used to tell were really scary, and the way he told them would frighten the pants off you. He was a young army officer in the First World War and then served in Egypt and the Sudan and anywhere the British army were based. His stories used to keep us spellbound about all his adventures. After leaving the army he became a master at Eton, for a few years, and then decided he wanted to become a priest. Although I believe he was quite well off, he wanted to work as a priest in the poorer parts of London and that is how he made his way to Paddington. I often wondered what happened to that old Vauxhall, maybe it's in a museum somewhere. What a wonderful, caring human being he was, a true gentleman. I have never forgotten his kindness and stories, and his love of his fellow man, he will no doubt now be sitting on the right hand side of the lord in heaven.

Poem

Father Franks on this earth he did dwell

A yarn and a story he could tell

He's now up in heaven, telling his tales

Angels are singing and are ringing them bells

Now sitting with God on his right hand side

With a smile on his face two feet wide

When I got back from the camping holiday and told Phillip all our stories, he was quite upset he was not asked to come but there was no room at the inn for him on the trip. The two church going boys from across the road called for me on a Sunday to see if I wanted to go to Hyde Park to feed the swans and ducks. Their mother had given them two large crusty stale loaves of bread to take with them. As soon as I saw them loaves of bread my eyes lit up, of course I'll come to feed the ducks I said, so they gave me one of the loaves to hold. So off we went. It was about a thirty minutes walk to Hyde Park and the ducks were in a large pond in Kensington Gardens. By the time we had got to the pond I had completely polished off the loaf, I had been eating it on the way without them knowing, that's how hungry I was. OK, John, you can start feeding the ducks now, they shouted. I ate it all, I had to admit, and you mean to say you ate stale bread? They said with a look of horror both together. Yes I replied, I was quite hungry. They must have told their mother about it because whenever she saw me, she used to ask if I would like a meal and whenever she asked me I was in there before she had finished the sentence with her knife and fork in my hand ready to tuck in. It doesn't matter how bad things are in life, like cramped conditions, poor food and sometimes very cold, you get used to it. Your body and mind seems to adapt to any situation and you make the best of what you've got. The streets were your playground where children of all ages used to play and let off steam in the summer evenings. We used to play cricket with the lamppost as the wicket as no-one could afford a car the streets were empty of traffic. In the winter football was played. When you think of the noise that was made nobody ever complained. This is the era where you could leave your door open all day and nobody would break in. A lot of households would have a key attached to a piece of string; it would hang inside the letter box. If any child wanted to get in they just pulled the string up and unlocked the door. How times have changed!

Poem

Kicking a ball about with your arse hanging out
The noise was deafening, oh how we did shout
Kicking that ball between the posts yes that's a goal
May play for England may get out of this hell hole
Or maybe I'll do better will play that game cricket
A good catcher of a ball I'll just keep wicket
I could play both sports and play for top teams
But its only make believe it's all in my dreams.

One way that us kids used to make a few bob was to collect newspapers and old rags. This was known as "toting". We would make an old cart up with four pram wheels with string in the front to pull it along. We used to pull the cart along to the better of parts of Paddington, which included

Maida vale, Queensway, St Johns Wood and roads off the Edgware road. Most of the houses had basements with a cellar and this is where all the dustbins were kept, if you managed to get a big bundle of newspapers you would get 6d for them, 2 p in today's money. Today you wouldn't be able to buy anything with it, but in them days you could get in Saturday morning pictures (a big thing in those days). On a good Saturday we could make 5s shillings (25p) and with that three of you could get in the cinema and have quite a good meal each. There was quite a few ways we were able to make money. In them days, red telephone boxes used to have a slot for putting your coins in and a button and chute for getting your money back. If you dialled a number and it was engaged, you would press the button B and your money would be returned out of the chute. What we used to do was bend a piece of cardboard into the chute so that it could not be seen. When someone pressed button "B" to get their money back the cardboard would hold the coins. We would be watching the telephone box from a safe distance. The people would keep pressing the "B" button and would give up trying and leave the telephone box mouthing profanities. On a night we would block about five boxes and after about two or three hours remove the cardboard and the coins would come tumbling out. On a good night we could make 4 shillings (20p) a lot of lolly in them days. The other scam we used to get up to was "bunking" in at the cinema. There were three ways of doing this - One way was for all of us to pool our money then give it to one person to get in. He would buy a ticket, go into the cinema and make his way to the exit doors at the back of the cinema. The doors had roll bars on them so he would lift the roll bar and hey presto, five or six of us would scamper in, hiding in the men's toilets and would wait a couple of minutes, then the first lad would make their way in, until we were all in. The other way to get in was to get a length of wire and make it into a circle and then thread one part of the circle in between the two doors, then manoeuvre the wire till you made contact with the rolling bar, then wiggle the wire onto the bar and with an upward pull of the wire the bar would release the door and you all piled in. I have to say I became an expert in opening the doors because I used extra thick wire used on orange boxes. The other way of getting in was waiting at the back doors and wait for people to come out and you would just walk in, but the trouble with this approach was the people coming out would sometimes tell the manager and he and his staff would come looking for kids, so whatever way you got in the golden rule was never to sit next to each other and try to find a couple with a spare seat next to them. They would think you were part of that family. The biggest menace to all of us kids in the cinema was the men that used to sit next to you if there was a spare seat. They would normally have a raincoat over their arm and the next thing you felt the raincoat on your leg, followed by a hand, these men to us were known as "bum boys". Once you felt that dreaded hand, you exited that seat in seconds and found another seat. The best seats in the house were priced at 3/6d (17.5p) and they were in the upstairs circle. Sometimes if I felt daring, I would make my way up to the circle and sit in the best seats but you had to sit with a couple up there because the staff knew that no urchins could afford the prices up there. I remember one time I was in the circle sitting with a couple and down below I could see all my mates being thrown out. They would just ask for your ticket and if you could not show them one you were out. But all of them had got to confident that night and sat with each other and that was that. For some reason Phillip and I always used to be in the wars as far as our health was concerned and I suppose as with most things if I got a health problem he would always get the same symptoms as myself. We had both been at home now for two years and it had been one year since we had returned from Goldie Leigh Hospital. We both started to notice that our eyes were getting very sore and that the eyelashes were caking up and sticking together. This was the condition called Bletherritis and in our case was quite bad, not a very common eye condition but there were a few cases about. So back to the clinic we went to be told by the doctor that you both need to go to hospital and get it treated and that the children's hospital we would go to was White Oak Hospital in Swanley, Kent. This was an eye hospital only, and patients came mainly from the London area. We thought the doctor meant only being there a few weeks in total but we were there for eight months. Within a week we were both taken to Swanley by a nurse.

White Oak Hospital

My first thought as we entered the gates was, thank the lord I don't have to top and tail for a while. Once again this was one of those Victorian hospitals with the main hospital block and large houses that made up the rest of the Hospital. Phillip was in the same house as myself and as with Goldie Leigh, White Oak Hospital had its own laundry and a large school. There were about ten houses in all with about fifteen children to each house. The ages ranged from five years to seventeen years, some of the older ones had been there most of their lives and the house mothers were looked on as their real mothers as some of them were orphans. Some of the house mothers had been army nurses in the war and were not married so this was an ideal job for them, the children they never had, I suppose. The grounds of the hospital were large. On one side was a large wood where we used to play. One day we were playing cowboys and Indians with made up bows and arrows, and I was hiding behind a tree but my right leg was showing. The next thing I knew there was an arrow sticking out of my leg. The pain was indescribable. As I fell to the ground the other lads gathered around looking very distressed and shocked and not knowing what to do. Well I thought to myself this has got to come out, so with my two hands clamped around the arrow I pulled it as hard as I could and out it popped. The surprising thing is that there was very little blood and looking at the arrow head it had penetrated in about two inches. The lads carried me to the main hospital block where the nurse took a look and saw a small neat hole in the leg and wrapped a bandage around it saying that will be fine in a few days. After a few days the pain started to really kick in, I could hardly walk on it but on seeing the nurse she said stop pretending you're hurt and walk properly. As the days went on my leg started to swell up and started to turn black. By now I could not walk on it. By now they realised that there was a problem with the leg so they had my leg raised on pillows with a hot poultice wrapped around it to draw out whatever was in it. The next day they took the poultice off and slightly squeezed my leg with that a large wooden splinter popped out followed by heaps of black tar like liquid. It must have been two inches long, they now realised that I was not making the pain up. It took about two months to get over it. The hospital had it's own football team and also a cricket team and fine laying fields, it was like being at a public school, from the back streets of Paddington to all this! Childhood days do not get better than this. Every Sunday was visiting Sunday but half the parents never wanted to show up. Some of the children had not seen their parents for years. Our mother never once paid us a visit although in them days it would have taken about two hours to get there but we were not bothered and just carried on with things. Two houses away from ours was one of the all girl houses. As Phillip and I were now thirteen we both started to take an interest in the young ladies. There was one girl that we both had a crush on and her name was Janet Price. Although it was only puppy love on both our parts we both did not have the courage to tell her how we felt about her. Janet Price came from the town of Sevenoaks in Kent, about ten miles from Swanley and Phillip, when he was in the army was talking to a fellow soldier and asked him where he came from, he told him he was from Sevenoaks. Phillip then said I knew a girl from Sevenoaks and she was in hospital in Swanley in Kent with me and here name was Janet Price. Well blow me down said the soldier, she's my girlfriend and has often talked about her time in that hospital, what an amazing coincidence they both thought. Phillip and myself were called into the nurses office one day and the doctor was sitting at his desk as we entered he looked up from a letter he was reading. Sit down boys, I've brought you in today to see me to tell you both that my staff and I think you are both well enough to be discharged and return home. This came as a bombshell as we were told we would be there for at least two more months. The doctor then said to us, I need to speak to a colleague and left the room. As he left the room I picked up the letter, it was from our mother asking the doctor to discharge us both as soon as possible as she needed both of us home so that she could get the extra housing points. With shaking hands and a heavy heart I put the letter back on the desk. So once again we were wanted just for the points, not for ourselves, a bitter pill to take. As the doctor returned, he said, I've had a word with my colleague and he agrees that you can both go home as soon as possible. So that was it, six fantastic months of good food, people who cared and a wonderful environment. It was now all to end; it was a sad day once more when we had to say our goodbyes to staff and all of the children.

Return to Paddington

Once again we found ourselves back in London again and having been away the past eight months you realise how dirty the whole area was. Having just returned from green fields and fresh air. Now Johnny boy, you've just got to get used to it again and be positive and you'll survive. One of the first persons I bumped into was one of the brothers who I used to knock around with, his name was Frank, who told me all about the things he had got up to and the news that he had joined the air cadets which was only five minutes walk away and would I be interested in joining them and as soon as he mentioned you also get tea and cakes! If I joined them he would give me two shillings (10p) because if he just got one more recruit to join, he would get a corporals strip which he really wanted. After the nights training I was in the recruiting office in a flash, the next thing I was standing in front of the group Captain. Why do you want to join the air cadets? Well sir, I lied, I've always been interested in Aircraft and when I'm older sir I would love to join the RAF. Well John, he replied, that's a very good reason to want to join us and with his outstretched hand he shook mine. I was now a member of the Paddington Air Cadets. We will see you Thursday night for your first nights training and if all goes well you will get your uniform three weeks after that. I left his office a very pleased lad as I had just earned two shillings, a fortune to me. Frank had been waiting outside the office and his first words were, well, have you joined up? Yes I have and you owe me two bob. Out of his picket he pulled out the coin, I nearly snatched his hand off grabbing it from him. It turned out to be one of the best things I had ever done, as far as things went in Paddington because joining the air cadets opened up new horizons for me. Not only did it get me out of the cold one night a week on some weekends we would travel up to RAF Hendon (RAF Hendon closed down in a bout 1970 and now is an aircraft museum) which was about six miles up the Harrow Road (Watling Street) and go flying in small aircraft. Sometimes flying to RAF Henley, or RAF Northolt and then on to RAF Hornchurch. RAF Hendon, Henley, Northolt and Hornchurch were the four airfields that were situated around London and played a major role in the defence of the capital in the war. The thrill of it all, being such young lads, flying all over the place with the RAF and seeing that they had now given me a brand new blue uniform, I felt like part of a team, a family if you like. In the summer we would all go camping in one of their operational airfields Thorny Island was one of the camps we would go for two weeks in the school holidays which was a boys dream come true. Going down to the firing range and shooting targets with 303 rifles which was fantastic. For some of us who were only fourteen a rifle was almost as tall as me. We also got to go on route marches with RAF instructors and what was most pleasing to me we were given three square meals a day. If I could have I would have signed up for the RAF just for the food but like all good things they all had to come to an end but having experienced the camping I detected a new self confidence in myself.

Poem

Soaring into the blue yonder we're up in the sky
Now up to twenty thousand feet and flying so high
Taking off from London it's the first time I've flown
With ten cadets with me I'm not on my own
Hey it's scary up here so what if we crash
Well Johnny boy if we do we are all ash
The pilots in front he's called the aviator
Sitting behind him is the navigator
It has Rolls Royce engines they sound so very sweet
But just look at my face white as a sheet
All of a sudden we have landed safe and sound
What a great feeling to have landed on the ground

Returning back from the camp for once I did not dread returning to London maybe I was finally getting used to this way of life. When I returned to Paddington, I thought I would expand my horizons, so I joined the boy scouts which were next door to the air cadet's hall. Most of my weekends were taken up in the scouts. We used to go on field craft camps in surrey or Kent, learning how to survive in the wild, which was great fun, but was always a bit wary of the scout master, making sure I was never alone with him. When we used to go to weekend camps, he insisted that he tucked all the scouts in their beds at night, I'm sure he would have liked to give us all a big kiss goodnight as well! One of the things we used to do in the scouts was to take part in bob-a-job scheme. What this involved was knocking on doors and asking the house holders if they would like any jobs done, like clean their cars, washing windows or shopping for them. This would cost them a bob. A job was worth one shilling (5p). We were given a white card and when the job was completed they would fill in the card of what work was done and the amount paid. This bob-a-job only went on for two weeks and in that time I collected about two pounds, a lot of money in them days. One of the houses I called at asked me to clean a boiler in the basement of this large house in Queensway (the posh part of Paddington). He was quite an old man so he asked me would I like to clean his boiler once a week and he would pay me. So I agreed to do this. Within a month not only was I cleaning the boiler, I was doing his shopping and cleaning his flat for him. He owned the large house and he had about ten flats in it, some families living in them and others had single people living in them. So in the end I was doing jobs for his tenants and sometimes I would earn about 10 shillings (50p) a week, which is probably worth today about £10, this was a kings ransom in them days. This was the start of my earning a living.

Phillip runs away

Although I had settled down quite well, Phillip was not very happy with life. He had never got used to living in Paddington and hated everything about the environment he was living in. He used to talk to me about the wonderful times we had in the homes and why should he still have to live at Westbury Terrace. So it came as no surprise to me when one Friday evening after school Phillip said, I won't be going home with you because I'm going to run away. I have had enough he said, I cannot take it anymore. Where will you go I asked? I know it was really terrible of me but my first thought was oh well, at least I won't have to top and tail anymore. I don't know, he replied, I will sleep rough. He had that look in his eye and I knew he was determined to go so I gave him the only money I had on me which was a one shilling coin that I had, I wished him the best of luck and he was gone. I don't know why but I never thought of going with him, I suppose I had settled in better and got used to this way of life, but I did have a lump in my throat, seeing him go as we had been through so much together and I was worried how he would be able to manage on his own as he was not street wise. His last words to me were, when you get in say that I've had enough and I have run away and I will never be coming back. On returning home I knocked on the door to get in as I was never allowed a key. I kept on knocking but there was no reply but I got quite used to this so I would either sit on the doorstep or go for a long walk. On this occasion I went for a long walk and returned two hours later and knocked on the door. I had mixed feelings in having to say Phillip had run away. One part of me was quite excited to be reporting the news but the other half of me was a bit worried as how it was going to effect me. I could see a light on so I knew someone was in and after sitting on the doorstep for half an hour the door opened and mother stood there. Where's Phillip, she said crossly, he's run away and has told me to tell you he won't be coming back. Oh, he has, she said crossly, don't worry, he will be back tomorrow you'll see. I must say that night was the best night's sleep that I had in ages but thinking about it I would have rather had his big smelly feet in my face than him not being around. Even that first night I was starting to miss him. The next day came and no sign of Phillip. By now I could see that mother was getting quite agitated and saying I'll have to report him to the police if he's not home by this evening. Eight o'clock had arrived and no sign of Phillip so off she went to the police station on returning she said they'll soon find him and bring him back. But Saturday went into Sunday and still no sign of him. On the Monday I made my way to school and at about ten o'clock I got called into the Headmasters office to be told by the headmaster that Phillip had been found by the Police and had been living at night in a coal cellar in Bayswater and has now been placed in a young persons hostel, as he insisted he did not ever want to return home. I was so pleased to hear he was alright. He had told the police the whole story about his life and had told them he would rather spend the rest of his life sleeping in that coal cellar than return home. He was dealt with very quickly by a juvenile court to see what was to become of him. On hearing his side of the story the Judge decided to place him permanently in a hostel in South London. His nightmare had now ended and his life now changed forever.

Poem

It took some courage to run away after school
All on his own with no one around to call
Sleeping in a coal cellar he had about enough
Even then he knew he would have to sleep rough
Laying amongst the coal dust and them smelly bins
With many other unknown bugs and lots of creepy things
Sometimes it pays to be bold if you want more
Taking a chance hoping it can open another door.

Things started to get a little better now that Phillip had left. I suppose mother did not want me to leave as well as the very reason for us being there was for the points and if I decided to leave the point's situation would be grim for her. I started to now make friends and one friend in particular lived just across the road. His name was Jimmy Gregg; he lived with his mother and step brothers and sisters. I thought where I lived was bad enough, but his house was even worse. It not only looked like a bombed building from the outside, the inside looked like a bomb had done its worse. The front door would not close properly and the framework had shrank, probably due to the damp conditions. Some floorboards were missing as you entered the house and the stairs looked like they would collapse at any moment. The house did have a cellar but nobody had ever plucked up the courage to have a look down there. I always understood that it was half full of water. It would explain all the dampness sometimes complete strangers would walk into the house, have a good look around and then leave empty handed, if you have nothing there is nothing to steal. Even the rats that occupied the house gave up on the house. It is said that they made a pact with each other, half of them bolted and found a warmer house with food, the other half stayed and committed suicide by jumping on to the rat traps. Preferring this way of dying than to be either frozen to death or starved to death. Jim had three other brothers living with him and two sisters. The sisters shared a bedroom upstairs but the brothers had to share the same bedroom downstairs. The walls had wallpaper hanging off, it was so old, and a print of Queen Victoria could be seen on it. The bed was a double one it must have been years since the bed had sheets on it but if you looked closely you could still see evidence that sheets were there once was but were now part of the blanket. The one blanket that covered them was years old and had probably never been washed in its lifetime, It was so hard and stiff. If it was whacked with a hammer the hammer would just bounce off. In them days no one had carpet to keep the house a bit warmer and in all my years visiting Jim's house I never once saw an open fire alight, however did we all manage to stay alive in those days? As the winters were very much colder than they are today, but survive we did.

Poem

The family were sharing their house with them large rats
Just one of them would have defeated an army of cats
No food in the house so rats ran away
Why would they live there no need to stay
The Gregg family were such a hardy bunch
Very little food they never heard of lunch
Most families just put up with near starvation
Them working class people throughout this nation
This family could be called the salt of the earth
Not in money terms as they had nothing of worth
Such wonderful kindness and friendship they had shown to me
As strong as ever like that solid oak tree.

I would soon be leaving school as I was approaching fifteen years old. The school was still as rough as ever but being older I did not get into any more fights. If I could see a fight was eminent I used to be able to talk my way out of it and one way was to agree with everything the potential attacker was saying and telling him why would I want to fight the best fighter in the school. This was reverse psychology and it worked every time, they went away feeling even harder than they thought they were and I ended up with just hurt pride but my face was still in once place. One of the pupils I used to sit next to went by the name of Roger Blair, how I could ever forget that name! He was a bit behind in all subjects and I used to try and help him in some of his projects that we may be working on. After helping him with yet another task he thanked me and asked me to meet him outside after school. On meeting him outside he felt into his jacket pocket and pulled out a ten shilling note and handed it to me saying this is for you for always helping me with my work, don't tell anyone about it. I was in total shock. Ten shillings at that time, housewives would have been able to buy her groceries for the week and still have change leftover, but what shocked me more was the other notes he had rolled up in a bundle. I not only spotted ten shilling notes but also one pound notes but what really made my legs go weak and my head spin was the sight of them big five pound notes, when you think the average wage at that time was less than five pounds a week. These white five pound notes were really large they were slightly larger than a birthday card with bold black writing on them; it was a remarkable and beautiful note. This was most definitely the finest note ever printed but it was taken out of circulation I believe because it was very easy to forge and many millions were printed. So rather than have millions of forgeries on the market overnight they recalled them all in and printed much smaller blue ones. Although the new blue five pound note still was the same value as the old one it felt like it had devalued in money terms. On each Thursday afternoon most of the school used to walk the two miles to Paddington recreation grounds for sporting activities. You could take part in running or many of the other things that were on offer. It also had a restaurant in the middle of the complex and this is where Roger Blair and myself headed to get some refreshments. Get what you like John; said Roger, I'll pay for it. So I brought a coke and a slice of cake, he ordered the same and pulled out from a wad of notes a big white five pound note. Handing it to the lady you could see the shock on her face as she probably didn't take five pounds over the counter in a week so you could understand why she was so shocked. I'm sorry she blurted out I have not got the change in the till to change that amount, so bring it with you next week, I think the bill came to about 9d (4 ½ p) (this is the equivalent of a fourteen year old today pulling out a £100 pounds) and paying for something worth 50p. As we sat there chatting away two policemen walked in, the lady pointing in our direction to the policemen. Right you two, you're both coming down to the Police station to explain how you came to be in possession of a five pound note. The police in those days were very much respected and people looked up to them. As we both were taken to the police car my heart was racing and I was quite frightened wondering what would be my fate. Within ten minutes we had arrived at Paddington Police Station which was on the Harrow Road. Right you two said the burly desk sergeant we're going to get to the bottom f this. Right you Blair go in room one and pointing to room two, you Banfield go into that room. As I was led into the room my heart felt like it was going to explode. As I sat in the chair a very aggressive detective walked in. Right Banfield, who have you robbed? How much did you steal? And where is the rest of the money? With his face about two inches from mine he shouted come clean son and tell me the whole truth because if I find you've lie to me I'll make sure you're locked up and I'll throw away the key. I haven't done anything I protested, I don't know where Blair got the money from, all I did was help him spend it. After a few more questions and shouting and screeching at me he said, sit still I'm going out for a minute. As I sat there my biggest fear was what Blair was saying as I had no idea how he obtained the money. As these thoughts were going around in my head the door opened and in walked a much younger man. Hello John, he started off, my name is Simon and I would like you to tell me the whole story about how you and Roger got this money from? After telling him all I knew about the money and did not know where Blair had got it from. He thanked me and said sit there John I won't be a minute and out he went. As I was sitting there I thought what a nice man and how friendly he was compared to the other one. Once again the door opened and in came the aggressive one. Right you tow-rag, Blair has admitted that you and him carried out a robbery and stole all that money he had on him, so own up now or you won't see the light of day anymore. With him waving his arms about then crashing his fist on the table it was quite frightening. I've told you the truth sir I blurted out, if he's saying we've committed a robbery he's a lying scumbag. Just at that moment Simon the nice cop came in. Ok Dave let me deal with this. So out of the room went the madman, John, said Simon, I know you must be thirsty so I've brought you in a cold drink and also a bar of chocolate. John, he went on, Blair has told us everything about how he got the money, and I know you don't know how he obtained it so I will tell you. He tells us his grandmother lives with his family and about six months ago he was looking in his grandmother's bedroom cupboard for some toys of his that she kept in there when he noticed a large box underneath some old magazines. On opening the box he couldn't believe his eyes; it was full of hundreds of different bank notes. So, at first, he only used to take ten shilling notes, and then it went on to one pound notes and then the five pound notes. I learned later that his mother and grandmother had been called to the Police Station and told of the story but the amazing thing was the grandmother refused to lay any charges against him so they had to let him go. I later found out that she had over three thousand pounds hidden away in the box and Blair had managed to steal about £500 of it. Older people in those days never had bank accounts and a lot of them didn't trust banks so they used to hide their money. The value of that money would now be something like £50,000 pounds. Blair admitted no one knew where he had got the money from so I was allowed to go with no charges against me, much to my relief. I don't know if they ever informed my mother that I was in the Police Station but I never mentioned it to her and if they had I'm not sure if she would have come anyway. The police probably still use this method of interrogation this is how it works when being questioned, for the first time you get the really nasty and aggressive policeman to intimidate and scare you, when his softened you up a bit you get the nice guy comes in as your friend and they hope you will feel that you can talk to your new friend. This method is called the stick and the carrot and I should think it works in a lot of cases. Once again back at school I somehow got involved in a fight that I was trying to stop between two kids but a teacher looking out of the window thought I was the one doing the fighting so up in front of the head master I was marched. In them days you were never called by your first name it was always by your surname. Right Banfield you have been seen fighting so I'm awarding you six stokes of the cane. It made no difference if you protested that you were innocent he was always right. With six canes of different thicknesses he always allowed you to pick the cane that you wanted to inflict the dreaded punishment on you. When I had first been given the cane I had picked the thinnest one out as I mistakenly thought that I would feel less pain with this one but with a thin one the pain is a stinging one that lasts for a few hours. I had been told to pick the thickest one as this gave you less pain. As he lifted the cane up he always uttered these words, this is going to hurt me more than it hurts you. You always knew this was complete rubbish as he brought he cane down on to your hand you could see the glee in his eyes, with a slight smile on his face he even gave you a choice, you could have six whacks on one hand or three whacks on both hands. I must report that with the thickest cane the pain was not half as bad. If the girls were naughty they got given the slipper on their backsides by a lady teacher which I thought was very unfair.

THE O'DONALD'S

Although everyone lived very close to each other in Paddington as all the houses were terraced ones and all back to back, after ten at night it would be quiet except for Friday and Saturday nights because next door to us lived the O'Donald family. They had the whole house, Grandfather and Grandmother in the top flat, Mother and Father in the middle flat with their children and uncles in the bottom flat. All hell would break out when they returned from the pub. They would be as drunk as skunks and used to fight and argue for at least two hours until usually the police would turn up and try to restore order. The funny thing is they were all family and all lived in the same house but would do exactly the same thing again the following weekend. For the readers information in the 1870s there was an Irish family in the East End of London who were always fighting amongst themselves and also fighting the Police. They were named the Hooligans and this is where anyone caught fighting and being an aggressive person is called a Hooligan named after that family all those years ago.

BED AND BREAKFAST JOB

One Saturday I was walking up Queensway, the posh part of Paddington when an advert caught my eye in the newspaper shop. It wanted a student to help prepare breakfasts and take them up to guests in their rooms. Free breakfast and five shillings a week was the wages. I went straight round the guest house and was able to get the job as I was prepared to start the following morning. I had got used to money by this time because of the Blair episode. At school I would start at seven in the morning, help prepare the meals then take them up to the guests. The best part of the job was the big breakfast I was allowed to tuck into. The guests were all professional people staying in London for five days then going home for the weekends. On the Friday they would always give a tip. It was usually a 6p piece (2 ½ p) so the job was worth ten shillings with wage and tips. One of the guests took a particular interest in me and as I brought the tray up to his bedside he would ask me to sit and talk with him but I had to refuse his request as I had another nine rooms to look after. One morning I was telling the guest house owner about the nice man in room six who used to give me a bigger tip than anyone else. Oh him, she replied, he's the other way. The other way miss, what do you mean? I mean she said he's a nancy boy. A nancy boy miss, what does that mean? Well John, she sighed, he likes people of his own sex, so you be careful in future. I will stand outside the door when you bring his tray up just to be on the safe side. It just shows you how innocent I was on most matters in them days but I thought he was a very pleasant man and I am quite certain I would have been safe with him. I always thought he was a very lonely young man in London and just wanted to talk to people. I know he was training to be a doctor and then go on to be a surgeon, I hope his dreams came true and he reached the top in his profession. I had never eaten so well in ages; I then used to collect all the empty plates left outside the guests rooms and get myself off to school. I would have done the job for no money but just for the food. I did not require second helpings from the school meals after them breakfasts.

That old saying (all work and no play makes jack a dull boy) was taken on board by our school. So every so often they used to take us on trips. On one of the trips was to the royal opera house at Covent garden in London. The head master used to arrange it all as he was a big opera fan and also liked classical music. You can imagine taking street urchins and slum dwelling kids to an opera house. As we were led into our seats the first thing everyone noticed was a pair of binoculars in a box behind every seat. To get the binoculars out of the box you had to put a coin in the box 6d (2 ½ p). The kids were not interested in the opera; all they were interested in was to get at any money that might be in the boxes. The other place the head used to take us to was the Royal Festival hall on the South Bank. This is where all the classical music and organ recitals take place. I remember the head master saying just before we all entered the festival hall if I can just get one of you interested in this sort of music then I feel I have done my job. Well headmaster, you got me interested in it and I thank you for that.

Poem

Classical music at its best such a wonderful sound
Elgar, Grieg and Wagner better composers never were found
Beautiful heavenly music composing it is a gift from god
Today's technology downloads it straight onto your new I-pod
Music that inspires you will last for ever more
Listening to the master pieces will make your spirits soar
Now making their music in heaven these wonderful gifted men
A polished performance each one like a well cut gem
A great job done headmaster you introduced great music to me
We all need that window to open for us to see

Museums – South Kensington

At weekends and on school holidays, I used to walk to the museums from home at south Kensington. It was about a four mile walk from Paddington. I sometimes spent a full day there as it was so interesting and in the winter it kept me out of the cold, also there is the science museum, the animal museum and the natural history museum. In one part of the science museum there was a room with a large television set and you could watch TV programs. As we didn't have a TV at home this was a real treat. Also in the science museum was a cinema which showed documentaries about the world at large so for free you could have a day's entertainment. In those days there was a 2p deposit on coca-cola glass bottles. This was before cans had made their way into this country. The deposit scheme was in place because there was still a huge shortage of glass in this country. So you would get that 2p back to you when you took the bottle back to the shop. The people who mainly went to museums were the middle classes and the better off; hardly any working class person would want to walk around a museum so the better off people could not be bothered to take their bottles back to the shop so this is where I came into my own. These people would have their lunch outside in the garden areas and put their bottles into the bins so with my bag I used to carry I gathered up these bottles and took them to a local shop. I could easily hold ten bottles in my bag so that was two shillings I had made. In those days this would have got me a meal, drink and still have change. I had now reached the age of fifteen and I was called into the headmaster's office. Right then Banfield, have you thought about what job you are going to do when you leave school? In them days there was no such thing as advice, a career officer that came to our school, and asked me what job I was thinking of doing? Well Sir, I was thinking of working in a factory or something like that. I thought he may be able to give me some good advice. Well Banfield, he said sharply, I notice that your school reports are not too encouraging, and it seems on your reports that you talk too much in class and you don't pay attention most of the time and looking at your grades you've achieved, you won't be setting the world alight, so I think factory word will be right up your street as you're not the brightest pupil around. Can you imagine a headmaster telling a pupil all this in today's world? You would be consulting with your lawyer in the view of suing him for deformation of character and slander. Right then Banfield; tell me what you think you have gained from being at this school. Well Sir,

I think I have learned to look after myself, because if I had not stood up for myself I would have been bullied all the time. Not the answer he wanted to hear from a boy not of his social class, as Mr Jones was a middle class snob, he used to wear a long black gown and a box type hat. He would have like to be teaching at Eton, but for him it must have been a big step down to be teaching at an inner London run down state school. He would often mention how he lived in Croydon, in a nice house and commuted every day. I often wondered if he had been a naughty boy in years gone by and teaching at this lowly school was his punishment. One of our teachers that used to teach us quite often was only about twenty five years old, quite shy and completely out of his depth in this rough house of a school. His name was Mr Wright. He could never keep the class quiet talking about science subjects so he used to ask anyone in the class to talk on any subject and then he would tell his stories about life. As it was a mixed class the class was mainly made up of girls and one in particular was a stunner. As all the other girls were flat chested but this girl Pauline Taylor had the figure of a goddess and liked to show it off. In class she would wear a tight fitting jumper and quite a short skirt. As she sat in the front of the class she was the centre of attention, it was not for nothing that Pauline Taylor had the nickname of PT which was prick teaser! As Mr Wright was teaching Pauline's skirt would ride up, the poor man could not keep his eyes of her. With Pauline you could look but not touch as one of the boys made a suggestion to her one day and got such a foul mouth rant from her it would have put a swearing sailor to shame, not the kind of girl you could take home to mother! Pauline was one of those girls that you wonder what became of her. With us slum boys we had no chance of even asking her out, this girl would want to be wined and dined and she probably ended up with a very rich playboy or a middle eastern prince. Like all things in life, one of the days you have been looking forward to and this day had finally come, it was the last day of my school days. I was called in to see Mr Jones, the headmaster. Well Banfield, it is your last day with us and let me just say I know you have had a difficult upbringing and I think you have coped quite well with it and I think you are a very positive person and that will stand you in good stead, so I want you go to out there in that great big world and try and do your best in everything you do, and I'm sure you'll be a hard working and good citizen. As his hand came out to shake mine he said, good luck and that was that. There I was thinking he was an uncaring aloof middle-class twit, at least he had shown a bit of compassion and kindness. On leaving the school for the last time I looked back and saw a building that I had managed to have some good times, but also some hard times but because it was such a rough school it taught me how to look after myself and survive, and it may have made me a better person because of the experience of being there.

Poem

That was a nightmare experience attending that school
Defending yourself and surviving was the golden rule
Teachers that cared not pupils that never wanted to learn
It's the positive ones in life that will surely earn
School days are the happiest days that's what they say
Should not be counting the days when you can get away
But we survived it when all was said and done
Had battled against the odds the fight I had won

STARTING WORK

My very first job was in a factory right behind Kings Cross station, London. The factory sharpened large and small blades that were used on printing presses that made and printed magazines and books. My job was to make sure jets of water were aimed at the blade as they were being sharpened by huge rollers. It was very boring and the heat was terrible. I used to start at 8 in the morning and finish at five thirty. As it was only 4 miles from home, I used to walk there and back to save the underground fare. My first weeks wages were £2 10s (£2.50p) so I thought it a bit much as I handed over my wages to my mother, she gave me back for myself 5 shillings (25p). With these words ringing in my ears, I've kept you these last few years now it's your turn to keep me! I Was sitting in the canteen at work one day having my usual grilling by the women that worked there. They used to tease me and say well John, have you ever kissed a girl and I bet you're still a virgin. Do you get wet dreams etc. And at fifteen I used to go as red as a beetroot which of course made it even worse, then they threatened to all grab me and pull my trousers down, oh them innocent days. When one of the workers asked me how much I was earning, I told him and he said you can earn more than that. A friend of mine, he went on, is the same age as you and he gets one pound more a week that you working as a trainee butcher. So the next day I took a day off and went to a local butchers which was in a road called Formosa Street just around the corner from Warwick Avenue Tube station. I walked in and asked if they had any vacancies for a trainee butcher and just my luck someone had left the previous day, so I got the job and at one pound more a week I thought I had hit the jackpot. I then went back to the factory and handed in my notice. When I explained to the manager he offered me one pound more a week to keep me as in his words, you are one of the best workers I've had for a long time and I would be very sorry to lose you, but I had by then made up my mind to leave as the new job was only ten minutes walk from home and seeing I had endured a whole year there I thought a change would do me good. So I started the new job the following Monday. The shop was named Dewhurst and there were hundreds of shops throughout Britain. Formosa Street was just off Warrington Crescent which was quite a middle class part of Maida vale and there were quite a few wealthy people who lived there. The butchers shop was next to an off licence and opposite that was a greengrocer shop named of Mark Levy. The rest of the street was made up of about nine other shops. Starting my first day was quite strange as it is with any new job. There was the manager Mr West and two butchers. Mr West was a dapper sort of man. He took a lot of care in his grooming. He seemed quite old to me (but everyone does when you're young). He was about forty five years old and when first meeting him, I liked him straight away with his happy go luck attitude. Call me Brian, he said, not Mr West, which was unusual in them days for a manager. My job was to cut up the meat and also deliver the meat on the carrier bike to all parts of the area. The manager used to take all the money coming into the ship and also serve the customers. What I thought quite strange was when serving lady customers he used to give them their meat but not charge them for it. I used to deliver on the bike twice a day so when I had made up my round, Brian used to give me extra packets to deliver to the same addresses every time I went out and at the end of the week used to give me five shilling (25p) tip which was quite a lot of money then. Some of the addresses I used to take the extra parcels to were not the usual houses I delivered to. When ringing the bell at these places the lady of the house would open the door with hardly a stitch on and made no attempt to cover up but they always gave a tip 6p pence (2 ½ p) surely I thought to myself, these cannot be ladies of the night? (old toms) but if they are it's nothing to do with me so I'll just accept my tip and be off. The best part of the job was going out on my deliveries as Maida vale is like most parts of London, you have the poorer parts but the next street is quite well off. I very rarely had to deliver to the poorer parts mainly to the middle class or the wealthy areas. Some houses in Maida vale were really posh. These were up near little Venice where the grand union canal splits three ways. One way going north, the other way going to the Paddington Basin, and the other heading east to Regents Park. Delivering to one of these canal side houses and you were in for healthy tip. In 1955 I was coming up to my sixteenth birthday and that morning I got to the butchers shop a bit later than normal and to my surprise the other three members of staff were still waiting outside the shop as the manager had not shown up. Just as I joined them, a police car pulled up outside the shop and also with the police was the area manager for the region. Right the area manager said, I have the keys and I'm opening up the shop, so these policemen can search the shop. That's odd I thought, search the shop, what for I wondered? Once the shop was opened, we were all ordered to sit in the staff room. None of us had a clue what was going on. After half an hour the older of the butchers was called into the manager's office. After about twenty minutes the other butchers was called. It must have been around about twenty minutes again when I was called in the office. As I entered, I recognised the large cop as the one that interviewed me about Blair's money saga. Oh it's you Banfield, he shouted. Do you know John, piped up the area manager? looking quite shocked, yes the cop said, I interviewed him about a matter when he was at school but never mind that. What I want to know from you Banfield, is what you can tell us about Brian your manager. Well I said, I think he is a very nice man, and has always looked after me very well. Then tell in what way did he look after you he shouted. Well, I replied, he was always kind and he used to give me 5 shillings (25p) extra every week. So tell me, he snapped, why would he give you 5 shillings extra a week. It now dawned on me Brian my manager was probably in deep trouble and this policeman thought that I was involved in what ever Brian had been up to as I still didn't know what was going on. Right, bad cop went on, if I don't get satisfactory answers from you I will carry on this interview at the police station, so tell me the truth you little punk. Now Banfield, can you tell me why when delivering the meat to No.20 Warrington Crescent Maida vale, you used to go inside the knocking shop. The knocking shop I said, what is a knocking shop? I have never heard of that name. You're not as naive as that he shouted. It's true I protested, I used to go in, to get the money off the lady. Look I shouted, I don't know what's going on. I have not done anything wrong. If the manager is in trouble its nothing to do with me, I uttered. OK, smart arse, turn your pockets out. Fortunately that day I had only two shillings (10p) on me. Ok, he said you can put your money back in your pocket. He voice changed from being aggressive to quite normal. I don't think I need to carry on interviewing you, get out of this office and don't cross my path again. I was pleased he never took me back to the police station and get the good cop, bad cop routine. As I walked into the staff room everyone was quite shocked at being interviewed and what we all wanted to know was what the manager had been up to. It didn't take us long to find out as the district manager walked in the staff room. The Police have now left; I will now explain what has happened. Look lads, he started, you all deserve an explanation as to what's going on. Right now here's the whole story. Last night your manager was arrested at home and charged with various charges which included stealing money off of the company, falsifying the books of the company, living off the earnings of the prostitutes and running a brothel. We all sat there open mouthed and found it very hard to believe what we were hearing. He went on to say, I've had my suspicions for a while as the takings of the shop were down, so I, and the police mounted a surveillance on the shop and even used to follow you John to see what houses you went to and how many meat parcels you delivered and counted the amount of customers entering the shop from the time of opening until closing. We then used to go back to the shop at night open it up and look at the books and the day's takings for that day. The takings were down from what they should have been and the customers coming in had been falsified (he admitted all the charges laid against him) and because of that he got a lighter sentence, but that lighter sentence was still seven years in prison. He did say in court that no-one else was involved so we were all in the clear. Being the manager of the shop was a perfect cover for all his dodgy dealings. What gave the case a bit of spice to it is he had served a five year prison sentence ten years previously for stealing and whilst inside had learned to be a "butcher". After all this I decided to look for another job for in spite of what the manager had got up to he was always kind to me and I missed him not being around. I had heard of a job as a trainee butcher in Connaught street just of the Edgware road near Marble Arch which was a very up market area with a lot of wealthy people living there. I went for the interview liked what I saw, got the job and started the following Monday.

Poem

What a lovely man was our manager Mr West

Taken away and locked up became her majesties prison guest

What a happy bunch we were working in that shop

Until the police called it was that aggressive cop

It seemed quite funny really that he sold meat and offal

And also running a knocking shop was the districts biggest brothel

Funny thinking of it he sold two kinds of meats

One was for consuming the other for gentlemen's treats

Start at Somers & Kirby –
aged Seventeen – Butchers

My first day at the new shop was getting used to the new set up because this shop had a touch of class about it. They sold the very best of meats and this was a very nice area. I was told that one of my duties would be to ride the carrier bike for all the phoned up orders. This could be up to fifty deliveries a day and sometimes three deliveries on the bike meant I was hardly in the shop. The shop was situated about half a mile from the north side of Hyde Park and some of the deliveries were made quite a way over to the south side of the park. One of our customers that lived at Hyde Park Gate, south side of Hyde Park was Winston Churchill's household, I would take a large order to them in the morning and then have to take an order back to them in the afternoon which sometimes consisted of only half a pound of mince a round journey of about six miles. I used to complain about this but the manager used to say I'm sorry about it john we cannot afford to lose their custom. Delivering to Churchill's house was an experience, because taking the order into the kitchen everyone was greeted by a huge parrot in his cage, f—k off it would squeal, the German cook would tell it to shut up but that would make it worse, you're a nancy boy, and you look like a pansy it would yell (nancy boy and pansy were the words in them days that today are known by the words poof, queer or gay boy). This parrot was an amazing bird, it would mimic the German cook's accent spot on and if you closed your eyes you would think you were talking to the cook. It didn't take it long to get my accent off and it was like hearing a recording of your own voice. The cook was explaining to me that the parrot had come from a naval shore base and that would explain some of his other navy sayings which included – All the girls love a sailor, your taking a load of bo—ocks, I see no ships, anchors away, jack tar went to far, The captains a sh-t, hello sailor, everything's ship-shape and one saying that really stood out was – lets go and shag some wrens tonight. This is the kind of parrot you need in your porch when the double glazing man calls, just open the door and he would let him have it. While serving at the shore base this parrot should have been given a medal and mentioned in dispatches.

Poem

Listening to that parrot my word it could swear
Anyone entering the room that's all they would hear
Out of its mouth came bad swearing from the bird
Could curse like a sailor words you'd never even heard
No wonder he had been discharged from the navy
This lovable swearing parrot who's first name was Davy
Now up in bird heaven this naughty swearing bird
Most deafening should be seen but never heard

Working in the butchers shop was the manager, the till girl and two other butchers. I was amazed to be listening to this strange language that they were talking between themselves. They would mainly utter this strange talk when customers were in the shop. This strange talking was called "backslange" so that nearly ever word said was reversed, so if a new customer would walk in and you wanted to get rid of all your old meats the manager would say to the butcher (give that man all of the old meat which in backslange is evig taht nam lla fo eht dlo team, with this talk the customer would not have a clue what was being said and after a while it was quite easy to pick it up and sometimes join in. Now the shop was really starting to get very busy and I could not keep up with all the phone orders with people deliveries, the manager, Mr George said to me John, we will have to get you some help so we will be looking for another lad to help you with your deliveries. The words had hardly left his mouth when I mentioned Jimmy Gregg, he's a friend of mine and he may be interested. Well John, he replied, if he is as good as you we will take him on. When I told Jim about the job he couldn't wait to start with me. After his interview, Jim got taken on, so my workload was much reduced. Jim got in the swing of things at the shop, but even with his help with an extra bike they had purchased we could not keep up with all the orders because now we were cycling about twenty miles a day each, which was shattering for both of us, so Mr George decided to buy two bikes with motors fitted to the back wheel with a little gear lever. At that time you did not require a licence for these bikes. These bikes were great fun to ride to Churchill's house. The other side of the park would normally take for the return journey about one hour with the motorised bikes we would do the return journey in about thirty minutes. The shop used to attract a very high class kind of customer with lords and ladies who lived in the better parts of London: Park Lane, Belgravia and Westminster. Of course we had to deliver goods to the tradesmen entrance but a decent tip was always waiting for you.

Mr George always said you could tell someone with money as they would just ask you to cut top quality meats without asking the price of how much the goods cost. It seemed that the upper class people who had money handed down to them and were the old school had impeccable manners and would treat the working class and everybody with the same respect as they would with their friends and family. In a lot of cases the people who had made their money the hard way and were also quite wealthy could be very loud and abrupt with no manners. You could always tell the people who had class. The owner of the shop was a Mr Kirby; he had gone into partnership with a Mr Sommer's years earlier. He also owned a wet fish shop nearby and other outlets. He was quite an elderly gentleman at this time and quite a wealthy man. He used to visit the shop every now and again and used to tell Jim and myself stories about his childhood and how he got started in business, but he admitted his greatest achievement in life was not how much he had accumulated in money terms or what he was worth, but at the age of seventeen scoring the winning goal for his local village team. That meant more to him that anything else he had achieved. He was a very humble man and a nice human being, the salt of the earth (a lesson for us all me thinks). Jim Gregg and I had now become firm friends, so not only working together; we used to meet up at night and at weekends. Jim's mother decided that their family deserved to own a car. Just up from Bourne Terrace was a used car showroom that was set up on an old bomb site. Most of the cars were falling apart and utter wrecks but she brought an old Austin seven which even in 1956 must have been built in about 1932. In those days there was no such thing as an MOT so cars could and were sold in many cases in very dangerous conditions. The tyres on this banger were non-existent they were so bald you could see your face reflecting in them. It was the handbrake that stopped the car as the foot break was useless. As jims mum could not drive she let Jim have the car. I think she paid about twenty five pounds for it. As there was no such thing as a driving school in the area we used to take it in turns to drive it, not having a clue how to even put it in gear but after a while getting the hang of it. When you think of here we were driving a wreck, we couldn't even drive properly with no licences the car was not even taxed or insured but we knew nothing of these matters we all took it in turns to drive it around the streets and after getting confident enough taking it out onto the main roads. How we managed not to hit pedestrians or anything else remains a miracle. This car really broadened our horizons; we were now able to get to places we had never seen before. Out on one of our trips one weekend we were driving along merrily with Jim in the driving seat as he went to turn a corner, near Wembley stadium the steering wheel came off in his hands. His words to us were, does anyone want to buy a steering wheel, but it was lucky he was able to stop the car and hammer it back on to the steering column. What was amazing we were never ever stopped by the police in all the time we were driving. At this stage of our lives we were never really interested in girls, just going out in the car. On one summer evening we drove to Runnymede where the Magna Carta was signed, parked the car beside the Thames and walked up a hill that overlooked the statue. There stood a collage that was not occupied in the evening but for some reason cars were still parked, over looking the steep hill. In them days people never bothered to lock their cars. The first time we went up there we were just having a look around the collage grounds when we heard this shout, quick come over here, this car isn't locked, shouted one of the lads. We quickly made our way over, one of Jims brothers Billy, had already opened all the car doors. Why don't we all get in the car said Billy and let the handbrake off and push the car over the hill. At first we all thought what a silly idea that was, but after thinking about it for a while said to each other, let's do it. With that the four of us pushed the car right near the edge of the hill and then all piled into it, with the doors still open we all waited until it started to really build up speed then jump out just before it flipped over. We never ever thought about the dangers involved. That evening we opened the doors of another car, and did the same again but this time Jims other brother John was sitting in the front seat, the car went hurtling down again and once again bailed out at the last moment except for Johnny in the front seat, as he went to jump out his left leg got caught up between the seat and the floor and he couldn't get out. We were horrified. Watching him still trapped in the car the car by this time was half way down the hill as it flipped over we saw Johnny flying out and landing with a heavy fall. We all rushed to his aid thinking the worse, but unbelievably he never had a scratch on him. His only words were that was great!! The two cars ended up right at the bottom of the hill and covered by trees and bushes. They were completely hidden from sight. We left it for another week and returned back again to have some more fun but this time we all agreed that no one should sit in the front driver seat again. We set off walking up to the college and once again all the cars were still parked near the edge and all unlocked. That evening we managed to ride three more cars down the hill before we called it a night. I told the other lads that it would now be silly to go back for more cars to ride as they would probably be watching in future. I always came to the conclusion that the owners of the cars must have thought the cars must have been stolen as no one would have guessed that anyone would want to push their cars over the top as they now were completely hidden by the undergrowth. The cars are probably still down there but now would be completely rusted away, we must have been mad.

Poem

They were all our yesterdays them days are now gone
What we did those evenings it was so wrong
We were only just young lads letting off hot steam
A little gang we were pulling together as a team
When growing up you get up to many new tricks
But what you call it is really getting your kicks
Yes we've all been young once and done such stupid things
But growing up and getting sense with all that learning brings

On another occasion we all decided to walk to Hyde Park one evening. We got to Hyde Park about eight o'clock that evening and made our way to the Serpentine which is a large lake in the park. You can hire boats out and it also has a swimming area. The bridge in the middle of the lake takes traffic from the north side of the park to the south side. For some reason that night we walked to where the Peter Pan statue stands, so we all started to climb all over it and I and two of the other lads started to swing on the pipes that peter the statue was blowing into. Peter's hands were clasped around the front of the pipes, when all of a sudden there was an almighty noise. The pipes had come away in our hands; we all ended up on the ground in a heap. Oh dear I thought, that was not meant to happen, what do we do now? We all talked it over and decided not to take the pipes home because if caught with them, we would be in big trouble. So with the only option left open to us I picked the pipes up (which were very heavy) went to the waters edge, and threw them as hard as I could into the water. They have now been in the Serpentine for fifty years and I don't think anyone has ever recovered them. The pipes were stolen once before a few years before this episode, but they were recovered and put back on the statue. In the evening news the next day was printed the headline (the pipes of peter are nicked again) and it went on to report that four youths were seen in the vicinity as dusk was falling, the only people who would have seen us was the ladies of the night (old toms) that were looking for business walking up and down the serpentine bridge. At the time of writing this I am now taking steps to inform the appropriate people as to where the pipes are located and hopefully they can be returned to their rightful place after all this time. Jim and I had now reached eighteen years old and now were both thinking that riding a bike most of the time was not a very smart thing to be doing. Although we made a few bob in tips, the wage we were paid was quite poor, we both asked for a rise but we were only offered a few pence a week more so we both decided to move on and find other employment. About two weeks after getting such a miserable pay rise we both handed in our notice as Jim had found a job with Mark Levy who owned a green grocers shop in Formosa Street, Maida vale and I found a job working in a timer yard on the Harrow Road near Paddington Green Police Station.

Joined Samuel Putney aged eighteen

The main reason for taking the job at the timber yard was the money. It paid about £2 more a week than being a butcher's boy and it was only a five minutes walk to get there. My job was as a machine hand. The wood operator would feed the wood into the machine and I would grab hold of it and stack it on a barrow, after a while this started to get boring and I had wished I had stayed at my old job but things were not all bad. There were a lot of young fellows working there so at lunch break we used to jump off the piles of wood that were stacked around. How anybody never got seriously hurt I'll never know. On one lunch break I was hiding from the other lads hidden behind a row of 6" x 2" (150mm x 50mm) timber floorboards. I still don't know what made me look up, but as I did, I could see these floorboards heading towards me. I just managed to jump clear as they came crashing down hitting the ground with an almighty thud. If I had not got out of the way I would not have had a chance, I would have been squashed to the size of a beetle and my story would have ended there, what made me look up? Is your lifetime planned? Was somebody looking after me? Is there such a thing as fate? The answers to all these questions I believe is definitely Yes, I have to admit I think the old Arab saying that says "it is written" is about as good as it gets and that your life is not only in your hands but is ruled by a higher force. But that's my humble view. At night Jim and I and his brothers never ever stayed in as no one owned a TV, so we used to have to make our own entertainment and although we still had the use of the old Austin 7 we all brought motor bikes which started to become the in thing to get at that time. This gave us much more freedom than the car as it meant we could all go out at the same time as the car only fitted four people in it. We met up with an experienced motorcycle rider who was about 45 years old. To us he was so old he got named granddad but he took it in good spirits, he was like a father figure to us and we used to go to all the motorbike race meetings with him. In them days it was not law to wear helmets so no one did. We were all coming back from brands hatch in Kent one evening and I was at the back of the group. On entering a crossroads I had to brake suddenly, the back wheel locked up and the bike skidded along the road on its side with me hanging on like grim death. All of a sudden the bike went one way and I went the other. My bike ended up smashing against a wall and I ended up under the front of a car. The driver of the car saw what was happening and braked hard. My head was about 4" (100mm) from making contact with the car engine. The car driver got out of his car as white as a ghost and shaking, thinking I was badly injured or worse. He couldn't believe his eyes when he pulled me from under the car as I only had a slight scratch on my head although all my clothes were ripped to pieces, I looked worse than I was. Once again I think someone was looking after me. I promptly picked my bike up which amazingly was not damaged and carried on with the pack and returned home.

Poem

My bikes going one way and me going the other
This is normally the time you try and take cover
Sliding across the road now is that me dead
About going to hit that car with my unprotected head
That lord up above please will you hear my plea
I have my faith in you, please look after me
I thought I was going to meet you that day
But you decreed I was not going to die that way
Have more years on earth my time not up yet
Thank you sweet lord forever in your debt

The other place we used to go at night and at weekends, was the ace cafe on the north circular road, near Wembley. Bikes from all parts of London used to park outside the cafe and watch as bikers used to race each other along the north circular. The cafe is where all the latest bikes were on display and you could spend an enjoyable evening looking at the bikes and chatting with their owners. This was the year 1957 and a popular fashion of the day was the teddy boy look. This look compromised the Edwardian look, hence the teddy boy. The dress code consisted of gelled back hair with the front of the hair in a roll and the back set into a DA (Ducks arse). The jacket had silk labels and it went almost down to the knees. The trousers were skin tight and the shoes were big wedge type things and the socks were as bright as you could get them. We were never teddy boys as the fad was dying out so it was a bit before out time. As I was still on "L" plates for my motor bike I decided to take my test to get a full licence. The day came for the test and I had to go to Acton in West London. On being introduced to the examiner he explained that as it's a motorbike, he stands on the pavements and watches you rather than sit on the pillion seat. So his instructions to me were turn right here, turn at that round-a-bout ahead, of you and then come back to where I'm standing. Simple enough I thought, so I set off. I did my right turn as instructed, came up to the round-a-bout and was just about to go round the round-a-bout when a man stepped off the pavement on to the road and my bike ran over his foot. You f-----g stupid idiot he screamed, what the f—k do you think your doing?   You should have looked where you were going. Look mate I said, I'm taking my test just now and the instructor is watching me over there. Taking your test you dick head he said, you shouldn't be on the road, you're a danger to the public and carried on and said I hope he fails you knob head, and with that, he put his shoe back on, and two passers by helped him pick up all his food shopping which was now all over the road and stormed away swearing and cursing as he went. Oh dear I thought what am I to say to the examiner, I had no time to think because all of a sudden I had pulled up beside the examiner. What the hell was that all about he shouted, I watched you run over that poor mans foot. Not my fault I said, he should have been looking where he was going. I'm sure he was swearing under his breath. Right he said, as he was making notes on his clipboard, I want you to turn left over there then turn first right the first right again and again first right. I will be somewhere on the pavement when you've turned your last right, I will hold my hand up and when I do I want you to make an emergency stop. Right he said, now have you got all of that, of course I said, right then carry on if you please, but the way he said it sounded as if he had given up on me and was thinking I've got a right one here. I was thinking to myself I must get this right and make no mistakes so off I set, now what did he say?? Turn first left, but hold on a minute first left is a service road supplying goods for shops, surely he didn't mean up there, well that's what the man said, first left so first left it is, so up this service road I headed. The men unloading the lorries were giving me vacant stares but he I'm not worried about them, I'm taking my test. I had driven up quite a way on this road and it just all of a sudden got very narrow and led into a high street. I now realised that maybe I had taken the wrong left. I'd better turn round and go back to where I started from but looking up I realised it was a one way road. Oh well I might as well get on to the high street, turn right, right again and right again and with luck meet up with the examiner. On turning the three rights he was nowhere in sight, this is a complete disaster I thought, where the hell is he. I was by now completely lost as I did not know the area, I didn't even know where the test centre was! This is not going very well I was thinking to myself, what do I do? I know what I'll do, I will keep doing a right turn on every road and I'm bound to bump into him. I must have been going for at least 15 minutes when joy of all joys I spotted him in the distance, as I got closer to him he looked a bit tight lipped and his eyes seemed to be bulging out, as I drew up along side him I was expecting his hand to raise for my emergency stop, instead he bellowed, did I tell you to go up that service road, you idiot? Charming I thought, you told me to go first left and first left is where I went I replied. Look mate, don't you know a service road is for lorries only, no cars, no motorbikes, just lorries. I'm sorry, I said, can I start again? No you cannot, he shouted, the test is finished, oh that's good I said, does that mean I've passed I pleaded. His face by this time was as bright as if he had a red light bulb in his mouth. Look son, you have just asked me if you've passed? First off you ran over a mans foot, then I ask you to go up a road and you go up a service road and then get yourself lost, now do you think you deserve to pass the test? Yes I replied we all make mistakes you know. By this time I thought he was just about to have a heart attack, as he handed me the failed certificate storming off shouting profanities, he must have got out of bed the wrong side that morning!

Poem

All I did was take my motorbike test
Made a couple of mistakes but did my best
What's the big deal driving up a service road?
Was told I had contravened the highway code
Well I only drove over that silly mans feet
Causing me to nearly fall off my seat
Never mind I'll just have to carry on with that L plate
Then confident will pass the test at a later date.

I had worked at the wood firm Samual Putney now for six months and what made me think it was time to leave was one day I caught three of my fingers in the circular saw. They were quite deep cuts and I was very lucky that they were still attached to my hand. When I pulled them clear and after a few stitches in the hospital I decided that my career in the timber industry should end. At night we all used to visit the fish and chip shop on the harrow road. The fish shop was run by an Italian family and in them days a lot of the customers would be paid their wages on the Friday and be broke on the Monday so they used to ask the fish shop owner to give them the fish and chips and they would pay him on the Friday, this was known as "tick". The owner had two cards in his window which I always thought quite amusing they read:

Limerick

Good people came and I did trust them
I lost my money and their custom
To lose them both did grieve me sore
So I decided to trust no more
Out clock has stopped "no tick"
Therefore
If I trust I bust if I bust I rust
No trust no bust, no bust, no rust
Our clock has stopped "no tick".

A ten minute walk from where we used to live was the grand union canal. This canal is the main canal that starts off in Paddington and goes up to Birmingham. They first started building it in about 1798 and if you fell in it you were supposed to go to hospital to get a jab as the water was so polluted. One day we were all walking along the canal path we saw this lad swimming away quite happily when suddenly he let out a sharp yell. We could see blood coming up from the water, it was fortunate he was quite near the edge and we all were able to pull him out. He had injured himself with cuts and slashes across his legs, arms and his back. It was probably an old bed or anyone of hundreds of junk items thrown in. As we dragged him out he smelt like a dead rat, his wounds were quite deep so we told him to get himself to hospital and get stitched up and make sure he got the jabs. He said he would, but probably went home, had a wash and came straight out. People used to throw all kinds of things in there and the people whose houses backed onto it, you would see them just open their top windows and throw old bikes, beds, kitchen rubbish and anything else they wanted to get rid of. People were known to put live unwanted pets in a bag, tie it up and throw it in but with all that some kids used to still swim in it, even as late as the late 1960s. Barges were still being pulled up the canal by shire horses, a wonderful sight. It is strange to think that I live 10 minutes away from the canal here in Milton Keynes.

Poem

Dug out by hand this canal waterway
An engineering marvel the great wonder of its day
These canals were first built for Britain's industrial revolution
Horses pulling along the barges became the ideal solution
Strong shires tugging the boats loaded up with goods
From the worlds forests many different kinds of woods
Pleasure boats now cruising along with them weekend sailors
From city wiz kids and even east end tailors.

Well, I am one of the water signs (Pieses) and after avoiding certain death with them floorboards that fell and nearly getting all my fingers sliced off, I decided the timber business was not for me, so I packed it in there and then. Without having another job to go to, Jim and I used to visit his uncle quite often. His name was Ron Hart and he had been in the motor trade all his life, so one day I was telling him all about my mishaps in the timber firm and now I was unemployed. He said he would try and get me a job working with him. By the following week he said he had got me a job as a flatter polisher. What's that I asked, well what it is John, he went on, you have to prepare a car for spraying with water and a very light sand paper, then the car is sprayed and then apply a very light compound to bring out the shine and for you to get the job, I told my boss that you have worked for Rolls Royce and was one of their star men! But don't worry about the job, as myself and the bloke who works with me whose name is Nick Franks will show you how it's done and will look after you. The boss has said because of your previous experience you can start on Monday and he wants me to introduce you to him, but Ron I pleaded what will I say if he starts asking me questions about how the jobs done, what do I say? Don't worry about that said Ron, I'll be next to you and if he starts asking you awkward questions, I'll be there to back you up, so just be confident, as he does not have a clue about the trade anyway.

Kennings Motors, Edgware Road

The Monday soon came around and I was feeling quite nervous when I met Ron and Nicky outside. Kennings motors, I have some very good news for your John, said Ron, the boss told me on the Friday that he was had to run a northern branch for two weeks but to take you on and he will meet you when he gets back. All I had to do was meet the assistant manager that morning who knew less about cars than I did. Welcome to kennings he said as he shook my hand. We have heard so much about your skills it's a pleasure you meet you (little did he know). Ron must have really gone over the top with my skills and knowledge, what did worry me a bit is here was I just 18 years old the youngest bloke in the whole garage and supposed to have worked for Rolls Royce and was this highly skilled artisan, and I hardly knew one end of a car from the other end! Ron quickly showed me how to prepare a car for spraying and how to finish polishing a car after being sprayed. I had to get it right before the boss came back. The boss duly arrived back and I was introduced to him. He went on to tell me that seeing I had joined the team, we would now be increasing the amount of cars coming in for spraying and I would be working on his own Austin princess. This car was a large black saloon and mostly used for weddings. What he mainly wanted was the bonnet polished up and made to look like new. No problem I said, consider it done. I need the car in the morning he said so I'll leave it overnight and pick it up tomorrow. With that he got one of the fitters to bring it round to our workshop. Ok John said Ron, put that compound that is in the tub and gently rub it in and that bonnet will come up a treat. After about an hour of rubbing the compound all over the bonnet as instructed Ron came back to see how I was getting on. Taking a look his jaw dropped open and he had this white look about his face. Stop, he screamed, you've ruined the bonnet, what the hell have you used on it? I used that compound you told me to, the one you pointed at, I said. He shouted, you used the one on the floor. Oh, no, you have used the wrong one, I told you to use the yellow tub not the white one! We will all be sacked. You have used the compound that is so course it's like using rough sandpaper and is used to get a stubborn paint work off. By this time Ron was talking to himself and having a nervous breakdown and then started to talk to the brick wall, my job, my job, he's cost me my job, he yelled. After a while Nicky came up with an idea. Why don't we spray the bonnet and start again. Ron had heard what Nicky had to say and stopped mumbling and said that's a good idea, but lets hope the manager is not around because if he comes in here we will all be sacked. Nicky you go and see where the manager, is and I will stand outside and make sure no one comes in. Five minutes later Nicky came running back. He's out for the rest of the day. With that Ron quickly got the spray gun ready and myself and Nicky prepared the car for spraying. Ron then sprayed it and told us to get in early the next morning. Give it a very light compound and no one will ever know. We all got in early the next day, worked on the bonnet and Nicky spotted the boss coming towards the work area so Ron and Nicky pretended to work on another car and left me to look like I was polishing the car. As the boss entered he let out a yell, my God that's fantastic, you have done such a good job on my car you would think it's been sprayed! As he shook my hand he said you'll go a long way my son and gave me a pound tip which in today's money would be worth £10. He then drove the car out with a happy simile on his face, both Ron and Nicky were relieved as they still both had their jobs but that was a narrow escape.

Poem

Never ever worked on a car just took a chance

Just accepted a job with Kennings in their London branch

As in life you sometimes have to dive and duck

Surfing on that crest of a wave riding your luck

From that flat path we walk then climb that mountain

Tasting the spa waters in that clear spring fountain

Maybe I can go through life with a positive attitude

My compass is pointing to the south that's my latitude

The weeks went by and I started to get quite good working on cars and I was enjoying the work. Some of the lads who were my age started to get their call up papers to go into the armed forces. After the age of eighteen all males were called up to do two years in one of the services. The army, navy or air force, so it was no surprise to me to receive a letter telling me to go to Acton West London for a medical to see if I was fit enough to join up. The following week I attended the medical and was quite pleased as I got graded A1 fit and seeing that I had been in such bad health when younger it came as quite a pleasant surprise. A month later I got my call up papers to join the army and this is why I never got myself my own flat as I new I would be going into the services, and my regiment was to be the Royal Engineers and the barracks were in Malvern, Worcestershire.

Joined the Royal Engineers – Aged 19, 1958

Waking up that morning it was with mixed emotions, on the one hand I was a bit nervous, but on the other hand quite excited about the new adventure that was about to unfold with my bag in my hand I left the house as if I was just going off to work. I'm off now I said, OK, my mother replied, no hug, no shake of the hand. See you then was the reply. Oh well I thought to myself, another chapter in your life so make the most of it. I walked the one mile journey to Paddington main line Station with a spring in my step, knowing that I would be sharing my life once again with a family, be it a very large family.

On reaching Paddington Station you cannot fail to be impressed with the wonderful architecture of the station with the huge glass atrium supported by great columns built of course by that amazing man, Brumal, the Victorian master builder. Standing there on the station platform I couldn't help notice that I was the only person standing on their own. You could tell all the other young fellows getting on the train were all new recruits with all their family members to see them off, but once again with me no one really cared! The train was packed out with new recruits and I was just able to get a seat. Of course steam trains were still running at this time so the journey time took about two hours. You could feel the atmosphere as everyone was apprehensive of what was to lie ahead. As the train pulled into Worcester station you could see many army lorries queuing up outside the station. As we all alighted from the train all we heard was this almighty roar. It was our first introduction to the Sergeant major, a six foot something built like a bear with a flattened nose and two cauliflower ears. Right all you mummy's boy's line up and when I call your name out get your arse in them lorries. There must have been about two hundred new recruits on this train but would be many more coming later from the north, Scotland and Wales. So it took quite a time before everyone was loaded on to the army lorries. We were then taken the six miles to the barracks which were at Great Malvern, just outside Worcester. The lorries made their way into the camp and we were ordered to climb down and told to form up in lines so we could be addressed by the senior officer. As he approached us I thought, he walks just like a girl, but never mind, it's just his way. Right men, he said, as you know this is a training base, you will be here for six weeks basic training and then you will go on to other units to get further training. If you have any problems my door is always open, so don't hesitate to come and see me. I thought to myself, I'm not going in any room with you on my own! I had never in all my life seen so many different kinds of men from all parts of Britain and all walks of life, from a millionaires son to a northern dustman's son, that's what made the mix so very interesting. As with everything in life your first day is always going to be a bit nerve racking knowing what lies ahead. It was quite frightening and overwhelming to say the least. The first thing you have to do is to make an orderly line to get checked out by the medical officer to make sure all your parts are in working order. The next step is to get the dreaded injections. In front of me were two men as big as gorillas and before it was their turn to get their jab they fainted with a loud thud as they hit the floor. No wonder the injection tool was the size of my arm. I found myself in the front of the queue; it was my turn to take the punishment. The next sound I heard was "next". I now started to feel quite faint, but before I knew it this huge great needle was in my behind, the dose was delivered, I have never felt pain like that, instead of changing the needle on every injection the needle was just dipped into a solution and then used repeatedly on the next guys so it was getting blunter and blunter so much for health and safety. The big lads who fainted didn't get away with it, because as soon as they came round the dreaded tool was inserted in them. The first day was also spent having bedding issued plus all your eating utensils, plus fitted out with your uniform and boots, also that day, dog-tags were made up for each man. God tags are issued to each man and worn round the neck. These are made up of metal discs that have your army number stamped on them plus your date of birth. If ever captured by the enemy it's alright them knowing your date of birth and army number but never the regiment you are in. The reason for dog-tags is in the event of your death or accident but mainly in action, with an enemy you can be identified by these tags, being put together with a load of strangers and knowing that you are all in this together you soon strike up conversations with your fellow recruits. By the time you have finished getting all your equipment together and sorting what billet you are housed in it is now the evening of the day, but there is to be no let up in the frantic pace everyone has been put through since arriving. The evening session consisted of the corporals showing everyone how to make up your bed for daily morning inspection. Blankets and sheets had to be folded in exactly the same way and made into a square box with all your equipment laid out in the front of it. By the time this had all finished it was 9.30 and lights out were ten o'clock by that time everyone was totally knackered and sleep was going to be heaven.

The first morning of training

I thought my whole world was turned upside down when on that first morning I was literally upended from my bed and went flying through the air. My mind had not quite registered what was going on as I had been in a lovely full sleep. Get up you f-----g w--k--r this voice bellowed as I lay on the floor with the bedding and the bed on top of me. I then realised this was it, this is the start of the punishment. Can you imagine this being allowed today? The shouting and swearing was unbelievable. This of course was to get everyone in a state of fear, and also to let you know who was in charge. You had to quickly get washed in freezing cold water, get dressed and make your bed as instructed. Then clean the billet from top to toe and then all line up outside, ready to proceed to breakfast. As the time had now reached 7am you all tried to march to breakfast but seeing we had not yet been taught to march we marched like a load of drunks out of step and falling all over the place, not knowing how to march you tend to fall over your own feet. After breakfast the real work is just about to start. As you all assembled on the parade ground for a day of learning how to march. Once again this is done with the same system, good guy, bad guy routine and the bad guy is the R.S.M (Regimental Sergeant Major). Who for some reason took an instant dislike to me. Maybe it could have been that I was the smallest man out of the 200 men being trained on parade, why did you turn the opposite way to all the other men when I told you to turn right, you horrible little man., shouted the R.S.M, what are you? I'm a horrible little man, Sergeant Major, I replied, and from that day he was on to me at every opportunity. Once everyone was able to march reasonably well which took about four days of constant drilling and marching, by the second week the standard had improved dramatically we were now all marching in step and working as a team. Once you have mastered the marching and drilling all the squadron got taken down to the rifle range to get used to firing the 303 rifle and the browning machine gun. Trouble with me was I was only slightly built and under nine stone so when first firing the 303 rifle my right shoulder blade became very sore because the recoil from it was quite strong but after a couple of days at it I became an expert shot, as most of my shots hit the inner bull of the target. I was selected with two others to take part in a test to see if we could get our marksman badge; this test involves laying down in the crouch position and the standing upright position. The course is over three days and takes in the browning machine gun. The skill is to know how to line up your sights and taking into account wind speed and weather conditions. I and the other two recruits managed to get the required pass marks and therefore became marksmen. This enables you to wear the marksmen badge on your uniform and we received a weekly allowance of 2/6p (12 ½ p). If I would have been in an infantry battalion and not an engineering corps I could have gone on to take a snipers course if I had wanted! After gaining my marksmen badge the R.S.M stopped shouting and cursing at me and picked on others as he also had the badge and he probably respected me a little for it. The marksman badge is made up of two rifles crossing over each other. It is worn on the lower sleeve of your uniform and I must say I felt quite proud when wearing it. The rifles we were using in 1958 were called the Lee Enfield rifle, I'm not sure but I think they were made in Enfield in Middlesex at that time (hence the name). After firing these weapons and without fail they had to be thoroughly cleaned with a slight lick of oil and a cord (pull through). This cord pulled all the way up and down the barrel until the barrel was shining. One day all the troop were cleaning their rifles when I happened to notice that stamped on the side of my rifle was a date stamp mark. The date of manufacture said 1910, making my rifle 48 years old. On asking the other men what their date stamps said the oldest was 1908 so we were using rifles that in some cases were 50 years old, but I must say even they were very old the were still nearly as good as when first manufactured.   Just to think a lot of these rifles were used in both the first world war and the second world war. They had a magazine that held six bullets and these rifles could kill a man at a mile distance. They had a bolt action mechanism and they were in use in the British army for over sixty years. Just as our intake had learnt to handle these rifles they were finally being replaced by a new rifle and this was the semi-automatic Belgian F.N. the next stage of the training was the dreaded route marches with full pack and rifle. These marches would start off at 5 miles one day and as the days went on build up until they had reached 20 miles a day. But we were all very fit young men and were all able to do these marches quite easily. Just before coming into the army I had bought an electric razor from a second hand shop just off the Edgware road. I had paid only a pound for it so I thought I would give it a try out after I had been shaving in cold water in the mornings, so plugging it in for the first time and switching it on there was one almighty bang and then followed by a blinding flash. The electric razor just flew out of my hand; this must have saved me because I had managed to fuse the entire billet. If it had stayed in my hand I would surely have been electrocuted and there would only have been ashes remaining of me. Of course I was not allowed to get away with this so the corporal who had a separate room in the billet and who was the N.C.O (non commissioned officer) could make his own rules up, deciding my punishment for this misdemeanour was that I for two hours of every evening for 7 days was to clean the urinals and clean the metal drain covers that stopped the urinal from getting blocked up. Not a very pleasant duty to perform but to make the punishment worse, I had to clean everything with a cleaning powder and to make it harder use a tooth brush. You have not got anytime to be bored whilst in training, because after the daytime training finishes, at night you have to get your kit polished, pressed and non-stop cleaning and by the time you have finished all that it is time for bed. There is no let up in the constant cycle of marching, running, drilling, marching drilling on the parade ground is known as square bashing, route marching and no days off until the end of training. But by now everyone was feeling super fit and you feel you could take on the world.

Poem

We fit young lads now really getting into shape
Stamina levels are high so toned and wide awake
Four weeks ago just a rabble that included everyone
Now we were fighting fit many miles we had run
All our training had paid off a complete fighting force
The battle nearly won almost the end of the course
It's surprising what can be achieved when pulling together
Having done all this in all kinds of weather

On three days of the training we all had to sleep out in tents in the Brecon beacons which in November in them days were very cold. The terrain is quite formidable, with rough ground with mountains and steep hills, ideal for army training. It was on such a backdrop that I and 3 others were ordered to make a team up, we were dropped off in the middle of the beacons and with only a compass and a map to guide us and just enough rations to last a few hours we were told to find our way to a stone farm building marked X on the map where we would be met by an army truck. Unfortunately we hadn't taken much notice of compass training and map reading which was taught to us a week previously so here we stood the four of us with not a clue about which way we should be heading to get to this farm. Looking at the map meant nothing to us. One of the men with us decided we should be heading south so we all went along with him but after about four hours of walking up and down mountains we were completely lost and to add to our misery one of the lads had pulled a muscle in his foot. As it was winter and very cold we could not get a fixing on the sun to get our position. As the hours went on we knew that we were not going to make the farm house as we didn't have a clue where we were. By now the light was fading so we decided to get cover with a shelter. We made it from brown ferns. By the time we had built the shelter darkness was upon us, so we each huddled together to get as much warmth as possible. I have never spent such an uncomfortable night in all my life. It was so cold and now with no food left we were now quite hungry. The lad with the injured foot is the one who slept throughout the night! The morning light could not have come soon enough and as soon as the light was good we decided to try and find our way out of this predicament but no-one knew which way we should go. All of us saying different ways to go (what a right bunch we were). As we were still arguing between ourselves which way we should be heading, we heard this dog barking, and then heard that wonderful sound of men's voices calling out. It was like music to our ears. These were our rescuers. There was a mountain rescue team as well as an army team. They had waited for first light to look for us as night-time would have been too risky. It turned out that we had been dropped off 30 miles north of the farmhouse. Where we had been found was thirty miles east of it (and we were supposed to be trained soldiers!!). We were the joke of the squadron.

At last the time had come when we were due to pass out from basic training. This was the day we had all been waiting for. We were all lined up in our best uniforms and shining boots to march past the General taking the salute, with our rifles resting on our shoulders and legs striding apart. We set off with a marching band accompanying us with every man in step and arms swinging in time. I have never felt so proud as that day. It was also quite sad really because of all the men you had trained with and been through so much together, would all now be going off to new postings at the end of the passing out parade.

Poem

The training is hard it is rough and tough

After six weeks square bashing it's just about enough

With twenty mile forced marches in full battle kit

But my body can take it oh so very fit

Finished with all our training and now passed out

All a band of brothers there is no doubt

Now a great team but had our highs and lows

What now will be our fate only the lord knows

All the relatives came to greet their sons but I wasn't surprised there was no-one to greet me, that day it just made me feel I was still not really wanted by anyone. But the army was to be my family for the next two years. The army camp we were stationed in used to be an American army hospital in world war 2 but they had condemned it as unsuitable to live in, the British army thought otherwise and thousands of men were trained there. The army's thinking was although it was run down and not suitable to live in it would make the soldiers tougher and hardier. After the passing out parade we all had to spend two more days in the camp and then had a weeks leave before getting posted to your next squadron. The next evening we decided we would all head off to a village hall not far from the camp where dancing was being held, but before we made our way there we found a pub which was quite near to the hall. All the men decided they were going to drink as much as possible that night. As I only drank very occasionally this was going to be a big test for me. Into the pub we all went there must have been about twenty of us in total. We all put one pound in the kitty (which was a huge sum in those days). We all started straight off drinking whiskeys and vodkas, most of the other lads were not used to drinking, so within half an hour a lot of them were the worst for ware. The pub had a roaring fire burning in the corner of the saloon bar, and the next thing I saw were glasses of vodka being consumed and the empty glasses being smashed into the brickwork of the fire (as was the custom in Russia). The locals were shocked, and were out of there within seconds. By this time my head was spinning like a top. Someone had shouted that the military police were on the way, so with my head spinning, I looked around the bar and I was the only one left in it, they had all bolted. Trying to make my way out my body wanted to move, but my legs refused. I realised then that I had drunk far too much but I managed to stagger out and noticed in front of me the village hall. So making my way to the door, I nearly fell through and in front of me was a table with two ladies sitting down taking the entrance money. Just at this time, I felt oh so very sick and could feel it coming up and so could the ladies. As they tried to get away, it came out with an almighty roar, and flowed like a volcano erupting all over the money on the table. Once the flow had stopped I crashed onto the table completely smashing it in two with the two ladies screeching. The next thing I remember is lying outside the hall face down with snow in my mouth, how I got outside or who put me there I never ever found out. Hearing a voice saying, you're coming with us I remember seeing their uniforms and red caps and realised they were military policemen, I do not remember any more until I woke up in what looked like a hospital which in fact was the sick bay of our training camp. I had never felt so ill as this. I had a drip in my arm and silver foil wrapped around me as I was suffering from hypothermia and the foil was to keep my body temperature up and me stabilised. It turned out that a passing man had found me in the morning when out walking his dog so I had been out all night and no one had noticed me. That night it had snowed all night, so I was lucky I had not been completely covered with snow. It took four days for me to eat anything. As soon as I tried to eat I would bring it all up. My whole head was spinning day and night for two days. The doctor told me that the only reason I had survived is I was young and very fit, but I think there was someone around looking after me (maybe it's my guardian angel?). As I believe everyone has one. I spent 8 days in the sick bay before I was discharged and by this time all my troop had been transferred to other bases so I never got to say my goodbyes which upset me a little as we had all helped each other through think and thin and achieved our goal together. After coming out of the sick bay I had to report to the C.O (commanding officer) as I was put on a charge under army rules that stated that no man should "self harm himself". As I stood in front of the C.O the charges were read out that I, sapper Banfield had abused himself with alcohol and after hearing more evidence against me he asked me what I had to say for myself. Well sir, I replied this was the first time that alcohol had passed through my lips and I am truly sorry for any inconvenience and trouble that I may have caused. I hoped that this stomach churning over the top pathetic grovelling would get me a lighter sentence and fortunately for me the C.O took pity on me and stated that I had already suffered enough and at eighteen years old, had got carried away and had lost the leave the was owed me so he summed up I hope this has been a lesson to you that you will take on board for the rest of your life. I find you not guilty on the charge but with immediate effect you will be transferred to Aldershot for training in Field Engineering, you are dismissed. Thank you Sir, I replied, a wise man indeed, if found guilty I could have received up to 28 days in the Guard House.

Aldershot – Field Engineering Course

Arriving in Aldershot I was pleased to be greeted by two lads who had been training with me so I was off to good start, or so I thought. It was a six week course in learning the art of bailey bridge building. Bailey bridge building is a very simple way of getting an army and all its equipment over a stretch of water in a very short time. This is done by sections of the bridge already prefabricated and with enough men, sections of the bridge can be bolted up and constructed very quickly and with a day you can have a bridge ready for use. After a week of learning how it all gets slotted together it's then out on site to build the real thing. So with toe-protector boots on and a hard hat I was ready to start a new experience. I had only been working on the bridge for about 3 hours and with men working on an above section I heard the cry "below" which was the warning shout of an article falling, before I had time to move a section of the bridging had landed right on to my right boot. I almost passed out with the pain but was supported by two men. When they took the section off, my boot was completely torn open, and the blood was filling up the rest of the boot and my sock. The medical team were quickly on the scene and managed to put a tourniquet on my lower leg to stop the bleeding. By this time I was quite weak but before I knew it I was being taken to a military hospital for urgent attention.

Poem

Bridge building can be dangerous as I soon found out
Hearing that cry from above or was it a shout
A section hitting the top of my right foot army boot
This is not supposed to happen to a new recruit
Should I thank the lord it never hit my head
If it had done I would have been brown bread
Am I being protected by some year mystic force?
Could it be that Viking legend from ancient Norse?
So who was this mythical giant that went into folklore?
It was the hammer wielding god of thunder the mighty Thor.

Tidworth Military Hospital

Arriving at the hospital I could see it was quite an imposing building and within minutes I was being examined by an army doctor and nurses. I could tell it was a military hospital by how efficient and highly trained the staff were. The medical staff on the bridge had bandaged the whole of my boot to stop the blood flow and they thought this was the best method as they did not know what the nature of the injury was. Lying on the operating bed I could see the nurses unwrapping the blood soaked bandages from the boot and my biggest fear is I may have lost a toe or other digits. Once they had unwrapped the bandages an x-ray was taken and I was given the news that I needed an operation to repair four bones in the foot that had been damaged and to treat some parts of the foot that had been squashed. Within half an hour I was in the theatre and I only remember waking up in a ward full of other soldiers from all other different regiments. A military hospital is run like a well oiled machine and everything is planed to the smallest detail, and you know that the care and attention is first class. If you are able to walk you work on the wards cleaning floors, making beds and anything else that needs to be taken car of but with my injury I was excused everything. The soldier in the next bed to mine had just come back from the operating theatre. He had a bullet wound in his backside of all places and had been flown back from Aden, in the Persian gulf where his regiment had come under fire from a group of rebels. He was in one of the highland regiments, he was telling me while out there that a RAF corporal who was attached to his battle group had sold a rifle to a rebel group and received 28 days detention for his crime. At that time a private in his regiment had hit an officer because he thought this officer was making the wrong decisions as they were fighting a battle. This soldier got six months in a military prison, as he pointed out you get one months detention for selling a rifle, but six months for hitting an officer (something wrong there me thinks) After four weeks in the hospital, the plaster cast was ready to come off, and on removing it they found it had healed up very well so within two days they decided the next step would be physiotherapy in the hospital gym. Waiting for me in the well kitted out gymnasium was a team of therapists headed by a female captain in the army nursing corps who was to be in charge of my treatment. All the rest of the team were friendly and very sweet, but the Captain whose name was Mason was a very manly lady and had the arms and muscles of a body-builder. I was only nine stone at the time but she must have been 14 stone at least. I'm sure she hated men and me in particular as her first words to me were this is going to hurt you more than it hurts me so you had better get used to it. I thought to myself, all those lovely young ladies in here, and I have to get the dragon of the litter. As I was now laid on the table she had hold of my foot and was turning it, this way and that. The pain was unbearable and the only words that came out of my mouth were mercy, please have mercy on me I cried. Mercy she bellowed, I'll give you mercy, and carried on the torture. I'm sure she enjoyed my screams of pain and my pleas for her to be gentle with me. After two weeks of sheer hell and punishment she decided that I was fit enough to end the treatment and be discharged from the hospital.

Poem

The army captain who treated me was an enormous big lump
Was built like a hippo with a massive big rump
She slammed me on the table with such a great force
Had the strength and power of a mighty shire horse
Then this huge great body bent right over me
At this point I'm thinking is this not a he
It was definitely female and was sure that she shaved
She smelt like a rancid skunk and had never bathed
Then getting hold of me and chucking me on a chair
It was like being gripped by a big brown grizzly bear
And underneath her armpits there she was a showing
A massive great forest of hair that needed mowing
Just a hundred of these dragons would win any fight
A trained battalion of Ghurkhas would retreat and take flight

As I made my way back to Aldershot barracks I had time to reflect on my hospital stay and thought to myself that "captain beast" who treated me would make a good interrogation officer, just one look at her and a prisoner of war would tell all without not being tortured. As I entered the office door at Aldershot camp I was met by the orderly officer who ordered me to do an about turn. As he handed me my new posting orders saying you will not be taking part in any more bridge building training so report to your new camp and good luck. Charming I thought to myself, their getting rid of me for something that I wasn't responsible for. Oh well, it's their loss and my gain.

School of Military Survey
nr Newbury, Berkshire

I was driven to my new camp from Aldershot and as we went through the main gates I noticed all the fields and farms that surrounded the camp. This is pleasant, I think I'm going to enjoy my stay here. I was quickly introduced to the O/C (officer commanding) and looking through my army papers noted that I had experience as a butcher in civilian life, just the man we are looking for he said, our last butcher left the regiment last week so get yourself sorted and you can start your new duties tomorrow and just before I left his office the O/C said oh, by the way Banfield, I believe you met my very good friend the O/C at Aldershot, we completed our officer training together and he is still a very good friend. Now I know why I was transferred to this camp, they wanted a butcher. I wasn't even asked if I wanted to job, I was told I was getting it! Just outside the camp was where all the married quarters for all ranks were situated, of course the higher up the rank you were the better house you were entitled to. And what a great job it turned out to be. My first job was to be introduced to the senior cook that was in charge of the cook house as SGT Murray he explained to me that daily he would give me what meats were required for the following day so I could make them up. That way we would always be a day in front of ourselves. Sergeant Murray had been an army cook for ages and was due to leave the army the following year after 25 years service. I had quite a long chat with him and found him to be a very friendly Scot who had this tinkle in his eye. He explained to me that the last butcher and him had a good arrangement together and hoped that we both could have a good working relationship together. On leaving his cookhouse his words to me were you play your cards right and we will get on fine, but I will come and have a chat with you and explain it all. As the weeks went by officers and senior NCOS (non commission officers) suddenly started to appear at my work and trying to be my best friend. Of course they were only there for the best cuts of meat that I could give them but it didn't take me long to barter with them. The best cuts of meat like rump steak and fillet steak all went to them and in return I got excused all parades and no drilling or marching and 72 hour (3 day) long weekend passes which were great. It meant you could pack up Thursday afternoon and report back to camp on the Monday morning. My butchers area were I worked overlooked the parade square and from the window

I used to watch all my mates marching up and down and I used to think to myself, life doesn't get much better than this. Then a knock at the door and an officer would say, morning John, the wife would like a nice bit of fillet steak for tonight and would you take it round to her. So as soon as I had finished all my duties for the day, I used to take the meat orders that I had been asked to deliver to the wives because of my status as the camps butcher I slept in a house on the camp with 3 other men from head quarters who were office workers. They also never had to do parades or drilling, we were the envy of the camp. Only a week had gone by when the cookhouse SGT came in my butcher's area. John he said, I would like to take you out for a drink tonight and we can get to know each other. Fine I said, look forward to it. That night I met SGT Murray in a pub not far from the camp and as the drinks started to flow he started to tell me how things were done in the cookhouse. Look John, I know I can trust you so I'll explain how things operate but I need your co-operation to make things work. I was all ears. It's like this SGT Murray went on, I order all the meat from the meat wholesellers from week to week and say I order 3 hind quarters and 3 fore quarters they only send 2 of each and the same with lamb quarters, there will put one less on the lorry. Now John, this is where you come in, seeing that you are the butcher, you are the one who has to sign for it. So John, what are you thoughts on all this. Well I said, the one question I have to ask is what's in it for me? Good John, he said, I was hoping you would say that. Now here's the deal, you sign for the meat products then you take delivery of them, then on your record card you will write that you have sent to the cookhouse more than you have, it's foolproof, no-one ever checks and if they did check you would have the record cards to say how much meat you have sent to the cookhouse and no-one knows what your stock is and how much meat I am holding in the cookhouse so lets talk money John, said SGT Murray. The meat for the week is delivered on the Monday of every week and this is when the driver who owns the meat firm pays me on the shortfall so if every Monday I was to give you £10 what would say to that. I would snap your hand off to get that money I said, good John, deal done. As the drinks were flowing SGT Murray said, now John, nobody must ever know about this, not even your best friends because if this fiddle was ever discovered, we would all be in serious trouble, trust me I replied my lips are sealed. Just before he left the pub, he said to me, just by looking at you John, I knew I could trust you and knew that you would go along with the deal, and he went on to explain the best cuts of meat the officers and NCO's used to ask you for were your test, if you would have reported it to someone then I would have not made an approach to you but because you kept quiet about it we knew we could make a deal with you.

Poem

Here I was in the army doing a bit of dealing
Losing a bit of meat here and there not really stealing
The army was paying me just two pounds a week
Earnt extra money by fiddling the army of their meat
Nothing wrong with that my friend with pay so low
Could not refuse the offer how could I say no
Some would say we were just plain greedy mean crooks
But all we really did was to cook the books.

Have I got such a dodgy face? To put the money he was offering me in perspective, at that time I was being paid by the army £2 a week, so with him offering me £10 a week extra was a king's ransom to me! I knew that this fiddle went higher up than with just SGT Murray and must have been going on for a long time and as everyone was happy in this arrangement so was I. As the weeks went on the arrangement was going along very smoothly with no problems. My hair was by this time getting longer as no-one bothered with me. The only time I wore my uniform was to go on leave in the working week I used to wear what cooks wear, spotted thin trousers and white jacket and hat. Once again Thursday afternoon came round and I set off on my 72 hour pass and to return as usual on the Monday morning. Just before the camp gates lived SGT Murray and this morning he was waiting for me at his front gate. Hi, Ian, I said, you don't look too happy today I said, John, quickly come in, I have something to tell you. By now I was thinking something is not quite right here. On entering his front room Ian blurted out John, I've had a tip off that all deliveries are now being watched, the owner-driver knows about it so when he makes a delivery you must sign whatever he delivers and also put the right amount of meat you send to the cookhouse on the order cards so if you do everything by the book we will have no problems, but I'm afraid this is the end of our fiddle and all my other fiddles. He went on, this tip off has come from high up so no-one knows that we know about the tip off. I just wondered to myself how many other fiddles was Ian up to? Ian and I could never see who was watching the butchers shop area or the cookhouse, but we knew we were being observed by someone. When I used to unlock the door of my shop I could tell things had been moved about and more likely had been weighed so they must have been coming in late at night but I knew as long as I did everything by the book they had nothing on us. For the next few weeks everything was done by the book and once again walking back to camp after my week's leave Ian was by his gate once again, but this time looking like the cat had got the cream. Hi, Ian I said, Hello John, come in, I have something to tell you that you may find interesting. First off, I will only be Sergeant cook for 4 weeks then I'm going on a course to train as a chef in a civilian hotel. This will be for 6 months and by this time I would have completed my 25 years in the army anyway because we did everything by the book for the last few weeks I've had no evidence against any of us and because of this I retire from the army with my full pension but I must warn you John a spy tells me there is going to be big changes afoot so be warned. I shook Ian warmly by the hand and wished him the very best and my parting shot was (nice to have done business with you Ian) and back to the camp I walked. Just as I was making my way to the block I was living at, I heard this almighty bellowing voice from a voice that I did not recognise. Sapper come over here, as I turned round, I faced this new RSM (Regimental Sergeant Major) What is your name he shouted, sapper Banfield I replied. Well Sapper Banfield, may I ask you when the last time you had a haircut he shouted, not for a while I meekly said. You're a disgrace to yourself and to your regiment, you are now on a charge, turn round and march yourself to the CO (commanding officer) office. Oh thinking to myself, I'm in a bit of trouble here. Within ten minutes I was standing in front of the C/O. Well Banfield, he shouted explain to me why you have grown your hair so long. Well sir as you know, I am the camp butcher and seeing that I was not required to go on parades it just slipped my mind, I lied. Well Banfield, for a start you are no longer the camp Butcher as we are going to buy it in daily from now on, already prepared and made up (I wonder why) you will be moving out of that block you are in and back to the main barrack huts with all the other men, there has been changes in the staff in the last 48 hours and the likes of you had better watch out. Right Banfield, for growing your hair so long and your uniform being in a terrible state you will serve 14 days detention; now get out of my office. Oh dear me, I thought I'm now back in the real world.

Poem

Losing my job as the camp butcher just was not on
Just wonder if it was to do with our con
Now standing in front of the C/O at attention
At least Ian never lost his pension
Must now again get used to living off two pounds a week
Will look for other revenue that's what I'll seek
Must count my blessings could have ended up in jail
Making and sewing up mail bags for the Royal Mail

I just wondered if I was being punished for the meat scam, but as they could not prove anything this was my punishment. After serving my 14 days detention which mainly involved me washing up the dishes in the officer's mess by day and going back to the guard room at night I was now billeted. In one of the large round huts with all the other men which was going to take some getting used to and that my new job was to be a batman to a few officers who were single. This involved cleaning their kit and tidying up their bedrooms and quarters. This turned out to be a great job and one of the best jobs on the camp. I used to start about 9 in the morning and finish at 4.30, the rest of your time was your own. I was always up for a laugh so one evening I went back to one of the officers bedrooms that I knew was on a weeks leave and dressed up in his captains uniform with his sam brown leather belt across my shoulder and waist and with his cap on and also his cane, I really looked the part. I had got one of my mates to be a look out so when the coast was clear, I walked from this officers quarters to my billet which was a five minute walk. On reaching the billet my mate pushed the doors open and shouted, officer approaching. I then entered the billet. On seeing me the whole billet stood at the end of their beds at attention as I slowly walked down the billet, not one of them recognised me. I did not talk as they would have known it was me. They were standing there as stiff as pokers not daring to move after walking the length of the billet I could hardly hold back the laughter and I couldn't resist talking to one of them. What's your name sapper I shouted at him, it's Jones sir, he replied, not a very tidy person are we Jones, look at the state of your bed man, I bellowed, sorry sir, he pleaded. Sorry, you'll be sorry I snapped. Just then I heard this laughing coming from the man next to him, he had recognised my voice and shouted it's Banney, that's the name I was known as by, this time the whole billet had erupted in howls of laughter as they had all been totally taken in and begged me to go into the next hut and do the same thing. So with the men from my hut now watching from the windows of the next hut I walked in. Officer approaching came the cry, once again I walked up to the billet there was total silence until I heard the door I had just walked through rattle open and turning around spotted what was to be my worst nightmare. It was a real officer and it was Major butts, and the thought want through my head, he even out ranks me! Turning to face him I felt like dying on the spot he gave me a smile and a nod of his head as one officer would do to a fellow officer. Oh my god I thought, what do I do now? I felt the whole world was crashing down on me and just couldn't believe my eyes. I thought this is a bad dream; it is at this point I removed my cap he looked at me in bewilderment, and amazement, what the hell is going on here he demanded to know. He screamed Banfield, what do you think you're playing at. I'm sorry sir, I said, but I only did it for a laugh sir. Did it for a laugh, he raged. By this time his face was the colour of a red London bus. You've just impersonated an officer, which is a serious offence, now take that uniform back where you got it and get yourself down to the guardroom.

Major Butts had only come in to the hut to get a pair of trouser pressed by one of his batman that was billeted there. Just my luck I thought. After spending the night in the guardroom, I was up before the C.O at 9 o'clock that morning. As I stood in front of him, the charge was read out to him and once he heard the charge looked at me with a pained expression. Now listen sapper Banfield, this is a very serious charge you are up in front of me, and it is so serious I'm now thinking that you should face a court marshal. What have you got to say for yourself? Well I thought to myself, I had better make this speech to him a good one as I don't fancy being on a court marshal as that meant an army prison. Well Sir, I know I dressed up as an officer and I'm very sorry about that, I did not mean any offence to anybody, but I only did it to get a laugh from the lads and bring them some cheer into their lives and also sir, I never realised it was an offence, I just looked at it as dressing up in fancy dress and the last thing I wanted to do was be disrespectful to anyone. After hearing what I had to say he turned to the officer sitting down taking notes of the meeting what are your views on this matter Lt Ross. Well Sir, Lt Ross said, I know sapper Banfield and I'm sure there would be no disrespect in the action he took; I feel it was just high spirits and a sense of fun that was behind all this. Thank you Lt Ross for that, right sapper Banfield the C.O. said, do you want to be tried by court Marshal or accept my punishment. Accept your punishment Sir. Right then, he went on, I have taken aboard what LT Ross has had to say and I agree that it was all done as a laugh as you put it and you were not being disrespectful to the rank or uniform, I therefore sentence you to 21 days confined to barracks. Thank you sir, I muttered, and then saluted. About turn, shouted the Sergeant Major. As I left the office, the RSM Major said, you were very lucky in there, you could have been court marshalled for what you did! So all it meant now is I would have to wash the dishes in the sergeants or officers mess. I was pleased that LT Ross had spoken up on my behalf as I'm sure he knew he owed me a favour as he was one of many officers that I had given meat to for nothing, so he got to repay me with his summing up. The 21 days detention soon went by and things started to get into a routine. As I was no longer the camp butcher I now started to do the daily morning parades and the big main parades. These were the queen's birthday, visiting senior officers or N.A.T.O top brass. It was on one of these parades that things didn't go down too well. It was a grand parade for senior officers from many foreign armies to show them how the British army trained, drilled and conducted themselves in all forms of military procedures. On this day, extra seating had been erected for all the visiting military personnel and their families also specialists were brought in the RAF regiment, who were experts in marching and performing hundreds of drill movements with their rifles plus the massed bands of different army units. Before the parade started we were all lined up near the parade ground and told by the RSM (sergeant Major) that the army wants a really good show put on, and that no man had better get it wrong or else. Being one of the shorter men on parade, I was in the front row of our troop and right in line with all the visiting generals as we began to march, the bands started to play and in no time we had formed up in our positions. The next step in the procedure is for the visiting senior officer to inspect the rows of troops, once he has inspected the men, he then returns to his rostrum. The next step is to fix your bayonet onto your rifle, this involves taking your bayonet that is sitting in a sheaf at the back of your waist belt and on the order to fix bayonets you pull the bayonet out of the sheaf and attach it to the end of the rifle barrel. There are two steps to complete the procedure of getting the bayonet onto the rifle. On the order of fix, you place your right hand onto the sheaf and grab hold of it. The second move on the order of bayonet, about three seconds after the word fix, inserts it into the top of the rifle barrel. We were now ready for the order. The major then shouted out fix. As soon as fix was shouted, my right hand went to grab hold of my bayonet but for some reason it wouldn't come out of the sheaf. I was still trying to get it out when the order was shouted bayonet. I managed to get it out of the sheaf but everyone had now fixed theirs. There was complete silence around the parade ground as I attempted to fix my bayonet as quietly as possible but it being metal to metal, it's just not possible to keep it silent. From the back of the ranks I could hear the R.S.M in hushed tones say, what the f—k are you playing at Banfield. When fixing the bayonet onto the rifle you have to turn it half a turn as it is spring loaded, it then slots into a groove. This makes the noise like a clunk click sound. But I had not turned it the full half turn and as I took my hand away it flew about 10 feet into the air and of course in front of all the spectators and from the packed stands I saw every head spin around to look at me. As it hit the ground the men behind were trying to suppress their laughter. The noise it made as it hit the ground was deafening and with the spectators groaning with the words OH and OUCH. If only the ground would open up and swallow me up. On all parades there are always men who have been excused boots and are not carrying rifles whose job it is to be on hand for anything that may crop up, mainly for men fainting or for men not able to connect their bayonets properly! For the rest of the parade I marched without the bayonet attached which must have looked really funny. It could only happen to me!! Of course the next day I was up in front of the O/C on a charge of failing to use my equipment properly (the army has a charge for everything). His first words to me were sapper Banfield, you are a disgrace to your uniform and you have made our regiment a laughing stock, in front of visiting general and hundreds of spectators. What have you got to say for yourself? Well Sir, I blurted out, I went to get my bayonet out of my sheaf but it wouldn't budge, and when I finally got it out, it would not fix onto the rifle barrel and I was trying to make it as quiet as possible hoping it was not noticed by anyone. He quickly cut me off, you are an incompetent soldier and a useless individual, my head will roll for all this, he shouted, I sentence you to 7 days detention, now get out of my sight, you are an embarrassment. With that insult ringing in my eyes, I did an about turn and stepped out his office. To wash more dishes and plates for the next 7 days, the cheek of it. Everyone is allowed to make the odd cock-up now and again. I once again completed my 7 days detention, and I was now more determined than ever to stay out of trouble, as I always seem to be in it. You'll be pleased to know Banfield that you will be going on manoeuvres on Monday, this voice behind me shouted. I turned to see it was the Sergeant Major with a grin on his face, and I'll be able to keep an eye on you.

The Brecon Beacons Manoeuvres

The Monday evening was upon us and we all assembled at the starting point loaded up with our equipment and taken aback as on the army lorry taking us there was only 20 men from the regiment but looking around I realised all the men had been in some sort of trouble or another and knew that this was a punishment thing. It took us about 4 hours to reach the beacons which in the summer are very beautiful but at night the picture changes as you cannot see a thing in front of you. (Why do they always hold manoeuvres at night?) As our small troop assembled for the action the sergeant Major gave us the run-down of what our roll was to be in the coming mock battle. We like many others from different regiments were to wear red arm bands and we were to be the hunted. So we were the enemy, we were to be given 2 hour start and walk about 20 miles without being captured. The hunters were made up of elite troops such as the Ghurkhas, the parachute regiment, and the Guards with our sergeant Major leading us; I felt I would not get into any trouble. Just before we set off our sergeant Major gave us a battle talk. Now listen men, if we can avoid being captured, it will be a feather in our caps and our C/O will be more than pleased, but if you do get captured the enemy will spray you with a red dry so you will be out of the battle and you will be taken by them to the battle headquarters as their prisoner. We are an engineering regiment and they are the experts so stick close to me and you all should be OK. It was 10pm when we started out; we could just make out our way, by the moon that was shiny. We knew we had been walking for two hours because all of a sudden all hell broke loose. There was mortar fire, machine guns opened up and thunder flashes exploding, the whole night sky was lit up and it was the most frightening sight I had ever witnessed. It went on for what seemed like hours and in the confusion we had all got separated. I was thinking at that time this is a mock battle, what a real one must be like. By this time I was crawling along the ground on all fours not knowing where I was going and came across a bush and thought to myself, I'll just get in amongst it till all the noise dies down and then be on my way. As I settled in amongst the bush it suddenly went all quiet and as I lay there I noticed thousands of stars glowing, the moon had now disappeared, what a wonderful sight to behold, I had never seen the stars in all their glory. The next thing I remember is feeling how damp my face felt but the biggest shock of all was to see night time had been replaced by the early dawn, and it was the dew that had dampened my face. Oh dear me, I think I'm in trouble once again, how could I have gone to sleep! What do I do now? Heaving myself out of the bush, I had an even worse shock, my rifle was missing.

Poem

The first start of the manoeuvres were on that night
Running around like a crazy man in a mock fight
After two hours of mayhem thought I would lie
Settled in to some bushes looked up at the sky
Pitch black by now I could now see afar
Amongst all the others even spotted the North Star
My eyes slowly closed just went into a sleep
And never even had to count them sheep
Woke up next morning with dew on my face
What made it worse still ten miles from base
Looked around all the bushes my rifle had disappeared
My worst nightmare had happened court marshal I feared
Would tell them I got hit with an almighty whack
That's all I can remember because it all went black

I don't believe it. This cannot be happening to me. As I was getting out of the bush, I noticed that parts of it were made up of a bramble bush and the razor like spikes had cut into my face and hands and as they had been bleeding I must have looked in a sorry mess. That's when the idea came into my head, I'll say all I remember is walking along and I don't recall anything after that, and I must have been knocked unconscious. As I woke up and it was the early morning and looked around for my rifle but some someone must have picked it up, that sounds a good excuse I thought to myself. As I prepared to set off, looking around me I hadn't a clue which way to go. Where was I? Where do I head for? Oh, good, I've just spotted a Path, I'll follow that and see where it takes me, of course by now all the army games were over and they had all packed up and gone back to barracks. So there was nobody about. By now I must have walked about 7 miles and in the distance spotted a road. Thank god for that, now I may be able to flag a car down. As I approached the road I saw on the other side of the road an army land-rover with four military policemen in it. Just my luck I thought they had spotted me and had stopped. What the hell have you been up to one of them shouted, look at the state of you, he cried, explain what has happened to you. I then went on to tell them I had been on manoeuvres last night and had somehow got knocked out by something or someone and only remembered waking up this morning with a very bad headache. That's all very well soldier, but where is your rifle, the senior one of the four shouted. Erm it's missing I meekly said. Missing he yapped, what do you mean it's missing? That's a very serious offence soldier, a court marshal offence in fact. Right he said, get in the back of the land rover we will take you to a field hospital for your wounds and find out what's to be done of you.

-The Field Hospital-

The Field Hospital was made up of canvas tents that the army can set up very quickly in times of battle or on manoeuvres. They are equipped with all the best medical equipment that nursing staff may need. One of the military policemen took me inside the tented hospital and explained to the nursing sister where I was found and what I had told them. OK the sister said, leave him with us and we will examine him. He then departed. The sister looked up at me and said, first off, let's get your first name. My first name in the army, that's a first. Am I hearing right, this lady is human. John I blurted out, well John, perhaps you can tell me your full name and army number. All this information I gave her and I noticed what an attractive young lady she was. I was falling in love with her as she was speaking. Just then the army doctor entered the tent. Well well, what have we got here nurse, it looks like he has been pulled through a hedge backwards. (If he would have said forward he would have been spot on). I have not questioned him yet doctor she said sweetly, well perhaps you can tell me what happened to you soldier. I went on to tell him that I was walking along but crouching down and that's all I remember. Right sapper lets get you onto the table and I'll give you a complete medical examination. Having looked all over me and found no evidence of any injury the doctor said the only thing I can come up with is you could have had some sort of blackout and this would explain why you didn't remember anything until you woke up, so I'm going to keep you in for 24 hours to observe and keep an eye on you. This is great news! I thought to myself it makes losing my rifle not so serious! Because my thinking was this if I was unconscious how would I know what happened to my rifle. The field hospital covered quite a large area and the tent I was in had about 40 beds in it. I was looked after very well as there was only two other soldiers in the beds. The next morning the doctor said I could b e discharged and they were going to take me back to my regiment's camp in an army ambulance. As the doctor handed me my medical notes, he said, hand these notes to your medical centre at your barracks, and an army nurse will be with you on the journey, just to make sure everything is OK. I did feel a bit guilty about deceiving the wonderful field army hospital staff, but losing a rifle can get you six months in a military prison so it had to be done. We finally arrived at my barracks and the ambulance pulled up outside the sick bay. They had already been informed all about me. As I handed the notes to the medical officer he looked over them and said, I'm putting you on light duties for a week so you're free to go back to your billet but you are due to see the commanding officer in the morning. As I left the sick bay the sergeant major who we had been on was waiting outside. We looked around for you for an hour Banfield, as we could not find you we thought you must have been captured so we pressed on and by the way Banfield, you're not supposed to know that your rifle was handed in at about midnight of that night so do not mention I told you, once again I was standing in front of the commanding officer. This time the charge was read out as follows – contrary to army rules and regulations and to good order and military discipline you have been charged with losing or abandoning a 303 lee Enfield rifle while on manoeuvres. How do you plead sapper Banfield, grunted the commanding officer. Not Guilty, Sir I replied in my humblest voice. Losing your rifle is one of the most serious charges a soldier can face Banfield and I want to know how you can plead not guilty when you clearly lost or abandoned the said weapon. Well Sir it's like this, on that night of the manoeuvres I was running along but crouching down and I don't remember anything after that, until I awoke in the early morning and looking around for my rifle was shocked to find it missing, but knew it must have been handed in. I was just about to add more when he cut me off. Sapper Banfield I find this episode and your story unbelievable and I just don't know what to make of it all. Sergeant Major, march him out and I will consider my verdict. With that I marched out his office and waited very nervously outside wondering if he had swallowed my pack of lies. The Sergeant Major could see how uptight I was and tried to reassure me by saying, for some reason Lt Ross likes you and he will try his best to help you in there so all is not lost son. We must have waited about half an hour when the door opened. Accused and escort, march in a voice bellowed. As I turned to face the C/O LT Ross gave me a knowing look. Banfield, you have pleaded not guilty to the charge so I now have to ask if you wish to be court marshalled, for the said offence or accept any punishment that I might hand out. I will accept Sir, anything that your good self thinks fit I said in a very soft voice, hoping that would make me appear as a little boy lost. He went straight into the attack, right Sapper Banfield, you know how serious the charge is and I find your own view of events unbelievable, however I have looked at all the evidence from your RSM, the field hospital and what you have had to say, I will not be sending you for court marshal (thank god for that I thought) and as you have agreed to take my punishment, then that is the road I will take. As there were no witnesses to how you ended up losing your rifle, how you got them injuries and what did happen that night, I must then take your version to be the truth, but things just don't add up. But you have to be punished for losing your rifle so with that in mind I sentence you to 28 days in detention in the guard house. Oh by the way Banfield, your rifle was handed in at 13:00 hours and if it had not been handed in you would have not escaped a court marshal. Thank you sir I replied. I marched out with a skip in my step knowing it could have been much worse (all this turmoil for a few hours of sleep). LT Ross came to visit me in the Guard house and told me that when I had completed my 28 days I was to be posted to a depot in Chatham in Kent as the commanding officer had tried to get me posted to the furthest location the British army served at but seeing I only had six months to do they decided it was not practical. LT Ross also confided in me that the C/O thought I was a bit of a wide boy and in his view the story I had told was a complete pack of lies but had no evidence or proof that it was a made up story! He also said it was a good job I was in that room because I was able to calm the C/O down and persuade him you had some good points and he should be lenient with you. The 28 days detention soon passed and on the last day of the sentence I was told I would be going to Chatham barracks the next day.

On packing all my kit in the kit bag I got a surprise visitor, it was LT Ross to wish me well. John he said, when you get to Chatham you will meet an old friend of mine, his name is Captain Walker. I have told him all about you and I think you will get on very well with him. He runs all the sports teams for the regiment. So my tip for you is to join his football squad. If you join the squad you will never look back, with a handshake and a wave to LT Ross I said my farewells to the school of military engineering – Newbury. My only regret in all this is I never got to see the lads in my regiment. I'm sure they would have enjoyed the stories I had to tell about my sleeping under the stars and losing my rifle and the story I made up to try and cover myself.

RE Transit Camp - Chatham — Kent

To make sure I arrived at my new posting I was driven by a staff car the 100 or so miles to Chatham. On reporting to the front gate I was directed to the C/Os office and found myself in front of this strange looking LT Colonel Johns with eyebrows that were as large as a hedge. It was very hard to keep a straight face when facing him. I'm just going to go over your army history sapper Banfield and to me it does not make good reading, in fact, it looks to me, you are treating your army service as a joke, well I'm here to tell you that this is all about to change, you have only six months service left but in that time if you step out of line I will stamp down hard on you, do I make myself clear? Yes Sir, I replied in a voice that was clear but not loud. He went on, you seemed to have got yourself on a few charges for various reasons but now that you are here try and make a go of it and keep out of trouble and to help you I'm going to send you to work in our headquarters office and I don't expect to see you in front of me for any reason. Thank you sir, I said as I saluted and left his office. Things seemed to be really looking up. But I still couldn't get them eyebrows out of my mind. This I thought was the best camp I had been in all the office staff were up for a laugh and I made many friends in the barracks and our nights were spent in the local pubs meeting and chatting up all the local talent that were in the many pubs that were in Chatham at that time. The river Medway runs through Chatham and out to the open sea and at this time, 1960, it still had a large navel base (the reason for so many pubs) so with a large army base there this made for many fights between the services. One of my jobs in the office was to log all prisoners being kept in our guard house. As more often than not, soldiers detained in their naval brig, in most cases they had all been fighting and as drunk as lords and kept in custody overnight and when sobered up escorted across the road to the navy base. I marched behind with all the relevant paper work and handed them over; we would then collect any soldiers that the navy might have picked up. I was working away doing some paperwork one day and I heard a voice say, got up to any fiddles yet sapper Banfield? I looked up and saw an officer with the rank of Captain standing by the main desk, fiddles I meekly said, let me introduce myself to you, as his hand stretched out to meet mine, Captain Walkers the name, LT Ross has told me all about you and as you may know we are very good friends at your last camp so I know everything there is to know about you and he tells me you looked after him very well and he appreciated it so I'm here to look after you. Firstly are you good at any sports he enquired? Yes Sir, I'm quite good at football I lied, OK, then be at the sports field at 13:50 hours on Wednesday and I'll give you a trial. If you're any good I'll consider you for the army football team (Wednesday afternoon is always the time all services carry out their sports). On this day the army team seemed to be enormous great beasts most of them over six feet tall and seem to enjoy inflicting pain on the opposition. As I was only a sub I was glad I was not taking part in this one sided battle. Fists and boots were flying in from all angles, this is not a football match I thought, its war. One of our forwards got a punch on the chin and he had to come off, right John, you're on Captain Walker said, get in there and make yourself useful. Being only 5ft 5ins tall this was going to be a one sided battle me thinks, but being small and agile I was able to get stuck in and with only my second touch of the ball I scored with an outrageous shot that hit about two of the three players before ending up in the net. We eventually won the game 2-1. After the game Captain Walker came up to me and said that I was in his team from now on. You are not technically a good player but a fighter and I like that in a player. Some of the players we have, he went on, play like big girls and are scared to go into a tackle so I was now in the regimental football team. Playing in the football team was a great skive as we played all over the UK but the best matches were the ones played in Germany at (BOAR) British Army of the Rhine, playing in knock out tournaments against all different regiments. Win or lose the drink ups after the matches were great, but like all things they come to an end. As the season had finished so back to Chatham once more but the time we got back, arrangements were well in hand for a parade to celebrate the queen's birthday, always a big occasion in the army. Her birthday celebrations are in June and this year it was a very hot day. As we all paraded on the main parade ground in front of the towns top people and many thousands of local people, once again, because of my height I was standing in the front row facing all the spectators. By the time all the seats were occupied we had been standing out in the sun for over an hour with a heavy uniform on, it was torture, with the sun beating down with no shade. I was thinking to myself how do I get out of this? 20 more minutes passed and still no sign of the General that was going to take the salute. By now I was really feeling hot under the collar, as they say and with no sign of the top man showing up drastic action was needed. Right, if he doesn't show up in another five minutes I'm going to pretend to faint. The five minutes went by and he still had not arrived, this is it John, down you go, but make it look real, these were the thoughts going through my head. I had been on other parades and watched as men fainted, they either fell forward or backwards, if they fell forward they went down as straight as a log and in some cases lost teeth or had face injuries. Both ways were not a pretty sight and I wasn't about to make it that real. Just before I collapsed I whispered to the lads next to me, that's it, I've had enough of this I'm out of here, and with that, I sort of stumbled down with my knees bent and my body crumbled in a heap, making sure I pushed my rifle to one side. I did not want to land on top of that. As it hit the ground, I heard this sigh from the spectators, oooooh and when I hit the ground the sound was Aaaaaah. As I lay on the ground I could hear ladies shouting, look that poor boys fainted, I hope he's going to be alright but the sound I feared was the colour Sergeant in the back of the ranks "Banfield" and a few choice swear words, in a voice, meaning to say it was a pretend faint, the other voice I heard was the officer in charge. Man fainted; stretcher bearers remove man to sick bay. The next thing the lads were bending over me whispering "nice one John, you've got some front" and other comments as they carried me away. I felt really pleased with myself entering the sickbay. I pretended to come round; the duty doctor asked the lads did you see this man fall and if so how did he fall. They said, we saw him fall and think he may have hit has head on the ground. After examining me, he said because of the heat, your body just shut down causing you to faint; you're also dehydrated so we need to get some fluids into you. Well at least one person thinks it's real. What made it better for me that day, two other soldiers had also fainted earlier on, but of course they were genuine, as they had both fallen in an upright position and both had facial injuries. But by this time I was feeling quite ill, the doctor was discussing with the nurse that they expected more faintings to take place as the temperature on the parade ground had now reached 85 Fahrenheit and when the parade was completed he would be confronting the commanding officer to complain about leaving men with full uniform out for so long in that heat. I just settled back in bed. All this was music to my ears. As I went into a relaxing sleep I was rudely awakened by loud shouting from outside the ward. The voice in question was the colour Sergeant and I could make out he was not too happy with the acting that he thought had taken place and the manner in which I had fallen as no one falls like that when they faint. He also implied I was malingering actor and there was nothing wrong with me. He just pretended to faint to get off that parade and he should and will be charged as soon as he comes out of here. On hearing this, the doctor was absolutely furious and went into a rage. How dare you come into my sick bay Sergeant Major and tell me one of my Patients is feigning a sickness, this soldier is quite ill and by the way how is a man supposed to faint? Is there a regulation way of falling? Some people faint without warning and others like sapper Banfield have time to stop themselves from falling badly, now get out of my sick bay and if anyone is to be charged it will be you! As I lay there chuckling thinking to myself people believe what they want to believe but a good act does help. After two days in sick bay the doctor said I was fit enough to return to my duties so back to the office I returned. I found out from the men that they stood out in the sun for 45 minutes after I had departed, in the pub the following night. We all had a great laugh about it all but what I didn't know is the lads had fixed my bed up before we went out to collapse as I got into it. It was a very heavy cast iron bed. As we all returned from a great night out I felt a bit merry and felt like talking. But they had all got to their beds quickly waiting for the big show as I got into mine. But I sat on the rail on the end of the bed with one foot under the main support bar. All of a sudden there was an almighty crash, the main support bar had caught my right foot with such force this time I really did feel like I was going to faint. I was yapping around like a terrier dog even though I had consumed a few drinks the pain nearly took my breath away. They quickly lifted the bed off my foot, it was now up like a balloon with a deep cut right across the foot with blood flowing out like a volcano erupting. Panic stations now set in; the lads quickly wrapped a towel around it and started to carry me down to sick bay which I had only left a day before. Now let's get this story right, how did it happen? I said we will just say someone must have come in our sleeping quarters and set my bed to crash down when I got in it, but it all backfired on them. On entering the sickbay the nurse cried out, oh not you again! You've only just left us, what happened to you? After explaining it all to her she said, the doctor won't be here until the morning so I'll bandage it up and he will look at it then. Right lads put him on that bed over there and bring some of his things over as he could be here for a while. The next morning the doctor came into the ward took one look at me and said, you must like this place. After taking the bandage off, he said we will need to get that foot x-rayed to see the full extent of the injury. After the x-ray the doctor said you'll be pleased to know it's not as bad as we thought, you have broke the top foot bone but we will put it in plaster and you should be OK in five to six weeks, you can return to your duties and seeing that you work in the office that will be fine. Back at work in the office the Sergeant Major paid me a visit. Banfield I'm putting you on a charge for a self inflicted injury. How could I inflict the injury on myself, I said. You can explain it all to the C/O, he said with a grin. This is all because of my fainting scam I thought. Be outside the C.O office at 14.00 hours, I always seems to be in trouble and on charges. Why me? When on a charge you stand outside the C/O office with a guard in front of you and one behind. This is of course in case the accused feels like attacking the C/O. We were waiting to go in, when the front guard let off a ripper, with that myself and the other guard were in fits of laughter, just then the door opened and the shouted words were, guards and accused march in, left right, left right, halt, turn round and face the C/O. I still had a grin on my face and as the C/O was looking down at the charge sheet all I could see were these massive bushy eye brows and still thinking about the ripper. The laughter I was trying to suppress suddenly erupted with full laughter. Are you laughing at me Banfield, he shouted. No Sir, I'm sorry sir I replied. Get out he shouted and when you have composed yourself you can come back in. Yes, Sir, sorry Sir and we marched out. Both the guards and myself were now in fits of laughter and after about two minutes the front guard said John, pull yourself together, if you laugh in front of him again you'll be in big trouble. So we all composed ourselves as best as we could, knocked at the door and all marched in again. Right Banfield, have we got over your school boy giggles now? Yes Sir, I answered. You are standing in front of me charged with causing self inflicted injuries upon yourself, what have you got to say in your defence on that said charge? Sir, I started, I just cannot understand why I am standing in front of you, because on the night in question I was ready to get to bed and standing by the foot of my bed and just sat on the rail and it collapsed on top of my foot, I believe it was done as a practical joke that went wrong, whoever set it up was hoping I would get in bed, then the whole bed would have caved in on me, so I don't see why I should be charged as I'm the one with a broken foot, through no fault of my own. Escort and accused, march out and I'll consider my verdict, left right, left right and once again we were standing outside the office. How I kept my laughter in check I will never know. We stood outside for five minutes when we were called back inside. As I once again stood in front of him, his first words were, I like you sapper Banfield, but find it very hard as to why you were even charged with this offence as it seems to me you are completely innocent of the charge and I will be looking into the reasons why certain people brought this charge against you and what indeed the motive behind it was, you are dismissed but before you go, I am awarding you a weeks leave in light of what you have had to suffer lately. Thank you Sir I beamed. I saluted and marched out a happy bunny. My foot took five weeks before the plaster came off as soon as it was taken off I started my weeks leave.

My Weeks Leave

On the first day back home in London I was walking by Warwick avenue tube station when a car pulled up beside me and a head popped out of the window. Hello John, what are you doing, I thought you were in the army? It was Mick Levy the green grocer owner whose shop was opposite the butcher's shop I used to work in. Yes Mick I'm still in the army but have a weeks leave. His eyes lit up, a weeks leave eh, fancy earning a few bob working for me? What would I be doing then if I said yes? Well Mick said, I've got a lorry spare and what you could do is if I load it up with fruit and veg, you go up to Kilburn, and off the high road there is long roads without any shops so instead of people walking to the high Street they could come to the lorry to shop. OK, I said, I'll try it, when do you want me to start? You can start tomorrow if you want, as its Saturday it should be quite busy there. The next day I helped Mick load up with a lorry full of fruit and veg and set off to Kilburn not knowing if people would be interested in buying from someone they had never seen before. Parking the lorry at about the half way mark where it was about ten minute walk to the shops I opened the side shutters and there displayed was all the fruit and veg. Within seconds I had my first customers. Have you taken over from old Bert, she cried, I hope so, he retired six months ago and we now have to walk all the way up to the shops. No I replied, well in that case you should do very well here. And she was right; within three hours I had sold out and had to return to tell Mick the good news. On seeing me return so soon Mick's face dropped, no good he shouted. No good I laughed, sold out old son, I have come back for more supplies. From a dropped face it became a beaming smile. Great John, get straight back up there and sell more, oh by the way John, how much did you make? Mick Levy, never owned the green grocer shop in Formosa Street, this belonged to his father. As his father was very elderly, Mick ran the whole show, his father only coming down from upstairs for two hours a day to take the money at the till. By the end of the week my takings were about £100, a huge sum in those days. I worked on the Saturday and on returning to the shop I said to Mick, I've to got go back to the army on Monday as I have had my weeks leave. What he shouted, go back, you must be mad as he handed me my wages of £10. Seeing I was only getting £2.50p (£2-10 shillings) army pay this was a fortune to me. Go sick, get yourself a doctor's certificate and we will both make some money, why not I thought. I know a bent Indian doctor just off the Edgware road in Praed Street Mick then said. So off to the bent doctor I went. Sitting down I noticed something unusual about the surgery, most of the people sitting around the place were all young men. On talking to them this doctor was known throughout London as the men were all from the services, army, navy and air force and from all parts of London. As you walked into his examination room he asked you who you were, why had you come to him and what was the matter with you. It was as simple as this, you told him your name, that you were in the army and the illness you were suffering from, in my case I said I had the runs, with that he produced his sick-note pad wrote what I had told him down and calmly put out his hand and said 10 shillings please (50p). If you need to review it again, come in next week. It was as simple as that. He must have been the richest Patel in all of London. He took great pride in telling me how he was a police doctor. Well that brought a smile to my face (if you were in the services and found yourself on sick leave you could go into any doctor to get a sick note) but they at least would examine you and you would get the sick note for free, not so with doctor Patel. Who would have sold his soul for a pound note! I carried on selling the fruit and veg on the second week and on the Friday as I was serving a customer a man with an identity badge came up to the lorry. Good morning Sir, can you show me your trading licence for selling goods on the roadway? I'm sorry I said, I don't own the lorry, it belongs to Mr Levy, he has probably got the licence. OK the man said, I will let you carry on trading today but if you return tomorrow I want to see a licence, if Mr Levy has not applied for one do not turn up here or anywhere else, if you do you will both be fined and with that he left. That's it, that's the end of our joint venture. I finished trading for the day and returned back to the shop. Bad news, I said to Mick, a man from the council wants to see your trading licence and if I don't show him it we will both be fined. That's OK, Mick said, you can trade in some other place. Sorry Mick, I cannot take the chance, if I get caught and they found out I was on sick leave I would be in deep trouble. Yes I suppose your right, Mick agreed. Well Mick it's been good working for you, maybe when I get out I'll come and look you up. You do that, he said, when you get out there will be a job waiting for you.

Last weeks of Army Service

Returning back to barracks I felt quite strange after two weeks off but I soon got back into army life. As I worked in head office I was given the job to sign all other ranks pay books. Each soldier was allowed two 72 hour leave passes with a rail warrant and four 48 hour passes with no rail warrants for the year. When issued with their 72 hour passes and rail warrant I was supposed to stamp their pay book but if a pay book was ready to be stamped and a pound note was sitting on the page, somehow I forgot to stamp the book, so some of the men always seemed to be on leave. My thinking was, by the time the fiddle was discovered I would have completed my service. I still managed to stay in the football team. We had another two weeks tour of BAOR (British Army of the Rhine). The sports captain said, we were all up for it, as it was a good skive and the German beer cellars were a great night out. We only arrived at a base in Hanover which belonged to the royal artillery. The night before the match we all went out on the town. The beer was flowing and German beer is very strong. The next morning we were all in a very bad way. The start of the match was about to take place, we could hardly stand up, let alone see the ball. The final whistle was a welcome relief for all of us and as we only lost by twelve goals to them, none to us, but felt we had not done too badly. The sports captain was not pleased and banned us from going out the night before the next match which was in Frankfurt. We all still managed to slip out for a good drink. The next match was against a Scots guard's team. They were huge men, not one of them under six feet, if you got in their way they just crashed into you. By the end of the game we had been slaughtered by the even worse score than the last one, it was 14-2 to them. We were getting worse. The next game was in the south of Germany, and this was in Stuttgart and this one was not a services team but a school for deaf and dumb pupils. It was all done for good relations to the host nation of course we had all been on the beer the night before the match with the usual hang-over. As they couldn't communicate between themselves we assumed we would beat them easily. How wrong we were. They were 6-0 up by halftime and by full time the score was an awful 11-3 to them. This was all too much for the sports captain, he cancelled all the remaining games and we were back in the UK the UK the next day. His final talk to us was you are all an embarrassment to the regiment team and to yourselves and as from now you are all sacked from the team. Ouch. Charming I thought, the ungrateful sod, what did he expect with eleven drunken players. I had almost come to the end of my service life now. I had to hand over my office duties to a new man and explain to him how all the fiddles worked. It was a very sad day when I woke up that morning and knew this day was my last day as a sapper in the royal engineers I had spent two years in the army and once again as with my past life felt I was losing a family. On your last day you have to sign off all your equipment, this takes you to most of the camp, so seeing all your old friends for the last time gives you a lump in your throat knowing that you will never see them again. You will never get that comradeship and camaraderie that bonds men together in the forces, we were like a band of brothers. My last duty to do was to see the C/O who hands out your army record and gives you a talk. By this time my army uniform had been handed in, so I was in my civilian clothes standing in front of the C/O felt quite strange. Now that I had completed my service he started off, well John, looking at your record you've had your ups and downs and it looks like it's been a roller coaster ride for you and I know from my experience and dealings with you I have found you to be quite a character, and can only wish you well in life as I'm sure you will do well. I hope you have enjoyed your stay with us, he smiled, Oh Yes I replied, I would not have missed it for the world. Was two years national service worth it, you bet it was one of those things that you'll always remember?

Poem

Millions were called up for two years or more

One hell of an experience and that's for sure

Two years I served it all went so fast

I was up for it and completed the task

There were happy times, bad times but proud to serve

As a sapper in the engineers a fantastic learning curve

I had tears in my eyes when we said our farewells

Leaving men from all over this nation, England, Ireland, Scotland and Wales

Now finished with army life and with the service

Soon will start civilian life and I'm feeling nervous

Finished Army – Mick Levy Greengrocer

The first thing I did on leaving the army was to find myself a flat and I found a nice one in Warrington crescent just around the corner where Mick Levy had the green grocer shop that I had worked in. I called in to see Mick and straight away asked me when I would be starting work. Tomorrow if you like I replied. OK Mick's eyes lit up, right your start time is six am, to 7pm (had he never heard of unions) he went on I will come with you on the first morning and we will be going to the old Covent garden fruit market and your job will be to pick up all the fruit and veg that I buy from the whole sellers. When we get back to the shop you will unload the stock and when that's finished serve the customers and refill any shelves that need restocking (not much to do then). I must be mad taking this job on. Thirteen hours a day, that's more working than rest and sleeping in the 24 hour clock. This reason we had a vacancy in the shop was because my old friend, Jim Gregg had left to immigrate to South Africa with his wife Alma. If I may, I will try and tell you a bit about Mick Levy. He was the product of an Irish mother and a Jewish father. He was at that time 35 years old with blonde curly hair and a bit of a character with a very good sense of humour. Mick was an orthodox Jew which is a lowly Jew. His wife was a liberal Jewess which in most cases were a lot wealthier and a higher class of Jew. Mick's whole purpose in life was to make that extra shekel and I had to take my hat off to him. He was an expert in how money could be made. He lived in Finchley North London, which has a large Jewish Community; his motto in life was money makes money. And his other saying was, when working with money, you'll make money. On the first day of getting back to the shop Mick showed me how things worked in the shop, in the basement was sacks of cabbages and every day using a hose pipe, would give them a good soaking as this increases their weight by about 20%. As they were sold by the weight this made them much heavier and therefore more expensive. Mick had one of those minds that was always thinking ahead. One morning I was in Covent Garden with Mick when he got his pen out and started to write the registration number of a brick lorry from the London brick company. When we got back to the ship I asked him why he had took the brick lorries number down. He then went on to explain that his wife had damaged the bonnet of her car that morning, hitting the front garden post. He got hold of the brick companies number, phoned them up, and the conversation went something like this:

I was driving my car this morning through Covent Garden and it was about 6:30am and I was travelling behind one of your brick lorries and two bricks fell onto my car bonnet as he braked. I tried to catch up with him but he just drove on, he probably never realised he had lost two bricks. All I could do was to get his registration number. I could hear the voice on the other end of the line, Oh dear Sir, I am sorry about that, leave it with me and we will trace the lorry and the driver and question him about this, leave me your telephone number sir and I will get back to you. About two hours later the phone rang, it was the London brick companies head office. Mr Levy, we have spoken to the driver of the lorry and he confirms your story that he was in Covent garden at that time, but he said he would not have known he had lost any bricks so may I personally apologise on his behalf for the damage to your car, please get the damage repaired and if you send us the repair bill we will gladly send you a cheque to cover the cost. Mick's wife got her car repaired for nothing. How about that, for cheek and front. But that old motto springs to mind, he who fiddles wins! Mick's father lived in a flat about the shop in Formosa Street and had lived there for the past five years. He had moved from his old flat in Covent Garden which he had lived in for most of his life. His grandparents had emigrated from Russia like thousands of other Jewish people and mainly settled in the east end of London and the most popular areas for the new arrivals were Dalston, Hackney and White Chapel. They had emigrated from Eastern Europe from the 18th century. They lived in complete squalor but they overcame their hardships and being an adaptable and hard working race they managed to survive, and in a lot of cases built up enough capital to start their own business up mainly as shop keepers. Each father would hand his business to his son, when he passed; in some cases the son would expand the business and so on. Just up the road from Mick's ship was Warwick Avenue underground station, and outside there used to be a barrow boy who sold fruit only. A lot of his trade was from passengers enlightening from the tube. They would buy their fruit from him and on the way home, and then call into Mick's shop just for their potatoes. This was like a red rag to a bull; he would put the potatoes in a bag and go to put them in the ladies shopping bag and with his other hand he would squash all their soft fruit without them knowing. What Mick was hoping is when they got home and took out the damaged fruit, they would never go back to that barrow boy again. Mick knew that the barrow boy never had a licence to trade there so he used to always be phoning up the council to try to get him removed. The barrow boy would be in fined in court but the next day is back, much to Mick's anger. The best part about working with Mick was working down Covent Garden. After a while I got to know most of the wholesalers and the porters, Mick's job was to buy all the produce from the wholesalers and I would collect it with my two wheeled trolley. Mick would hand me the buying receipt for the goods he had purchased and I would pick them up. One morning Mick gave me a receipt for six boxes of eating apples that he had purchased so I made my way to the warehouse and with receipt in hand looked for a porter to hand it to him. As there was no one around I loaded the apples on my trolley myself. I waited a couple of minutes for a porter to arrive but no one came, so I just walked out with them and loaded them onto my lorry. As I finished loading them, Mick appeared I said, you're not going to believe this but I have just taken these apples from the warehouse and no-one took the receipt off me. Mick's smile was as broad as a Cheshire cat; in that case he beamed I'll take the receipt back to the wholesaler and ask for the porter to deliver them to the lorry. It could work out to be the perfect fiddle. If the salesmen says that your boy has already taken them I'll say to him, oh sorry, I have not seen him all morning and didn't know he took them and hand him the receipt, but if he says I'll get the porter to bring them, we're on a winner. Ten minutes later the porter duly arrived with six boxes of apples (fiddle completed) that worked a treat smiled Mick. We will split everything in half. I bought them for £4 a box so your share is £12, a lot of money at that time. Why don't we do this on every order I purchase and if we are lucky we will clean up Mick greedily said, and I being as greedy as him shouted, why not, let's do it. So this was the start of a very worthwhile partnership. It was not long before I was making more on the fiddle than Mick was paying me wages! As the months went by I said to Mick I think we should change our whole sellers as we have been hitting them too much and give them a rest and go for the other whole sellers in the other part of the market. That's a good idea said Mick agreeing with me. We will change whole sellers tomorrow. The next morning we set off to the other side of the market. On this order Mick purchased ten boxes of tomatoes, then me the buying ticket and off I went to the back of the whole seller's warehouse, nobody was about so I took a few boxes of tomatoes and wheeled them out to my lorry. That was so easy, I said to Mick, well John get enough, ten boxes Mick smiled, so off I went again, loaded up, came back to the lorry, unloaded the boxes, this time Mick said, I will come with you this time and hand the buying ticket in and say that my boy will pick this order up. As I went to the warehouse and started to load up, I found myself surrounded by six of the biggest mean looking crew-cut men that had ever been born. The man mountain of a brute, the foreman, he looked like he could snap me in half with just two fingers. We have been watching you and this is the third time you have been back to pick up the same load and you took it back to your lorry as we followed you. Right George, the big foreman bear said to his sidekick, phone the police, your getting put inside for this sunny Jim. It's all a mistake I pleaded; this is the amount I thought my boss had ordered. You little runt, he yelled, honest mate, I meekly blurted out. All I could think of is where is that Mick, I looked up and there was Mick. Hello boys, is there a problem here? Is there a problem, big bear growled? I can see you nicking three loads of tomatoes, a big problem. Mate, no no Mick quickly piped in, he's my boy and he's as honest a lad as you could ever meet. You could leave this boy a bank full of money and he wouldn't touch a penny. At this stage I'm sure I could see Mick's nose growing by the second. Are you old man Levy's son, big bear shouted at Mick? Yes I am, Mick replied in a very nervous coward's way. Well because of that I'm not going to knock you both into next week, as your old man was a good customer with us for years and as honest a man you will ever get. Now both of you bring all my f-----g tomatoes back and don't ever show your faces around here again. That was close Mick; I thought I was going to be mincemeat in there. Mick still could not say anything. I think he was still in a stage of shock. We never tried the fiddle again. Mick often had salesmen dropping in his shop trying to sell their wares. One day, a nice car pulled up outside the shop, out stepped quite a well dressed young man and walked into the ship. He had a large black box with him. With his hand outstretched, took Mick's hand and warmly shook it. Hello, my name is Mr Ross, and I represent a new company, Ross & Company, selling frozen foods. In my box, I have all the products that our company produces. Mick's first words to the salesmen were what's in it for me then. I'm sorry the salesman said, I don't understand what you mean. Well old son, it's like this, Mick replied, I'll take a small order from you like five packs of frozen peas, five packs of fish and five packs of peas then you get the lads at the factory to smuggle out a few boxes of the same things I had ordered and then you and I can split it 50/50. Mr Ross the salesmen at this point looked quite shocked and bewildered, but Mr Levy, he blurted out, I have just started the company up myself, I own it and I am trying to build it up. Well good luck to you mate, Mick snapped, but unless I get fiddles I'm not interested. Mr Ross went away, shaking his head with his tail between his legs. He had been given a lesson in how hard it was going to be to sell his products to small shopkeepers without the fiddles. Mick had three large fridges in the downstairs of his basement full up of other frozen companies products all brought on the fiddle. Mr Ross had no chance of a sell. One of the other salesmen that used to come in weekly was Jim, from Fyffes bananas, Mick used to have four boxes of Bananas, one Mick paid for and the other three were fiddled. This Jim had been supplying bananas to Mick for years and was fyffes top salesman. One day Jim came in with only one box and said, sorry Mick it's all changed down the depot right now, because the other week they took on a new manager and he was looking out of the office window and noticed that the workers car park had the biggest and newest cars in it. The directors and managers car park had mostly much older cars in it. He called one of the directors over to the window to witness a young chap getting out of a state of the art latest sports car and parking it in the workers car park and came to the conclusion that something was not quite right here. He then had all of the lorries followed at various times and watched how many boxes the drivers took off and how many were on their invoice sheets and realised that every driver was on the fiddle, along with the warehousemen. Jim was saying that this would be his last delivery as he had been called into the office and told, we know you have been fiddling Jim, but because you know the warehouse inside out and must know all the fiddles we will not sack you but promote you to manager and this way you will be able to detect any stock that goes missing. So rather than be sacked like most of the drivers and warehousemen, Jim took the promotion, never to carry any more bananas. The other scam Mick got up to was mainly with women customers. I think this is because he was worried that if a man got wind of the scam he would get a smack! Mick would serve them their purchases put their goods into their shopping bags and in the palm of his hand have their change ready for them. He would then turn his hand round so they would receive the change and as he did so his thumb would trap a coin to the palm of his hand. Ninety-Nine out of a hundred people don't bother checking their change. How right he was with saying "work with money, make money!" It was a Friday and Mick had to have a rare afternoon off to take his child to the dentist. On arriving back home he noticed from his kitchen window a man was jumping up and down on the other side of his back garden fence. Mick was out of his house within seconds and confronted the man. What the hell are you doing? Err; nothing really, replied the man. Mick then noticed that the man had a clip-board and an identity badge hanging around his neck, Mick shouted at him, if you don't tell me what you're doing mate I will call the police or better still give you a smack, so which is it to be? Ok, the man blurted out, I'm from the council and we are looking at the size of all the back gardens along this road and we are thinking of purchasing about 10 foot from the end of each garden and making each household an offer as we want to store sand and grit and salt for the winter months, but please sir, I would appreciate it if you kept it to yourself and not to mention it to your neighbours as this information is not supposed to be known yet. No sooner had the council man left with Mick telling him the secret was safe with him, he was knocking on every door in the Street to warn then what the council had in mind and to form a committee to get a group payment rather than a lower payment for each house. The plan worked for them, all because they all agreed to sell their land for the same amount and each received £5,000, a huge amount for that time. Once again, money goes to money! Jimmy Gregg had worked with Mick before me and was there for a few years, and one of the storied he told me was he used to drive the lorry to Covent Garden and the route he took was through Regents Park and as always was half asleep at five in the morning. He was just turning into the park when all of a sudden there was this almighty bang, what he crashed into was the gun-carriage belonging to the royal horse artillery. Every morning they exercise all of their horses with gun-carriages in tow. The officer in charge of the mounted troop had dismounted from his horse and let rip into Jim, calling him stupid xxxxxx idiot and accused him of trying to kill his horses and will be claiming damages from him for the dent in his gun carriage and stress to the horses. On getting back to the shop, Jim had told Mick the full story and outlined exactly what had occurred. After listening to Jims story, Mick had only one question to ask Jim and it was - was their a light on the back of the Gun Carriage? To which Jim replied, even thought I was half asleep I definitely did not see a light on it. That's all I need to know Mick said and was on to his solicitor within minutes. After explaining all the facts to the solicitor, the solicitor then informed Mick that no-one had ever successfully sued the army in a court case and won against them, we will see about that Mick replied, I want you to take the case on and I want damages from them. As my van has extensive damages to the body work the case took quite a long time to come to court, so on the day of the court case Mick was quietly confident of winning because there was no light on the gun carriage. As the judge summed up the case he found in favour of Mick's argument about no light attached to the carriage and therefore it could not have been seen in the dark, the army had lost the case and had to pay all the costs of the case and the repair of the van and Mick was awarded other costs. This was the first time the army had been successfully sued by anybody and to think it was all Jims fault entirely but Mick once again saw some money to be made out of it and was successful. Jim had been writing to me about how he was enjoying South Africa and how he knew how much I would like it out there so with the letters from Jim and getting quite bored with working 13 hours a day I decided to apply to South Africa House, as an immigrate, and as I had trained as a butcher this is the trade I hoped would get me out there. Mick used to give me Wednesday afternoons off so on one of these days I was given an interview at South Africa house and was pleased to hear that they were short of butchers and I would be accepted on an assisted passage to immigrate and I could immigrate in eight weeks from the interview. The hardest Job for me now was to find the right time to tell Mick about my leaving. Mick had two sides to his personality; one was a happy go-lucky kind of guy, salt of the earth and one of the boys. The other side of him was don't ever cross me or else and I knew if I was to tell him I would be leaving in eight weeks to work in South Africa he would see this as an employee who was making him good money which was about to come to an end and worried he would not be able to get someone else to work the long hours that he demanded. So I knew he would not think twice about phoning South Africa house and informing them that I was an untrustworthy bone idle type and one of natures useless individuals, so with this in mind my plan was to inform him of my intentions a week before I was due to leave and to tell him I was going to Australia and not South Africa. But life seems to throw up some funny twists and turns it was now three weeks before I was due to leave for south Africa and as usual, I was loading the lorry with market produce at Covent garden and overheard two porters discussing the bad accident that had taken place at the flower market side of Covent garden. It seemed a man had been knocked down by a lorry. My thought was "poor man". On loading the lorry up with all the usual produce I made my way to my usual cafe for a well earned cup of tea and on entering the cafe wondered why Mick was not sitting there in his favourite seat. Where's Mick I enquired to one of the porters. Where's Mick, he replied, he's in Hospital, that's were he is he said. Seeing the look of shock on my face he quickly said you obviously don't know John, but Mick was knocked down by a market lorry that reversed backwards onto the pavement and knocked him down into the basement of the flower showroom and it seems he's in a very bad way. I just could not believe what I was hearing. Here was Mick, the sun shines out of his backside, the wheeler dealer, the man whose favourite word was profit, was now lying in a hospital bed with serious injuries. So quickly going to the scene of the accident I was told that the lorry had reversed onto the pavement, hit Mick, and knocked him onto some railings which had collapsed throwing him down into a cellar. I told a policeman on the scene that it was my boss who was knocked down. So after giving him my details and where our shop was he advised me to drive back to the shop and wait for news back there. No sooner had I got back to the shop, Mick's wife was on the phone telling me Mick was in a bad way but business is business and to carry on as normal opening the shop and going to Covent Garden daily and she would be in to see me shortly. About 3 days later Mick's wife Glory paid me a visit in the shop and thanked me for running the show all by myself and she told me that Mick would reward me when he was discharged. I felt like a traitor, hearing them words but I thought now is the time to tell her I would be leaving. After I told her the news, she took it quite well but said to me of course I cannot tell Mick you're leaving at this time; I will have to wait till he gets a bit better. I did promise her I would probably be able to get a replacement for me which made her feel better. My last week of working there I was able to get a friend to replace me so everything worked out fine. Mick took about 8 weeks to recover from his injuries and I believe he was very well compensated for the accident. My last day of working was a Saturday and on the Monday I was all set to start a new life in South Africa.

Start of South Africa

It was a Sunday night and a few friends were with me in a pub in Maida vale for a few drinks to wish me a bon voyage which was the next day. Goodbyes are always hard and you always think to yourself, am I doing the right thing? But the old saying "in for a penny in for a pound" and "who dares wins" gives you confidence that all will be well. After saying our goodbyes I made my way back to my flat, but did not get much sleep that night as I was quite excited about what the next day would bring. The door bell was ringing and opening the door there standing was my friend Brian smith who had kindly offered to see me off at Southampton docks. As I handed the flat keys to the landlady I knew that this was the beginning of my new life. The landlady had her radio on and the record being played was "ticket to ride" by the Beatles. I thought to myself, how appropriate with my ticket in hand. Brian and I hailed a taxi and asked to be taken to waterloo station. On the way the taxi driver heard me talking to Brian about south Africa and butted in, my friend is in south Africa and is doing very well there and I'll tell you this young man, you'll either become a rich man or an alcoholic. These London taxi drivers, it must be said, do have a way with words. Thanks mate I said, I'll remember to make plenty of money, but keep away from the drink! On reaching the station I noticed our train which was for the docks seemed to be quite full, could all these people be going to South Africa? On boarding we both managed to get a seat and in the carriage, with drinks in hand, were a group of young ladies who were also picking up the ship in Southampton. All these girls were nurses and had two year contracts to work in a Durban hospital. They had come well prepared with bottles of wine in tow, we soon got chatting and the wine was shared with us. By the time we had reached the docks I could hardly stand up, we all agreed to meet up on the ship and carry on the celebrations. It was sad to be saying my farewells to Brian as he was a good friend so turning round I started to climb up the gang plank and only then did I realise how big this passenger liner was. On the side of the ship in bold letters proclaiming that this ship was the Edinburgh Castle-Union Castle Liner.

Poem

The time had arrived about to make a new start
My beginning of a new life such a beating heart
Sailing half way round the world for just fifteen pounds
Looking forward to taking in all the sights and sounds
This is a floating palace a sight to behold
It's got facilities for everyone whether young or old
Please don't wake me up from this lovely dream
Feeling like the cat that just licked the cream
A life changing experience and I'm just about to sail
Hoping in the future many stories I'll be able to tell
Let's start them new tomorrows I wonder what's in store
I'm about to be in a new chapter that's for sure
Now looking forward to the future forgetting the past
She's called the Edinburgh Castle is almost ready to cast
Holding ropes were released the tugs took up the slack
Now started to move forward there's now no turning back

The Union Castle line had six ships that only sailed between South Africa and Britain and each ship was named after a castle in Britain. The crew in them days was made up of 90% British crew as the unions were very strong back then. On reaching the top of the gang plank I handed my ticket to the steward and thought to myself here I am, about to depart on a passenger liner for seventeen days and all its cost me was fifteen pounds!! This was the year of 1965 and even up to 1980 you could still immigrate to South Africa for that amount. If you wanted to immigrate to Australia the cost was even lower at ten pounds! These two countries needed workers to fill thousands of unfilled vacancies so they came up with a plan, it was called the assisted passage scheme and tens of thousands of people took up the offer. The Edinburgh Castle was able to carry about 750 passengers and about the same number of crew. I was really excited about this trip as in my back pocket I had £2000, quite a big sum in 1965, most of this I had acquired through my little fiddles with Mick. I thought it would be a good idea to look around the ship before it sailed and was thrilled that this was to be my home for the next three weeks. I made my way to the top deck and could see the ship was making ready to sail, the band in attendance played the tune "A life on the ocean waves". I could just pick out Brian waving at me as the mooring ropes were let loose. I had a lump in my throat, but this was to be expected as I was sailing into the unknown. With the tugs now slowly pulling and guiding the big ship out of Southampton docks and then departing it quickly built up speed and with an hour the coastline had disappeared. I was shown to my cabin by a steward that looked the spitting image of Julian Clary as he wiggled up the corridor he looked back at me and blinked his eyes at me and pouted, you'll be alright in here ducky as there are three other men you'll be sharing with and with that with his hand on his hip, he minced up the passageway. I thought to myself this ship must be quite a happy and gay ship! On opening the door to the cabin I was pleased to see my three cabin mates had already settled in. Hi, a voice said, my name is Jim and this is Russell and this is Jock. Hi guys, my name is John, pleased to meet you all. Jim had just obtained his degree from Imperial Collage in mechanical engineering and was going out to South Africa as a trainee mine manager. Russell was a computer programmer working on a two year contract and jock was the most interesting one of the three. He had worked on the castle line ships for fifteen years as a boiler man in the engine rooms before joining the castle line ships. He was a very good amateur boxer. The then became a professional welterweight boxer and won quite a few cups and medals and had all of these displayed in a cabinet in the first class lounge. Thanks to the captain of the ship who was a very keen boxing fan a year before I met Jock, a very wealthy American publisher was a first class passenger on one of the sailings and he too was a boxing fan and was talking with the captain in the first class lounge and noticed the cabinet with all the cups and silverware and was most impressed and asked the captain why he had them on display. The captain told him, the reason being, was that one of his crew members had won them and he worked in the engine room. The millionaire asked the captain, I would like to meet this man as I would like to shake his hand and congratulate him. The next day a meeting was arranged between Jock and the millionaire and the outcome of that meeting was Jock was offered a Job with the millionaire as his bodyguard, minder, driver and any other jobs that may come up! As soon as the ship arrived in Southampton Jock signed off the ship and started work with him. The millionaire had businesses all over the world, so on his business trips he would sometimes fly but in most cases go by boat. So he could relax with him on the trips he took his wife, his two children, a school teacher and also a nanny so wherever he went in the world they would all go with him. Whenever he didn't require the school teacher, the nanny or Jock, he had a large villa in Spain where they could stay if they wanted to or go home to the UK. Jock had been working for him for about a year when I met him and was going out to South Africa to chauffeur him around in his Aston Martin which was stored on board. The other two cabin lads and myself soon got used to life on board soaking up the sun by day and dancing and drinking by night. We would get up about the same time in the morning and that would be the last time we would see Jock until the next morning. I asked him one morning what did he get up to all day and night? He said, I visit all my old crew mates in the crew quarters; I eat with them and drink late in the night with them. He did admit to me that although he had a fantastic job with the millionaire and was doing really well, he missed the life at sea and really missed all his crew mates. So we saw very little of him on the trip. The other lads and myself really got into the spirit of things with the bars open all day and cheap drink we were having a great time as the nurses that I had met on the train. I think their mission was to try and drink the ship dry!

The Stowaway

We were into the fourth day of the trip and started to really get to know quite a few fellow passengers. One of the passengers stuck out from the rest. He was about twenty four years old and wore a black suite and white shirt. What was strange about him is that he never changed into shorts or put a swimming costume on, even though the temperature was boiling, we were all at the bar on this day when he came over to us and asked if he might join us, of course young man, take a seat, what's your name I asked, Peter he said. I brought him a drink and as the drinks started to flow he blurted out, have you not noticed anything about me? We all shook our heads, no not really, we politely said. Before we could say anymore he said he was a stowaway! So that's why he wore his suit all the time and had that smell of a rotting carcass! It seemed like he had to tell someone. After a few more drinks he told us the full story. He had just walked up the gang plank at Southampton and was not asked for his boarding pass and just stayed on and thought he would get a free cruise holiday! We asked him where he had been sleeping? Peter said, I have been sleeping in one of the lifeboats and finding bits of food on the tables. We all agreed you cannot carry on like that, you must stay in our cabin at night but you will have to sleep on the floor and we will get you some grub when we have our meals in a doggie bag. Peter became quite a celebrity on board as nearly everyone knew he was a stowaway and seeing that he had not brought any money on board with him, people were giving him money to keep him going but his luck ran out when one of the officers found out about him and the master-at-arms arrested him where he was sent to the captains office and was informed by the captain that he had the power to lock him in the brig for the rest of the journey. But he was very lenient with him and offered him a cabin with his food thrown in, if he would work in the kitchens for the journey to South Africa and back to Southampton but was to be handed to the police in Southampton. He accepted this offer with open arms as he would now get good nights sleep in a bunk and plenty of rum.

Poem

Our stowaway on board the ship his name was peter lee
He wanted a free trip sailing on the sea
Climbing into a lifeboat it was his night time home
This took some guts seeing he was all alone
Seven days since he had washed and it was telling
He stunk like an unwashed armpit peter was smelling
Got him washed and cleaned gave him a new shirt
Looked like a new man no trace of any dirt
Now working in the kitchen with his new found mates
Washing them pots and pans and them greasy plates

After a few days on board ship you get to know many of your fellow passengers and also some of the crew members. As this was in the mid sixties British ships were crewed by UK people. The waiters in the dining room were all young fellows, and being 1965 they were hippies. This was the age of "flower power". Kevin was our table waiter a young lad from the east end of London. He was a good looking young man. One morning after serving everyone on the table, he said, how would you all like to come to a wedding party tonight? It's in the crew bar and two poofs are getting married so it should be a good night! Kevin had got us all permission to go to the crew bar for the night. The wedding was conducted by the biggest and hairiest stoker you ever saw. The bride and bride groom exchanged rings to much applause from the crowded bar and a great night was had by all and all us passengers were treated as honoured guests. Kevin said, he thought that 20% of the crew were gay but everyone got on well together. We asked Kevin did he intent to make the merchant navy his career? You must be joking he replied, my plan is to meet one of those rich single or married woman on board. I don't care how old they are, I wonder if he ever got lucky?

On board ship was a large group of catholic priests travelling out to South Africa for a convention. They were everywhere. One evening I was walking up a corridor with Jock to enter the dining hall; two priests were coming up the other way. As Jock and I drew level with them one of the priests made the sign of the cross at Jock. Jock went mad, swearing like a trooper, how dare he make the sign of the cross to me he cried, Jock was a protestant. He was very upset about it. Don't worry Jock, I said, he just wanted to give you a blessing. We all had our meal that evening and as usual jock went down to the crew quarters for some heaving drinking session. We all went on drinking and dancing and we all came back down to the cabin about three in the morning very much the worse for ware. I managed to get the key in the door but the door only opened about six inches and would not open anymore. So with the three of us pushing as hard as we could we managed to push it open and I was able to squeeze in. Inside the cabin I found Jock lying on the floor, his legs wedged up against the door. Come on Jock, get up you drunken sod I cried. He was out for the count so I managed to pull him away from the door. With that my other cabin mates came in. We all then tried to wake Jock up until one of the lads noticed how his face colour was grey-white in appearance. He quickly checked for a pulse and to our shock he did not have one. I think he is dead someone shouted! We all agreed that he was indeed dead and that's when the shock sets in. I was only walking up the corridor with him a few hours ago, I just cannot believe it. We all decided that we must phone a member of the crew. Before we had time to phone an officer was walking near our cabin, we shouted over to him that one of our cabin mates looked as he was dead. On inspecting Jock he seemed more shocked than us and said I have known jock for many years, Jock and I have sailed on many ships in the past. I will now have to get the ships doctor and with that he disappeared down the corridor, returning ten minutes later with a very young ships doctor. Who for the next ten minutes tried to resuscitate Jock, and then said, this man is dead and although none of us had ever seen a dead body before, it was quite obvious that Jock had died and it was the doctors inexperience that showed and as he was saying that his face went white and his hands were trembling. It turned out that he had only recently qualified as a doctor and this was his first job at sea. What a baptism of fire for the poor man! The doctor called up on the phone for crew members that were still on night duty to make their way to the cabin and remove the body to the sick bay. When the crew members arrived they refused to touch the body as it seemed that an old navy tradition was not to touch a body until the sun was up so they quickly left as quickly as they had come! The doctor then asked us if we would move the body and of course we all agreed but what a sad and painful experience that was for all of us. The doctor said that an inquest will have to be held on the cause of death and this would be held in Cape Town as this was our first port of call. It was only two days until the ship docked in Cape Town so there was a sombre mood with us all. On reflecting what had taken place my mind went back to when I was walking with Jock up the corridor when that priest made the sign of the cross at Jock, that maybe he was about to depart from this earth? Why did he give him a blessing, very strange but in all this there are more questions than answers! Some people may have thought that I was just a little cynical when I knocked on the cabin door of Jocks Employer the next day as I had got to know him quite well as he was always knocking on our cabin door with a pair of shoes to clean or a shirt to iron and he used to see Jock out for the count through the effect of drink and I would volunteer to clean his shoes and take them back to his cabin. As he opened the door to me he greeted me with a firm handshake and invited me in. He of course was in a first class cabin. We talked about the loss of Jock and how it had affected all of us. I then took the bull by the horns and said to him, Sir, is it possible that I could take Jocks old job on? I am a young man, honest and trustworthy, and I'm sure that I would prove to be highly suitable to you. I am sure you would John, he replied, but my wife and I have talked about this very subject and she feels as I do, that we would like a married man to fill this position; in that way his wife could be a companion for my wife. We feel having a single man for this job is not ideal as there is a lot of free time and temptations that goes with the job. As I left his cabin he gave me a warm handshake and said, I wish you all the very best John and hope you make a success in your new life in South Africa and with that I left his cabin. With quite a heavy heart, but thinking to myself at least I tried and if you don't ask you don't get. As I left his cabin I made my way back to my cabin I noticed the cabin door was open and my two cabin mates were standing inside with the ships captain and the first mate, also the doctor. Just the man we wanted to see said the doctor. I think you lads would like to know the likely cause of death of Mr Kierney. I am certain that his death was due to him choking on his own fluid but this can only be confirmed at the post mortem. We are looking into the circumstances and how Mr Kierney was found. Your cabin mates have already given me their account as they saw it so we would like yours. After going through the details and roughly what time of day, the Captain thanked us all and said there will be a Post Mortem on Mr Kierney when we arrive in Cape Town and we just want to be sure of all the facts. As the captain made his way out he said thank you for your time gentlemen and I have to tell you that you may be called as witnesses at the hearing into his death in Cape Town, this is standard procedure in these cases and they all left the cabin. We all decided to have a few drinks at the bar in memory of Jock. We were due to dock in Cape Town at 6am the next day but we were told by the Purser that we would not be allowed off the ship until the local police had interviewed the three of us to make sure there was no foul play involved and to get at all the facts. The next morning the three of us made our way to the top deck to watch the ship sail into Cape Town harbour. As the quayside came into view we noticed an ambulance parked there and also four police cars, quite a sad sight, knowing that our friend would never be seeing his home in Scotland again. It was mixed emotions that we viewed Cape Town, in one way quite excited arriving in South Africa, but on the other hand sad that our journey had ended with the passing of our cabin mate. As the ship tied up the purser took us to his office and said, wait here lads and the police will come in to interview you. When the police arrived we were interviewed in separate rooms for about twenty minutes each, we then had to wait an hour while they discussed our three statements. The head detective then said to us you are free to carry on with your journey each of you, but write down on this form where you will be staying. When you reach your final destination you may be required to attend the inquest on Mr Keirney and the inquest should be in about two weeks time. My two cabin mates were getting off in Cape Town and I was carrying on the journey by the boat to Durban. About 70% of the passengers alighted at Cape Town, some settling in Cape Town but most of them getting the train and making their way up country to Johannesburg. I spent the day sight-seeing all over the cape and made my way up table Mountain, a sight to behold. There cannot be a better view from the top in this entire world. Getting back to the ship which would be leaving in the morning at 6am, I took one more look at Cape Town before we sailed to our next port of call which was Port Elizabeth. Joining the ship at Cape Town were local people taking their holidays to Durban and doing the round trip back to Cape Town. I now had my cabin all to myself and the good news was that the group of nurses were going up to Durban so I knew that the next five days would not be dull as they could all drink most people under the table. The sea journey from Cape Town to Port Elizabeth takes about 36 hours in them days, it was quite a small place and the ship stopped only for twelve hours. The ship then makes its way to East London, sailing for another day to get there taking on more passengers, cargo and provisions and once again 12 hours stop and then the final hop to Durban which takes about 34 hours. We all had to celebrate the last night of the cruise as our total days at sea would have been seventeen in all and some very firm friendships had been forged. It proved to be an unforgettable night with the celebrations going on to the wee small hours. But like all good thing, they all come to an end. The ship was due into Durban at eight that morning but it had to zigzag through many merchant vessels that were moored outside the harbour waiting to get into the docks. At that time there was supposed to be a world trade boycott of Rhodesia (now Zimbabwe) and no country was allowed to trade with them. All Rhodesian goods came in through South Africa but many counties thought money was more important than boycotts. Through bleary eyes we all watched as the coastline came into view. What a beautiful sight with the sun beating down, I thought to myself, this will do for me. As the ship docked it was now the time to say all our goodbyes. It is often said that when saying your farewells you get a lump in your throat. Well I must have had a tennis ball in mine or it felt like one. I'm not very good with goodbyes and when you have shared so many happy days with people and you know you will never see them again, it seems that much sadder!

Start of new life in Durban

As I walked down the gangplank, I was directed into an immigration office after checking my name I was told I would be staying in the esplanade hotel as were quite a few of my fellow passengers which was good news! We all climbed into coaches laid on for us and made our way to our hotel. My first thought on seeing Durban was what a lovely clean city this is; I think I'm going to like it here. It only took twenty minutes to reach the esplanade hotel, it seemed to be built in the 1930s and very clean with its own night club attached to the building with the best of Durban's groups playing every night. I have hit the jackpot, me thinks. It overlooked the Durban Yacht Club all very posh and being a four star hotel we could not have found better and as it only cost us each £5 per room, two of us sharing with all meals thrown in, you could not get off to a better start. I got to share a room with a fellow named Ron Flitham who was from Yorkshire. I had seen him on board ship a few times had thought him to be a bit loud and always at the bar, typical northerner was my opinion. Everything was going just great but now I've got to share with this loud mouth yob. My name is Ron, I heard this voice in front of me say, and I believe your name is John, I believe we are to be room mates. As I shook his outstretched hand I was thinking he sounds much quieter than he was on board, maybe he was just showing off in front of all his mates. We were both shown up to our room which had two single beds in it and very clean and comfortable. As we got chatting I realised this Ron was not the loud mouth I had took him for, but was quite a nice lad and it turned out to be the case over the two years. He was a carpenter by trade and was hoping to work on building sites and make loads of money. The hotel guests were made up of about half being immigrants from all over the world and the other half tourists and South Africans taking their vacations. It was quite a large hotel and always had something going on. A union Castle ship would dock in Durban every two weeks so there was always new people coming in from Britain as this time in South Africa they did not yet have TV so it was very much a social thing. So at night in the hotel if you did not want to dance to the group that was playing in the club you could all meet in the lounge and have a great night of drinking with all different nationalities. For the first week in the hotel, Ron and I used to have a big breakfast, and then make our way down to the beach soak up the sun and try our hand at surfing. Who wanted to work when you had all this? After a week of being beach bums we both decided we had better find work as to much of this life would get one lazy so Ron found a job on a building site and I managed to get a job working in a butchers shop a stones throw from the beach. Just the man we are looking for the manager of the butchers shop said, within two years you could be a manager of one of our branches. Yer Right, I thought, I have not come out here for a career, I have come out here for a good time, the beach, the sun and the beach babes! I started on the Monday at the shop and by the Tuesday I knew this job was not for me. Hearing the waves crashing against the beach and watching the surfing lads riding the waves from the shop window was all too much and with two thousand pounds tucked up in my back pocket, which today (2008) would be worth about £8,000 why would I want to work? On the Tuesday I had a word with the Manager, Sorry boss but this job is not for me, I need my freedom I said, I'm too young to be cooped up in here all day. So I will be leaving today. I thought he would be mad at me for wasting his time but he fully understood. He then paid me for the two days and I was off as free as a bird. That evening I met Ron, my room mate, in the hotel and told him I had left my job. That's nothing he said, I was sacked today but got myself a new building site contract. For the next few weeks life was great, every one else was working but for me it was one glorious holiday. Because of this I was known as "Lord John". After about two months without working and my savings dwindling at an alarming rate I decided to seek work, but what should I do? The work problem was solved when I bumped into a friend who told me of a job that would be just up my Street. He told me it was a meat firm that had many vans and the job was to drive to factory, warehouses, clubs or pubs selling all types of meat products. This sounded just the job for me, so off I went for a job interview. The manager was a very aggressive type of man and very blunt. Well John, he started, the pay is low, but sell well and you can earn good commission, bad sells and your out that door, well do you still want to work for me? I'll give it a go I said, nothing ventured, nothing gained I replied. You can start Monday and I will let you have my best Zulu boy. He's big and strong and will take care of you if you ever get in to trouble. That last sentence of his made me think a bit. Why would I get into trouble? And why do I need someone to look after me? Oh well, I need the money and I can talk my way out of any trouble, I hope! Monday came round and I reported to the manager who introduced me to Leroy, my new van friend. Pleased to meet you Leroy as I stuck out my hand, my hand met his and it was like being gripped by a mechanically attached hand. I was glad to see my hand was still in one place, nice to meet you boss John he replied. I was so glad this man mountain was going to be my friend! The large van was already loaded up to the hilt and with a list of all the different prices for all the goods I drove out of the gates with high expectations. The last words the manager had said to me is whatever you do John, do not attempt to sell your goods in any of the townships as you would sell well in them but you may not come out of them alive. Your best bet is to try and sell to clubs, hotels and building sites canteens and places like that. Well Leroy, where would you say we make for. Sorry boss came his reply, no much English, no understand you. Great I thought the big bear talks and speaks very little English. As I did not know Durban too well and Leroy could not understand me, but as I had on board mostly meats that the Africans eat so I assumed the best places would be where lots of Africans congregate like markets and such, so I made for Durban Market and parked in the middle of the square. Looking round at Leroy I could see he seemed to be quite nervous. Leroy you talk Zulu and sell goods to people I pleaded. He just looked at me blankly and just sat in the corner hiding out of the way. I could only speak a few words of Zulu so the Africans were looking at me in amazement. After about two hours without selling not so much as a sausage I decided to leave the market and try my luck elsewhere but where do I head for. No wonder the last sales man didn't last. He probably starved to death. I remembered that the docks in Durban employed hundreds of workers. Leroy will we do well in the dock area I asked? No understand boss he grunted, why did I ask? Positioning the van in what I thought would be a likely selling place I was now ready for a busy afternoon, it all turned out to be a complete waste of time. After about two hours I had only sold 10 Rand's worth of goods with Leroy sleeping soundly in the back of the van I decided to return back to base. On entering the gats the manager was shouting at me, you must have had a great day to be returning so early. Great day I shouted, you must be joking I'd only taken ten rand. It's a waste of time; I might as well pack it in here and now. No No, John, don't do that he said, none of the vans are making any money and you know I told you not to go to the townships well I have to say that is where you can make some good money but it can be risky so it's up to you. I'll give it a try I said but you will have to tell Leroy he cannot sit there like a dummy; like he has done and not only that he speaks hardly any English so he's useless to me. The manager shouted, Leroy come here, John he speaks perfect English, and he was just trying it on with you. I have told him if he does not help you all day I will sack him when he returns back, but he has promised to help and assist you in any way. The next day we set off to the nearest township to Durban which was about twenty miles west of the city. It was one of these townships that surrounded Durban and with a population of about 100,000 people, this one west of the city was quite a size. On entering I felt just a little nervous but quite excited of what might be. Now Leroy I said, you must tell me the best place to trade as you know the township. Yes Boss John, you must go to the market square, plenty of people gather there, we make plenty of money, all in perfect English if you please. As I stopped the van, where Leroy had directed, the first person that came up to the van said, I am an off duty police officer and you should not really be trading in here boss, but seeing you're here now you might as well stay, but please make sure you leave by four this afternoon as it can get quite violent when the evening comes round. As he left he shouted, good luck, you should do well today. Soon the word got round that a white van had lots of meats on board and they were all quite cheap, it did not take long before lots of people wanted to be served but the trouble was they all wanted to be served at the same time. Leroy really got into it with gusto talking in Zulu and calming everyone down and thinking to myself he's finally come good. Within two hours we had we had managed to sell half the stock and with one or two people who could speak English asking if we could come everyday I had visions of making a small fortune. As quickly as the crowds had arrived they simply disappeared. Where have they all gone to I asked Leroy, don't worry boss John, they have all gone for a drink and then a lie down but they will be back later and also there is a funeral taking place this afternoon but we should be alright boss John. The next step for us both was to get all the rest of stock from the back of the van and sort it all out for the next round of mass selling. We had already sold about R100 worth of goods (£50) which was a huge amount for them days. It was about two hours since our last customer and I was thinking, are they coming back. Just then I heard the sounds of singing and clapping in the distance. I asked Leroy what was going on, he said it sounds like the people from the Funeral are celebrating the life and then the death of the departed and it looks like they are making their way over here. Five minutes later they had completely surrounded the van and I could see a lot of the people had been earlier customers. All happy and in good humour but now the mood had changed and they were very aggressive and threatening. Most of them had glazed eyes so much drink had been consumed so I knew we were now in for a hard time. Looking back at Leroy his eyes were now glazed but this was due to the fact he was terrified and as it turned out a complete coward and a yellow belly. With groups of men now reaching over the shelf and helping themselves to anything that came into their hands I knew we were now in for big trouble. The mood of the crowd was getting uglier by the second and it did not help matters very much because my protector minder and new found friend Leroy had opened the vans back door and bolted. Watching him running at an amazing speed, he would have won an Olympic gold medal in all of the disciplines from the hundred metres to the mile. I quickly grabbed the door and shut it tight with the bolt pulled across now what do I do? I had to come up with a plan and quickly or I'm in big trouble what made the situation worse they were climbing on the roof and they were ready to get into the van only one thing for it now I will throw the stock to them and that may quieten them down, so with handfuls of sausages, pies and meats of all descriptions I just threw them in all directions to the mob hoping that this might give me time to maybe make a quick exit. The sight that pleased me the most was to see them fighting between themselves for the spoils. I had now made up my mind what I was going to do. My plan was to get them so engrossed in all the free meat flying out of the van. Hopefully they would not notice until I was too late my van disappearing into the night. There was not very little left of the stock so with my last few handfuls I threw the goods as far as I could to keep the mob as far away from the van as possible, then jumping into the driver's seat I started the engine and fortunately for me it started up first time with a clear path ahead I noticed in my rear view mirror some of them fighting each other, but also I could see some of the mob chasing after the van (the ungrateful sods) with no windows now left in the van and the wind rushing in from all sides it just seemed so unreal (is this a dream?) At last the exit sign came into view, phew that's a relief, I have made it, all in one piece, I was now outside the township so I pulled up into a lay-by switched off the engine and with shaking hands calmed myself down with a much needed cigarette and just sat there reflecting on the last few hours and how lucky I had been.

Poem

Hundreds of Zulus had returned back having buried a friend
They looked mean and nasty is this to be my end
We were surrounded like in the film called Zulu dawn
Had visions of my head arms and legs from my body torn
Suddenly the van started rocking from side to side
I'm not staying here boss the coward Leroy cried
The back door he opened he was out like a shot
So long my body my friend this is definitely my lot
They were angry and hostile had been drinking all day
Is this going to be the spot where I finally lay?
So in all directions those goods went flying
My stock they would now not be buying
Started up the engine then slammed it in gear
Thinking of that old saying I'm out of here.

All this was now in the past and now I better start thinking about the future, and how was I going to explain to the manager the nearly wrecked van and even worse all the stock had disappeared and of course returning without Leroy in the end, I decided that I would come clean and tell the whole truth as I knew the manager and the firm would be in big trouble with the authorities if they found out one of their vans had been selling in a township. He would automatically lose his trading licence. I had calmed down by now, so I started the engine once again and made my way to the main highway to Durban. I had just got onto the highway and would you believe it, in front of me was Leroy with his thumb in the air hitch-hiking without a care in the world. As I pulled up along side him, the look on his face was a picture but you could see that he was pleased to see me jump in Leroy I said. After apologising a thousand times and explaining all the facts to me. I said to Leroy at least we are both in one piece and that's the main thing, we will tell the boss the truth, but you know Leroy, we will be sacked or shot on the spot. But we will not say anything about you leaving me as this could jeopardise any future jobs you may apply for. We arrived back five minutes before the place closed for the night as we drove through the gates I have never seen that look on a man that the owner had it was a combination of shock horror and complete disbelief. My van he shouted, it's a write off! What the hell have you two been up to? Well boss, I said, the truth is, we were making no money anywhere so I decided to sell in the township before I could explain further I thought the poor man was about to experience a massive heart attack ranting and raving, shouting and swearing like a demented orang-utan. I told you not to go to the townships you bird brained idiot. After he had calmed down a little I explained the whole story to him. Just tell me one thing he asked did you report this to the police? He shouted. No, I replied thank god for that he yelled I would have lost my trading licence, if you had! You threw all my stock to them he cried, I cannot believe it! Just give me the money you made and both of you get out of my sight, you're both fired. As I handed over the money I thought what a selfish excuse of a man, he was not even interested in our welfare only interested in his van and stock. I said my good byes to Leroy and as I shook his hand was that tear I detected in his eye? Getting back to the hotel and in the bar I told Ron my flat mate all about my plight and how luck I was able to walk away from that episode. He then asked me what job I will be going for. Job, I said, I won't be working for a while, and I will be spending my days on the beach for now. But after a month of lazing around just swimming and surfing it can start to become quite boring so I started to look around for a job. In the meantime Ron and I decided to leave the Hotel and get ourselves a flat which would give us more freedom than the confines of the hotel. We found a really nice flat in Smith Street in the nice part of Durban. I also got myself a small Volkswagen Beetle which was the cool car of that time. This I hoped would be my pulling passion wagon. I was told that the railway people were looking for staff so along I went for an interview. They were looking for amongst other positions a job as a trainee welder this mainly involved welding broken railway tracks and repairing Bridges. I worked in the Durban area for two months and then was driven up country to the Tugela River Bridge. This is about 150 miles north of Durban. The welder who was teaching me also came with me to Tugela. We were driven up there by one of the Railway managers who was rough and tough sort of man whose name was Carl and was a very proud Afrikaner and hated anything British and seemed to hate the world and almost anybody who lived on it and what made it worse with him he liked a drink. We both had to meet him at the depot and we were to be driven to Tugela in a large American type Pick up truck by him. The trouble was he could hardly stand up, his speech was slurred. As I shook his hand and said hello how are you. He said, Oh, not a bloody Roenik (redneck) this goes back to the days of the South African War of 1898 to 1901 between Britain and the Afrikaans boars in them days the British army still wore bright red tunics with a white pith helmet protecting there heads from the sun, but not there necks. That is why they got the name of rednecks and they were hated by the Afrikaans. The journey time was about four hours to the Tugela River Bridge. As we made our way off the Main Highway we had about fifty miles left on the journey. The rest of the way was on a dirt track. As he was still drinking out a large bottle, his driving at this time getting steadily worse the further up the dirt track we went. His speed was getting dangerously fast, we had just turned a large bend in the track and within seconds we were twenty feet behind a station wagon with a couple in the front with two small children sitting in the back, trying to avoid the major smash that was certain to take place he slammed on the brakes as hard as he could, this in turn flipped the truck onto it's side. It was now sliding at great speed into a village area with me trapped near the door with the ground almost touching my face and with the welder and the driver pressing down on me I said to myself this is where it ends for me, what seemed like ages the truck finally came to a stop about three feet from a group of African women sitting round a tree. All I could feel was now the driver's boots in my face in his haste to get out, the welder also had his boots in my face as they both scrambled out I was trapped between the seat and the dashboard and with the smell of diesel now very strong. I was certain that the truck was now about to go up in flames. I somehow managed to free myself after a couple of minutes of sheer terror; I forced my body through the windowless driver's door. The two heroes who had abandoned me were nowhere to be seen. They had run as far away as possible in case the truck exploded. After about five minutes they came back to the truck when they realised it was not going to explode. Carl the drivers words to me were sorry John, but in a situation like that it's every man, for himself. Charming I thought who needs friends like these. As the truck was a complete write off we had to walk the rest of the way to the Tugela Bridge which was about five miles and with no hat on, by the time we reached Tugela I was fried the colour of a lobster as we came out of a clearing there in front of me was a magnificent sight, the Tugela river flowing from west to east in all it's glory. The Bridge that spanned it was a double arched rivet type construction, the Tugela River is about two hundred feet wide so it was a very long Bridge. I thought came into my mind as I was taking in this wonderful view, that only sixty five years ago British troops had been crossing this river fighting the boars in the boar war. It was thirty more minutes before we reached the permanent camp site, set up near the Bridge inside the compound were a few metal huts. They were for the white staff and to the back of them were all the Africans quarters which were just shacks. The workforce consisted of just three white men and about 30 Africans. The head African boy was named Jess and as all the Africans answered to him he was known as "boss boy" and his word was law. A fine human being and a gentleman his job was to clean the huts out and cook all our meals as well as is in charge of the African workers but they had to fend for themselves. Let me show you around the compound Jess said, this is where you sleep, pointing to a very small hut with just a straw mattress on a wooden bed with a small window above the bed on the table was an oil lamp for any reading you needed to do as there was no electricity in the camp. All the cooking was done on an open fire and if it rained, cooked on a stove in one of the huts. All the Africans working on site were Zulus as there would have been big trouble if they had any other tribe mixed in with them. In those days all white men were given a name by the Zulus as I was twenty six at the time my name in Zulu was Korsan, which means young master and that's what the workforce called me. In those days and it was now 1966, the fashion of the day was for young men to have long hair just like members of the Rolling Stones and the Beatles, which were the big groups of the day. As the Africans had never seen a man with long hair before, my nick-name became "Tomershan" which in Zulu is "Girl". When they talked to me my name was always Kolsan but between themselves it was "Tomershan". We had our first evening meal that first day around the camp fire and as Jessee was the boss boy, he was allowed to eat with us. The African workforce had their own fire and food. In South Africa the evenings draw in very quickly and by six at night it is in total darkness. The first night around the camp fire was spent mainly asking me why I had come to South Africa and why I would have wanted a job like this? Jessee was really fascinated with me talking about television and how a box in your front room could bring pictures to you and looked in amazement when telling him football matches were played regular (South Africa did not introduce television to the nation till the seventies). The first morning at the camp was how the days would start from now on, Jess, would knock your cabin door saying that breakfast would be in ten minutes. The breakfast consisted of Millie Meal, this was cooked the same as porridge and it tasted very much the same with a type of breakfast that jess was able to bake with jam on the bread it was sheer magic. Tea was also made in a billy can over the fire. After that first breakfast Carl the foreman called me over and asked me what I was like on heights as the Bridge at its highest part was over 150 feet above the river. Not for the faint hearted he pointed out. I'm OK with heights I lied, trying to stop my legs shaking too much. I will give you my best two boys to help you and teach you how things are done. Carl the foreman called the two Africans over to me and spoke to them in English. This is Master John, and you will be working with him. He has never done this work before so you must show him how things are done. The bigger one of the two reached out and shook my hand. Pleased to meet you Kousan, my name is Enpagaini; the younger one also reached out his hand my name is Moses, also in Perfect English. Do you speak Zulu, Enpagaini asked, no I replied, but I would like to learn I said. OK then we will only talk to you in Zulu starting tomorrow and you will then have to pick it up. Enpagaini and Moses could both speak four languages, their own tongue Zulu, then Afrikaans, English and Portuguese. This was truly amazing, as they had very little schooling. As I walked towards the Bridge with both the boys I became aware how big this Bridge really was. As we were getting closer the Bridge was now getting bigger. We were not standing right by the Bridge and Moses then explained what my job in the set up would be. The Bridge was a steel structure and held together by rounded ball type rivets. These rivets over the years would corrode and have to be hammered out and be replaced by new ones. Enpagaini's job was to light up the kiln, place the rounded rivets in it and when red hot, remove them with a large pair of tongs and place them in a large bucket and pull up the bucket to Moses who in turn would remove them with tongs then put one on to the hold, where the old rivet had been and my job was with a large air gun, hammer it into the Bridge. So as not to be in your own way you have to start from the very top of the Bridge and work down. So before we started work that day the boys suggested that I walked up the Bridge with them to get used to the height. So with Enpagaini in front of me and Moses behind me we slowly began to climb in a crouched position up to the top. The part of the Bridge we were climbing up was about 30 inches (760mm) wide with no safety net or harness to rely on and with man eating ugly 20 foot crocodiles swimming below with their flesh tearing teeth glistening in the sun, if the fall never killed you the any meat will do crocs certainly would.

Poem

Climbing up that Bridge that day was not very nice
Was I scared and nervous yes those words will suffice
Those ugly great monster crocs were waiting for a meal
Just one slip they would been in for the kill
My lord have you seen the size of them teeth
Clamped in those huge jaws your life would be brief
Hold on tight John don't fall in them waters
They will eat anything and snap you in four quarters
I will make certain they won't be eating me
Avoiding them at all cost not having me for tea.

Having stopped three times on the way up and with them both telling me not to look down as we neared the top that saying came into my mind, it was "stop the world, I want to get off" We had now reached the very top and with my whole body shaking like someone who is having a fit. The boys were saying how well I had done. Just sit here for a while Moses was saying and get used to the height and you will be fine. As I started to relax my white knuckle grip that was holding the sides of the Bridge. I sat there taking in a scene that can only be described as truly outstanding with the Tugela river snaking its through tree lined valleys with flocks of buzzards making lazy circles in the sky and the sun beating down relentlessly on this white skinned frightened young man sitting on this Bridge in the heart of Africa. By now, having got over my fears and taking in all this wonderful gift of nature. Just one of them sights that I will remember forever. Time to go down now Kossan, Moses said, just crouch down and go down backwards. Going down seemed to be much easier that climbing up and it was not long before I was standing safely on the ground. It is best that you start work tomorrow said Moses it is better if you climb up and down the Bridge all day and get confident in climbing. We will be preparing the equipment and gear for the job. After climbing up and down the Bridge a few times in my own time I started to get the hang of it and now felt quite confident. By the end of the day I could walk up the Bridge in a crouching type way without holding onto the sides. As night fell it was the usual set up, have your evening meal and with the sun setting talk for a few hours around the camp fire. Both Enpagaini and Moses were pleased I had mastered the art of climbing as I would have been a liability to them. The next morning we started work with me sitting on top of the Bridge with my air powered rivet gun, with Moses knocking out the worn rivets and then placing the new red hot ones in position I attached the head of the gun to the rivet pulled the trigger, this then pushed the rivet into the hole and formed a shiny new rivet. The worst part of the job was the relentless sun beating down with no shade cover to be had it was so hot by midday Moses used to get some eggs out and fry them on the specially prepared part of the lower Bridge. Within one minute these were now ready for eating. We used to work up till noon on the Friday and then make our way home for the weekend and after a long drive we used to be back in Durban by four thirty in the afternoon. The social life in and around Durban was fantastic always a party to go to or take your beers down to the beach. I had by this time made many friends of all different nationalities a few of them in the hotel, but a lot of them were from a friend of a friend. I used to go up to the better part of Durban to visit my old friend, Jim Gregg and his wife, Alma who with Alma's mother used to live in a fabulous flat, even though there were married they still used to join in with all us singletons. One of the venues in particular that we all used to make for was the Ocean View Hotel which was perched amongst the hills over looking Durban. There was so many of us we formed and named ourselves "The Jungle Mongrels". The ocean view used to have a large stage for acts to perform. When we all had one too many, we would make our way up on stage and try and sing in harmony, it was truly awful but for some reason we were greeted with wild applause as they were as drunk as us! The founder member of the Jungle Mongrels was a proud welsh man from the valleys by the name of Ron (taffy) Rymer who was once a merchant seaman. We all met Ron and his beautiful wife Dorothy. She was a local girl. Ron had been out there two years before me so he knew far more people than me. He was employed as a traffic cop in the Durban City Police. It has to be said he was not your average cop as we know them; his main beat was the Indian market and the railway station part of Durban. His job entailed finding the owners of illegally parked vans or cars and issuing parking tickets for any motoring offences committed. It is said that when he first started Patrolling his Patch hundreds of tickets were issued out by Ron but as time went on, less and less tickets were given out. It is allegedly suggested that he was known as "backhand Ron", it is believed that he made a small fortune from his dealings and returned to Britain with a nice nest egg and now lives in happy retirement in Southampton with Dorothy.

Poem

That Durban city policeman went by the name of Ron
Managed to make a fortune with a well worked con
Was a son of the valleys and also the dales
His heart was always in that lovely country of Wales
This old merchant navy seadog who went off to sea
All so long ago now retired and taking afternoon tea
Will remember his happy memories like all the mongrel gang
Farewell those African adventures that Welsh voice choir sang

It was about this time that my old mate Jim Gregg's wife Alma and her mother Edna returned back to the UK. This was mainly due to homesickness. South Africa was at that time a man's place. I also purchased a Volkswagen Beetle car. These cars are a must for a hot country; they do not have radiators and as they are air cooled having a car made me much more mobile. The first weekend off went so fast that before I knew it the alarm clock was showing four thirty on the Monday morning. I had only a short time to get ready before I had to meet the foreman at 5am outside my flat for the long journey back to the Tugela Bridge. I had now adapted to the Bridge work with the help of my two boys Enpagaini and Moses and as with the first week the physical work was no problem but the relentless sun beating down with very high humidity causing me to lose bucketfuls of sweat, so plenty of liquid had to be taken. As with most nights the camp fire stories were told and this night Enpagaini and Moses had been invited to the evening meal. Moses was really keen to tell us the story that happened to him at the last job he had. He was explaining to us that his last job was working in a gold mine in Kimberley. All the African workers were paid quite well as the mines were deep and could be quite dangerous at times. They were all paid once a month in cash and most of them used to send some of their wages home to their families. One Friday it was the end of the month and pay day once again. As they were lining up to receive their pay in the distance they noticed two large American cars driving into their large compound and out stepped from the cars eight well dressed African men with clip boards and a large blackboard and easel and set it up outside the pay office and spoke to hundreds of miners who had by now gathered to listen to these big shots from the capital city. Moses then went on to say that the man who seemed to be in charge spoke. We are investment bankers from Johannesburg and we have come to speak to you today to make you some money. He then drew diagrams on the blackboard of how their money would increase if they wanted to invest some money. He went on to explain how it all worked. Gentlemen you are honest miners and we are honest bankers so for every rand you invest with us today, we will come back next month on your pay day and give you double. So if you were to invest five rand today, we will come back next month and you will receive ten rand. Moses then said there must have been about two thousand miners listening and about one hundred of them gave various amounts which were recorded in a large accounts book. The rest of the miners thought it was some sort of fiddle. Once the last miner had handed over their money the men with the black suits and shades packed up and left with a passing comment, you men who have not invested are silly, because you have lost money. The men who trusted us are wise men and next month when we return will be rich men. The next month came round and it was the day the bankers promised to return. The men who hadn't invested were saying to the men who had, they won't be coming back. You have lost your money. But true to their word, the bankers did arrive at the same time as the last time. Right gather round everybody, the head man shouted, all the names I call out please come forward and pick up double what you invested with us. Sure enough every man who had invested picked up double their money. When the last man had been paid out the head banker shouted to the miners, now do you trust us, you have seen how rewarded were the men who invested with us, once again we shall be back next month with double money for anyone who invests with us. Moses went on; he had hardly finished speaking when there was a surge of bodies with most of their wages in hand scrambling to get money in the investment book. One of the men took the money the other man put the name of the miner and how much he had invested, while the other man gave a receipt for the sum invested. Long queues had formed to hand over their money and it was quite late, before the last man had invested. The average wage for one months work for a miner in them days was about R100 (£50). Moses reckoned about two thousand miners took up the offer so roughly about R200,000 (£100,000) was invested that day. The following month could not come round quickly enough as the excitement was mounting men were making big plans as to what they would be doing with all this money. The big day had now arrived, the cars were due, large crowds were getting very excited; men were straining their eyes to be the first one to catch a sight of the cars. As the minutes ticked away the miners were now getting restless. Where can the cars be? What's happening? Half an hour had now gone by and still no sign of the cars. Men were now getting very agitated and by now it was dawning on them that they had been conned. Once the hour had gone by and no cars came, near riots were taking place, most of them had been well and truly stuffed. Moses lost R40 (£20) in the scam and felt he had got away lightly. It was one of the biggest scams ever seen. The so called bankers were never seen again, nor were the money. If you think of it, it was a very successful operation planed to the last detail; no one was hurt except in their pockets. The weeks now seemed to fly by as we only worked till 12.30 on the Friday and made our way home. But on this Friday the foreman informed me I would have to make my own way home as he had to visit his mother up country on that day but you'll be alright he said, hitch a lift, just stick your thumb out and you will have no problem getting home. So with my bag resting on my shoulders I set off along the track to walk to the highway which was about a mile from our camp. On reaching the highway I duly stuck out my thumb and low and behold the first car that passed then stopped a few feet in front of me. Running to the car an African voice said, in broken English, where's you going, to Durban I replied, step in man the voice said. No sooner had I opened the back door the car sped away at high speed. Sitting in the back seat were two other Africans and another one in the front and the driver the car was a very old American Cadillac, these cars have quite a lot of room in them but with these four enormous bears sitting there it felt like a mini car. My first thought was big mistake Johnny boy, getting in this motor. The car smelled like a brewery, they were all drinking beer out of bottles but more worrying even the driver was pouring it down his throat. The car was swerving all over the road and to make matters worse they were all smoking "hemp" which is marijuana also known as cannabis. Today it would be called a spliff. They were really high on the stuff and were quite threatening. As Enpagaini and Moses had only talked in Zulu to me I was able to pick out a few words they were saying. The main words I picked up on were money, white man and overseas to putting two and two together it didn't take much logic to realise that these big bears were going to rob me or even worse so I had to think up some plan pretty quickly but before I could say anything the driver said sharply in broken English, why you hitch on road? My response to his question was I work for the railway company and I am on such a poor wage that I cannot afford to get the train home for the weekend. That should help my case letting them know I had no money. They then started to talk in Zulu and then the driver asked, you not from here. Where you from? It was now very plain that the only one who spoke English was the driver. Oh I'm from Britain, I replied and I lived in London. He cut me off very sharply, why you work in this country? The next answer I gave I thought would determine how the outcome of this situation I found myself in would be resolved. Well I nervously answered, I have heard so much about your beautiful country and heard how badly the Africans are so badly treated and I wanted to see this for myself and seeing that the Africans were here first before the white men, this country belongs to you and what I have witnessed you are all treated so very badly and I found myself saying you should all rise up against this government and take over this country and to get my final grovelling point over I said in Britain everyone is treated equal, whatever their race or colour and it has really shocked me how you are all treated and how bad your living conditions are. The next thing I noticed is that the driver was starting to get very excited and talking in Zulu with the other three in the car. After what seemed like hours the driver shouted at me. We stop soon in township but now you must drink a beer. By now my head was searching for answers, had I said all the wrong things? Why was I being offered a beer? But more the point, why were we they stopping, Is this were I met my waterloo? A bottle of beer was handed to me from a bag that was on the floor. As I began to drink these newspaper headlines flashed before my eyes, young white man found murdered in bush. I was suddenly brought back to earth with a jolt as the car screeched around a sharp corner and then came to a sudden halt. You stay in car the driver said, looking round at me he then got out and left me in the car with just one of the Africans. He must have seen the fear on my face as he said, they get more beer boss, you be alright, and we all have a drink together. This was all said in broken English, but I got the message. For the first time felt a bit more secure as they returned to the car each of the men were carrying a crate of beer. After stacking the crates on the floor the driver drove off once again at high speed. You have smoke boss the driver said, I was then handed a large hand rolled cigarette. As I used to smoke at that time I took the fag which I knew was one of their "specials" as I had been breathing the stuff in for the last hour and felt quite light headed. I took my first puff, I felt my eyes bulging out of my sockets and I started to feel quite faint but once I had taken a second puff I felt really good. I noticed that the men were now much friendlier towards me; maybe it was something to do with my little speech I had given them about how badly they were treated. You our friend, now have another beer shouted the driver. That sounded very good news to me! My name Zimbi, said the driver, what name do you have he asked. My name is John, I said and I am very pleased to have met you I said I my best grovelling manner. We drove on ever more erratically than before but with a couple more puffs and plenty of drink I no longer cared anymore. We were still about seventy miles from Durban when my very best friend in the world Zimbi the driver said, John, we don't take you now to Durban, we must stop off in township, you get another lift on Highway. Ok I said, thank you for taking me this far, it's been great travelling with you guys. The car came to a stop just outside a township, but still near the main highway as they all got out the car, they could hardly stand up and Zimbi was even worse than the others as the fresh air reached his lungs, he was staggering around like a punch drunk boxer. They all in turn gave me a hug, which nearly squeezed all the air that was in my lungs. Now it was Zimbi's turn to hug me, this man mountain of a man, he picked me up and gave me an enormous hug, it felt like being gripped by large mechanical vice like claws. After putting me down, my ribs felt like they had all been crushed by this bear of a man. Look after yourselves I shouted as the car sped away. I was happy to be alive, but quite sad in a way as they had been really good company. As I approached the highway I noticed a police car coming towards me, as it drew up alongside me it stopped and the two policemen got out. We noticed you have just got out of that car, with the four black men inside, said the sergeant, yes I replied, they were very kind to me. Where did they pick you up from the sergeant wanted to know, oh it was at the Tugela River, I said. The sergeant's face was now very stern looking. Listen to me young man, you are far from overseas and you do not ever get into a car with Africans in it, you are very luck to be alive right now. We recognised the men in that car, and they are all very dangerous individuals. You are a so lucky you were not robbed and killed, then dumped in the bush. If you must hitch a lift in future you must make sure it's with white people. Where are you heading for, he asked. Durban I said, the next thing I knew the first car that came along he waved it down are you going to Durban, he asked the driver, yes I am he said, right in that case, I would like you to give this young man a lift and after explaining it all to the driver and his family and make sure he gets out in Durban. After thanking the sergeant for his help I got into the family car and was driven to Durban. Talking to the family in the car, they made it quite plain to me what a risk I had taken but how was I to know as no-one had ever told me! After dropping me off in Durban, right near my flat I had time to reflect on my journey and wondered if my talk had in any way saved me or was it a bit of help from up above? A bit of both I felt.

Poem

I needed to hitch a lift from Tugela it was getting late

Being in this backwater your safety was down to fate

My lucks in is that car now slowing down

I shouted out please are you going to Durban town

Once in the car I realised this was a big mistake

But surely this is a dream and I will soon awake

And why are you hitching white man, why are you here

Then sat in the back seat and was handed a beer

With the drink and the pot the car was zigzagging

Like a dogs tail going side to side happily wagging

Looking at the biggest man was he was twenty five stone

With the neck of a hippo all muscle and bone

Finally getting out of the car with hugs all around
And so lucky I was not found tied and bound
Dropped off on the main highway that's where I alighted
A highway police Patrol car I had just sighted
The policeman came up to me and was quite alarmed
Thinking that in some way that I may be harmed
Don't ever risk your life like that you're lucky to be alive
I'll arrange a lift for you so that you'll safely arrive

It was now time to meet up with all my friends for a few well earned drinks. These friends were a very mixed bunch and from all corners of the world. One of the places that we all used to visit was called the "1820 settlers club". This club was named after the first settlers from Britain that colonised natal province. Many different nationalities went there so it had an international flavour and with some of the best rock bands taking part it was always a great night out. The girls outnumbered the lads by four to one, so there was no shortage on that score. On this Saturday night I met up with a few lads and by the time we had made our way to the club we had all had a fair amount to drink. We all settled down at a large table and as guys to checked out all the talent. I have been given the job of ordering all the drinks at the bar. Looking over to our table I noticed that the lads were all in deep conversation I wondered what sort of discussion they were having?? After ordering the drinks I sat down and waited for the drinks to arrive. There seemed to be great excitement at the table come on lads, let me in on the secret. There's no secret John, said one of them, we think that if anyone would be willing to take a bet on it would be you. Ok I said firstly what is the bet? And is there a reward if I win this bet? Well John, one of them said, there are ten of us here and we all will give you 4 rand each (£2) making 40 rand (£20) a huge amount then, if you dance with that girl over there with the dark hair and stay on her table for the night, make a date with her and bring her here next week. And if you manage that you win all the money. You're on I said, for that kind of money I would dance and date the ugliest women in the world, little did I know what awaited me. Oh and by the way John, you only get the money if we see you bring her into the club next week. Ok I replied. The bets on.

Poem

The 1820's club was a place for all different ages
Some of the women there needed locking up in cages
The bet was to date this girl and bring her back
She was as skinny as a pole with hair so black
Facing it for the first time my heart missed a beat
She was what they call the chaff never ever the wheat
It was frightening and scary but the bet will be won
Now stuck with the worlds most ugliest woman under the sun

As I approached the table where my 40 rand bet was sitting she had her back to me and she was sitting with another girl. I moved round to the front of her and saw her face for the first time. I was in total shock, my god she was so ugly. Instead of a face that launched a thousand ships, she looked like she had been hit broadside by one. My first thought was sod the bet I'm out of here! But being a person who was quite prudent with money and 40 rand was a week's wages then, the sensible side of me kicked in and I uttered those words, would you like to dance. She looked at me in complete disbelief, dance, she said, you want to dance with me? Later learning from her that this was the very first time a man had asked her to dance normally it was always with her girlfriends. No not really I said to myself but money is to be made here. Looking over her very quickly I noticed there wasn't much meat on her, as skinny as a pole, but hey who cares, it's only a money date. But worse was to come as it stood up and reached her full height, it towered above me by about eight inches. I could have died on the spot, the next thing I knew she had reached down at my hand and firmly dragged me across the dance floor. Looking over to my table I could see that all the lads were in fits of laughter some holding their sides and doubled up with there knees on the floor. I then realised I had been set up and they had known how tall and ugly she was. As we got into the middle of the dance floor she asked me my name, John, I said and what's yours I asked. Frida and I am Afrikaans and you John sound as if you are from England? That's correct I replied, I'm originally from London. As I had many drinks before approaching her table I had not looked at her really well but as we moved around the dance floor I noticed what a very long neck she had, it reminded me of a giraffes neck and horrors of horrors I saw this long neck stooping down on me, the next thing I felt was this huge mouth locked onto my lips, it felt like a suction pad had gripped me, what seemed like a lifetime she finally released the suction. I have never heard such a roar in all my life as the one that came from the other tables, that were in on the set up. It must have been an amazing and comical sight watching this six foot plus lady and this five foot five man trying to dance. As I looked up into her face I noticed a large spot on her cheek. On closer inspection I realised this was not a spot but a mole with black hairs protruding from it. My god I thought this lanky giraffe necked witch with a hairy mole has just kissed me, this cannot get any worse. I have just lost the will to live. I was now sobering up but needed another drink to get over the shock to my system. I'm going to get a drink I said and quickly ran to the bar, but this thing was not going to let me out of her sight. I'm buying the drinks John, she shouted, as she stood behind me at the bar, right then I said, I'll have two large Bacardi's and cokes and two pints of lager, she paid for all the drinks and we sat down at her table where's your friend I asked. Oh she's gone home I think she's upset I've found myself a man, I was certain that she had told her best friend to bugger off in case I chatted her up. This bet is now going horribly wrong will somebody please pass me a gun, I would now like to shoot myself and end it all. We took the drinks back to her table and I started to pour the drinks down my throat, in the hope as I became a little drunk the face I was looking at would seem less ugly, once again because I had consumed more drink I was able to pluck up the courage and look at her ugly face and noticed her right eye was slightly lower than her left one and it drooped somewhat. I could have drunk the entire contents of the bar and she still would have looked like a dragon. The silence that followed was only broken when she said, do you know John, you are the first man that has ever asked me to dance, really I said, but thinking to myself why am I not surprised you ugly cow, because for a man to ask her for a dance would b e either as drunk as a lord, or be high on drugs! A waiter appeared with a tray full of drinks and he said, these drinks have been sent over to you with the compliments of the table in the corner. I'll give them something to shout about and give them a good laugh and plucked up the courage and reached across the table and planted a kiss on her cheek taking care to miss the cheek with the fallen eye as I did not want to kiss an eye socket! This was greeted by loud clapping and cheering from my friends table. I know they are your mates over there she said, I think they are all uncouth and are acting like school boys and are probably jealous of you John as you have managed to get yourself a girl, did she just call herself a girl? Oh my lord I thought, I cannot believe what I'm hearing, please help me someone I would like to die! She then asked if I had a car when I replied I had, oh please can you take me home now, as I told my father I wouldn't be home late tonight. As we got up to leave the venue the band were playing the rolling stones, hit of that time called "I can't get no satisfaction" how appropriate I thought there will be chance of me getting satisfaction with this thing. Which by now had attached her arm in mine, as we walked off the floor to deafening and wild applause from some of the tables? Before I left I had finished all the drinks brought for me and some of hers so by now I was well and truly hammered. The 1820's settlers club stayed open 'till about 1am most nights and as I opened the car door for her, that old saying, "even the ugly ones start to look pretty after a few drinks" as I got ready to drive away I looked across at her and through my misty and blood shot eyes it seemed I was looking at this lovely princess so being a normal guy I made a grab for her thinking I would have my wicked way with her, John, behave yourself, what the hell do you think you are doing she shouted, no man is ever going to touch me until a wedding ring is on my finger, for her to get a wedding ring on her finger was like asking the pope to change his religion to a Muslim, it will never happen. I'm sorry but that's the kind of girl I am. she just called herself a girl again, to me she looked more like a melon that had been hit with a hammer and squashed beyond all recognition. Well I thought about it later and with all the drink in me I could just about manage to raise my arm let alone anything else!! How I managed to get to her house I will never know, but there were no drink drive laws in South Africa at this time. Stopping outside her house she said, thank you John, that was the best night I have ever had, I would like to see more of you, and I hope you like me she said. Yes of course I like you I lied, I will pick you up next Saturday and we will go back to the club again, oh thank you John she cried I will look forward to that and with that her neck came down as quick as a lightning strike followed by her head and once again her mouth acted like a suction pad. Please call me about six, John as I would like to introduce you to my father before we go out. The next day of course I had to face all my friends and the ribbing I had to take was unmerciful. Some of the kinder comments were like, when are you going to marry the witch. How could I tell them that in my drunken state she had started to look quite attractive to me, just have that money ready for me next Saturday as I intend to win the bet I said. The Monday morning soon arrived and at the crack of dawn I was once again driven up to the Bridge at Tugela for another weeks work and for the whole week I thought about how I had to face that dragon once again. But my fears were soon overcome with the thought of the winning bet I would pick up. The working week soon came to an end and once again it was Saturday. Well John, old son, this is your big day, where you get to win that bet, driving up to her house I felt a bit nervous, not so much seeing miss ugly but I was about to meet her father! With one knock of the door it opened suddenly and standing there was the biggest thing I have ever laid my eyes on, his whole frame filled the doorway; he was built like a Congolese gorilla. Ducking his head as he stepped out onto the drive I am very pleased to meet you, I quietly said, as I lifted my hand to shake his. You're a redneck, he shouted, I'm a boar farmer and we hate the English. He then went on to tell me the crimes the British had done to his people in the boar war at this stage I thought it best if I withdrew my hand as he looked like he was about to rip it off. Hearing all the commotion the daughter from hell appeared please father, don't be angry. This is my date John, you're date John, he bellowed, you never told me he was English. Does it matter father, you cannot live in the past all your life, she shouted, just come in John and don't mind him, his bark is worse that his bite and really he is just a pussy cat. He didn't look like a pussy cat, to me more like a pussy cats much larger cousin a huge big male lion and he could crush me in just one of his hands. As the ugly one led me into the front room she said, this is my mother, she looked like a typical farmer's wife, extremely ugly, big broad shoulders, a massive cleavage and hands the size of shovels and probably used to be a prize fighter other than that, quite a feminine lady. Pleased to meet you I said, we shook hands; she gripped my hand with such force I thought every bone would now be broken in it. The saying goes if you ever want to marry the daughter take a look at the mother first, well looking at this mother, all I can say is like mother like daughter. She looked like a pig that had been in a fight with a pit bull, I was sure any words she may have said to me would start off with oink, oink, oink. As her father entered the room we all sat down on the settee and the conversation between us became quite pleasant and starting off with why don't you f**k off back to your own country you British are all scum, but we gave you bastards a good licking in the boar war, so what have you got to say for yourself he yelled??   At this point my tongue seemed to turn to stone and no words were forthcoming and I sat there like a naughty child that had just been scolded by his father. I meekly replied I agree with everything you have said. I admire the Afrikaans people and their fight against the British army in the boar war. It was won with outstanding bravery and at great cost to the boar people, (a small band of boars managed to hold out and in some cases win battles against the might of the British army they were the first people to use guerrilla war tactics and mastered the art of hit and run warfare). After that speech I felt the atmosphere in the room change suddenly, well he said, nothing to do with you was it! Have a beer, my name is Pieter, and I believe you have come to take my daughter on a date, yes sir I replied politely, with your permission of course. Yes of course, you have John, he smiled take a drink with me would you. The family all sat round the table. Frida sat next to her sister whose name was Litta; she also had inherited this family's look, the ugly look! As the drinks started to flow I became much more relaxed and was really being made to feel at home. I was sitting opposite to Frida and her sister and the sight I witnessed next was so unbelievable, I thought my eyes were deceiving me as the two ugly sisters were talking away to each other a flea jumped from Frida's head to her sister's head. Oh, my god, it cannot get any worse than this, I was feeling quite ill at this stage, but to my amazement things took a turn for the worse because five minutes later a flea jumped from Litta's head to Freda's, I don't know if it was the same flea or it's brother or sister. I was in total shock and Pieter asked me if I was alright. As the colour had drained out of my face, I hope you're not going to be sick John, he said. I need some fresh air; I blurted out and quickly retreated to the garden. I'm getting straight in my car now and getting away from this house of horrors and leaving that flea ridded gruesome deformed ugly cow date of mine to wallow in her flea infested house. I was just about to jump into my car and get the hell out of there when I suddenly remembered the money bet, a little voice in my head was saying "John, if you have to share a flea or two with her, so be it, don't risk losing the bet" to quote my hero the bard "to flea or not to flea" tut-tut. I reluctantly turned towards the house again, just as her father came out to see how I was feeling. I must be going now I said, it will be too late to get into the club, that's OK, her man mountain father grinned, you two have a great time and crushing my hand in his, he bellowed you take good care of my daughter and bring her home before twelve tonight. What is this thing about being home before 12, would it be that if she is not home by then she turns into the ugly frog! And I don't want any funny business taking place, my daughter is a sweet and innocent young girl and I want her to remain that way. I thought to myself, make no mistake mate, she will still be ugly and innocent when she is ninety years old, of course I replied, I shall bring her home safe and sound. As I entered the house the ugly one linked her arm in mine and rested her head on my shoulders. I quickly broke free from her grip and ran to the driver's side of the car and hoped infestation had not taken place in my car or on my head. As we drove towards Durban she calmly said to me, John, have you thought about settling down, buying a house and having kids?? Because I was a bit stressed about the hair hopping fleas and not thinking about the bet money I was going to win, I blurted out, no not with you ugly cow. What did you say? I came back quickly what I said was you are cuddly and how! Oh, thank god for that I thought you said something else! I really put my foot down to get to the night club. The quicker I got shot of her with her flea infested head the better. We entered the club to much applause from my friends and sat her down at a table as far away from my friends as possible. I then said to her sit here, I will get the drinks in but before I do I just want to have a word with my friends over there. That's OK, she said, don't be too long. Making my way to my friends table I had my hand outstretched, where's my bet money, give it to me quickly and then I'm out of here. True to their word I was handed my R40 bet money and I said to them I've been through hell and back for this money never again will I ever attempt anything like that again. Well boys I'm off now and I will see you all for a drink tomorrow and will explain everything that has happened, if miss ugly comes over to find out where I am tell her I fell ill and went home. I did feel a bit of a rotter walking out on her like that but she was strictly a business proposition and anyway alls fair in love and war!

Poem

That's her sitting there the bet has now started
Asking a stranger to dance not for the faint hearted
With her back to me she was looking really swell
Hoping when she turned around she will ring my bell
Then standing in front of her I witnessed this sight
Because something about this thing does not seem right
Looking her up and down god is this for real
That face has been battered by that grinding water mill
With her being so ugly is that such a crime
She only needs a face job a stitch in time
Have put myself in this position just for the bet
And now I am wishing we had never met
Is it a were wolf and has a dropped eye
Just get out of here John, please walk on by
Walking onto the dance floor it gave me a snog
Ten times worse than being kissed by a slimy bullfrog
It gave her character this eye that rested on her cheek
This amazing ugly dragon lady some say she was a freak
It even hinted of getting married hoping of a wedding ring
Imagine what life would be like being married to that thing
In days of old she would have been shackled to stocks
Rotten fruit would then be thrown at her even large blocks

Back to the Tugela River again the weekend came around so quickly and again I found myself on the long journey to the Tugela Bridge and by now I had settled down nicely into the job. Although the conditions were quite hard but it was a joy to be working out in the bush with the Tugela River as a magnificent backdrop, it was on that Tuesday morning that Jesse as usual woke me up with a knock on the door. As I went to get out of my bed, my legs gave way and I collapsed back down on the bed. What a strange feeling. Having no energy and feeling so very weak. I once again tried to get up, but could hardly move now. After about ten minutes Jesse once again knocked at my door, Jesse come in I shouted, I'm not feeling very well. As he entered I could see the concern on his face. Boss John, he said, tell me what's the matter with you. After explaining my symptoms to him, he said, boss John, I have seen what I think you are suffering from before and it is called tick bite fever so we must get you to hospital as soon as possible. Jesse then left the hut saying he would tell the foreman and explain all about it to him. As the foreman came in he laughed you'll do anything to miss a day's work. As more men appeared they lifted me on to a makeshift stretcher and carried me out to the company land rover and with all my workmates looking on, loaded me onto the Landrover's floor. The foreman said I will be driving you to the hospital and Jesse is coming to look after you. Now it's going to be a very bumpy ride with you on the floor so you'll have to hang on as best you can. He drove out of the compound with all my workmates shouting their best wishes. The long journey to the Durban hospital took what seemed like days but in fact it was only a few hours. Little did I realise that I would not be ever working at the Tugela Bridge or in deed working for the railway company any more.

Poem

Waking up one morning not feeling very well
Tried to get up that's when I fell
My legs were a shaking my knees were weak
Where is that Jesse his help did I seek
I'm in a bad way felt really ill and sick
All because of that parasite it was that dreaded tick
But Jesse the boss boy was quickly by my side
Help this young man he's very sick he cried
I am certain I've seen these same symptoms before
A tick has bitten you and that's for sure
Tick bite years ago sometimes proved fatal and you could die
Without swift action your home became that place in the sky
Finally made it to hospital getting there late at night
Should get better now and everything should turn at right

By the time we drove into the hospital I was now feeling very weak and could hardly move. The fever had really taken hold of my whole body. I was expected as they had telephoned the hospital explaining the state of my health and what they thought I might be suffering from. A trolley was wheeled out to meet the land rover and I was placed on it. I could just about remember both the foreman and Jesse saying their farewells because by now I was quite delirious and really spaced out and was not of this world. All I can remember is being prodded and probed and on waking up the next morning seeing a doctor examining me and on the other side of the bed was a beautiful blonde nurse, am I in heaven? And is this an angel that has come to greet me? I am doctor Van-da-Merwe a soft voice said and we have examined you and you have tick bite fever. We shall treat you by giving you penicillin injections on the hour and hope this will eradicate the blighter. (Tick bit fever starts when a tiny tick that thrives on long grass and then gets into the human body normally through a cut or an open wound) They had examined me and found a small cut on my right leg and suspected that's where the tick entered my body. Before penicillin was invented the tick bite fever was very dangerous and if not treated very quickly could prove to be fatal. The hospital that I was being treated at was for only employees of the railway network so it was like a private hospital with first class treatment. The majority of the Patients were Afrikaans so very little English was spoken on the wards. The man in the bed next to me made it clear he did not like the British for what they had done in the boar war (and who can blame him) but we got on quite well. After I pointed out to him that was in the past and this is now. On finding out my name ha asked what's up with you then? When I explained that I had tick bite fever. Tick bite fever, he shouted, twenty years ago, my brother caught that and guess what, 24hours later he was a corpse. I watched as the man opposite him was waving frantically and shouting in Afrikaans at him. He then realized that the had said the wrong thing and said you'll be alright because now they have penicillin so don't worry, don't worry you complete idiot, here I am, 26 years old in a foreign country and you have just informed me I am about to die! The way to treat tick bite is to pump as much penicillin into your system as it is safe to. This should kill off the tick before it kills you off. I had now been in hospital for seven days and it was Christmas Eve and all my friends came and paid me a visit and crowding around my bed informing me that a very special friend would be coming to see me later on and said with much chuckling and laughing. It was evening visiting hour so being my friends they all were extremely drunk. Some were riding in the wheelchairs and racing each other down the corridors. One of them had managed to obtain a doctors white coat and started to chat with the Patients and talk about their ailments. He was so convincing the Patients were discussing all their ailments with him! What finally persuaded the matron to have them removed was when they all managed to wheel my bed out of the ward, having detached my drip and monitor lines. They were stopped just short of the exit from the hospital. I was told by the matron that their behaviour was unacceptable and to inform them all that in future only two people would be allowed to visit it me at any one time. Have you ever felt like burying your head in a deep hole because the sight I just witnessed. I wanted to bury mine because walking in through the doors of the ward was my winning bet money dragon (they have set me up again!). Walking towards the bed the long necked thing was smiling at me like a Cheshire cat on heat. Her first words to me were I knew we were meant for each other, your friends told me how much you loved me and I am the girl of your dreams and I am certain we will be with each other for ever! She went on when you failed to return to my table that night I went searching for you. I went to your friends table and they said you were not feeling very well and then told me all the lovely things you had said about me so I went outside looking for you but returned as there was no sign of you and all your friends let me sit with them for the rest of the night. (With friends like these who needs enemies). I left one of them my telephone number and he phoned me to say you were in hospital and was asked if you will visit him. So here I am, surely I'm having a horrible nightmare. This is all a wild dream. What brought me back from my dream like state was nearly being suffocated by here suction pad lips that had clamped around my mouth. I was speechless, what could I say to her. My so called friends had really dropped me in it, wait till I see them. The most important thing now is to get rid of the drooped eye long necked witch who by now has most likely infested me and my bed and half the hospital with the battalion of fleas that it carried around in her hair. It's been a long day I said in a weak voice and I am very tired and need sleep. Of course she said, I will leave you now but I shall come back and visit you after I come back from Christmas holidays with my parents and this time it was a quick peck on the cheek and she left with the words that horrified me "I love you Johnny"!!! After she had left Heidi the nurse came over to me and said, so that's your girlfriend then? You must be joking and told her the whole story; she laughed out loud and thought it was the funniest thing she had heard of in ages. I woke up to the sounds of a choir and as it was Christmas day the nurses had formed a circle in the middle of the ward and were singing and Heidi looked quite beautiful with the lights of the Christmas tree lighting up her wonderful features I watched as tears ran down her delicate cheeks. As she looked over to me she gave me a gentle smile and my heart skipped a beat, is there such a thing as love at first sight? The choir then made their way on to the next ward and it gave me time to reflect on all that had happened to me recently. As I lay in deep thought a gentle voice whispered, Merry Christmas John, as I looked up Heidi was standing beside my bed. That was a lovely carol service I said, it brought a lump to my throat, yes and I felt quite emotional as well Heidi replied, as this is my first time away from home, I said to her with your slight accent I thought you were Afrikaans, Oh no laughed Heidi, I'm from Norway and I see from your medical records John, you're from overseas as well. It's my day off today she said but I wanted to sing in the choir so I will sit with you for a while if you like, and then I have volunteered to help serve the Christmas dinner to all the Patients. What a kind a noble gesture I told her, well it's better than sitting in my flat on my own, she replied. Why would a beautiful living doll like her be on her own I wondered? The days moved on and the injections had done their Job and had destroyed all traces of the tick and in the afternoon the doctor said I could go home the next day. On the one hand I was so pleased to have been told I would be discharged but on the other hand sad that I would not be seeing Heidi ever again. I was just laying there in deep thought when this voice to the side of me was saying, so you're going home tomorrow John? Maybe we can meet for a drink sometime if you want? Am I hearing this from her? Or is this a dream? Would I like a drink with her? I would walk a hundred miles with two heavy sacks of coal on my back, just to see her beautiful smile.

Poem

Was working up country that's were I caught that beastly tick

The size of a pin head that made me so sick

Never in all my life have I felt so ill

That small but deadly bug has been known to kill

But with first class care and penicillin in the injections

This wonder drug can fight and destroy most infections

With a dedicated doctor and a very pretty nurse

They both made sure I would not be requiring a hearse

Hiding in the long grass a whole army of ticks

That's what you get for working out in the sticks

To be put into hospital by a creature so small

Why was it not an elephant or something as tall

Would rather have been attacked by such a big beast

It's a bit of an embarrassment to say the least.

You get plenty of thinking time when you're in hospital and my last night there I had much to dwell on and I decided that I would not be returning back to working on the railways but find myself some other employment.

Selling Encyclopaedias

I made my way back to my flat in Durban and told my flatmate Ron I would not be returning to the Tugela Bridge and that I was looking for another Job. I know a job that might suit you he beamed, what's that then I asked, well he said, I know a couple who sell encyclopaedias for a living and see what they say about taking you on. Ron had arranged a meeting with the couple in a Milk bar of all places. John, this is George and his wife May. George was a thick set man in his middle forties and his wife may in her middle thirties and quite attractive women but as soon as her mouth opened every other word was a swear one and with her east end accent added in the mix you knew she was a very formidable lady. Ron tells us you are looking for a job so what makes you think you can sell encyclopaedias she snapped? I was not ready for questions so early in the morning, all that came out of my mouth was err, erm, she quickly cut me off, that's not a f-ing answer she yelled at me, I could certainly see who wore the trousers in the household. George her husband piped in, I think you're being a bit harsh on the lad. Yes I realise that she said and I'm sorry John, we will try and explain to you a bit a about ourselves and our company that we run. George then explained we are both originally from London and have been in South Africa for the last 15 years. We both used to sell encyclopaedias in London but never did any good there. As we were fighting a losing battle because of television we would make an appointment to see a customer walk into their place and try and sell the books, whilst the television was on. In the end we used to have to switch the TV off ourselves which used to cause major rows between the kids and their parents and mostly did not make any sales. So we decided to come to a country that did not have any TV and now we make a very good living between us. We now employ six salesmen and they all make a good living. So John, this is how it works, we don't pay a wage to our salesmen, they make their money on commission so the more books sold the more commission they make. I quickly interjected, what happens if I work for you and I don't sell any books all week? Well in that case May said, I'm afraid you won't earn any money, it's as simple as that. Talk about heads they win, tails they win. So John, May asked, do you want to give it a try? Ok, I said, I'll give it a go, nothing ventured nothing gained. Welcome aboard George said, I will take you out with me and show you how to sell to people and show you all the tricks of the trade. Our main business is selling children's encyclopaedia so we target families with children. We go for the soft sell and if that does not work we revert to hard sale tactics. What's the hard sell tactics I innocently enquired? I'm not going to tell you now George replied but you will be coming out with me for a couple of weeks to learn how to sell these books and what Patter you have to give to customers to get that sell and John, this is strictly an evening and weekend Job, because it is a must that both the parents of the children are present when selling because both parents have to agree to buy these books as we don't want one parent agreeing to buy them and the other parent disagreeing as you will lose the sell. And to answer your question, what is hard sell? If I have not made a sale after all your sales talk, and they are not interested in buying then you will see what hard sell is all about. So John, meet me tomorrow night at seven around my house and I will show you how to sell and how to make some serious money. So what I want you to do tomorrow in the day is to practise this speech that you have to give to the customers. Then I think you're ready to go out selling on your own. Oh, by the way you must wear a suit and look smart, as this creates a good impression. I duly arrived at the large detached house that George owned, heavens above was my first thought, he is certainly doing very well. George could see how impressed I was with his house and said, you could you own something like this John if you became a good salesman. Lets go I said full of enthusiasm, OK John, I can see your eager to get started and don't worry we don't have to cold call as I have a list of customers that have phoned the office and made enquiries about the books so we are half way there and making a sale. We approached a rather run down looking house with the paintwork peeling off the front door and windows, before we rang the bell George whispered to me, I will tell them you are my nephew helping me to carry the books etc and please John don't look surprised when I tell them that you are from the education department and as no one ever questions me about it I get away with the lie. Later ringing the door bell a large woman appeared come in she shouted. After George had introduced himself he said this is my nephew and he is at college and is studying to be a primary school teacher so he is very interested in children's education (the lying toe rag) I found it very hard not to burst out laughing at this unbelievable rubbish coming out of his mouth. The woman's husband was an enormous bloke and he was surrounded by lots of empty beer cans and looked very aggressive, you better not upset me sort of character. They had three children with ages between seven and eleven, just the right age to target selling encyclopaedias to. The mother was really keen on her kids getting a good education and believed that these books would give her children a head start; on the other hand the father was dead against them as they would cost money and this would be less money for drink for him. After about an hour and George trying to convince him the benefits of the books, he turned to me, John, as a school teacher, will you tell the gentleman how beneficial these encyclopaedias will be for his children's education? Fancy asking me to make a speech about education with me not having a clue about children's educational needs. Thanks a bunch George for using me as your ace card in the pack. I rambled on about how every child's education mattered to me and how these books could help them to achieve excellent results in most subjects. I must have been as convincing as a drunken man trying to act sober in front of a Judge. The man staggered up from his chair and turned on me, well Mr School Teacher, you can see we are a poor family so if you're so concerned about my children's education why don't you give them free private lessons and that way I will not have to purchase the books and you will have the satisfaction that comes from helping poorer children. Although the man was drunk, I have never heard so much common sense and wisdom spoken. I was like a rabbit in the dark, caught in the headlights of a car completely transfixed. I was stunned into silence. George must have seen how uncomfortable I was and quickly interjected, look, if you don't care about your children's education, that's fine, but in years to come if they all have low paid jobs and have no futures it's all down to you. I realised that this was where the last throw of the dice came into play and George was into the hard sale mode and as George explained if this didn't get a sale, pack up and go as you're only wasting your time. The mans face turned to rage when George mentioned low pay, as this man was more than likely only paid a pittance. He shouted if you two are not out of my house in ten seconds I'm going to pick you both up and fling you out. For someone who hates violence and any sort of pain and a born coward I was out of that door in five seconds flat with George right behind me. George was so frightened, in his rush to get out he had left three of the encyclopaedias on the table. He only realised his mistake when the three books followed him out of the door. The drunken slob, the man's a waster and a loser George yelled, if he wasn't so drunk I would have laid him out, yer right George. I don't think so! I'm sorry John, that was not a very good start to your selling career but you will meet a nutter like that every now and again. Fancy a drink John, George said? Yes that would be a very good idea I agreed. We made for a quiet bar in town and all George wanted to talk about was encyclopaedias and making money. As the drinks stared to flow, he started to open up and felt he had to tell me about his wife May and what a great sales person she was. For every set of books George sold, she was able to sell three; her success was due to the fact that she wore the most revealing outfits, with the shortest mini skirts ever made and a low cut top that left nothing to the imagination. When selling to a couple, she would make sure that she was sitting opposite the husband so she could flash as much leg as she could at him. George was saying it normally took her on average about an hour to get him to sign for the books as they always were in quite a state of excitement by this time. She would say, men are weak and it's like taking candy from a baby. It seemed to me that George was jealous on two fronts, the first one was his wife was flaunting her wears in front of a strange man and secondly she was earning much more than him. For the next two weeks I went with George to about ten homes and he managed to sell three sets of books but some nights we were there till very late before he got them to put pen to paper. They more likely signed for the books just to get rid of him! He only had to sell one set of books a week and as there were six books in a set, he would be on big commission. Tomorrow night John I want you to go out on your own and see how you get on selling by yourself. I have arranged for you to see a family so good luck. It was a rainy night and I was thinking what am I doing selling books on a Saturday night, I must be mad. Arriving at a house in a working class area I packed my book samples in a large bag, had a quick glance at the scripts so I could confidently talk about the benefits and merits of purchasing such a wonderful set of books. The door opened by a women with the greeting, come on in, you must be the man from the education authority. Thanks a bunch George, once again, you have told them I am a school teacher! Please sit down. As I sat their nervously going over in my mind the script I was about to give, and hopefully make my very first sell. The husband walked into the room, hello my name is mark and my wife's name is Pam, you will be pleased to know that our children are staying with my mother for the weekend so there won't be any interruptions. My over all impressions of the couple was what a very nice and down to earth couple they were. As I began to get the sample books out the bag, Pam asked me if I would like a drink, yes please I replied and with a cup of tea in hand I stated to recite the script. It goes on about how these books will benefit their children etc, after about ten minutes I noticed that the husband's eyes had that glazed look about them and was that his right eye slowly closing? Surely I'm not boring the balls off him? I'd better bring this speech to an end or he will be collapsing in a heap in a sleep induced coma. Pam, his wife said they sounded just what our kid's need, now the main thing is John, we don't have much money and we are on a tight budget and every cent counts. Ok John, never mind about the hard up story and tight budget and go for the hard sell and make some money for yourself. These books were very overpriced and most people paid a monthly sum for them and it could take up to five years to pay for them. After informing them of the price of the books they reluctantly agreed to purchase a full set. Out of my pocket I took the acceptance forms and laid them out on the table in front of them, but I heard this voice in my head saying how could you do this to such a nice couple, have you no principles. They deserve better than this, how will you ever be able to hold your head up in society. Do the right thing John. As the voice faded I grabbed the form and shouted please don't sign that form, it's all a con, you could get the same information that's in them books from the library and to tell you the truth I have nothing to do with the education authority, you are a nice couple and I don't want to see you being ripped off. I could see the shock on their faces, I then went on to explain how I had to memorise a script, get you both to sign and not worry if or how you could pay for it, I would just pick up my commission and run. Well, well Pam said, I am quite shocked but very pleased you have been so honest with us, please let me get you a drink. One drink became two, and in the end it ended up being a serious drink up. As the drinks were flowing Pam did say that she thought it strange a young fellow would be selling books on a Saturday night when he could be out with friends chasing girls! I left their house in the early morning with warm handshakes and friendly embracing. Both of them would go on to be very good friends of mine. The next morning as arranged I paid George a visit. On opening his door, the first words he spoke were did you manage a sell? Don't tell me, you probably had them eating out of your hand. Actually George, I replied in a rather stern voice, I did not make a sell, but I did end up having a great drink with them both. To be perfectly honest, with you I find your method of selling to people who are considered to be the have-nots in life quite distressing and totally out of order. I was now at full steam, how you manage to sleep at night I will never know, I am puzzled how you live with your conscience so you will not be seeing e again. The look on his face was a picture.

John Wall the Journalist

I was not worried that I had not made any money for the past three weeks as I still had a healthy bank balance so I will soak up the sun and chill out. When I first arrived in Durban and was booking in at the esplanade hotel I noticed sitting at the bar a man with a wild mop of dark hair dressed in a safari jacket and short trousers with long socks. He had the appearance of a game warden. Over a drink I got chatting to him and was surprised to learn that he was a journalist and his name was John Wall. He originally came from Southern Ireland and had worked in South Africa for the past twenty years, he was in his late thirties and liked a drink (two gallons a day) and must have smoked a hundred fags a day, a typical journalist trait. He could write about politics and equally be at home writing about sport. He was a true wordsmith. Looking at his appearance you knew his face never came into contact with the sun because he hated it. John worked for the biggest selling newspaper in Durban which was called The Daily Mercury, and there were many perks that went with the Job. Firms are well aware the power of the press so the office he worked in would have lots of requests from companies to write favourable articles about their products. He was given first class accommodation on a cruise ship sailing between Durban and Capetown. He then gave a glowing report about the ship. There were all different kinds of freebies on offer for the staff of the newspaper. I became quite friendly with John and he would ask me to accompany him to various functions. One of the many ones that I recall was when he was asked to cover a story about three visiting mediums from the UK who were doing a tour of South Africa. His editor wanted him to see if he could detect if they were fraudulent. We arrived at a large hall and paid our entrance fee. John did not want anyone to know he was from the press. The majority of the audience were made up of Women so John and I stuck out somewhat. We were sat in about the middle of the hall and had just taken our seats when there was a round of applause as the three mediums walked onto the raised stage. John had taken his notepad out and was ready to note down anything that may be of interest. One of the mediums went into a trance and then pointed at a lady not far from where we were sitting and started to tell her about her departed husband and he sends her his regards. She seemed to get his name right and the lady seemed to be most impressed with her description of him. I turned to John and said what a load of rubbish; she has more likely been planted there by the three mediums. It all then became a bit bizarre. The middle medium drank her water and then proceeded to go into a trance and after about two minutes started to talk in a deep mans voice. She explained that she had now been taken over by a ninetieth century physician and he wanted to help a lady in the front row who had a lung problem. Yes you know who you are don't you, Margaret said the medium, evidently he was going to give her spiritual healing right there and then. After about five minutes and still talking in a deep voice she took another drink of water and returned back to her normal voice, well Margaret he has left me now and has given you healing, so how do you feel now? Wonderful, came the reply, I feel like a new woman she shouted. Turning to John again I said that the deep voice was probably coming from a tape recorder and Margaret was a plant. Next it was the third medium on the stage who took a drink of water and also appeared to go into some sort of trance. She then stood up and said, I'm getting some strong connections with a young man in this hall and I could see that she was pointing in my direction. Oh, no, surely its not me she's wanting to talk to. As I slipped down in my seat I hoped she would go on to someone else! But I could hear her raising her voice, Yes, you young man, the one with the blue shirt on, who is sitting behind the lady in red. I could hide no more as the whole row in front of me turned around and were saying it's you she wants to address! I now sat upright in my seat and I was looking directly at the lady. John whispered to me, this should be interesting! Her opening words to me were you are from overseas and I see that a large liner brought you to this country (correct) I am told you suffered quite a serious illness recently (who told her, correct) you were in hospital but now you have made a full recovery (also correct) I am being told you had quite a mixed childhood with some of it good and some not so good. As I see many different houses that you were brought up in (correct) I just cannot believe what I am hearing she is so correct so far, it's unbelievable as she has never met me, it's all so weird, she then proceeded to tell me about the passing of my father, just after the war at quite a young age and this was the reason I was not brought up with the family. She carried on talking about a few more very accurate details on my life, I can picture you arriving in this country and stepping down a gang plank and in your life you will be stepping down and up many more (how did she know that I would get to love cruising so much??) she finished her talk to me by saying when the daffodils come into bloom I can see you walking up a gang plank and you will be sailing away from these shores and I am seeing another young man with you and it appears that you will help to keep this man from danger. Well, well I thought you have been right with all your predictions and summing up of my past life but that last statement about me going home was rubbish as I was really enjoying my life and had no intentions of returning back to Britain. She then asked me if any of her talk had made sense to me, yes I replied, you were very good and thank you, then sat down. She took a sip of water then the other lady pointed to another person and gave her a reading. Once that reading had ended the host came onto the stage and thanked the three mediums for a very entertaining evening and reminded the audience that free light refreshments were now available at the back of the hall. Well John, what did you make of her? Just give me an idea how good you thought she was say from one to ten. Well, John, I would give her a nine out of ten, that's how accurate she was. John said, seeing refreshments are on offer I shall take the opportunity to interview the people who were given a reading and find out their comments on the three mediums. He soon found the first woman who had a reading and introduced himself as a reporter and told her he was writing an article for a newspaper on mediums and would she mind if her views and comments were used, she readily agreed. He asked her how she found the experience. The woman was quick to point out to John that she had been to many meetings like this, but this one was the best one she had ever attended. As she pointed out, a few mediums ask if you know a certain person but with this medium she would say I have a person here that you know and went on to name her or him as she put it, she told me facts even my family never knew and I was totally blown away with her. John, interviewed most of the people and the same answers came back the mediums were genuine and very accurate. John asked me to sum up the whole experience and I told him that I went to that hall as an unbeliever and thought all mediums and their like were a load of rubbish but have to admit, my views have changed somewhat and I was very impressed with the proceedings and now have an open mind. The article was duly printed the following week.

I still had enough money in the bank to still not have to work and enjoy a life of leisure. This is where I picked up the name of Lord John because I had not worked for the past two months. Word had got to me that a young lady had visited the 1820's club looking for me and left her telephone number for me. I had told Heidi that I used to go there quite often with my friends. On receiving this news I was on the phone to her quicker than a rat up a drainpipe. Fancy Heidi a Norwegian goddess trying to get in touch with me! I phoned her and arranged to meet her the following evening. On meeting her, she wondered why I had not contacted her like I had promised to? Where are we off to she enquired, I hope it's to the 1820's club that you were always talking about? We will not be going anywhere near that place I said, Frida the mad woman will be there and she will be all over me like a rash! So started a friendship that was to last about three months and you couldn't get a better place anywhere to be young with the sun and sea surfing and great night clubs to be found. I had now found my paradise. Heidi and I went everywhere together and had wonderful days that never seemed to end, but I used to see that sometimes she had such sad eyes and asking her one day that sometimes why she had such sad eyes, she replied, I trained to be a nurse in Norway and came out to South Africa with my parents and have now been here for three years and although I like the lifestyle out here I so miss my homeland so much. She then went on to tell me how very homesick she was and was thinking of returning home shortly without them. She was going to book up a ship to Southampton for the end of the month which was three weeks off and gave her notice in at work so that we could have her remaining time in Durban to be as fun-filled as possible. What goes around comes around as the saying goes and the day of Heidi's sailing had arrived on the Windsor castle. As the bard once quoted (parting in such sweet sorrow) and there was my Heidi Jennssen sailing away from my life forever. All goodbyes are said and addresses are exchanged and promises are made to meet up with each other and before you know it the ship had slipped its moorings and with its fog horn blasting the customary farewell salute it slowly slide away from the quayside gaining a steady speed with Heidi waving with one hand and with the other one wiping away the tears. A few of the tears I should think would be the missing of her family and the unknown future that awaited her. Soon the ship was just a dot on the horizon then saying my good byes to Heidi's family I returned back to my flat with a heavy heart and thinking to myself well John, you have had your fun days so it's about time you got your self some work days.

Poem

Lying in my hospital bed did get my first sighting

She was to become my nurse this young and Nordic Viking

Her name was Heidi she was twenty five and sweet

Was younger than springtime observing her became a treat

And with hair the colour of sand naturally blonde of course

Heide was born in that ancient land sometimes known as Norse

The land of the midnight sun with such majestic mountains

Crystal waterfalls cascading down into the fjords making rainbow fountains

With the sweet crisp air and the clear deep waters

So proud to be Norwegian those Viking sons and daughters

The country that gave us Grieg his composing and cords

Listening to his music is like sailing down the fjords

A better place on earth has yet to be found

Heidi was now returning to her roots going homeward bound

On the Buses

Looking at the Job section in the natal mercury what caught my eye was a job for trainee bus drivers working for the Durban Corporation. That sounds just the job for me I thought, driving a big red bus around, is that not every boys dream?? The next day I took myself off to the bus station and was promptly given an interview and was told I was just the sort of candidate they were looking for so it was just a simple matter of taking an aptitude and intelligence test, a mere formality in your case Mr Banfield, said the interviewer, if you would like to go in the room next door, my assistant will give you a test paper. The test paper is quite easy and it is split into three parts: part one is general knowledge, the second part is written English and the third part is maths which is so simple my eight your old son would have no trouble completing. He went on, you have 30 minutes to finish the test and the average time to complete it is twenty minutes. The general Knowledge part of the test was quite easy and I finished it in about five minutes, the written English part proved to be also very straight forward and easy then came the maths part, this was in three parts, long division was the first sum to work out, I just found myself staring at the sum, not having the faintest idea how to even start working it out. Time was moving on so I went on to the next sum which was multiplying, once again my mind went blank and I didn't have a clue how to even start it off, never mind, just a small hiccup, I will go in to the last part of the maths test and this was the fractions part. I could not get my head around this at all; I might as well be looking at Mongolian. This is the time I wished that smart-arse eight year old son of the interviewer was sitting beside me! The bell sounded to end the test and the test papers were collected up and handed in. There were five other people taking the test and we all sat their nervously awaiting the results of the exam. The pass mark was 75% or better. The examiner then walked back into the room with all the completed test papers and then proceeded to read out all the other five men in the room and with the words congratulations chaps you have all passed the test, please make your way to the room next door and we will discuss the contract and conditions of your employment. Mr Banfield, please stay where you are! Oh dear, this does not look very good. As the last person closed the door, the examiner turned to me and said, you did very well on your general knowledge and written English but you failed to complete any of the maths questions and as it stands in your test you have only reached the 45% pass mark, but you don't have to tell me the reasons why because I know your mind froze when confronted with the maths questions, am I right? Yes sir, I found myself grovelling, my mind went blank, and I feel so silly not getting one question right. Look Mr Banfield, it happens to the best of us, I know you can answer the maths questions but you need to leave this place and clear your head so go away for two hours return back here and you can re-sit the maths test and I'm sure you will pass with flying colours. It should now be clear to the reader that I was rubbish at maths! So the big question is how do I, in two hours, understand and be able to complete and pass a maths test? I know I will head on down to Millie's cafe and I hope I can find some answers. (Millie and Dennis had lived in South Africa for a few years and decided to open up a restaurant in the centre of Durban, it did a roaring trade, supplying office workers with freshly made rolls and sandwiches and it is where most of the ex-Pats would hang out). On entering the restaurant Millie greeted me with her usual broad smile, Hi Lord John, got yourself a Job yet? Well Millie, I replied in a nervous way, that's why I have called in to see you. After explaining all about my failed attempt at the maths test to her, I asked, is your daughter home. Yes she is home from school, Millie answered, thank the lord for that, she may be able to give me some lessons in Maths. Millie called out to Lesley, her daughter; Lord John would like to see you! Lesley was only eleven years old but a maths boffin. You have got to help me Lesley I found myself saying to her and explained all the sums that I had failed on. Oh they're so easy Lord John (I was even called Lord John by an eleven year old) you must be very thick if you can't do these simple sums, even an eight year old could do them (where have I heard that before). Lesley then sat me down like a school teacher would do and got her exercise book out and laid it out on the table. Right she went on, you tell me all the sums that were on the test paper and we will go through them all and I will explain how to approach them and for the next hour teacher aged eleven and pupil aged twenty-six worked on all the maths questions that were in the test paper. That's it Lesley said, I think you have got the basic idea, just remember what I have taught you and you should easily pass the test. She must have had a great laugh with all her school friends the next day explaining how she'd helped a grown up thick-o to do simple maths. (Lesley grew up to become one of South Africa's top surgeons!) After giving Lesley a big thank you hug for all her time and Patience, I made my leave of the restaurant with both Millie and Lesley shouting Good Luck John. Ten minutes later I was entering the bus station again. On reaching the test centre I was greeted by the examiner. Right John, here's your test paper on maths only and you have fifteen minutes to complete it and your time starts now. As I nervously turned the opening page I noticed that every maths question was similar to the ones that Lesley had shown me. Within ten minutes I had finished all the questions and hoped that they were correct. The examiner took the test paper off me and started to mark it, I could see he was ticking all the questions and sums so I was quite confident. He looked up and said you will be pleased to know you John, that you answered every sum and question correctly and you will be offered a job with the other candidates as a trainee bus driver. Well I never, I know Lesley had taught me very well so well in fact the examiner went on to tell me that I had the best maths result of all the candidates with a 100% pass mark! It was Thursday and we were due to start training on the following Monday. I went straight round to the restaurant to tell Millie and Lesley the good news an they were both highly delighted that I passed the test.

Poem

Her name was Lesley and she was still at school

Young girls her age do not teach as a rule

Never met anyone like me as think as they come

Not a clue about maths even the most simplest sum

Her teaching paid off, I became a willing learner

Play my cards right good wages I could be earning

Had not even reached her teen years this young girl

A jewel in the crown lets call her a pearl

She had that gift of teaching in my maths lesson

Lesley went on to become highly skilled in her profession

I was going to make the most of my weekend because come Monday I was due to start work which after all this time I was not looking forward to because in life the less you do the less you want to do. So this weekend I was determined to party. As it was 1966 South Africa was not yet receiving television so no-one stayed in at night so every night was party night. Of course I could not show my face at the 1820's club because long neck was still looking all over town for me. We all made for the esplanade hotel, the first hotel I stayed in on arriving in Durban. The nightclub attached to it was the best in town and the best groups played there. Being 1966 the Rolling Stones, who's big hit at the time was I can't get no satisfaction and also the Kinks with one of their greatest tunes ever it was, lazing on a Sunday afternoon, they were at their peak then. As well as the Beatles, who's hit at the time was Ticket to ride and also a South African young man made a hit record in London which became a world wide hit, it was called "Pretty Flamingo" and his name was Manfred Mann. Most of the groups that performed at the hotel played "Stones" and

"Beatles" hits so you felt quite at home, but I still missed Heidi, I wonder if she is looking at the midnight sun with her thermals on and a thick overcoat wrapped around her, plus her hat and scarf keeping out the cold and thinking of me with my tee shirt and shorts and sweating with temperatures in the nineties. Like all good things the weekend passed so quickly and on the Monday morning I found myself reporting for work as a new recruit as a trainee bus driver for "The Durban Corporation Bus Company". I and four other new recruits assembled in the training school office. The training instructors name was Mr Walker, a large and jolly man, a third generation South African who was very proud of the fact that his forbears were originally from the UK. Right lads, his first words to us were, put up your hand if any of you drive a vehicle? Four out of the five of us put up our hands. Well gentlemen you may find this hard to believe but I generally prefer people that have no experience of driving at all and I can then start from scratch, but with people that drive they bring with them bad habits. It was the youngest in the group at twenty five who never raised his hand saying he couldn't drive, his name was Hendrick, and he was an Afrikaner from the Orange Free State and could hardly speak any English. He used to work in the gold mines in Kimberly but after a rock fall deep in the mine he decided it would be safer driving a bus for a living. The driving course lasted three weeks and if you passed it, you would be issued with a public vehicle licence (PVL). We were all taken out to the back of the offices and there stood the bus test track. The instructor then jumped in and said to all of us, I want you all to watch me on the test track and this is what I expect from all of you. Jets of water were then sprayed on the track. He then demonstrated how to remedy a full skid and how to correct locking wheels, most impressive I thought. We were then all introduced to the red bus that we would be training on. We all piled aboard and sat in the front seats. The instructor then showed us the workings of the bus. There was no clutch as it had a pre-select gearbox so to change the gear you just flicked a lever on the steering column. So gentlemen I am going to show you how easy driving this bus is. Hendrick as you have never driven before I would like you to be the first one to drive the bus in the large circle that has been set out. As Hendrick sat in the driving seat he looked terrified but with the instructor sitting behind him he was told to put it into gear, press down the accelerator pedal and drive and within five minutes of a bit of zigzagging he had got the general ideal of steering and within fifteen minutes was able to change gear when needed. Right Hendrick, you can pull over now, you have done very well. Now gentlemen, said the instructor, here is a man who has never driven in his life but within twenty minutes had mastered it, that's how easy it is, child of ten could drive it. For the rest of the day we all took turns in driving round the same set course and by the end of the day all felt confident that we could drive on the main roads.

If I can tell you about the other trainees that made up the group, there was Roberto who was in his late forties and came from Portugal, and had been in South Africa for two years, he hoped to save up enough money to buy a cafe back home with a good sense of humour and a ready smile even when he heard that his nick name which was "pork and cheese". Then we had Harry, he was from Liverpool and had worked in south Africa twice, the first time he had brought his young family out twenty years previously, but only stayed two years because his wife became very homesick and missed her family and persuaded him (with a bit of nagging) that they should return home. The first time they immigrated it only cost them £15 each to go after about three months back home in Liverpool, his wife found it not as good back home as she thought even though she was with family, she now realised that it was not all that bad in South Africa, so she nagged him even more to immigrate once again but this time they had to pay the whole fare themselves. Harry had worked on the buses when last out here but had to retrain because the gap was too long since he had last drove buses. A typical scouser was Harry, with an accent so thick the locals thought he was an eastern European, as they could not understand a word he said. The last of the group was a local lad who was born in Durban, his name was Paul, he was in his mid-twenties in his short working life he had so many jobs he had lost count of them, he had been as sailor, a cook, and too many other jobs to mention but the strangest job he confessed to having was working in a women's dress shop but there again not so strange as he was very effeminate and talked with a lisp and with his pouting lips was some character and asked that we should call him "Pauline". When the instructor was not about as management in those days had a very tinted view on anything they did not understand! But our view was live and let live. We were just one day away from passing out driving bus course, the day was Wednesday and this day we were all practicing out driving skills in and around Durban. We all took turns to practise and I was very impressed with the way Hendrick handled driving a bus as he had never driven anything before. The next day soon came round and I was picked out to be the first trainee to take the test. I was introduced to the two test inspectors that would be marking my test results. Just relax John, the younger of the two said. We will be testing you all over the Durban area and finish up on the skid Patch back at the garage, so when ready take it away. As I set off quietly confident although bus tests are much harder than car ones because passengers are involved and therefore a higher driving standard is required. After driving around for an hour I was told to make my way back to the garage to take the skid test. This held no fears for me and I was able to complete all the manoeuvres. I was then told to switch the engine off and answer Highway Code questions and general driving ones. The older examiner of the two then fired questions at me most were quite straight forward but two questions really had me stumped. One was this: if you were driving your bus and you came across a Bridge that you know you couldn't drive through because it was too low and you could not reverse backwards, how would you resolve the problem? I just looked at them with a blank expression and just for a laugh said, I would let all the tyres down. Good that is the correct answer. I was amazed; I had only said it in jest. The other question that had me stumped was: if you were driving up a steep hill with passengers on board and your brakes failed and you found the bus was going over the edge what would you do/ would you stay on the bus, or jump out just before it went over/ I really had to think about this one. But quickly came up with the reply, I would stay with the bus as there could be a chance I could somehow steer the bus out of danger and save the passengers. By jumping out the passengers would be left to their fate and like a captain of a ship they are all your responsibility. After a few more highway questions the older examiner offered his hand to mine with the words Congratulations young man, you have passed the test, you're driving skills were very good as was your highway code. I was then directed to the training room so await my fellow trainees completing their tests. I felt highly delighted to have passed the test, not only was I about to start a job I knew I would enjoy but I could now earn a decent wage and it was of course all down to a young school girl! After what seemed like eternity, into the room entered Harry the scouser with a wide beam lighting up his face, no need to ask if you passed then Harry I said. Yes he replied, and by the look on your face you passed he interjected. He then gave me a bear like hug which nearly drained all the air out of my lungs. Harry was built like a heavyweight wrestler. We sat there chatting about the time we had all spent in the training school. When the door opened and in walked Hendrick, he also had a smile that went from ear to ear and it was handshakes all round. A man of few words was our Hendrick. After a while he was followed in by Roberto, me pass, me pass, he shouted with glee, you all pass as well no, he excitedly said in his broken English as he tried to dance with us all. The talk now turned to Pauline as he was known by us all, when a group of people get together for training or courses you all strike up a friendship and bond with each other and hope that all the group fare well. It was not long before Pauline entered the room, giving a high pitched scream it sounded like an Australian wombat on heat. I've passed, I've passed, and he wailed and then proceeded to give us all a big kiss. He then said when the examiners told me that I had passed I was so excited I gave them both a big kiss and they looked at me in utter amazement, I think they were quite shocked, yes I think so Pauline! The following week we had to attend the classroom for a week of training to get us used to all the different vehicles and passes that were issued and available and to study all the many routes that were covered by the bus corporation. The week soon came to an end. On the Monday morning is where all our training was going to be put to the test. We were each assigned a mentor, who for the first week would show you the ropes and guide you through the job. When you first passed out as a driver, you had to work on a double Decker trolley bus as a conductor for the first two months. This was to get you used to selling tickets to passengers and knowing what fare to stage at each stage of the journey. I had to strap a ticket machine around my waist which had a handle attached to it. If someone wanted say a 20 cent fare you would tap in 20 cents on the buttons turn the handle and out would come a printed ticket. This was state of the art technology for those days. You needed a mentor with you in them first days because these machines often jammed up and he had to untangle the squashed and mangled tickets that had spued from the mouth of the often unreliable pieces of junk. We had practiced on these machines in training school, on how to remedy a malfunction but in the training school you had time to sort things out but under pressure with a bus load of sometimes rude, grumpy and aggressive passengers it was a different story. The first morning on the job I was introduced to my mentor for the week, he was a man in his late fifties and went by the name of George who had worked on the buses for 25 years. As we shook hands he said what made you take this crap Job, I hate everything about it, I cannot wait 'till I retire and get away from the low life's and the pits of humanity that call themselves passengers. So you enjoy your work I interjected with a wry smile. I thought a bit of humour would cheer him up a bit but he was not finished yet. And I have to stand on my feet all day and I have very bad varicose veins. I've asked for a desk job because of it but they have refused my request (I wonder why). He was now in full flow, I hate getting up every morning knowing I have to face the world and meet those disgusting people who travel on buses. A thought went through my head, is he for real? Is this a set up? Or is he a nutcase? I think George boy you need a shrink me thinks! I was thinking if he did go to a shrink he would listen to him for five minutes and would make a choice, do I shoot myself or throw myself out of my twentieth floor office window or shoot him with a 45 pistol and put him out of his misery and to think that I had to work with this crazy mad man for a whole week! I'll just have to try and humour him a bit. There I was on that first day as a conductor standing beside a No43 bus with George (the nutcase) and my driver for that week who went by the name of Piers Van Der Merwe, a proud Afrikaner who did not take kindly to me, knowing I came from Britain because as I lifted my hand to shake his he completely ignored it and spoke a few words in Afrikaans. He was at least six foot four in height and looked very athletic and my first thought was that I wouldn't like to get on the wrong side of this man mountain. He only speaks Afrikaans George said so it's no good you speaking to him in English because he will not answer you. Well that's great, I'm working with George the head case and piers the non-talking chip on his shoulder driver, this should prove to be a very testing week. As we drove out the bus garage I felt a b it nervous on how I was going to manage this day. And it did not help matters when George my mentor whispered to me, Pier's hates the sound of the bell ringing so try not to ring it too much. I have seen him shout and swear not only at the conductor but the passengers as well. Did he just tell me that or am I dreaming? Surely these two have just escaped from the Asylum? As the bus approached the first stop on the route I made sure my ticket machine was firmly attached around my shoulders and waist. The route we were doing was a mile then we went another mile along the beach front and returned back to the city hall again. The journey was only about three miles but it was the busiest route undertaken by the buses. There were no doors on these double Decker trolley buses so passengers were able to board the bus from the front and rear. As we pulled up next to the bus stop an almighty surge of bodies came flying past me, knocking me onto the bus floor, as I picked myself up I uttered the these words in a very quiet and meek voice, steady on there folks, lets have a bit of order please. My mentor George and the now seated passengers looked at me in complete amazement. George pulled me aside, now listen here limey (that was my name as far as George was concerned, as I came from Britain) a bit of advice he said, don't ever talk nicely to passengers and do not show them any respect, just be as aggressive as they are and you will survive. Am I now on a different planet? What happened to manners? Like please and thank you? The standard fare from the city hall to the beach front was 10 cents so as most of the passengers wanted to go there you did not have to change the machine dials so it made it that much easier. I was now starting to get the hand of this conducting job and had taken all the fares on the bottom deck and was about to walk up the stairs of the bus when it only happens to others and not yourself occurred. Suddenly without warning the straps of my ticket machine and money bag came flying off and fell with a thud onto the road. The reason this must have happened is when I was knocked to the bus floor, when the mob first came on. This cannot be happening to me! My first hour on the job. This is my second worse nightmare! Passengers who had seen the mishap quickly rang the bell to get the bus to stop but piers the bus driver did not like the sound of the bell, especially now that it had rung more than three times, so the bus went ploughing on. He must have seen it unfold but being piers he would have been chuckling to himself, knowing that the redneck conductor was in trouble. The bus finally stopped at the next stop, I ran as fast as I could up the road to retrieve my ticket machine and cash bag with George my mentor running behind me shouting you're going to be in big trouble now man. It must have taken me five minutes to get to where the machine and bag fell and what greeted me was a ticket machine all in pieces and the cash bag with no money left in it. As I had only been collecting fares for about ten minutes there wasn't much money in the bag so that was a blessing. Picking up what was left of my ticket machine and empty money bag I had George who by now was enjoying the whole episode that had befallen me, made our way back to the bus which was still waiting at the stop. What happens now I asked George? Do we go back to the depot or carry on I enquired? Not sure said George, we had better ask the driver, who was not a happy man. The passengers had been giving him an ear bashing for stopping for so long and wanted him to drive off and leave us behind. What do we do piers we asked him? We carry on the journey, he snapped, these passengers have paid their fare so we have to complete the route but the ticket machine is all in pieces and tickets cannot be issued to new passengers. That's too bad he shouted, I'm completing the journey with or without you both. Ok, Ok, said George, we had better finish the route with you. So we both climbed aboard with much shouting and cursing from most of the irate passengers. As people alighted at stops, more people got on and the sight that greeted them was two of the bus crew sitting there like dummies. When they asked for tickets were told there are no tickets as the machine has broken. Most of them then had broad smiles come over their faces while others just laughed out loud. I for my part just sat there feeling quite glum and thinking not a very good start to your new career Johnny boy, why me?? Was just one of the many thoughts that crossed my mind. Well looking at things in a positive frame of mind things cannot get any worse, and that's for sure. How wrong I was. For some unknown reason the driver decided to miss stopping at the next bus stop, knowing full well that passengers had rung the bell wanting to get off, they were shouting and swearing at him to stop the bus immediately. His back was not protected by a glass screen so he was turning his head and shouting swearing back at them. Amongst the uproar I could make out this well to do lady with a very polished accent shout, driver stop this bus at once. He in turn shouted back at her in English, why don't you shut your big mouth, you ugly old cow. She had been carrying a book and the next thing she threw the book and it hit him right on the back of the head. I could not believe what I was witnessing, the bus came to a grinding halt and all the passengers who had wanted to get off at the other stop quickly alighted with the pair of them now engaged in a slagging match and the passengers and the bus in complete uproar. My mentor by this time had jumped of the bus in what I thought was a very cowardly act and leaving me to sort out the rumpus. Give my back my book you uncouth, poor excuse for a man, the lady shouted. No you're not having your book back you bitch, he shouted in English, you hit me with it, so I'm keeping it and that is that, now get off my bus he raged. I'm not leaving this bus until I get my book back so there and if you don't give it back to me I am calling the police she snapped. Well John, this is the time where you have got to stand up and be counted, because this looks like it could get ugly, so getting off my seat and raising up to my full height of 5'5" i stood between where the bus driver was sitting and the by now hysterical lady. Ok folks let us all calm down now, this shouting is getting us no-where and looking at the lady I said that was a very silly thing you did throwing that book at the driver, because he could have swerved and it could have resulted in a nasty accident and I think that if you called the police they would be charging you with assault on the driver. Then a remarkable thing happened, the driver turned around and said to the lady, in English, I'm sorry that I passed the last stop, my mind was elsewhere (you little liar, it was the ringing of the bell that made you do it) but there was no need to throw that book at me. So let's forget the whole thing and get on with the journey. My words about assault may have had a bearing on the outcome because the lady said, yes I agree, if I can have my book back now we will forget the matter. The driver then handed back the book, the lady then reached out here hand and shook the drivers hand and with tears in her eyes sobbed, I am a Christian woman and what has upset me more than anything is that the book I threw at you was the holy bible and for that I am truly sorry. I felt really pleased with myself that I had settled the dispute, maybe I should apply for a post in the diplomatic service or maybe involved in counselling.

Once the incident was over, out from nowhere came my mentor as if nothing had happened. Where did you get to I enquired? Oh as soon as I saw there was trouble kicking off I made myself scarce, I don't like getting involved in arguments and fights. Thanks a bunch mate I said, you are supposed to be looking after me! Never mind about that he said, lets get this bus rolling. As I was still standing near the driver I heard him softly say, John, thanks for standing up to me and resolving the dispute, I thought you handled it very well and with that he turned around and his large hand reached out and grasped my hand and firmly shook it. I am sorry I haven't introduced myself, my name is Piers, I hope we can be friends, I think you're an OK bloke. Well that's a turn up for the books I thought. He went on, I'm sorry you're equipment came flying off; I did feel sorry for you as it was your first day on the buses. I have made up my mind he then said, when we get to the beach front, all the passengers will get off, don't let any more people get on we will then get back to the bus garage and you can get a new ticket machine. What a turn around in a man, he is actually talking to me. Could it have anything to do with the fact that he was hit on the head with the holy bible? He is now all sweetness and light. After dropping all the passengers off at the beach front, we then made our way back to the depot.

Poem

Working with the driver and mentor they both seem quite mad
Both men hated their jobs I found that a little sad
That bible throwing lady most certainly lost the plot
Aiming at the drivers head a bible bashing he got
With the machine in bits fares I could not take
Just why is this happening to me for heavens sake
I then stopped this heated spat turning into blows
But alls well that ends well how the saying goes
Things can only get better it's only my first day
Won't want another day like that I have to say.

We had all agreed between ourselves that we would not mention anything about the book throwing incident as the lady that threw the book promised to forget the whole episode. We knew we would have to explain the smashed up ticket machine and loss of fare money, when standing in front of the transport manager. As soon as we got back to the bus garage I found myself explaining to the manager all the details of what had taken place, I thought I may get the sack but to my relief he was more concerned about my welfare and if I had suffered any stress over it as I was new on the job, he hoped it had not put me off working for the company. What a true gentleman, but as he pointed out you won't work harder than you do on that beach front circle line route but you will get the best experience working on it. So if you agree young man we will keep you on it for one month, without your mentor, but with the same driver. That's fine I replied, so for the next month Pier's the driver and myself worked quite happily together and forged a good working relationship with each other. So much so, that Pier's asked me if I was interested in him teaching me surfing. I told him I would love to surf the waves. He said he would show me the ropes on the weekend. It was Friday and this was my last day working with piers on the circle line because on the Monday I was going to have my own bus and work as a one man operator. This being a large single deck bus with no conductor the driver taking the fares with the ticket machine mounted on a framework next to him. South Africa had introduced one man operations on buses a year earlier and was the first country in the world to introduce it. As Pier's drove out of the bus garage for what was to be my last day working with him he said, I am sorry John that I was quite rude to you by only speaking in Afrikaans for the first three weeks but I am a boar man and have been brought up not to trust English speaking people. I now see how wrong it was of me, you seem a nice sort of bloke so I hope we can be friends. Of course piers I replied, you can start this weekend by showing me all the tricks of the trade with the surf board. That's agreed then he smiled and he shook my hand warmly. Our first pick up point for the first passengers was outside the city hall and with about two minutes before we reached city hall Pier's said, John, its going to be really hectic today, as this is the last Friday in the month and it is always busy then. As we approached the stop the city hall steps were packed with people waiting for the first bus of the day. Good luck piers shouted, as he stopped the bus. I quickly got off the bus as I did not want to be crushed in the sheer weight of passengers trying to get on board. Within three minutes the bus was packed solid, so packed in fact, I could not get on board myself, it was then I heard that dreaded sound and it was the sound of the bell and someone had rung it twice, which tells the driver it's OK to move off. I could only watch in horror as the bus pulled away with me stranded on the pavement and of course there is no way Pier's would know I was not on board. As long as the bell rang once for passengers to get off and twice for him to proceed he would just go merrily on his way. It was just left for me to sit on the city hall steps and wait the return of my bus. After sitting there for about forty five minutes I spotted my hijacked bus coming towards its final stop. As I stood up I could see the astonished look on piers face. What, how why, was his first words, I cannot believe it, you have been here all the time. I don't know whether to laugh or cry. But hey, John, them passengers certainly put one over on both of us, don't you think he said with a glint in his eye. Can you imagine what it was like on that bus with the missing conductor the passengers getting off, telling the ones getting on we have left the conductor behind so when you want to get off ring the bell once, and ring it twice and it will go. They must have all been in stitches, plus of course no one had to pay a fare. We made three more trips around the circle line that day which proved uneventful, which was just as well because we would have to report what happened. The bus company would know how much is taken in fares daily on that route. A lot of people that day must have had a good laugh on that bus. Both piers and I both had a good laugh about it and wondered what would have happened if an inspector would have got on, and found no conductor on board. Once more we both found ourselves in front of the boss explaining what had taken place. The procedure is that you explain in detail all the facts then told to leave the room while they come to a conclusion on the case. When called back into the room the men that made up the panel seemed to have seen the funny side of it as the senior manager said, this is the first time this has ever happened in the history of this bus company and we all find it quite an amusing story and we find that it was not the fault of the driver and also the conductor was blameless and this episode will not go onto your work records. We will just put it down to one of them things that happens. Pier's and I became quite firm friends and I was determined that I was going to take up his offer for him to teach me the art of surfing. As we were both off work for the weekend, Pier's made good his promise and I agreed to meet him on Addington beach at six in the morning for my first lessons in surfing. On reaching the beach I could see that he had with him a spare surf board. Hey man, he shouted, I've been surfing since five this morning, grab that board and I'll give you a few hints of the dos and don'ts of surfing. Right John, that's all the basics of surfing, now lets surf. What an amazing experience, frightening at first but slowly as you get used to the sitting on top of a wave and being propelled with an unstoppable force riding the surf until the sheer weight of water unmercifully dumps your aching body onto the beach. For the first hour or two you're off your board more than you're on it, but with practise you start to get the hang of it. The thrill of it all so magical and having mastered it I thought to myself this is nature's way of giving a reason to be living. And this was the time when the group called the "beach boys" had really made surfing the in thing to do with their "surfing sound".

Poem

It was early Saturday morning walking down to the beach
Waiting for me was Pier's who was ready to teach
Will give you some lessons before you enter the surf
Because this is the best surfing spot on this earth
Take a look over there that's called the Indian Ocean
You should be riding those waves like poetry in motion
Standing on my surf board paradise I think I've found
This has just got to be the greatest thrill around
It's just me against the elements I feel so free
Keep me young forever sweet lord that is my plea
Them lazy days of summer is this all a dream
Because now I have become a lean mean surfing machine

By the Sunday I had really got the hang of this surfing craze and dragging myself back onto the beach I felt physically exhausted but feeling a great sense of achievement that I had mastered surfing. Thanking piers for all his help and encouragement and promised I would be surfing as soon as possible, depending on the new shifts I would be working.

Driving my own bus

Mondays seem to come round so quickly and this one was no exception and all the five of us who had completed our driver training together were each given our own bus. We were now called "a one man operator" this means you drive and take the fares. In the driver training school we had gone over all the bus routes but we were told if not sure of the route ask one of the passengers. They liked you to be able to know all the bus routes because if you were a spare driver and someone went sick you could cover for them whatever the destination. My first day went well as it did with all us new drivers, unfortunately except for Hendrick. As I parked my bus in the bus garage I made my way to the canteen and was greeted by my fellow trainee Harry the scouser. Have you heard what happened to Hendrick this morning, he said, in a shocked voice? No what happened to him, I replied. He went on to tell me that Hendrick had taken his bus out, filled up with passengers at his first stop in the city centre, drove along for about one minute, mounted the pavement and went straight through a large departmental store shop window! He was in hospital for a week and fortunately his passengers escaped with just cuts and bruises. Hendrick you will remember was the trainee who had never driven before in his life and finished the course as top driver. We never saw him again after that, there was an enquiry into the crash and the bus was found to have no defects so it was driver error it was assumed because of his lack of driving experience he came across a situation he had not come across in the driving school and panicked and lost control of the bus. And to think he was the outstanding trainee driver and they all thought he was the dog's testicles. On my first week of driving I was given a straight forward route but they got changed ever week. I had been given for my second week a very hard route and it took in three housing estates in the not so very well off part of town so it was an awkward journey but was told by the boss if you're not sure ask the passengers and they will put you right. This week was the early shift, six 'till two and it was mainly working class people building or construction workers and taking night-shift workers home. I had taken the entire morning shift to work and on jumped the night shift ones and on entering the first of the estates realised I had forgotten the way. Can anyone point me in the right direction, I pleaded. First time on the route then mate, a cheeky chappy enquired. Yes and I seem to have lost my way a bit I replied sheepishly. Don't worry mate I'll show you the way. The same man shouted to all the other passengers, the drivers lost his way! I must have had about twenty passengers on board and it wasn't long before the first many came up to me and said I live about 3 stops away but if you go down the next road on the right it will be a short cut to my house. Being naive and a bit green I agreed to this request. No sooner had I dropped him at his house the next passenger stepped up and he knew a better and quicker way to his house and so it went on. By this time I was completely lost and was now at the mercy of these (taking the micky) passengers. I had now just two people left on the bus and had just dropped the second from last one off when a lady jumped on the bus and said, I didn't know the bus company had started a new route out here? When I explained I had got myself lost and the passengers were helping me with the route, she gave a loud screech, jumped back off again and watched as she walked up the road shaking her head and in fits of laughter. What's the matter with her I asked the last man on the bus? Oh, she's a bit of a head case that one; she is like the village idiot. Ok I said, how do I get back on my route. Well first the main said, you can drop me off at the end of this road and I'll put you on the right route. As I drew up where the man requested he moaned, just my luck, my mate who normally picks me up every morning is not here, so if you don't mind could you drop me near my house? It's only about a mile away. Ok I said but you must point me in the right direction to get back on my route. Trust me, he replied (I wondered if he, and the other passengers had seen a big sign across my forehead in neon lights that read "idiot"). Within five minutes I found myself on an isolated dirt track. Hold on I said, I cannot take this bus up this track, it may get stuck. Don't worry mate, he calmly said, the track opens up shortly. Did I also have "gullible fool" written across my forehead? This is where I get off mate, he shouted, thanks very much for taking me home. Now if you carry on with this road (did he not mean dirt track? It will get you onto the main highway and you'll know you're way from there. Within seconds he had disappeared from sight. Well at least I'll be able to get back on my route! Carrying on up the track, I noticed a farm house to my left, but more worryingly beyond the farmhouse the track finished once again. I was like a rabbit caught in car headlights, rooted to the spot and in a complete shock. Oh dear, or words to that effect, I muttered to myself, I'm in big trouble here, I cannot turn this large bus around as the banks on either side of the track were raised and I could not reverse the bus all the way back as I found it difficult enough driving forward. Now John, don't panic, lets take stock of the situation, you cannot go forward or back, so another solution must be found, but what? I have the answer I'll scream!! But hey, I'll see if the farmer is at home and maybe he can help me. And if he's not in then I am in big trouble. As I stepped off the bus a huge man was standing there, is this a new bus route, he said with a grin?? Ha, ha, how very droll I thought to myself. I explained to him how

I had got lost and had literally been taken for a ride by the passengers. Well mate he said, I may be able to help you, but it's going to cost you 10 rand for me to get my tow truck. Although 10rand was two days pay then how could I argue? That's OK I said, alright I'll get my big tow truck out, the one if lift my tractors and farm machinery, I will hook it onto the front of the bus and hopefully be able to lift it up and spin it around, facing the other way. But be warned, it could damage the front suspension as I have never lifted something so heavy. Just do it I said in a nervous voice, what will be will be I said boldly. I'll be quite a while he said, my pick up truck is housed in a barn a fair way from here so don't go anywhere while I'm away will you, he chuckled. Ho ho, very funny I don't think. All I could do now was sit and wait in my driver's seat and wonder what the outcome to this nightmare would be. I then drifted into a deep sleep and remembered in my dream like state phoning the bus manager Mr Hill and explaining the situation that I found myself in and the conversation went something like this:

(me) can I speak to the manager Mr Hill

(Mr Hill) Mr Hill Speaking, how can I help?

(Me) This is driver Banfield and I'm phoning about my bus

(Mr hill) why would you want to talk to me about your bus?

(me) well I'm phoning you because I had a problem with my bus

(Mr hill) if you have a problem with your bus, you should be speaking to the engineers in the workshop

(me) yes in normal circumstances I would need them, but this is not your normal problem sir

(Mr hill) (Now getting a bit angry) what are you talking about man? Spit it out so what is this so called problem?

(me) well sir, I'll be as brief as I can it's quite a long story

(Mr hill) get on with it man, I haven't got all day

(me) well sir, I was assigned number 18b bus today as you may know, it's a difficult route for a new driver and I must admit I got lost and was given false directions by some very unpleasant and shady passengers and to cut a long story short ended up on a dirt road that went nowhere and found to my dismay I could go neither back or forward as the dirt track became so narrow.

(Mr Hill) what the hell were you doing on a dirt road?

(me) as I have explained to you sir, some passengers gave me the wrong directions

(Mr hill) Well Banfield, it appears you are a complete idiot and a moron and also a half-wit and seemed to got yourself in a right mess and you don't seem to have even half a brain and it's my opinion you haven't a clue how to get out of the situation you find yourself in so give me your exact location and I will get the fitters with a tow truck to get you off that track.

(me) there will be no need for a tow truck Mr hill as I used my initiative and asked a farmer to help me and he kindly said he would use his own tow truck to turn me around.

(Mr hill) well Banfield if he used his own tow truck and was able to turn you around why the hell are you phoning me?

(me) that's the reason I am phoning you to inform you the farmer was able to get his chains attached around the front suspension bar of the bus and lifted the front of the bus very successfully but unfortunately as he lifted the bus completely off the ground the front suspension snapped, but Mr hill you still have a bus but the front end is no longer attached to the back end because the front end of the bus fell right on top of a police car that was called to investigate why a bus was stuck up a dirt road and unfortunately Mr hill it completely crushed it and to make matters worse the back half of the bus is now sitting on top of the farmhouse roof and the farmhouse roof is now where the front room was. I know this is a state of the art brand new bus but accidents to happen, I'm hoping this little incident won't affect my future employment prospects with the bus company.

(Mr hill) I cannot believe what I'm hearing as my day couldn't get any worse because only this morning my wife walked out on me and has gone to live with a man twenty years younger than her but I'm not too bothered, maybe we could meet up for a drink tonight as I find you quite an attractive young man! I don't know if it was the prospect that I was about to become gay or the voice of the farmer shouting, Driver wake up. But I woke up from my heavy dream sweating profusely with the farmer saying I'm ready to do the lifting now. Well if this all goes wrong the worst the bus company can do to me is give me the sack or then again castration could take place so it's going to be an achievement or disaster. The farmer certainly knew how to handle a long armed jib because within seconds he had the bus lifted up and turned completely the right way with no damage done to any part of the bus. No how am I going to explain being about three hours late on my bus route to my manager! Help was at hand from an unexpected source in the form of the farmer. Hey, listen, the farmer shouted, I have had a word with my eldest son and we have come up with a plan of how you can get over the problem of how you became late on your bus route. This is the plan, I think you will agree it is a good one: my son will set off down the track and you follow him, when he gets to the edge of town he will pull up and you stop behind him. He will then proceed to hammer a large nail into your front tyre, you then phone the manager and explain you have a puncture and have had to walk two miles to get to the nearest phone and as you have no passengers on board its the perfect story. After paying the farmer his fee for getting me out of the mess I thanked him for being so helpful and friendly and for coming up with such a devious story. The farmer's son duly carried out the scam by banging a large nail into the tyre. It deflated within seconds. He then drove me to a telephone box and shaking me by the hand said, it's been nice doing business with you. All my fears vanished when I phoned Mr Hill and explained about getting lost and then picking up a puncture and his reply was, don't worry about it John, you're not the first driver to get lost on that route and you won't be the last and as for the puncture I will send someone out to you right away. Phew that's a relief; I thought he was going to chew by balls off. It wasn't long before the tow truck turned up; the fitter took one look at the tyre and said are you sure you didn't bang that nail in yourself, so that you could have an easy day? He seemed to have hit the nail right on top of the head so to speak. He towed the bus away to the workshop and I heard no more about the matter.

Poem

Just one hour into my route I lost my way

This was going to be such a very long day

How did I manage to end up on a dirt track?

It then became one of those days to hell and back

Think I will ask for help now from this farmer

Hope he will be able to help in this unfolding drama

The lift was successful it cost me just ten rand

That farmer saved my job by giving me a hand

The weeks went by and I started to really enjoy the job and after a while got to know all the routes and you get to know many of the passengers. Mrs Robinson was one such passenger she was a nursing sister that worked *night shifts and I used to pick her up every morning after her shift as she used to be the only person on board and we used to chat. It turned out that she was divorced and had been for a few years and admitted to me she was quite lonely. So taking the bull by the horns I said to her how can an attractive young lady like you be so lonely you must have men queuing up wanting to take you out? Well that's where you're wrong, what with my shift work I don't get to meet people. Well, I quickly said, I would love to take you out. Before I could finish the sentence she interjected why would a young man like you want to take me out? I'm old enough to be your mother. You must have young girls queuing up wanting to go out with you? Not at all I said, I am like you, on shift work I don't get to meet people I lied and anyway I think you are a very attractive and interesting lady, oh thank you, that's very sweet of you she said. We agreed to meet at the weekend, when we would both be off work. She introduced herself as Pam. We met as arranged on the Saturday morning at a coffee bar in town. Pam looked so sophisticated and chic, she certainly new how to dress stylish. We talked about everything on that first date and were getting on like a house on fire until I asked the question: how old are you Pam? Her mood changed from being very pleasant and bubbly. Why is it that men always want to know a woman's age? Oh dear, I've hit a sore point, here I think I had better redeem myself. And in my best grovelling voice I meekly said, you have told me Pam, that you have been nursing for years and I thought, that's not possible as you only look like you're in your early thirties (I figured out she was probably in her early fifties) Flattery will get you everywhere she smiled but John, the golden rule is that a man never asks a woman her age. Point taken and remembered, I found myself thinking. After getting on to such a bad start with Pam we became very good friends and I have to say nature had been very kind to Pam, not only was her face unlined her body parts were still very firm and had not dropped the dreaded inches and still with silky naturally dark hair. She was a picture of health. I met up with her and was due to take her to a drive in move one Saturday evening, why don't you introduce me to your friends she asked? Are you ashamed to be seen with me? Of course not my passion flower I replied, so instead of going to the movies we met up with my friends in the 1820's club. They had told me that the dragon no longer went there. I had already told them about Pam and the age difference between us and had taken so much stick from them. Among some of the nicer comments were, do old lady pensioners turn you on? And did you meet her at a grab a granny tea dance? I introduced Pam to them and they were all gentlemen to her on the night, but of course when I saw them the next day they all asked why I was taking out the oldest great granny in town.*

I was still doing different shifts on the buses the one I preferred best was the early one which was the 6am to 2pm one. The other one was 2pm to 10pm. On one of the late shifts I had reached the end of the route where I did my turn round to return back to Durban. I was about five miles out of town and I made my first stop on the way home. That night the rain was lashing down as I approached to the stop. To my dismay I saw a crowd of Bantu (black people) queuing waiting to get on (the rule in them days was you were only allowed to fill the six rows both sides of the back seats with either Bantu, Indian or coloured people, all the rest of the seats were exclusively for whites) The six back seats held about twenty people and the whole bus held up to seventy five passengers. As I counted the twenty Bantu on, I said that's it sorry but the black seats are full. Oh, boss, please, please let us on, we are all soaked through and you are the last bus tonight. I could see the desperation and despair in their eyes and it was then that I made up my mind; they're all coming aboard how can I leave my fellow human beings out in them appalling conditions. All right, I said you can all come on. Thank you, thank you, the ones who could talk English shouted, I felt great seeing the happiness and joy on their faces. By the time they had all got on there was only about two vacant seats left on the bus. That will be alright I thought to myself, I have done this same route a few times and on the return trip very rarely pick up anyone with only about ten minutes to go before the last stop and three stops from the end. I would see white people waiting to come on as they got on board, I saw the look of horror and disbelief on their faces. A big mean looking fat slob shouted, why have you filled the bus with blacks?? You know the rules. Throw them off, we have got nowhere to sit man, I'm sorry, I firmly said, they have paid their fares and I cannot throw them off, I let them on because of the appalling weather conditions. You should have picked none of them up, like most of the driver's fat slob shouted, but you being a roeneck, you just don't understand, well I said two of you can sit down. We are not sitting with Kaffers you kaffer lover, he screeched. I thought this is where fat slob is about to rip the head from my body. There must have been about twelve white passengers who got on and one of them came to my rescue. I'm a police officer and I don't want any trouble on this bus, what's done is done and I agree with the driver, he cannot throw these people off, maybe he should not have let them all on, but as they have paid their fares so if you people that have just got on don't want to stand for the rest of the journey, I suggest that you leave the bus. That little speech seemed to have done the trick because fat slob quietened down. All the rest of them were not happy but all stood the rest of the journey. I was quite pleased fat slob had not attacked me as I had got used to my head being attached to my shoulders for the past twenty seven years. I would still meet piers down at Addington beach and ride the waves with him. Addington beach was exclusively for the use of white people only; all other races had their own segregated beaches. The Indians had their own part of a beach area, the coloured population beach was next to theirs with the Bantus (black Zulus) having their own beach a bit further away. No different race was allowed on any other races beach. It was also the same with seats in the parks; these were for whites only, unless it had written on it that said "non-whites only". Non-whites could not go in to cinemas, restaurants, pubs or clubs, they were barred from everything and had no rights whatsoever but these were the dark days of apartheid. Most of the African Zulus lived in the natal area and supplied the majority of the workforce for Durban and the surrounding districts. The few Afrocans that lived in Durban were either nannies looking after white peoples gardens and houses. They would have there own quarters within the house and in many cases became part of the family but the vast majority lived in townships that surrounded Durban and every morning made the trip by train to work and late evening return back to their homes or shacks in the townships They were a very cheap and ready workforce. A white person could earn in a week what it would take an African six weeks to earn. But as history shows you cannot hold people down by force forever and with the unrest and uprising that followed change was only a matter of time and it was all down to one man and that was nelson Mandela.

Poem

What a great man he was this hero nelson Mandela
Brought much needed change to his homeland a splendid fellow
Locked up in Robin Island for well over twenty years
Just sitting in prison with his hopes and his fears
Planning how he would lead his country from his cell
And was finally pardoned and released from that awful jail
After becoming the president his job was to unite the races
All men should be equal whatever the colour of their faces
A legend in his lifetime awarded the Nobel peace prize
This man of the people so very worldly and wise

Long Neck comes aboard

I was half way through my early morning shift and was making my way out of Durban in one of the trips that was about a thirty mile round trip and getting ready to stop at the second bus stop on the trip as I pulled in I recognised a face that would be very hard to forget, Yes it was the dragon lady, she was third in the queue and had not noticed me yet. What do I do? Do I stop and let her on or as I am a born coward just put my foot down and get the hell out of there. But with about five people wanting to get off I was forced to stop. The passengers whose stop it was alighted. Just what do I say to her, there's no hiding place, and I'll just have to play it by ear. The first in the queue paid his fare as the second passenger was paying his fare she looked straight at me it's you John she shouted, where have you been? How come you're driving a bus? I was totally tongue tied, more in shock than anything, all I could say was where are you going? Pinetown she blurted out, then that will be seventy five cents please I said in a harsh voice. I'm going to see my granny, but on second thoughts I think I will do the round trip with you and find out why you have been avoiding me all this time.> Well if you want to do the round trip that will cost you two rand and to my horror she promptly paid up and sat down in the front seat nearest to my seat and then it started. Cross examining me the questions were coming at me thick and fast, I just don't understand you're friends all told me you had met the girl of your dreams and you loved me! And wanted to settle down with a girl like me! Strange as it may seem the Kinks wrote a song at that time and it was called "I want to spend my life with a girl like you". Have you ever wanted a big hole to appear and swallow you up? Well this was one of those times. I realised this problem was not going away so to give me thinking time I thought I would pacify her a little, it's best we don't talk now as I am concentrating on driving, so we will talk when I have finished the shift. OK she said, but I want an explanation. She looked quite menacing and reminded me of a time bomb ready to explode and them words of wisdom from my hero the bard came to mind. "Hell hath no fury like a woman scorned" So John boy, you have got to tread very carefully on this one. I had dropped the last passenger off and on my route display screen flicked it to show "depot only" with droop eye still sitting there. I still did not have a clue what I was going to say to her. As I approached the depot I said, you get out here and I will meet you in the soda bar across the road. I duly parked the bus in its bay and walked over to the soda bar. As I got nearer to it I was saying to myself be bold John, don't be intimidated by her. She's only a woman. Tell her she's an ugly old cow and to get lost. As I entered the soda bar I noticed droop eyes light up and as I sat down next to her she let fly at me, why have you been avoiding me? That's the second time she's asked me that. All I could say in reply was, err, erm, I have not been avoiding you at all, I have been working up country and haven't been back to Durban for ages. Well that's a lie for a start, she snapped, your friends told me that you packed the railway job in when you came out of hospital. "Ouch" how do I get out of that one? And another thing, your friends told me how much you loved me and wanted to settle down with the girl of your dreams. I suppose that's a lie as well?? She was now in full flow. I have been searching all over Durban for you and I cannot believe I have found you driving a bus! Come on Johnny boy, now's the time to go on the attack, stop being Mr Nice guy and make sure she won't want to see you again, be bold. Look, lady, my friends have been leading you up the garden Path, they are drunk most of the time and would just be having you on. I never said I love you, the only person I love is myself and the only settling down I want to do is with a crate of beer, laying on the beach and anyway I have a girlfriend so why would I want to take you out? I had to be cruel to be kind because I realised if I didn't give her the elbow now she would forever be hanging around the bus depot like a demented groupie. She was looking at me opened mouthed, I could see tears welling up in her eyes but my tactics paid off because she stood up, pulled her arm up and gave me one almighty slap round the face with her man sized hand and shouted, you bastard then turned around and stormed out. Boy was my face stinging but as the bard might have said "no pain, no gain". A sore face was well worth the price for seeing the last of her.

Poem

Oh what a beautiful morning driving down the esplanade way
Was on top of the world on that glorious day
I just cannot believe it, that's Miss ugly I fear
Could be seen for miles in her old fashioned gear
Catching a glance of her recognised that flea ridden hair
Those jumping hopping flying fleas would make any man stare
I have found you John it's now just me and you
Knew that we were made for each other just us two
Sat her down at the soda bar I must be bold
She's about to be dumped and she must be told
I will ditch the thing and she will be dispatched

How could she think we were the perfect match?
A smack in the face was a small price to pay
Her going was just heaven a time for rejoicing I'd say

I was still seeing Pam on a regular basis and one evening, she asked me if I would like to meet a great aunt of hers who lived just around the corner from her flat. Why do you want me to see her I enquired? Well John, she is a very special lady and has an amazing gift. She then went on to explain that her aunt was able to read tea leafs when a person had drunk a cup of tea. That sounds interesting I said, but thinking what a load of rubbish, still anything for a laugh. When we arrived at her house I was quite surprised at her aunt's appearance. I was expecting to see a little grey haired old lady with a black shawl wrapped around her shoulders. Instead I was surprised to find a young at heart and quite an attractive woman. Ah this is the young man you have been telling me about Pam. After exchanging small talk for a while she said, right lets get down to business. Right Pam, make the tea and use loose tea with no strainer. Have I been set up? And has this all been pre-planned, was the first thing that came into my mind. As I had finished my tea first, Pam's aunt had my cup in her hands and within seconds she was swilling the tea leafs around the cup in a circular motion and I could hear a faint chanting. Ye gods, this woman is a loony witch I decided. After studying my tea cup for a while the lady turned to me and said, young man, I see a large ship in your tea leaves and you will be sailing on it and it shows me it will be a long journey. On hearing this I was quite taken aback as I was told the same thing by the three medium ladies which I attended with the journalist John Wall a few months ago, how spooky! And having been told this the last time and yet once again I dismissed it as nonsense as I had no intentions at that time of going anywhere. We said our good byes to Pam's aunt and made our way back to Pam's flat. On the way Pam turned to me and said, I didn't know you were leaving South Africa, you have kept that pretty quiet! Don't be silly Pam I calmly replied, how can some one look at tea leafs and predict what's going to happen to them its absolute rubbish as far as I'm concerned. You may believe it but I don't. Well John, I can tell you my aunts readings are normally very accurate, she said crossly and only time will tell on this one.

The Undercover Inspectors

I had now been a bus driver for six months and was really enjoying the job with a varied shift-work Pattern you were able to meet the early morning commuters on the early ships and the late night ones on the night shifts. Unbeknown to me the bus company employed inspectors whose job was to assess how the bus crews were performing in their duties i.e. were they polite and courteous to passengers, did they have any attitude problems and did they have a happy or sharp disposition. I always tried to be friendly to passengers and be as helpful as possible. Sometimes I would be travelling as a passenger myself and would in many cases see how rude and aggressive some of the drivers were to people and in one case one driver swore at a lady and had her in tears because she didn't have the right change on her. I had finished my early shift one day and was having a cup of tea in the canteen and saw the shift manager coming towards me. Oh, no, what have I done now, was my first thought. Hi John, were his first words, when you've finished your tea and before you sign off can you come up to the personal office, we would like to see you. Oh, dear, I don't like the sound of this. I made my way to the office and a voice said, come in driver Banfield, close the door and sit down. As I sat down I noticed in front of me a large circular table with five people sitting around it, one of them being a woman. The general manager spoke first, right driver Banfield, just relax, now we have a few points to discuss with you. Firstly we have had some complaints about you, allowing non-whites to fill all available seats on one of your night shift routes, and as you know this is not permitted in the rules and regulations of this bus company, what have you got to say about this? I was quite taken aback by the question as I had no idea why I was sitting before the panel. So this is why I'm here for, oh well, if I'm going to be sacked for it, so be it, but I will leave with all guns blazing, "in for a penny, in for a pound". Yes I did fill my bus up with non-whites on that night and the reason I did so was because the bus was empty at the time and those poor souls were standing in the pouring rain soaked through and cold and to leave them there would have been callous and cruel. OK you have explained your reasons for filling your bus full of non-whites he said, now tell me what your thoughts are about the passengers who complained about your actions. (Well if I am about to be sacked I might as well shoot from the hip) to me those passengers who complained to you have no feelings or compassion for those fellow men and I feel disgusted and quite upset by their attitude. I could see from all busy writing things down on papers in front of them it was now the turn of the assistant manager to question me. As well as having complaints about your actions that night we have had some letters from passengers praising your good manners and helpfulness and your happy disposition, he went on, well driver Banfield, my colleagues and I have listened to your comments for allowing your bus to be filled with non-whites and also the reasons, so now driver Banfield we would like you to wait outside this office so we can discuss your comments. After waiting about ten minutes I was called back into the office and the general manager spoke. We all take the view that you took the right action although it is not in the bus company's rules to do so. But that is not the main reason you are here. It may be a surprise to you to learn that we would like to offer you the job as a tour bus driver. As you may know, this involves taking tourists to places of interest and beauty spots. We all feel you have proved to us that you get on well with people which are very important in this touring roll. OF course there is no shift work involved, it's a nine-to-five job and of course you will be on a different pay structure that a bus route driver and it will be a higher salary than you are now earning, so what we would like you to do now is think about the offer and let us know by the end of the week. No need to wait for the end of the week, sir I said, I accept the job, I blurted out.

Poem

Called into the office again now that's never much fun
Now what's a matter this time what have I done
Filling my bus with Zulus they call them non-whites
But surely there human they have got their rights
Offered a job tour bus driving right up my Street
No longer fare paying passengers its tourists I'll meet
At least now I won't ever be in that awkward position
Judging people by their colour it's what you call partition

Tour Bus Driver

Being a tour bus driver was a complete change to being a one-man operator driver. There were no fares to take or tickets to issue. All tickets were purchased by tourists at the Durban bus office or other outlets. The main attraction in the natal area and the place most tourists wanted to see was the "valley of the thousand hills" where Zulus fought the might of the British army in the late ninetieth century. The other venues they wanted to see were game reserves. The hardest part of the job was learning all the history of the place you were visiting and you had to relay all the facts about a place from a microphone just above your had. I received two weeks training, sitting next to an experienced tour driver, while he was explaining all the facts and the history to tourists on different tours. After two weeks of training I was quite confident that I was ready for the challenge. Before I was allowed out on my own I had to have the experience driver sitting near me to remind me of the route and to prompt me if I had forgotten my lines. The training week with the experienced driving soon came to an end and I absorbed as much information in my head as I could and making sure I took notes to get all the facts right. The Monday came around and this was to be my first time on my own. I called into the office to see what trip I would be doing. As I walked in the manager greeted me by saying, we have a prestige assignment for your first tour driver Banfield, and it is to drive the springbok rugby team around for two weeks between their training ground and the hotel they are staying in. You will also be driving the French Rugby team around. There will be another driver working with you so sometimes you will take the French team about. He then will take the springbok team around. I duly arrived at Durban airport to await the springboks who were flying in from Pretoria. There was a small crowd waiting to greet them and the aircraft door opened. The steps were placed in position. It nearly took my breath away for coming down the steps was the biggest bears I have ever seen. All of the rugby players were enormous, everyone well over six feet tall and was wide as barrels a frightening sight. As the first player boarded my coach he greeted me in Afrikaans ----------, when I replied in English, he was very annoyed. I would make out the word Redneck, followed by a lot of swear words in Afrikaans (it's funny how you always pick up the swear words of a foreign language) The manager of the rugby players heard the swearing and said to me in English, this is an insult, we should have had an Afrikaner driving us, I shall be taking this up with the rugby board. I guess they had a point, as the whole team were made up of Afrikaans and they should have been driven by one of their own and not by a foreigner. Each one of the players was so huge they had to duck their heads to walk up the aisle of the bus. Most of these rugby players were Afrikaan farmers and just like Lions. Formidable in a pack with the strength and speed to eat up anyone in their way. Watching them at the training ground I knew that the French rugby side were in for a hammering. The next day it was my turn to pick up the French team from their hotel. As I got my first sight of them I thought I was picking up a football team, only two of them were six footers all the rest were stocky but quite small. I knew that they would be squashed by the much larger springbok team. The first test match in Durban proved the point because the French side were beaten sixty points to three and in the other tests were also beaten.

The Schooner

My favourite trip was the valley of the thousand hills and in particular taking the tourists to see the site of Rorkes drift. This is where three thousand Zulu warriors surrounded a British fort, which had about six hundred defenders. The soldiers were mainly made up of a Welsh regiment and a few natal frontier scouts. The battle raged from morning to dusk and lasted for three days. Zulu warrior bodies were piled high next to the fort but the defenders refused to give up. They had lost three quarters of their men and the end was nearly up for them but suddenly the Zulus withdrew a few hundred feet and all turned towards the fort and all smacked their shears against their shields and started signing Zulu songs that signified the respect and bravery of their enemy and then turned away and left the battle. On that last day both sides had tremendous admiration for each other as they had all lost so many. Seven Victoria crosses were won in that siege, the highest amount ever won in any battle.

Every two weeks a passenger liner would arrive in Durban from Southampton, packed out with immigrants. Some would get off in Durban to settle in South Africa, the remainder would carry on with the ship which would be making its way to Australia or New Zealand. Durban was the half way stop for these ships so they would take on fuel and provisions and stay in port for forty eight hours before setting sail. I with three other buses would wait at the docks for the ships arrival then take the passengers on different tours in the natal area. I myself had arrived on the one of these ships eighteen months earlier so knew then how excited everyone on board was feeling. The passengers that were continuing their journey were the ones who wanted to go on the trips. As they boarded my bus I would welcome them aboard and as soon as they realised I was from the UK would be asking me how I liked it over here and have I settled in OK and they would then tell me about the hopes and dreams that they were expecting in either one of the new countries that awaited them. On some of these tours just before the end of the trip, a passenger would go down the bus collecting tips for the driver; I would make so much in tips I never had to open my wages, so money wise I was quite well off. My flat mate Ron and I decided to go for a drink one night at a tavern near the beach front. The customers who visited there were made up of lots of sailors from all over the world, these were merchant navy sailors from large tankers to cruise ships and you would normally have a great night hearing about all their adventures and exploits. As we entered the place I noticed how crowded the tavern was. As we sat down we got chatting to two lads, they were telling us they were crewing a schooner that had been built in Southampton and that where they signed on as crew members. The schooner had been brought by a very wealthy client in Australia and they were delivering it to him. There were ten crew members and they had an agreement that they could all fly home to the United Kingdom when the ship was delivered or apply to the Australian immigration people to see if they would be allowed to settle. They went on to explain that they had made their first and only stop in Durban which had taken them twenty one days at sea and were here to restock provisions. Jim was the younger of the two and he had signed off the ship that day as he was going to settle down in Durban and was having a last drink with his crew mates. As the drinks started flowing I was explaining to all the other crew members who had now joined us how I had always wanted to be a sailor and sail the seven seas. Well your wish could come true, shouted one crew, Jim has left the ship today so we are looking for someone to replace him, and do you fancy it a middle aged suntanned man said? Who turned out to be the skipper of the schooner. Erm, err; the words would not come out! Because if you are interested we are sailing tomorrow morning at about 6am, all you will need is your passport and a few clothes, you don't get paid but you get all your food and get the chance to sail half way round the world for free. I turned to Ron, what do you think, should I go or what?? Ron's words of wisdom were if you fancy it, go for it but remember John, you have a very good paying Job now which you seem to enjoy but you're only young once and this is a lifetime opportunity. That's it then Ron I excitedly shouted, I'm going to be a sailor! I need a new challenge anyway. I then went over to the captain and said, I would like to be one of your crew. He then shook my hand and shouted out loud, right lads, meet your new crew member, John and as he sat me down, told me all about the tasks that I would be expected to carry out, mainly preparing food in the gallery which sounded a great job. As it was past midnight I decided I had better return to the flat as I would not get up in time for my new adventure so Ron and I said our farewells to the crew and I promised to see them in the morning. As we made our way back to the flat, I said to Ron, I think I will get to the ship at 5am, instead of 5.30 just in case it leaves early. The next morning I threw my worldly possessions into a large bad, making sure I had my passport and set off to the docks. Ron had kindly agreed to see me off and to make sure that my work was informed and my bank details were sorted out and forwarded on to where ever I ended up. Just then doubts started to kick in, was it the drink doing the talking last night? What am I doing? I'm leaving a good paying job, I have made many good friends and I like living here. And here I am, facing the unknown. But the voice in my head won the day, it was saying listen John, nothing ventured nothing gained and what have you got to lose? So with a spring in my step we set off to the docks. It was about a twenty minute walk and just as we were about to enter the dock, I became a little nervous but also very excited, Ron said, this is it John, you're new life starts here. By now I was deep in thought, thinking what might be when Ron's voice brought me back out of my day dreams. I cannot see the schooner, he shouted, where is it? Oh, it's probably around the other side of the dock, I said quite confidently, so we walked to the other side of the docks and low and behold there were no ships of any sort moored at the berths. Something's wrong here Ron, shouted, I just don't understand it. Where the bloody hell is it? I know I ill find the harbour master and he will tell me where it is. As it was still only 5:15am I knew it was not due to sail till 6am. We found the harbour master standing outside his office. Good morning lads, are you looking for something he said, yes can you tell us where the schooner Annabelle is moored? The Annabelle he said with a smile on his face is the dot you can see on the horizon over there. What I shouted, it cannot be! It was not due to sail until 6am. Yes that's correct he said, but the tide turned early so the captain decided to leave earlier than planned, what about me I cried I'm supposed to be one of the crew. Well you won't be now will you he chuckled, it was not meant to be, just put it down to experience and walked back into his office. I think it had really made his day. A case of one mans misfortune another mans glee. Never mind John Ron said showing genuine sympathy, it may have worked out, but then again you may have not liked it out there and you may have wished you had stayed put (such wisdom and common sense from someone only twenty three years of age). I of course was very disappointed to have not sailed but it just wasn't to be and I looked at it as fate and as the bard would say "to be or not to be" and this proved it was not to be.

Poem

Have always wanted to be a sailor going to sea
Hoping a voyage of discovery this is going to be
I'll be joining up with the yacht at the docks
But in life you must learn to take the knocks
The sky had just lightened up daytime was just dawning
That yacht had sailed without me on that grey morning
Looking out to sea I could still see the yacht
In the blink of my eye it became a tiny dot

As the morning was breaking it would soon be light
All my hopes and dreams were disappearing out of sight
It changed my whole life the morning that yacht cast
But life's not about regrets its now in the past
Now a dot on the radar screen just a small blip
It's all just history now and so was that trip.

For the next few months I carried on with my tour bus driving and having a great social life but felt something was missing. I met up with Jim Gregg in a bar one night and we were discussing how things were and how our lives were in general. And Jim happened to mention that he was thinking about rejoining his wife back in Britain as he was missing married life and like me found that Durban had everything a man could want but there was that something missing. It could have been home sickness kicking in. As the drinks started to flow Jim said do you fancy going home? Because I've made up my mind I will be going home and it would be great if you could accompany me on the trip. I'm thinking of going back on the best ship in the fleet, the "Windsor castle", what do you reckon John? We could have seventeen days of fun filled days on that liner. The more the drinks flowed the more the idea of a cruise appealed to me. Jim knew my weak spot and this was I could be talked into anything and with drink in me I was putty in his hands. On that night it was agreed that we would both book up together in a month's time which would be the middle of October and by that time we could both pay our flat rents up to date and give our work notices in. The month went so quickly and it was the eve of Jim and myself departure. We had arranged for all our friends to meet us in a bar for a final send off party, you don't realise how many friends you have until they are all together. Good friends in life become like family so it is very hard to say your good byes to them. But we all face this sometimes in our lives. The leaving party went with a bang, the day of sailing a few of our friends were able to come and see us off and it was the last time we saw our friends, a sad day indeed.

Poem

The African sunrise and sunset magnificent in all it's glory
Displaying a blaze of colour in this never ending story
This is heaven on earth in this amazing beautiful land
A golden treasure chest discovered like that grain of sand
Early morning in all it's splendour from its sleep has awoken

Watching those acrobatic larks soaring dawn at last has broken
Them eager birds on the wing I watch them fly
As the rising sun casts magical pictures in the sky
Farewell my African odyssey the time has come to depart
I do so with many regrets and a heavy heart.

This South Africa

How do I even try to start summing up this amazing country with Johannesburg to the east a fine modern city and then to it's south lies cape-town a beautiful place with a temperate climate with the backdrop of table mountain no wonder early explorers named it "the fair cape" with thousands of miles golden beaches with views to take your breath away. Then up from Capetown on the east coast is Durban, a sub-tropical mix of all races and the warm Indian Ocean with Zulu people making up the population. A happy people with the most amazing singing voices. My best memories of this nation would be when I was working on the railways next to the Tugela river and one morning watching the sun rise showing the beauty of the Veldt and in the evening watching the sunset and the poem above summed it all up for me.

Both Jim and I found ourselves walking up the gang plank of a very stylish and beautiful ship. It was one of the most modern liners afloat and it was called the Windsor Castle, the pride of the Union Castle fleet.

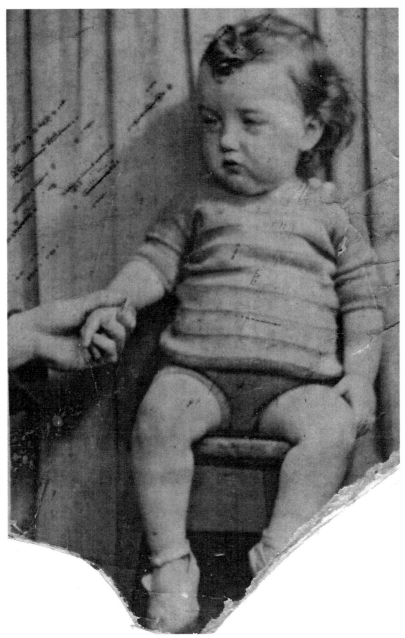

Baby Picture

Herne Bay 1955

School of Military Survey Boys 1960 – Author back row – 4th from the left

Army 1960

PRETORIA CASTLE

Enroute to Durban 1965

Durban 1966

Durban 1966

Sept 1973 - Devon

August 1974 – Guns at War Museum London

My family May 2008

The Windsor Castle

As Jim and I were shown to our cabin we wondered who else would be sharing it with us as we had booked economy class. The cabins in that class were for four people. We were pleasantly surprised to find just one more person was to be our cabin mate. He was a Scot named Alex and was the same age as us. He had been working in Durban for three years and had decided threes years of constant sunshine was just about all he could take. We all became firm friends but by looking at his appearance you would be forgiven for thinking he had spent the last three years working in a weather station at the North Pole. His face was a deadly white, even a ghost on meeting him would have turned around and bolted, thinking he was a living ghost! As with the outward voyage it took seventeen days to reach Southampton and we all intended to enjoy every minute of it. As with most cruises the day and nights fall into Pattern i.e. drinking, gambling and filling your face with food and then more drinking and the cycle just repeats itself. It's not long before you get to know your fellow passengers and the majority of them were returning Brits going home for holidays or returning permanently to the UK. But some were people who had come out on the £15 assisted passage scheme and had a few weeks holiday and were now returning home. They had found a scam to have a holiday on the cheap. As you get to know your fellow passengers you also get to know some of the crew members and as I was recalling my trip out to South Africa on the Edinburgh Castle and that the boxer Jock Kierney had died in my cabin. They knew Jock very well and remembered happy drinking times with him when he was a crew member. They said how bizarre it was to be meeting me as I was the last one to see him alive. Right up till the middle eighties British merchant and cruise whips were manned by British seamen but in the late eighties to save money shipping lines took on foreign crews so now there are only a few British crew members left, mainly first officers and captains. The moment I stepped aboard the ship I seemed to be getting strange stares and nods as if people knew me. All was revealed when a passenger came up to me and said you were the best player for Durban united this season, I hope your not going home and signing for a club in the UK. What the hell is he talking about? All I could do was give him a blank frown and my best simpleton look. I'm sorry I replied I think you must have got me mixed up with someone else. Well stone the crows he said, you are the spitting image of a footballer that plays for Durban United. Well they do say that everyone has a double and this footballer must have been mine. It did not matter what time of the day it was, there would always be something going on most of the day and well into the night. There would be a lecture being held in the theatre, or a beauty contest but Jim, Alex and I found what we liked doing the best and that was playing cards. The card games we started playing were three card brag poker or nine card brag. At first we were playing between ourselves and then a couple of other passengers would ask what we were playing and asked if we could teach them. As we were all quite flushed (sorry about the pun) with money the three of us were able to put decent bets on our card hands. We had been playing for two days when first class passengers who had just been to a lecture were passing through the lounge bar near where we used to play. What are you playing there lads, a well spoken man said in a rather clipped tone. After we explained the game to him he asked if he and his friends could join in. Yes of course you can we said. So we set about explaining how the game of three card and nine card brag as well as poker was played. The ladies in their party were all jolly jockey sticks type of gals; they were more likely to have been boarders at Cheltenham Ladies College when younger. Oh gosh, one of them shrieked, this looks awfully good fun. But despite their toffee nosed accents they were very good company and rather than use the facilities of first class they spent all their time with all us low life's in second class. As one of them put it, they are all a lot of boring stuck up sods in first class but they had never met anyone like Jim, myself and Alex in all their lives but as John Wall the journalist used to say about Jim and I, you two are just a pair of "barrow boys" and that probably summed us both up. The journey time from Durban to Cape-town takes five days. The ship stops off at East London and Port Elizabeth to take on and let off passengers sailing into Capetown is an outstanding sight with a beautiful natural harbour and the magnificent table mountain overlooking Capetown. Twenty four hours after entering Capetown the ship is once again on its way. The next port of call is Las-Palmas in the Canary Islands, off the North West coast of Africa and this takes ten days of sailing to reach. As Jim, Alex and I watched Capetown slowly disappearing on the horizon; my thoughts went back to when I was sailing into Capetown and the tragic death of Jock, our cabin mate on that day. It was now two days since we had sailed out from Capetown and Jim Alex and I had played cards in the evening, watched a show and stayed in the bar till closing time which was about 1am and managed to purchase a bottle of rum. We then headed up to the top deck where one of the swimming pools was located. All three of us were sharing this bottle of rum, it was so strong, and it must have been 20% proof. Just one sip caused an explosion in your stomach and then your head. Right Johnny boy, take it easy as you will be in trouble with this demon drink, a voice was saying in my head, so I eased up on it. But Jim and Alex were determined to finish the bottle. By this time I was quite merry but Jim and Alex were as drunk as lords. Alex had then decided it would be a good idea to throw deck chairs into the swimming pool followed by empty glasses that had been left on the tables. As I was trying to tell Alex that children could get injured by the broken glass in the morning when swimming and it was a stupid thing to do. I noticed from the corner of my eye what appeared to be a man walking a tightrope. On turning my head around I could not believe my eyes because there was Jim walking along the ships rail doing a balancing act with one arm sticking out seaward and in the hand of the other a glass and a half of Rum. Alex had also spotted Jim and let out a yell and I could see the horror on his face, even though I was quite merry at this time I still had my wits about me. My first thought was how the hell did Jim climb up on that rail as it is four foot high (1200mm) and my other thought was if I don't get to him quickly it will be "man overboard" because now Jim was stopping and taking a drink from the glass and carrying on walking singing at the top of his voice. I'm sure as far as he was concerned he was just walking down the corridor towards our cabin. I knew that I had to approach him from his back and try and yank him off the rail. I figured if he came in from his front he would see me and that could cause him to lose his balance. I never sobered up so quickly, and so quietly as I could, I crept behind Jim and to my horror he stared to drink from his glass without stopping, he just kept walking on, so without hesitation I sprang up and grabbed his arm and pulled him off the rail as hard as I could. He came crashing down on the deck with the glass still in his hand would you believe it, and all I got for my troubles was a mouthful of abusive language. What did you do that for he shouted, I was enjoying that. If he had fallen overboard he was so drunk he probably would have thought he was jumping into the swimming pool. But this time Alex had joined me and together we half carried and half dragged him to our cabin and somehow managed to get him onto his bunk and with seconds he was out for the count. Laying on my bunk I went through the events of that night and on how very lucky Jim was. The sea was as still as a duck pond and the ship sailed on an even keel. There is no doubt that if there had been a slight swell the boat would have been pitching just slightly and Jim would have ended up in the Indian Ocean and that would have been the end of Jim. He would have thought to himself, I know I've had a few drinks but this swimming pool seems to have got bigger somewhat. I also reminded myself that I was told by other people that I would be sailing on a ship with a friend the first lady to inform me was one of the three mediums on the stage when I attended a meeting with my friend the journalist John Wall and the other time was when Pam's aunt read tea leaves in my cup and predicted I would help a friend in some way when on board. How strange is that? The next morning in our cabin I was woken up by Jim shouting come on you two lazy sods, I'm starving he said, I could eat a whole pig and half a cow. Is this man human? Last night he had drunk so much drink it could have filled an Olympic size swimming pool and this morning he had no sign of a hangover and now all he wanted was a huge breakfast. We sat down with Jim at the breakfast table and both Alex and I were keen to know if Jim remembered last night's episode. After we both explained what took place on the night, he said, what are you two talking about you two were as drunk as skunks but I eased up on the drink he said proudly. When we explained about him walking along the hand rail that's rubbish he said, it was probably one of you doing a balancing act.

Poem

Holding ropes were let loose homeward bound we were making

A life changing journey in life we now were both taking

Jim was so lucky nearly ending up in the drink

If he had gone in would he then swim or sink

Had been drinking all night and as drunk as a lord

And would have had no chance of climbing back on board

You can thank me Jim for pulling you off that rail

And because I was sober you lived to tell the tale

Then settled in Scotland best move he ever made ye ken

And went on to have two great sons now grown men

Still waiting for him to thank me and buy me a beer

That will never happen because he's as tight as a pig's ear.

The rest of the voyage went without incident but we both kept an eye on Jim, especially if he had a glass in his hand as we did not want any more walking the rail games. Before we knew it we were sailing into Las-Palmas part of the Canary Islands and taking in a day sightseeing and then it was back on the ship and the next stop was Southampton and home with now just two days before the end of the trip. The card games were played for much higher stakes and the drinking now became non-stop. We knew we would never be doing anything like this ever again. It was our last night on board and the drinks flowed into the early hours and as everyone seems to do exchange addresses and telephone numbers but you all know no one will bother to make contact ever again. What brought me out of my deep slumber was the ships fog horn sounding off with an almighty blast. It seemed like I had only just shut my eyes.

A noise you don't want to be hearing when you have the mother of all hang over's. By the time we had all got dressed and managed a quick breakfast we looked out the portholes, Southampton docks were coming into view so making our way onto the top deck you couldn't help notice how bitterly cold it was and with the mist and fog swirling about it looked bleak and gloomy home coming. My thoughts were what have I done? Why did I leave roasting hot Durban for this freezing place? The ship duly docked at the terminal Jim and I said our goodbyes to Alex and caught the train to London. The African adventure was now well and truly over and now I was hoping to embark on a new life but what that was going to be? I had no idea only time will tell. Looking at the green fields as the train was speeding towards waterloo station, I could not help but notice, what a truly green and pleasant land this Britain really is! But was this a wise move to be returning home? Because in Durban, I had a nice flat, a good paying job and great social life and right now, sitting on this train, I have no fixed abode, I am unemployed, and have spent all of my savings, but I must not give way to such negative thoughts! And be in a positive state of mind. The train eventually pulled into waterloo station, and with butterflies pounding away in my stomach and feeling very apprehensive, and not knowing what the future held, Jim and I boarded a tube train for the journey to Paddington. As we both made our way up the escalators and onto the Street, I had that same feeling. I had all those years previously when I came up to London from Bournemouth as a young boy. Stepping onto the pavement, I noticed how dirty the buildings were, and the traffic at a near stand still and everyone rushing around like demented bees. Welcome home John! Jim and I hailed a taxi and asked to be taken to Maida vale, where Jim's wife Alma had managed to rent a flat in a leafy part of Maida vale. The taxi dropped Jim off and I carried on the journey to a tower block where my mother lived and hoping she was at home and if she was, ask if I might stay for a while, until I had got myself sorted. Fortunately she was in and agreed I could stay, as long as I liked, so that was a good start. The tower block my mother lived in was built in the middle sixties and replaced the Victorian terrace houses that stood where it was, the same old houses that as a young lad lived after coming up from Bournemouth. These tower blocks were soulless monstrosities that were twenty five stories high and a blot on the landscape. The day these blocks were erected, the community spirit died with the old terraced houses. Everyone knew each other, and helped any neighbours that found themselves fall on hard times. But in the tower blocks, once you shut your flat door, you never saw or spoke to anyone! These tower blocks were built all over Britain in the sixties and seventies and were the governments plan for the regeneration and development of the slums and the poor housing the widely existed but was a total failure and was a lesson on how not to herd people into a concrete eyesore.

Jim Gregg in the meantime had settled down well with Alma his wife in the mansions and got himself a job in an engineering company. Just off the Edgware road in Maida vale but he was not very happy working there! I now needed to find work so I went for an interview in the head office of Dewhurst the butchers. They had at that time shops in all cities and towns in the UK. I never wanted to go back and be a butcher but I needed the work and refill the bank balance and this seemed like the quickest way to achieve this and I was hoping, once I had saved enough money, get myself a better job! As I sat in the office being interviewed I was asked why I wanted to work for Dewhurst and all the other silly questions you are asked in an interview. I have always thought the best thing to do at an interview is say what you think they would like to hear¬ So when asked why I wanted to work for them again I said, I like the way this company is run and I wasn't to make something of myself within this set up and my aim would be to become a manager of this flag-ship company! I watched as the three men interviewing me relaxed back in their chairs and gave each other a nod of approval. When can you start one of them said (Cor that was easy I had them eating out of my hand). As soon as possible I replied and if I may, I would like to work with my old manager Mr James that I used to work with! No sooner I had finished, I could see the pained expressions on their faces whoops, what have I said? Why would you want to work with Mr James, the boss of the three piped in? Well I said, he was very fair with all the staff and a happy man and a gentleman and I enjoyed coming in to work everyday. For the next half an hour they were firing questions at me in all directions. Why did you like Mr James so much?? Did he do you any favours?? And was he generous in a way to you?? I just could not understand why I was being grilled so enthusiastically. Big boss spoke again What if you were not allowed to work with Mr James, would you still want to work for us?? I would be disappointed I replied but yes, I would still be very interested! OK wait outside, we have things to discuss. As I closed the door, I wondered why their attitude had changed so dramatically. After about ten minutes I was ushered back inside the office by a secretary who was so ugly she had the appearance of Miss Piggy. They would like you to go back in she grunted. I could just imagine in the staff canteen all the staff would save all their left-over dinners then throw them into a large bucket and place it in front of her where she could get her snout in amongst the swill! Sit down the boss man uttered. First of all John, we have to tell you that Mr James no longer works for us so what you got to say about that? Well I'm sorry to hear that, why did he leave I enquired? Boss man cut me short, suffice to say, he is no longer employed by us! And that's the end of the matter! (Something not quite right here I thought) Now Mr Banfield, we can offer you apposition as a butcher in our Notting Hill branch, the manager Mr Wright normally works on his own, but needs help with the heavy lifting and we have decided he must have two working in his shop at all times. That sounds good to me I replied. Right you start Monday and good luck in your new career, boss man said shaking my hand.

The bus ride to the shop was only twenty minutes away and just before entering the shop I wondered how I was going to get on with the Mr Wright? It didn't take to long to find out, as I approached the shop counter, I noticed Mr Wright standing there with what looked like a growl on his face, you must be the new bloke sent by the office, he snapped. I'm used to working on my own and I don't much want help but it looks like I'm stuck with you! (Thanks a bunch you sad sod I thought).

After only working with Mr Wright a couple of hours, I knew he must have many issues one of them issues was that he was a complete idiot. He was about sixty years old but acted eighty. He was very rude and abrupt with all the customers and a miserable git and I'm sure he hated all of mankind. And I knew I wouldn't be working with him for long! My first day of working in the shop was about to close and the shop had been heaving all day with customer (about two in total) and I really wanted to know from Mr happy why Mr James no longer worked for the company. Did Mr James find a better job I asked in a matter of fact way. Mr James he shouted, don't mention that mans name to me, that thieving lying scoundrel, they should have shot him and all he got was two years inside! Hearing this I was in total shock. Two years I said, what did he get two years for? Well he raged, they made him relief manager covering other manager's shops. When they went on holidays he fiddled the books in every shop he worked in, and stole thousands of pounds over a two year period but thankfully he got caught, he beamed proudly. It now all clicked into place, when I was being interviewed for the Job. Why the kept on asking why I like Mr James so much with him nicking thousands of pounds. They may have thought I was also a till robber! The way the idiot was going on anyone would have thought it was his own money that was nicked! Because he was such a doom and gloom merchant I had this picture of him at weekends of walking up and down Oxford Street in London, with a double board both to his front and back on the front board would be written "be warned – you're all going to die" and on the back board "the end is nigh". I had now been working at the shop for three weeks and had now had enough of being a butcher and working for Mr Doom and gloom which was really cracking me up. So on the Friday, I picked the right moment when he was moaning and groaning and I told him I'm giving you a weeks notice as from today. You can't leave he shouted, where's your loyalty. Loyalty, there's no such animal I replied, he seemed quite shocked, and went on to moan about how no one cares anymore and the lack of loyalty etc. But this was all to be expected from the boring, miserable git! Even though I never had a new job to go to, but as long as I got away from him I was quite happy. In them days finding work was quite easy so I had no worries there.

Poem

Interviewed at head office, all I want is a job
Need to make a living and earn a few bob
Wanted to work with Mr James but his doing time
Robbed every shop he worked at that was his crime
Such a lovely man was he and a true gent
He paid the price and to prison he was sent
The shop I was sent to was at Notting hill gate
Working with a man, all humanity he did hate
Dewhurst packed up trading and no wonder they went broke
Such a doom and gloom manager a real sad joke
The next job I get will be a much better one
It's all about being happy when all is said and done

I was now twenty eight years old and needed a flat on my own and was lucky to find a one-bedroom flat in Maida vale which was just off the Edgware road so it was a good location to be living and not too far from where Jim and Alma were staying. Now all I had to do was find myself a job. The weekly rent for the flat was £7 a week, this being 1968, when the average wage was about £25 a week, for living in central London this was a fair rent! I used to drink in the Warrington pub with Jims step dad Ted Cunningham. Ted was born in southern Ireland round about 1919. His family were very poor but happy as he had seven brothers and three sisters and lived on a small farm near Killarney on the west coast. He left home when he reached seventeen. He also left a heartbroken mother. He made his way to Kilburn in west London and stayed with an Uncle. His uncle worked as a plasterer and Ted was taught the trade by him. Just before the Second World War stated Ted joined the Royal Navy and served throughout the war, rising to the rank of a Petty Officer as Ted put it, not bad for a boy from the bogs! After the war, Ted returned back to plastering and bricklaying. I hear you're looking for a job he said, as I sat down with my pint. Yes that's right but I haven't a clue what job to go for I replied. Why don't you come and work for me he said, I have this job in Hamilton Terrace, St Johns Wood. Hamilton Terrace is one of the most sought after addresses to be in London with large mansion type houses on both sides.

Hamilton Terrace was named after Lady Hamilton who was the mistress of Lord Nelson. I will be working on day rates to the builder so I will tell the builder that you are the bricklayer and this way you will be paid the top rate! Sounds good to me I smiled. The next day, Ted and I showed up on the job and met the builder. This is John the brickie Ted proudly informed him. Well if Ted has brought you along you must be good! We have had three so called brickies in the last month and they have all been useless and I have had to sack them all! Ted had told me before we entered the house to stick closely to him in case the builder asks me any awkward questions about the bricklaying. But that plan backfired straight away as Ted got into a deep conversation with an old workmate of his. The builder called me over and politely asked, John, would you measure the distance between (and at that point his words were drowned out by loud banging noises from the next room) so taking the initiative and wanting to make a name for myself I took out from my pocket a tape that I had brought that morning for two shillings (10p). Now then I did not catch what exactly he wanted me to measure but surely it cannot be that window frame over there? Why would he want a window frame measured up? He must mean them two round steel bars in front of the window that are taking the weight of the floor above, six foot fix inches I proudly shouted. After carefully making sure the measurement was spot on, turning round waiting for him to thank me for that information I noticed a strange look on his face with his mouth wide open. It was as it he had just been told he had inherited two mother-in-laws! Ted, he shouted, I cannot believe it! John has just measured up between two support bars! Ted, quickly came over to me and must have noticed my cock-up, and calmly said, yes boss, I'm still training John as a bricklayer. Well I'm not paying him as one he shouted; I'll pay him labourer's money. As Ted didn't want to lose this good paying job, he agreed to that. I should be paid a labourers rate of pay! How embarrassing for both Ted and myself, I felt like a right knob-head. Fancy me measuring up between two steel pillars! You cannot get any thicker than that.

Poem

Served in the Royal Navy just an old sea dog
Reached quite a high rank this lad from the bog
Was from the emerald isle this man known as Ted
Come and work for me John that's what he said
We will say you're a brickie I'll look after you
Shall stick to you closer than a tube of superglue
Because of my cock up a brick I never laid

A bricklayer was not ever going to be my trade
Everyone had a good laugh about it thought it funny
But being paid labourers rate cost me lots of money
The moral of this story is be a good bluffer
Because if you get it wrong financially you will suffer

I went on to work with Ted on a few Jobs and got to know him quite well. He was a man of stories, and one of them was as follows, when Ted was demobbed from the Navy in 1945, he went back to plastering in the Maida vale and St John woods part of London at that time food was on ration. (At the beginning of the war the government realised that rationing had to be introduced for the whole nation because being an island, Britain could be cut off from food supplies from abroad so every family was given a ration book that had coupons attached to every page. So on one of the pages there could be coupons for eggs and on other page coupons for meat and so on... A family would be allowed say eight eggs a week, so eight coupons would be handed over. Rationing came to an end in about 1952, Rationing was a bitter pill to swallow, but the nation knew the sacrifice was worth the hardships involved, also rationed were building materials so Ted really struggled to make a living with his coupons. He was only allowed to purchase two bags of plaster a week, unless he went on the black market but this he could not afford to do. So his customers had to get most of his materials on the black market (the black market was a way of getting goods when you did not have any ration coupons you had to pay above the market price for any goods. The goods could be brought at shops of stores, from shady characters with little or no integrity who would sell their own grandmother for the right price. Buying this way was called "buying under the counter". The story that stuck in my mind was about the shortages that Ted experienced soon after him, leaving the navy. He went to price a job up at Hamilton Terrace, it was a large detached house and the owner of the house wanted some plastering carried out and the roof repaired due to bomb damage. After inspecting all over the house, Ted informed the lady owner that the house needed a lot of work done on it and he would not be able to carry out the work because he would be unable to purchase the supplies unless she could get hold of the supplies. She said this was not possible. OK, Ted said, I'll be off then. Don't go, the frail little Jewess lady shouted, wait there, Ted waited for a couple of minutes and the lady appeared with a set of keys in her hand and said seeing that you cannot repair my house and you say it could be months before you can get hold of any materials I will be moving to my other house in Bournemouth so here are the keys to this house. You can have it for nothing and I will sign all the paperwork relating to this house over to you. Ted stood there flabbergasted and completely shocked and could not believe what he was hearing. But Ted was not in any way materialistic as he lived in a small one- bedroom rented flat and said to the lady in his Irish brogue, now Mrs, what would I be wanting your house for/ I'm perfectly happy where I'm living. So I'm not interested in taking off you your hands! The lady must have been astonished with this remark but to be fair to Ted in 1946 hardly anybody who was working class owned a house. It only started to get popular with the working classes to buy a house in the middle sixties. I remember walking with Ted past the house in about 1978 and him pointing at the house and saying that could have been my house! He said it in a matter-of-fact way and seemed to have no regrets. This house today if-sold would fetch in the region of four to five million pounds. I enjoyed working with Ted, but sometimes work would get scarce and he would be out of work for a while, so I decided to look around for something more permanent. It was now 1968 and I was 29 years old. A friend of mine had walked into the office of a firm called Matthew hall, which had a warehouse and office in Amberly Road in Paddington and because they liked the look of his face, he was offered a Job as a trainee electrician and as he was the same age as me I thought I would try my luck as well. Have you got any jobs going as a trainee electrician I asked the personal officer? No we haven't he shouted, so bugger off you just can't walk in off the Street without an appointment and ask for a job! But my mate did who might that be he asked, Brian Martin, I replied firmly. He raised his eyebrows slightly. YES! I offered him a position straight away. A very intelligent and likeable young man is Brian and we have no vacancies for you. And the next time you want to talk to someone in this office see the receptionist and get her to make you an appointment, goodbye.   I should have raised my right arm level with my eyes and shouted "FUHRER", thanks for nothing. Charming I thought what a rude and arrogant twat he turned out to be, Brian had walked off of the Street the same as himself and got myself a job maybe he didn't like the look of me and thought I looked a bit dense. (He may have been right).

As I passed the young lady on the reception desk she asked how did you get on? When I told her I was not offered anything. She whispered Matthew halls main office is at Tottenham Court Road, why don't you try there and if you do good luck. This nice kind lady was to change my whole working life! |So not to be beaten I made my way to Matthew Halls main office. On entering the lady in reception asked what department do you require? I didn't have a clue, but just above her head was a board that read, Fire Protection division Third Floor, I need to speak to the manager on the third floor, if I may. OK, either take the lift, or climb the stairs. That's the first hurdle out of the way! Knocking on the door marked (Mr Petis Personal) come in this voice called out. Hello my name is John Banfield and I'm wondering if you have any vacancies. Exactly what vacancy are you looking for? He said sharply. His question took me off guard for a moment, UM, ERM, I stuttered, I would like to work in Engineering is all I could think of. What kind of work have you been doing in the past he asked? Well I have been butchering, a bus driver, and a salesmen, I answered. The look on his face told me he was somewhat a little peeved, by my job selection. I'm sorry, he snapped, with that work background, I cannot offer you a job in the engineering field. Whoops, I'd better think of something quickly, as I am out here without a job! And once again I have to thank that little voice in my head that said tell him about your army days in the royal engineers, you fool. Ah Mr Petis, I was in engineering when I was in the army with the engineers. You were in the Royal Engineers, he beamed!!

Yes sir I grovelled, I was a field engineer, building bailey bridges, by now. His whole demeanour had changed, well he excitedly burbled I was in the royal engineers during the war and loved every minute of it. And for the next twenty minutes or so, he bored the pants off me, telling me a bout all his exploits while serving with them. Of course I was nodding and agreeing with every word he was telling me and thinking I am listening to the most boring war-time reminiscing I have ever heard. I just hope for all my Patient listening that a job offer will be forthcoming! He at last said you haven't come here to listen to me talking about my army service. (me thinks, yes how right you are and if I had not wanted a job so badly, I would have told you that you are without doubt the most boring old bastard that I have had the displeasure to listening to. You came here for a job?? Yes sir, I would like a job in engineering, if you're good self has a vacancy, I stopped short of calling him your highness! I should have just got down on my hands and knees and kissed his feet, it would have saved all the Pathetic grovelling. Well John, do you think you would be able to get to Heathrow airport as we have a large contract starting next week, if you are able to travel there. I can offer you a position as a fitters mate; this involves assisting the pipe fitter and helping out on site when needed. The work entails installing complete sprinkler systems in factories, offices, shops and all kinds of buildings. On the fire protection division, how does that sound? That sounds great to me sir, OK, then, you will start at six shillings (30p) an hour plus bonus and any overtime that is required! Now let me give you some advice John. Work hard; learn the trade and you should do well. I have taken on young fellows like you over the years with no previous experience and who are now site managers! As he shook my hand he said good luck and happy hunting! Well what a turn up! When walking in his office within a minute he had rejected me and was about to tell me to get lost, but by mentioning my army days changed it all around. His decision to take me on effected and changed my life completely.

Poem

Arriving at Amberly road, a sparks I wanted to be
But the manager did not like the look of me
Don't ever come back here again, appointments must be made
What made you think I would offer you a trade?
But that kind lady who had such a nasty boss
Said keep on trying a rolling stone gathers no moss
Found myself in the main office. I'll try once more
This time I hope I'm not shown that dreaded door
Interviewed by this ex army man which was just great
Was offered a good job is that down to fate
It's being in the right place at the right time
Maybe I can reach the top like that clinging vine
Have you wondered if your destiny is decided when you born
Till your last breath when family and friends do mourn

It was the Thursday that I had the interview and I was told that I must buy myself a pair of overalls and a tape measure and report on site with my P45 over the weekend. I was quite excited about working for a company like Matthew hall and for an amazing hourly rate of 6 shillings and 6 pence (32p). This was considered, in 1969, just above the going rate at the time! But now in 2007 seems an incredible low sum! Monday morning had arrived and I was now to make my way to Heathrow airport. At that time the underground tube train only went as far as Hatton cross on the Piccadilly Line. Once at Hatton cross you had to get a bus to Heathrow. Even only coming from Paddington it could take over two hours in journey time. I finally made it to Heathrow airport and in front of my were two large buildings one was named British European Airways (BAE) and I noticed in a field to the far side of the buildings a tin hut with a sign board with the words (Matthew Hall Fire Protection Div). Walking through this quagmire was an endurance feat in itself. It looked like this land used to be a grazing field and was more like a bog! I must be the first person on site because this hut looks deserted. On opening the door I was surprised to see a young fellow sitting on a work bench. Are you Ben Welch the site supervisor I asked? Are you kidding, he frowned, I hope I never get like that miserable f--k pig, most detestable man that you ever likely to meet, you'll see what I mean when you meet him. My name is Keith Holmes and

I'm a pipe fitter, what's yours? My Names John I said, and I'm started as a fitters mate. Me thinks what have I let myself in for, it's a terrible journey, its freezing cold and the supervisor sounds like a right horror. As I was chatting to Keith I noticed him look out of the hut window. He then said I can see Ben walking across the field and by the look of his face he's not too happy. He pushed open the door and on entering looked at me and shouted, who are you? My names John and I've started today as a fitters mate, I quickly replied. Is that so, well for a start you can vacate that chair and wait near the car park. I have two lorries coming this morning, with all the materials to make a site compound. Charming I thought he didn't even say good morning and introduce himself! Ben still looked very fit for his age and I found out later that he used to be a fair ground boxer and would box anyone who thought they could beat him. They would pay him one pound to box and the deal was if anyone could beat him, he would give them £5, suffice to say Ben never paid out! The two lorries duly arrived and Keith and I, for the next two weeks, set up site. This job was a two year contract so we had to erect many cabins as there was going to be up to fifty men employed. Once all the huts were up twenty men arrived on the Monday morning and Bens health and safety talk was, get out there and get some pipe up, now f—k off and get started, and if I come round on site and see anyone talking and not working I will sack you on the spot! (Ben Walsh was from the East end of London and had been on Matthew Hall for about forty-five years and first started as a plumber, this was to be his last job as he was sixty three years old. Ben was of the old school a real rough diamond and in his day had been a right hard nut.) While he was helping us erect the huts he would tell me stories of life on sites in the past. He used to run big jobs with many men and he said he had to show his authority with a large workforce so if any worker tried to put one over him or gave him any backchat he would take them round the back of the hut and give him a good hiding. Once he was finished with him he would give him two choices, either go back on site and behave himself or be sacked there and then. Ben had two passions in life, the first was Leyton orient football club and the other was his German Sheppard dog. Ben had been married twice and twice divorced. His first wife had for years been used as a punch bag by Ben. When Ben came home late one night having had a skin full at the pub he once again started to hit her around but this night she was ready for him and conveniently had a saucepan handy and gave him one almighty whack with it and then departed from his life forever. Ben awoke from that episode hating women even more! The second and last wife of bens only lasted one year as one day in a fit of temper he drove his car at her while she was on the driveway. He only managed to break one of her legs as she managed to avoid the full impact.

Poem

Made it to the airport that cold and freezing day
What an awful journey was finding out the hard way
Watched a figure charging across the field, is that Ben
Was told he put a lot of fear into men
Hope it's not my arse he will be trying to kick
Charm is what is needed here that should do the trick
Heard about his stories when he was scraping and fighting
Love to be in a brawl punching kicking and biting
But his best years were behind him more bark than bite
But if he offered me out I would quickly take flight
His nickname suited him really it was Ben the beast
Because if he hit someone they would need a priest
Ben seemed to like me we just seemed to bond
Not a man to suffer fools gladly or be conned
Now sparing up in heaven in the prize fighters section
But will always remember basher Ben with much affection

Matthew Hall had three divisions, electrical, plumbing and the side I was on the fire protection (sprinklers). Ben teamed me up with Keith, who I had met in the hut that first day, which was a good thing for me, because he was a very good fitter and I was able to learn all the aspects of the trade from him. Although there were fifty men on our division, only three out of them had cars and one of them who was an Australian lived near me, so kindly gave me a lift, which saved me a hassle free journey and charged me two pounds ten shillings (£2.50p) a week!

The reader may be interested in how Matthew hall came about and what the fire protection division side entails. Round about 1897 a plumber whose name was Matthew hall, used to do small plumbing jobs around the Newcastle area. All his tools were carried around in a wooden card. Being quite an ambitious kind of man decided that if he was to make a decent living, London would be where that would be achieved, so leaving his barrow behind he caught the train to London, rented a flat in Paddington and bought himself a barrow and put a sign on each side of the barrow which read Matthew Hall – Master Plumber. It proved to be a good move for him as plumbing was still in its infancy and the work poured in. He then purchased a second barrow and employed another plumber. As word spread of this skilled plumber, with this strange accent he then decided he needed a place to store all of his tools and plant. So he rented a large shed in Amberly Road in Paddington. By the turn of the century Mr Hall had acquired large contracts to lay sewers down and lay water mains and lead piping coming off these mains for house holder's water supply. By the mid fifties Matthew Hall was one of the big players in the mechanical engineering field and this time he formed the fire protection division. This new group was set up as the "sprinkler" side. What an amazing achievement from a near penniless young man, from Newcastle a virtually unknown plumber with just his hand tools and built one of the larges companies of it's kind in less than 40 years.

The "Sprinkler System"

I will try and explain to the reader how the sprinkler system works and the benefits of such a system and the trade I was to spend thirty seven years working in.

The main aim of the Sprinkler system is to help put out any fires that may occur in all types of buildings i.e. a warehouse, office building, factory etc. Into a building that is going to be covered by the system, an incoming main with a pipe size normally 6" (150mm) is the first step. Off that main is erected a valve set that controls the water flows and pipe pressures. You can fill up the system, opening a large sluice valve on the valve set and also drain the system down by a drain valve from the valve set. The 6" (150mm) pipe rises up to roof level where smaller range pipes cover the whole building coming off these pipes is fitted every 9ft (10mm) a sprinkler head which in most cases is a small glass bulb attached to a brass rounded frame. This bulb has a liquid alcohol based inside it. All the pipes are full of water and under pressure in the event of a fire the heat melts the glass bulb which activates a small cylinder allowing the water which is under pressure to pour out, helping to extinguish the fire. If the fire spreads the next sprinkler head activates and so on! As well as protecting the roof and void area where a false ceiling has been fitted this is normally protected. The benefit of the system is that it is a fully automatic system and once installed requires very little maintenance. Bigger premises have fitted a large diesel and electric pump set with a water tank so a greater capacity of water is available! So this is the basic workings of a sprinkler system. For those of you who have not fallen asleep after all this useless information are there any questions? I was still living in my little one bedroom flat in Randolph Avenue, Maida vale and still kept in touch with Jim Grieg, often drinking at the Warrington pub in Maida vale. Jims step dad Ted used to drink there and the pub was mainly used by the Irish community rough diamonds most of them but the salt of the earth. The pub was well known for its big money card games that took place all over the weekends. There were four tables that had card games played on them. Like Jim I used to play on the table that poker was played, this table was the most popular as big money could be won (and lost). When playing we all noticed a man standing at the bar watching us play, none of us knew this stranger and he always seemed to be looking at us playing. After about three times coming into the pub he came over to our table and asked, do you men mind if I watch you, no problem with that one of the players said. So for the next two weeks this man watched us playing then asked did we mind if he could join us in a hand, if you want to came the reply. He then started playing and then to strike up a conversation, my name is Alex he said and I have just moved into this area and I'm hoping to make some new friends. But something was not quite right with this man Alex. He was in his late twenties, quite tall, and spoke with a middle class accent, but what was getting the card players backs up were the amount of questions. This so called Alex was asking, after joining in the first time and wanting to buy the whole bar a drink and become everybody's friend. He left the bar and promised he would return the next evening. After he had departed one of the customers that had been standing by the bar came over to our table and said, be careful what you say to that man, because I have had dealings with that scumbag and he is a special branch officer from Scotland yard and he more than likely was taping every word you said. He went on, he is so full of himself, he never even recognised me, also playing in the card school was paddy, a man mountain of a man and he said if that tosser comes into the pub tomorrow night, I'll deal with him. The next evening as promised, Alex walked into the pub wanting to buy everyone a drink, but we all refused his offer. After sitting down at the card table and quizzing everyone, big paddy had just about enough of his questions and let rip at him, who the hell do you think you are coming in here, cross examining all of us. Some of us may be paddy's and you may think we are all thick, be we all guessed you were either an informer or a Cop, now pick your money up and leave while your head is still attached to your shoulders and don't show your face again. I have never seen such horror on a man's face and without saying a word, grabbed his money and quickly departed the pub.

Poem

Playing our usual game of cards just for the crack
But staring at us was a man wearing a mack
Three of the school were Paddy, Shaun and Mick
Maybe he figured these Irishmen were all so very thick
Everyone knew this stranger was a cop from Scotland Yard
Was plain to see he had never shuffled a card
Why would they plant someone really stupid and so green?
Like sending that lovable nerd that hapless rascal Mr bean
Paddy sent him packing be on your way muppet
You have no brain just like a stringed wooden puppet

(ever since the troubles in northern Ireland that started in the sixties informers and plain clothes officers mixed with people in Irish clubs and pubs listening to any loose talk that may suggest support, funding and even equipping them with arms and a lot of useful information was obtained in this way).

Mick, a likeable rogue who used to play in our card school heard I was looking for a car and offered to sell me his Austin A40. It was in a bit of a state and even then was about 15 years old with no MOT or TAX but I knew it was quite a good runner so I agreed to buy it from him for the princely sum of £50. (Today's value in year 2008 would roughly be £250). I needed a car of my own as I was still working at Heathrow and if the lift I used to get failed to turn up it used to cause a lot of hassle because by the time you realized your lift was not going to turn up and making your own way it would cost you a mornings pay. (Mobile phones were not invented at this time). I brought the car on the Saturday and dove it around all the weekend with no trouble at all and was pleased that I had a reliable run about and I planned to get a MOT the following week. The Monday morning came and I picked up at Maida vale tube station a fitter named George who worked on the same firm as myself. He was to be my paying passenger. Petrol at this time (1971) cost about 5/6d (27p) a gallon. As we drove off from the station George said I don' t want to upset you John, but that engine sounds none too healthy and that gearbox is rattling as if it is on it's last legs. Have no worries, about this car I said, I've taken it on a long test drive and every thing is fine. We had only covered about two miles and George shouted I'm bloody freezing; have you got the heater on? Yes I replied, well it's not working then. Give it time George, I said in a confident manor, it's an old car and probably takes time to warm up. And also there seems to be cold air coming from the floor area, where my feet are. (I now was thinking give it a rest George, lets hear something positive about my new purchase!) But George wasn't finished yet. As I looked round I could see him pulling up the carpet where his feet were and he pulled the carpet back a cry like a banshee came from his mouth, I think every swear word that was known then flooded out! An almighty blast of cold air came rushing up, from a hole in the floor, the size of a large dinner plate. It was a strange sight watching the road rushing by from the hole, stop the car George cried, this is a death trap. You've bought a right pig in the poke John he spluttered. We both got out of the car and the look on George's said it all. He looked shell shocked. The next thing he did was to open the back door of the car and pull the carpet back, right he shouted I'll sit in the back seat the rest of the journey. And lay my feet on the seat as the floor is full of rust and any weight on it could cause it to collapse. The rest of the journey to the airport was driven in silence and I realised George was still in shock poor man. At last we made it to the job and parked in the car park and as was custom before we started work we went to the canteen for tea. As George sat down, he was asked George, are you all right? It looks like you have seen a Ghost. George went on to explain to the men at work about the pig car as he called it. The men were fascinated with him describing what a heap it was. They were all looking forward at the lunch break to take a closer look at the "death trap". Just another description George had for my car. Lunch break had arrived and no-one went to the canteen, instead crowded around my pride and Joy! I of course was quite happy for them all to give it a once over, also joining the party looking over the car was the site agent named Ray. From the main contractor McAlpines. It was widely known that this guy knew everything about anything, so a good man to get. An honest assessment relating to the car. His first sight of the car was not good, a rust bucket he snapped and that was just the outside of the car. I then lifted up both front and rear carpets and waited for his verdict. He stepped back in horror, My God! There are more holes than floor was his frank answer but it got worse. Banging the back passenger's floor to see how solid it was a large section of the floor fell to the ground. After a few swear words he said this car is a death trap, open the bonnet, I can't wait to see what state that is in. Of course the bonnet catch was broken so the bonnet had to be forced open with a screw driver. As it sprung open the engine compartment was a sore for sire eyes. The support brackets and the metal shelf holding the battery was tied up with string onto the frame of the car. The whole engine compartment was covered with a thick layer of engine oil and when ray asked me to start it up, on turning the key sparks were jumping between all the voltage terminal leads. That's it he shouted, I've seen enough, switch off. I'm amazed you drove it here. If I was a priest, I would read the last rites to this wreck and if you intent to drive it back home it will not make it. And he went on, in my opinion, this wreck has been sitting somewhere for over two years without moving that's why it is such a rust bucket, but thanks for letting us all look at it because we have all never had such a good laugh.

Poem

Proudly sitting at the table was an Irishman named Mick
Some called him a simpleton with others just pain thick
But he sold me a wreck that was falling apart
Would have been better off buying a horse and cart
Was it written on my forehead this man is dumb?
He looks so stupid I can charge him any sum
A fool and his money are soon parted
Being conned by Mick made me feel a little down hearted

The banger he sold me had more holes than floor
Was an infested rust bucket and rotten to the core
But how was I to know things would get worse
Just a miracle I never ended up in a hearse

George was the only one who stayed and said there's no chance of me ever getting back in that car again. As I have a wife and two kids and that wreck is a widow maker! George gave me this advice, if you have to drive that pig home, go very slowly and make sure you leave work earlier to make sure it's not dark when setting off! I managed to slip away early from work and started up the pig-wreck. The noise it made sounded like a challenger tank but let's be positive and keep calm, it will get me home! I managed to get onto the M4. This motorway starts at the Chiswick flyover and ends up in the West Country. George who had told me to drive slowly and this is what I was doing. Not because I wanted to but the wreck would not go any faster than 20mph. It was now making a horrendous banging noise from the engine and it became a bit frightening, but I knew if I pulled over the car would just fade and die. The good news for me was just a few hundred feet in front of me, was the welcoming sight of the Chiswick flyover. But by now I was getting some very strange looks from other motorists and some were pointing at the front of the wreck. What they could they see that I couldn't see? Thankfully I had finally made it into the flyover. The Chiswick flyover rises about ten metres above a combination of round-a-bouts below it. I had just reached the highest point when to my dismay I noticed steam pouring out of the bonnet and within seconds by an ear splitting bang that came from the engine compartment. The wreck came to a grinding halt. For ever the optimist I was hoping it would just find a broken hose or a leaking radiator. After the steam had cleared away I managed to force the bonnet open and what greeted me was an unbelievable sight. One of the piston rods had snapped off and was sticking out of the engine casing and oil and water everywhere! Oh dear me, the pig is dead! The flyover side I was on is only two lanes so traffic quickly built up behind me. This in turn brought the traffic to a near standstill as it was about 5pm, rush hour had started I had only stopped there for five minutes and already sustained a barrage of abuse. On both sides of the fly-over are two tall buildings with traffic monitoring cameras attached to the top of them. I could see they were both aimed at me so I knew that at least someone knew about my predicament and in the distance I could see help was on hand. I could make out the blue flashing lights of a police land rover but because of the traffic jam it took about twenty minutes to get to me. As the land rover pulled up level with me a cop shouted at me what's the problem mate?

Well, one of the pistons has smashed through the engine I said. Why am I not surprised, look at the state of the old banger, he chimed in, right, we're going to have to tow you out of here so I'll pull up in front of you and fit the tow rope under the car, you sit in the car and we will get you out of here. So, positioning the land rover in front of my car he then laid down under the front of my cars rear to attach it. As he disappeared under my car I was amazed to hear from under the front of my car profanities unbefitting a police officer! As he emerged from the car still with the tow rope in his hand he was covered from head to toe in thick black oil. What made it worse; his colleague erupted into fits of laughter. He looked like one of the cast from the black and white minstrels. He was shaking with rage with the whites of his eyes, now showing up against his oily black face. I thought he was going to give us a deep south rendering of "Old Man River". I really wanted to laugh but thought better of it, there's nowhere under this wreck I can attach a tow rope, he managed to blurt out. The car is riddled with rust. His colleague suggested he threw the tow rope under the front of the car so it could be hooked on somewhere at the back so that no one had to get covered in oil. They managed to find the only rust free part near the back axel. The cop that was covered in oil told me to sit in the front of the land rover and as he put it, if you were stupid enough to buy and then drive a wreck like that, I don't trust you to steer it behind the land rover. You are an idiot. Oh dear, I believe he doesn't like me too much! With the oily one sitting in the car (the cheek of it, getting my drivers seat oily!) we set off. The biggest fear for me now was the fact I had no tax, insurance or MOT so I knew I would get the book thrown at me as soon as they had towed me from the fly-over. We came to a stop on the first turning on the left up a side Street. As the oily cop uncoupled the tow rope from the wreck his mate reached into his jacket pocket and pulled out his notebook. Right Sir, this is question and answer time and with no visible tax disc showing on your windscreen, and the state of your car you have a lot of explaining to do. Right sir, first question: why are you not displaying a tax disc? I was just about to sing like a canary and admit having neither tax, insurance nor a MOT when his jacket two-way radio burst into life. I could make out a voice on his radio saying we have a RTA at Hammersmith, please respond immediately. He called his mate over and said, we've got a job in Hammersmith so we will have to leave this one and to me he said, we have to respond to a road traffic accident so this young man is your lucky day. And with that they sped off at break neck speed. Watching all this on the other side of the road was a tall man of West Indian appearance and he walked over to me. Hi man, were his first words. Did them cops give you hassle? I explained how I had broken down on the flyover and the engine blew up. I'm a mechanic, lift up the bonnet and let's have a look. Blimey what a mess, the rings on that piston rod are worn away, how long have you had the car he asked?

Three days I replied and it cost me £50. Man, you were done up like a kipper, he laughed. If you want my opinion it is only worth scrapping, I have a similar model to this one and I will take it off your hands and the best offer I can make is £5, it's up to you, because if you get someone else to look at it they will have to tow it away and you will probably only get £2 for it! Ok it's yours I reluctantly agreed. But you will have to drive me home to Maida vale to get the documents for it. That's no problem he beamed. But first thing we must get your car off the road and into my garage because those cops will be back to take details of your car and then you will be getting a knock at the door. I then helped push my car into his garage which looked like a breakers yard with car parts from all kind of makes. By the way, my name is Earl and with a handshake I replied, pleased to meet you, my name is John. On the journey to Maida vale we got talking and earl told me he worked for London transport at Chiswick bus garage and I am the head mechanic and also have a second job selling car part spares on the side. He went o n to tell me that when the red double decker had a serious accident and became a right off, his mate would buy the bus and between them repair it with all the spare parts that had been saved from other damaged buses, and then sell it at a high profit. What an enterprising team them were! Earl is probably now living in one of the West Indian islands in the lap of luxury! Arriving at my flat, I handed over all the documents relating to the wreck and with a shake of the hand and with the sum of £5 handed over by earl he was gone. It left me to reflect on what a bad day it had been but I suppose it could have been worse. Anything could have happened with a wreck as lethal and unbelievable dangerous as it was. The next evening I went back to the Warrington pub, hoping to find Mick who sold me the pig on wheels. Are you looking for Mick the barman asked? That's right, how did you know? I just guessed he said with a slight smirk on his face, but I doubt if you'll ever see him again because he moved back to Ireland for good this morning.

Poem

George had named the wreck I owned the widow maker

I could even add to that a terrible bone shaker

It was all or nothing now the engine had started

Had pulled out of the airport I had now departed

But it lacked any power it was going so slow

The lump in the front was just about to blow

All of a sudden I heard this banging and hissing

One of the piston rods decided it would go missing

It shot out the engine block before finally exploding
The feeling inside of me was a sense of foreboding
That journey was a nightmare on my cars last ride
On top of the fly over the pig thing had just died
But some folks just don't seem to care a damn
Even meek men get angry when stuck in a jam
Swearing and cursing these uncouth men in cars were bawling
The words coming out of there mouths was simply appalling
But to my rescue came them traffic cops to help
Hoping I was not about to get my collar felt
There's nowhere to fix this tow rope this is a joke
It's a lethal weapon just a pig in a poke
At last a bracket was found to secure a fixing
But with some very blue language that he was mixing
Now covered in oil and grease not a happy bunny
But his partner and I found it so very funny
This notebook was at the ready its curtains for me
Prison is beckoning son will they throw away the key
My luck was in they were wanted on another case
Right up their Street it was a stolen car chase
The saga ended when earl agreed to buy it off me
Just to think the only thing not rusted was the key

I now had to find another way to get to the airport and as luck would have it a plumber who worked for Matthew hall and lived 5 minutes from my flat offered to drive me there in his car as long as I paid the petrol, deal done! The airport contract was a massive undertaking with a workforce of about a hundred men, but the mood of the men was quite militant as they had heard of men working for other contractors that were getting far higher weekly bonuses than them. The most militant of them approached me and demanded action, John seeing that you get on with Ben so well and you seem to be his favourite, we all reckon that you should demand that we all get a higher weekly bonus. You can be our spokesman you can do all the talking but we will be right behind you. At the time we were getting about £5 a week in bonus, not that bad when you think the average weekly wage was only about £20. I agreed to be there leader in the negotiations but told them I needed a few days to convince Ben that the workforce deserved and warranted the £5 a week they were seeking. For a few days I was formulating a plan in my head as to the best way to approach Ben because if Ben got upset he would lose his head and I did not want to lose mine. I had now worked out how I was going to handle Ben and calling the men over I went through the plan with them. Firstly only five of you and me must go to see him and once we get to his hut you all wait outside, I will go in, talk with him and if he wants to hear what comments you have you go in and explain them to him. We all represented the workforce and with a shuffling of feet, and a few looks of panic and despair they reluctantly agreed to my plan of action. It was agreed that we would wait until Friday as Ben was always in a better mood on that day. As this was the last working day! The Friday came round and at about 10 o'clock I met up with the five men who were joining me, right men, I shouted in a firm voice, lets be bold, not only should we ask him for more bonus, lets demand better site conditions as they are a disgrace. All I could hear from their mouths after dropping that bombshell was the words of um, err, ah, erm, but no proper words. Ok I said, I won't mention site conditions, we'll drop that demand and bring it up again in our next meeting. I watched as the colour returned back to all their faces. This was a demand to far and suddenly they all seemed to all get Dutch courage and the fighting talk took over. Let's go for it, be bold lads, we are all in this together, all for one and one for all! Let's show Ben we all mean business. Most impressive, I thought, just like on the eve of a battle talk! As we all set off on the long walk to bens hut I could hear the men behind me, shouting out what was in store for Ben and how he had better not mess with them, united we all were. I t would normally take about five minutes to get to bens hut, and we were only half way there and already give minutes had gone, the walking pace had now slowed down dramatically and looking behind me noticed only three of us, a few more strides into the walk. A voice said meekly, we think it's best if you talk to Ben on your own John, because he may lose his temper if he sees us and with that they too did a quick about turn and were off as quick as their shaking legs could carry them. Even though I was quite a distance from the hut I could see Ben staring out of the window. Oh dear me, what do I do now? Do I turn around and go back to site? Or proceed with my mission, and inform him of all the men's demands and feeling very nervous as I got near the door it suddenly opened and there stood Ben with braces supporting his trousers. Cowards the lot of them he shouted! I know why you've come to see me, and it's all about the bonus scheme, I have my spies you know. I watched them yellow bellies from my window and saw them depart 'till you were left on your own, come in John, sit down and talk me through the men's grievances. I still cannot get over your so called mates abandoning you like that. I then went through all the issues and site concerns and was amazed to find that Ben agreed that the bonus rate should be better and site conditions improved and after discussing other minor concerns, Ben made me a cup of tea and said, I have had good reports from site about your work and you will be pleased to know that as from Monday I am making you up to a fitter, so well done. I am starting a new fitter on Monday, he lives local and I will team him up with you. Thanks Ben, I replied gleefully. You deserve it, he beamed and I'm pleased you had the balls to come and discuss site issues on your own, more can be said about them other spineless tow rags who set out with you! He went on; they have all shot themselves in the foot because when layoffs come along they will be the first ones to go! But let's keep that between you and me! And with a shake of his hand I departed his office a very happy man.

Poem

Marching boldly towards bens hut men with this fighting talk
What started off as a sprint slowed down to a walk
This walk became a shuffle lets call it dragging feet
It was this man named Ben they feared to meet
All for one and one for all the saying goes
These men are supposed to be my friends not foes
Watched them from my window John they have no balls
Left you in no mans land just deserters and fools
The bad news for them their actions I have noted
And the good news for you John you are promoted
Never to be forgotten Ben who liked a fight
Who's bark was certainly worse than his bite

On the following Monday, Ben introduced me to Brian the new fitter that was to work with me. Shaking his hand he seemed to be on edge and slightly nervous which was odd because he was built like a man mountain. We both walked onto the floor that I was working on and he blurted out before I start work with you John I have something to tell you. I am not a fitter, I do not know anything about fittings or pipe, my last job was a labourer in a factory but I was made redundant. I have been out of work for the past year and I am desperate to earn a living again, I have a wife and three kids to support so you can send me on my way now and I'll have no hard feelings. Well Brian thanks for being so honest with me but I have to say you have got some front to tell them you were a fitter, so Brian I won't shop you but as long as you work hard and are willing to learn the trade I will teach you. But you must not tell anyone else if you do they will report you and I will be in big trouble. My view in life is never kick a man when he's down and always be willing to do a good turn to someone, rather than a bad one. The weeks went rolling by and Brian absorbed as much knowledge of pipe fitting that I could teach him. He asked me one day if I would like to have an evening meal round his house with his family, as his wife wanted to meet me and thank me for giving him the opportunity to learn a trade and to get their life back on track. The meal was arranged for a Friday night and Brian drove me to his house after work, on entering his house I thought they must be welcoming a conquering hero home with balloons and bunting decked out through the front room, with a banner that read "thanks John" and she had invited most of the family members. I was speechless and felt quite humbled; after all, I only did what I hope most people would do. The meal turned into a drinking session and Brian's wife, Jane could not thank me enough and hugging me and crying her eyes out and what I had done had changed all their lives and how my act of kindness would never be forgotten. My reply to her was if you cannot do a good turn for someone don't do them a bad one! I woke up the next morning sleeping on the sofa having planned to only stay a couple of hours. It's nice to feel appreciated in life and nice to know a few people have benefited through your deeds. Brian had now been working with me for over a year now and had become a very good fitter and had grasped all aspects of pipe fittings. I've been offered a very challenging position with an oil company Brian gleefully said one day. That's great news Brian, what work will you be doing? He then went on to tell me it would be working on newly constructed oil platforms, in the North Sea. The job he had applied for and managed to get, was a foreman pipe fitter in charge of a group of pipe fitters. Their task was to fit out all the rigs with all types of mechanical valve sets and pipework. This would be a huge task for an experienced mechanical engineer, but with Brian's limited knowledge of pipe work I would have thought an impossible talk. He had applied for the job and made up a lot of his C.V and he had made such a good job of pretend work experience that he was offered the job there and then. What do you think John? Do you think I should accept the job? As Brian had a great personality and was a very quick learner and had the one ingredient that could pull this scam off and he had an abundance of that word "front". I told him to go for it and reminded him of that saying "who dares wins" so with a warm shake of my hand and thanking me for everything Brian started on his new working adventure. The reader will meet up with Brian and what became of him in a later chapter. I had now worked at Heathrow for three years and the job was almost completed. Ben was looking forward to his long awaited retirement; all the testing was now completed all and that was needed was to hand the finished contract over to the clients. But in life one should always expect the unexpected. We had on test the main cargo shed on 150 lbs water pressure and Murphy's Law took over at the highest point of the huge shed a leak had broken out and dripped into a tiny gap and onto an electrical circuit board that powered the baggage handling conveyor belt, this knocked out the whole computerised system. There were many anxious faces around at this point, but the main concern was how was this leak going to be resolved with all the scaffolding having being taken down? The leak was above two metre wide heating panels with no way of getting at the pipe even with a scaffold. For some reason Ben's top engineer and the concerned clients seemed to be looking in my direction. Surely not? They are not going to ask me to climb on the heating panels are they? Ben made the first move. John we have a slight problem even with scaffolding we would not be able to get at the pipe and anyway it would cost thousands to erect it so the only solution we can come up with is for someone to crawl along the panels and fix the leak! Ben had that hound-dog look on his face. I also detected in his eyes, I made you up son, so this is payback time! But I pleaded how am I supposed to get up to the panels in the first place? Ah, he said smugly, the builder has a four rung extension ladder that we can place adjacent to the panels. Just one question Ben, I enquired, why me? Well John, you are the smallest of the lads, and also the lightest, will you do it? And to make this suicide mission seem more attractive he added, you get to have tomorrow off when the job is done (big deal). I noticed all the other men had vanished as they knew a "volunteer" was about to be nominated. I was put on the spot, as Ben had done a lot for me, I felt obliged to agree to this task. The words health and safety had not yet been invented and as this was about 23m (70 feet) up with no safety harness a fall would be ending my time on earth! I reluctantly agreed to this, legs turning to jelly mission. The idea was for me to cork the leak while the pipework was still under pressure (most leaks occur between the pipe and the fitting and to stop the leak using a small chisel and hammer, knock into the fittings a rope type yarn. This normally does the trick so with a hammer in my belt and a yarn and chisel in my overalls, I composed myself at the foot of the ladder ready for the stomach churning heart pounding climb and like most dangerous situations you think to yourself what am I doing and why me? There was no getting out of it now; I had agreed to do it so here goes. I started to climb the first rungs of the ladder; it looked like the longest ladder that had ever been manufactured. I had only climbed about ten rungs and already both legs felt like a ton weight. But what was worse was the uncontrollable shaking in both legs. But I had to press on and just hoped my bodily functions would remain intact and not let me down! I was now about half way up, and the movement of the ladder was going forward and back was not as bad as when I was lower so this gave me more confidence. After what seemed like hours i had finally reached the heating panels I was able to step onto the panel and as they were all interlinked together I would be able to crawl along them to reach the leaking fitting. Oh what a relief what Joy, I had made it! But now I had to be very careful. As I crawled along the panels as they were only being supported by ½" (10mm) rod if I shuffled along the panels too quickly they all started to sway alarmingly so I had to proceed in a very slow manner but to add to my woes the panels were also on test as they were heating panels they were very hot. So by the time I had reached the leaking pipe I was leaking sweat. I was right under the leaking fitting and pulling my hammer out and with the chisel and cord hemp in position gave the chisel a good thump and withdrawing the chisel and cord found I had sealed the leak. What luck, sometimes it can take ages to cure a leak, I needed this lucky break. Normally you have to watch a cured leak for ten minutes to make sure it doesn't leak out again, but the panels were now so hot they became unbearable. So I made my way slowly back towards the ladder and getting my legs onto the first rung started to make my way down. Climbing down a ladder is oh so very easy than climbing up one. I now felt very elated with the task completed and knowing I was now not going to be scrapped and body bagged off the floor! The last step off the ladder was the sweetest. Ben was the first one to come over to me and warmly shake my hand for a job well done, as he put it go home now John and as promised you have tomorrow off with pay and by the way, Friday you are being transferred to Watney Mann in Islesworth south west London. If the same job was to be done these days a scissor lift would have been used. This is a flexible battery driven platform. Standing on four wheels you just press a button and it takes you as high as you require. It also has a moveable platform that extends out to get to awkward areas. You also have to wear a safety harness and the rope from the safety harness is attached to the safety rail of the platform. That's how health and safety is today, but in them days it was non existent!

Poem

It's Murphy's Law a leak in the most awkward spot
And in addition to that heating panels so piping hot
Did they think I would survive such a high fall?
Humpty dumpty I was not even though I was small
Ben treating me so well how could I say no
Being an easy going chap I just went with the flow

Only half way up the ladder it suddenly started swaying
And I'm not afraid to say I was nervously praying
Phew at last I had reached the top of the ladder
And was pleased to say no problem with the bladder
I steadily crawled along the panels and found the leak
And completed this tricky task in spite of the heat
Jobs done now let's get the hell out of here
Never in all my life have I known such fear
Stepping off the last rung I just felt so proud
With the clapping of those hands from the watching crowd
Health and safety at work them days no such thing
It took three decades more before legislation was brought in

The year was 1971 and I was still living in my one bedroom flat in Maida vale, the flat overlooked the Edgware road, which was handy as marble arch was only about three miles heading south and the start of the M1 motorway going north was about four miles. So Maida vale had a lot going for it. I still used to frequent the Warrington pub in Maida vale and felt quite at home with all the rough diamonds that used the public bar. I was drinking there one night with Jim Greggs step dad, Ted and all the regulars and through the door entered this enormous brute of a man. He was in his forties with scars all down his ugly fat and the shape and size of a prop forward with his cauliflower ears and smashed in nose, it was a frightening sight indeed! Enough to send not a cold chill, but an icy blast down your spine! His first words were I'll take on any man in here! His loud and frightening voice echoed all around the pub. Ted whispered to me don't look at him, I know him and is an animal. His name is Mick Clance and his nickname is Mick the beast and he enjoys beating people up. He would take great pleasure in beating his granny up! So with all eyes firmly looking into their drinks or glued to the floor the pub fell silent. Not the response Mick the beast had wanted, so, going up to the biggest man in the pub, he shouted, your mothers a whore and you're a big queer, now what have you got to say about that? He was talking to paddy Marlong, who was sitting down minding his own business with his eyes fixed on his beer glass and you couldn't get a meeker man than paddy, a gentle giant and he wasn't going to take the bait and just carried on looking into his glass. The beast then looked around the pub to see if anyone was staring at him! As no-one was he turned his attention to the young barman who had politely asked him, can I get you a drink sir?

(This young barman was either trying to defuse the tense situation or was just tired of living!) Within seconds Mick the beast had one hand around the now totally shocked barman's neck. How dare you talk to me before I have spoken to you without all the swear-words added. The madman was just about to knock him into the next world when the front door of the pub opened and in the doorway stood the biggest and tallest cooper the met police must have had on their books. He must have been 20 stone plus and about 6'6" (2m, 150mm) and no visible neck. He had to duck his head to make his entrance. Then Mick the beast turned around to see an even bigger beast than himself, his grip on the barman's neck was released instantly and then the strangest thing happened. Mick the beast collapsed on the floor in a heap. No neck Cop shouted, Get up Mick, you're nicked. But Mick was playing dead. No neck Cop knew Mick was acting as he had dealt with him before, but the rule was if a man collapses they were duty bound to call an ambulance. Mick the best was duly carted off to hospital and order was once more restored. Why did Mick the beast pretend to faint, I asked Ted? Well, Ted replied, there's two reasons, the first is that copper is the reining met police heavyweight boxing champion and Mick knew that, and realised he would have been flattened by him and he only came out of prison six months ago and his release from jail terms were if he was arrested within a year of his release for any offence, he would go straight back inside and he knows the law backwards and knows that you cannot be arrested if you are unconscious. Because your rights have to be verbally read out to you.

Poem

Then appearing in the doorway was this massive big cop
One look at him brought the rumpus to a stop
Mick the beast was mad but he was not thick
And did not want to be going back to nick
So pretending to pass out he fell to the floor
Knowing you can't arrest an unconscious man that's the law
Ending up in casualty and free to fight more days
As day follows night will end up in more affrays

Mick Levy, who owned the Green grocer shop in Formosa Street, brought another green grocers shop on the Edgware road. The shop was situated in a group of shops just before the boundary and the start of Kilburn. He had installed Jim Gregg as the manager and hoped as that part of Maida vale was quite well-off area and people were well heeled and wedged, he would make himself even richer! One of Jim's very wealthy customers a single lady in her late fifties asked Jim if he would be interested in accompanying her on a world cruise, all expenses paid. She was just looking for a presentable young man to be seen with throughout the world cruise. Jim had to politely refuse this offer as he was a happily married man with a young son. If had been a single man, I often wondered, if he would have escorted this old granny around? But it shows how much serious money was to be found in this manor. Calling in the shop one Saturday afternoon, Jim asked me if I was doing anything that evening, not really I replied. That's good said Jim, one of my customers has told me he's going to a drink-up tonight, and it's on board a cargo ship moored in the London docks. His best mate is the captain and it sets sail on the Sunday and is bound for its home country, which is New Zealand. The customer had written the name of the ship on notepaper as he was going on board earlier. The ships name was the Ricki Ticki Tarmi and this was its Maori name. Mick had a large red van, used for market work and for both his shops. Jim said we'll drive down in that so off we set and reached the Albert docks about 8pm. On giving the name of the ship to the police at the gate we were directed to the ship. It was a large refrigerated meat carrier. On stepping on board we were duly shown to the dining area. There the party was in full swing. Once the drinks started flowing, total strangers become buddies. As the night wore on Jim was trying to match the kiwi crew shot for shot in a drink contest. These seamen were hardened drinkers, but Jim was matching them like for like! As I was just drinking steadily I was able to observe how wrecked everyone was. It was now well after 2am and everyone was not totally paralytic, including the captain and the ship was due to sail at 8am that morning! As Jim was now in a comatose state it was decided we had better leave the ship with about four crew members who could hardly stand themselves. We all managed to somehow grab different parts of Jim's body and slowly make our way down the gang plank. The obscenities we were now shouting made it all the funnier. Fortunately Jim had parked right on the quayside next to the ship and opening the back doors of the van we managed to pull and shove Jim into the back, laying him on some old cardboard boxes. With handshakes all round to our new best Kiwi mates in the world I slowly drove to the dockside police post. With the window down I drew up to the hut. The officer wrote down the number plate looked in the back of the van but failed to see Jim underneath the cardboard boxes. Right Sir, said one of them to me, what ship have you come from? I had completely forgotten the name of the ship and was not even sure what planet I was on. The name of the ship, I slurred, I can't remember, you must be able to know what ship you were on he snapped angrily. All I know it was a kiwi ship I said sheepishly. The silence that followed was only broken by a loud pitched yell that came from the back off the van. It's the Ricki Ticki

Tarmi, you stupid f**ker the voice yelled, the two officers looked shocked. Where did that voice come from the demanded to know? Oh that my mate Jim who's had too much to drink, so we flung him in the back! But they saw the funny side of it and said, mind how you go and opened the gates and I made my way gingerly home! How times have changed. Can you imagine two cops wishing you well knowing you have had a skin-full. But there were no drink driving laws then! Myself driving home in my state was bad enough but the crew of the kiwi ship all the officers and the crew were completely leg-less and they had to navigate their ship up the river Thames and then to the open sea. It makes the blood run cold thinking about it. Driving Jim back home through the deserted Streets of Wapping then up to Hyde park corner, then on to Paddington I was serenaded by Jim trying to sing and then interrupting his singing shouting in a loud voice "your my best friend John" and more worrying for me was him constantly saying "I love you John" is Jim on the change? Or is this just the large amount of drink still in his system talking? I hoped and preyed it was the latter!

Poem

The Ricki tiki Tarki was in London Docks and moored

Jim and I invited to a party being held aboard

Now ready for its return journey home this kiwi ship

Twenty four hours to go would make its homeward trip

All liquor was free so of course it was flowing

And looking at our Jim's drunkard state, behavioural signs were showing

Three hours later Jim was drunk as skunk

Two barrels of beer and many whiskey's he had sunk

How can a man consume so much and stay alive

Was his bodies fail safe system helping him survive?

Carried down the gang plank in the van he was slung

With all the rotten fruit and cardboard he was among

Driving to the dock gates Jim was swearing and cursing

A sore head the next morning he will be nursing

Grabbing and pulling Jim now to face his wife indoors

This should prove interesting as he was on all fours

I suspect the dreaded dog-house he will be in

Just take your punishment like a man my old mate Jim

WATNEY MANN

It was now the spring of 1971 and aged 32 years I was pleased that the Heathrow job had finally finished. I had been transferred to one of the largest and oldest breweries in London. The brewery Watney Mann was established in about 1740, in Isleworth south-west London and just a short walk to the river Thames. As I was now the proud owner of a 3 year old car called a Singer Vogue, so driving to Watney Mann was easy, as it was only about 6 miles from Maida vale. I met up with Richard outside the brewery, just a couple of years older than myself this was going to be his first job in charge. As he was a plumber by trade, the plan was that I would give advice when needed. An extended bottling plant was added to the existing building so a complete sprinkler system was needed. The brewery brewed all types of beers and one of them was Carlsberg Extra Strong larger. You knew after drinking just about two bottles of this potent larger how strong it was. Working along side our trade was every trade that a building site needs, so there must have been at least two hundred men on site. The bottling plant conveyor belt passed between the two buildings so if a site worker wanted a drink he just walked to the conveyor belt and helped himself. As the job stated to progress we took on two more fitters. I used to meet Richard the so called supervisor, in the morning and discuss what had to be done that day and would not see him most of the day. When I did catch up with him he would explain how he had been in a different part of the building measuring up and ordering fittings. I knew this was a load of cobblers so I followed him after a dinner break and watched him fill his flask up from bottles on the conveyor belt (naughty boy Richard!) It all came to a head one day. Richard and the two new fitters were working on a suspended scaffold installing 6" (150mm) main pipe. The way to the scaffold was by means of a very tall ladder. When two had climbed the ladder after their dinner break they had probably only drunk a couple of bottles off Carlsberg so as finishing time was 5.30pm and there was no sight of them getting changed, I thought I had better see where they were. As I stepped out of the site hut, a worried manager of the brewery shouted to me, I don't know what the trouble is but your men for some reason, can't get down the ladder, so you had better see what's up. I didn't take much working out as to why they couldn't get down! There were a few workmen milling around under the scaffold thinking it all highly hilarious as they realised the men were so drunk they couldn't get down. Climbing up the ladder

I reached the scaffold and all over the boards were loads of empty beer bottles and the lads were so drunk they found it impossible to stand up. Richard slurred, John, we've been drinking all afternoon and we're smashed and there is no chance of us getting down that ladder. Well I said, you're going to need help down the ladder, that's for sure so I will find someone. But who I thought to myself. As I reached the bottom of the ladder the manager asked, what's the matter with them men? There not too well I replied, you mean they're pissed, he yelled! He was furious, and stormed off in a huff, shouting, heads will roll for this! What did he mean? About 10 minutes passed and through the doors walked the fire brigade. Oh my lord, I thought, there is going to be big trouble ahead, because this is going to have to be reported! The firemen had with them winches, tackles and harnesses and once one of the firemen had climbed the ladder he lowered a rope and pulled all the equipment up. Other firemen then went up and opened the scaffold up and with the three men now harnessed up, they were lowered one by one. I could have died, as each man was brought down; there was much applause from all the other trades. I've spoken to your firm, the manager snapped at me and they have told me to tell you that all four of you must report to head office in the morning! Oh dear, that sounds like the sack to me! We all nervously waited outside the construction manager's office, the next morning. I was told to stay where I was and the other three were called in to see him. About 10 minutes and then they all marched out with glum faces I knew they had got the chop. I was then called in. His first words to me were, I have sacked them three idiots for showing themselves up and also the good name of the firm, but I know you were not involved in all this so seeing that you know the job I'm putting you in charge and I'll send you two good fitters. Phew, that's good news; I thought I was for the chop as well! Because of the fire brigade incident anyone found so much as alcohol on their breath was liable for instant dismissal, suffice to say the drinking at work culture stopped immediately and the job was completed on time.

Poem

Watney Mann happened to be the name of the brewery
Where the manager to me one day vented his fury
The men that day had been drinking extra strong larger
That day was remembered for ending in quite a saga
These fools still had their senses but were really petrified
They knew stepping onto the ladder would be plain suicide
The fire-brigade were called to get down these fools

With them a vast array of kit and special tools
With the harness strapped on and a large tackle
An eyebolt securing the harness made safe with a shackle
Were winched down to earth in a most undignified way
Was all over for them there very last days pay
The moral of the story is don't work and booze
For it's not only your job that you could lose

Meeting Pat

I use to drink around the Paddington St Johns wood and Maida vale areas and occasionally I would meet up with Jim Gregg's younger brother Freddy. The pubs one visited were all up market and the one we used to use were very plush as was the area. It was in St Johns wood on entering the Pub I noticed two young ladies sitting at a table, chatting merrily between themselves. We both decided it would be a good ideal to go and "chat them up". Before we drew near to their table Freddy whispered "I'll chat to the blonde one, you chat to the ginger one!" My chat up line proved not to be the best around because I boldly remarked, I like a girl with ginger hair! It's not ginger, thank you very much, the colour of is auburn, she snapped. Well that put me in my place! That was the first meeting with Pat, who of course went on to become my wife! At about the same time this was still 1971 and Jim Gregg and his wife Alma, decided to move to Scotland would be a good idea. Alma's mother hailed from there and as they had a young son, named Simon, they thought it would be a better environment to bring up their children. They later went on to have another son named Graham. Having grown up with Jim, I have to admit I missed him at first, no longer able to set off for our long walks and plan our futures, hopes and our dreams, but you all move on.

Peter Beesworth

After finishing the Watney Mann Job I was transferred to other small jobs and then I was asked if I would fancy working on the mobiles at the weekends. I knew there was plenty of money to made working on them. The mobile carried around all the equipment needed to complete any job. In charge was Peter Beesworth, a stocky ex army man. He was a fitter-welder and could fly off the handle sometimes if someone or something upset him, but in spite of that a very nice person and to add to the mix a devout Christian. I agreed to join the mobile, as I knew you could earn well on it. The only downside about it was Peter was a workaholic and sometimes stayed on a job late at night, even if it was many miles away! The reason the head office wanted us to team up together was that peter lived in Paddington and I lived in Maida vale, a distance of about two miles. They also knew that I was a good worker and was always willing to work weekends. The main ingredients for a successful working partnership! Peter was in his middle fifties and had a grown up family and had been with the firm for twenty five years so knew the trade inside out. Once I had agreed to work on the mobile I arranged to meet peter at head office on a Friday afternoon. I hadn't bumped into him for sometime. On meeting him his first words to me were, I specially asked for you John I knew we would make a winning team! He went on; I will guarantee working with me you will earn £5000 a year. This being 1972, a huge sum for them days, the average yearly wages for that year was about £2,500. Right John, I will pick you up on Monday morning for a weeks work in an office block in the city, he beamed. We worked in the office block for the first week and the biggest hurdle to overcome was still being on the job at 8pm. It seemed the more overtime he could get the better! When he picked me up on the Wednesday morning he was not his normal happy self, and seemed a bit agitated. John, I have been told to ask you if you would be willing to work in Manchester for two nights next week. He went on to tell me that the work was on a building site, that was being picketed by all the work force, who had now been on strike for the past 4 weeks and if the job was not completed and tested by the end of the week, our firm would be hit with massive daily penalty clauses. So the workforce was hoping that the builders would cave-in to their demands because of the penalty clauses, but our firm and the builders had other ideas. Of course I agreed to go. It all sounded an adventure to me! The Monday came round and we set off for Manchester at noon.

The idea was we were to meet 3 men who were on the picket line in the day but at night no-one picketed the site and as they worked for our firm, then knew all the work that had to be done. The work was mainly welding and Peter being the best and fastest welder on the firm it was right up his Street. We met the 3 men who would be working with us, a couple of Streets away from the building site. A shiftier bunch of men you've ever seen, but of course, they were taking a big risk, because if their fellow pickets had got wind of their treachery I hate to think what would have happened. Making sure the coast was clear we all slipped in a side door, opened by one of the turn coats. As all the work involved was in the basement, power could be used and lights and electric tools and welding equipment also used, and as it was the bottom basement, there were no worries about noise levels. We worked through the night and sometimes in the night you stated to think "what if", what if we were discovered by them men on the picket line?> I had visions of being found working by the now very angry and hungry, not being paid men and with my four limbs having being ripped off, battered over the head with one of them (ouch). One of the men throughout the night had kept watch from an upstairs window making sure no-one suspected anything. We were booked in a hotel and that's were we headed after we finished the night shift. We made sure we left the site at 6am, knowing that the picket line started forming at 7am. After a few hours sleep, Peter and myself decided that we would see for our selves the men manning the picket line. On approaching the site, on opposite side of the roads there were roughly 50 men shouting their demands, with their posters demanding "all for one, and one for all" and "united we stand, divided we fall" but the one poster that stood out had written on it "no scab labour here" (a scab is sometimes known as a blackleg). This is a person who won't support any action taking place by a trade union. On dear, sorry men, we have 3 "scabs" and us two outsiders, working in your building. Looking how big, mean looking, and angry they were I was glad we were only there for one more night! But I decided if caught working by them, my coward side would shine and I would tell them I'm a pacifist and believed any form of violence is unjustifiable and all disputes should be settled by dialogue and hoped they would take pity on this coward now before them that was kneeling down with his hands in a praying position with sad begging eyes. The next night we carried on the same as the previous night but what was different was the site was now full of other trades. We must have been the guinea pigs, to see how things went. The builders had now brought labour from far and wide! I asked the three lads why they had worked, instead of joining the picket line. They all said they couldn't afford to strike and knew all the men now on the picket line would be sacked as soon as the dispute was over. Even their partners were sworn to secrecy as they put it. If they found out we had double crossed them our lives would not be worth living. After finishing all our work, we were able to leave at 5am, I was never so happy to be leaving a place, never ever, would I repeat this episode. On the long drive home, we got chatting and I asked Peter if he had ever been in a situation like the one we had just experienced. My worst working experience Peter recalled, was when I had only worked for this firm for two years and was by myself on the mobile, and went to do some welding in a newly built bakery in Hertfordshire, he went on, the bakery had four floors and most of the building was made of wood and I was just welding the last pipe of the new sprinkler system that had been installed. I was welding on the top floor next to some newly erected ducking. I had been welding for about an hour when I heard this shout, everybody out, there's a fire! Peter then said, I did wonder if I my have caused the fire as the ducting was open at the spot were I was welding. By the time I got out the building it was totally alight and by the time the fire brigades had arrived, not much was left of this two hundred year old bakery, not all that old then Peter! While the first fire brigade were still damping down what little remained of the building the site engineer called all the shocked building workers together and asked if anyone had any idea how the fire started. Peter, being a good Christian, held his hand up and said, it was probably my fault I was welding near some open ducting and some sparks must have fallen down the duct. The site manager shook Peter by the hand and said I have been in the building trade all my life and you're the first man that has ever admitted to anything, let alone admitting to causing the fire that burnt this listed building down! (Whoops) Our firm, we're not best pleased, that firstly Peter owned up to causing the fire and secondly admitting it! Peter did say he heard the cost of the fire was nearly £250,000 a whopping sum at that time. What surprised Peter, he didn't lose his Job! A few years after this experience, I was working at a firm called Standard Telephone Company (S.T.C), this was situated in a Southgate off of the north circular road, north London and merrily working away installing pipe, when a voice behind me shouted, hello John, and turning around I saw that it was one of the Manchester men, that had worked on the picketed site. He went on to tell me that six months after that picketed job, he and nine other men, were asked if they would work of another picketed job, but with a difference, as this was in Sydney, Australia. They were offered a handsome bonus once the job was finished. They all of course said yes to the offer, it was for six weeks. He said as on the Manchester job, if they had been caught working, they would have been strung up and lynched by the Aussie's.

The idea having the mobile was to do small jobs that two men could handle and it required a lot of weekend working, where staff would not be there. So over the months, Peter and myself worked on many small jobs, but one job that was for a much longer period was at STC. We worked there for about 3 months and the story that springs to mind is the one about Chris, a ceiling fixer, who owned the firm erecting all the false ceilings. In the four large buildings that made up the complex, he had worked on the same buildings five years previously, then for another large ceiling fixing company. He then went on to tell us his story. He said they had a weeks work left on the job, and the management approached his boss, and asked them, if they would give a price, for a small canteen that had been built. His bosses told STC they weren't interested in quoting for such a small job, STC Management were furious with them, they then asked Chris if he would be willing to do it, yes I will help you out, but I could only do it in the evenings and probably two weekends. He pointed out you would have to supply the materials, as I have no savings. They agreed to do this and paid him an hourly rate. He completed the job to his usual high standard, and then they said to him, your firm, have in the past two years, have had a million pounds worth of work from us, and they couldn't even be bothered to quote for this small job! So what we have decided to do is to ask you if you would quote for our work in the future. Before he has time to answer, the manager said in the early stages, we would supply all the material and equipment, and we would allow you to do the jobs on day work rates, and once you get on your feet, you could give us quotes for jobs, what's your answer to that? Chris was flabbergasted, he went on to say, here I was, an ordinary working class man, in my middle thirties, living in a council hose in Basildon, Essex, with a wife and three kids, and given this opportunity, I couldn't believe my luck, so naturally I accepted this once in a lifetime opportunity, as he put it. Within two years I not only did work for STC but built my firm up so was able to price for other contracts and within five years was the third largest ceiling firm in London. He had now a new house in leafy part of Essex, and owned a house built in Florida. It just goes to show you in life, being in the right place at the right time gets its reward, and also in this case, the saying goes, from acorn a mighty oak tree can grow! And it couldn't of happened to a nicer man!

Even though with Peter, we seemed forever working, I still tried to fit in a social life with Pat, and living so close to the West End, we used to be able to go to the latest shows, and clubs and one of the pubs that we visited quite frequently was a pub just on the edge of Regents park, named the price regent, with quite a good mix of customers, mainly middle class people that live in the area, and a few hippies that were allowed to smoke their spliffs by the young manager. (Pat and I) after a while got friendly with these, spaced out, laid back, spliff smoking, peace to the world types. You could nearly get yourself high on just the puff floating around. On this Saturday I parked the car as usual, we entered the pub and for some reason it was unusually busy for that time of the evening we just managed to spot two empty seats and asking the hippies why the pub was so full they said it was a lot of the landlords and landlord's relations celebrating his birthday. He also said that the wife's side of the family came from the east end and their husbands came from south London but they had mixed together before with no trouble. But to me most of them looked to be very unsavoury characters. As the evening went on they seemed to be in a threatening mood and I decided it would probably be prudent to make ourselves scarce as I felt something was about to kick off and looking at Pat, I could see that she also sensed something was not quite right. The landlord and his wife were both serving behind the bar, the chatter of the customers was instantly silenced, because of this huge man standing at the bar shouted at the manager, you're wife's an old slag and half the men in this pub have shagged her! Am I dreaming? Did he really say that? This only happens in movies right? The saga, then took a turn for the worse because by the time the huge aggressive man had finished his sentence the landlord had unscrewed the beer dispensing handle and whacked big man right over his head, with it. But it didn't make the slightest difference on big man because he grabbed hold of the landlord and gave him a Glasgow kiss. Within seconds the pub was in total uproar. Chairs were being used as weapons and beer glasses went flying just like a scene from a Wild West bar brawl. It seemed strange but it all seemed to be taking place in slow motion. This was now getting serious, especially as the next sound we heard were the large window panes being shattered. As it was now too dangerous to make a run for it with chairs, glasses and bottles whizzing about, I decided the best course of action was to seek protection under the table we were sitting at. So grabbing Pat we both sheltered under it and looking from both sides of the table saw that all the other customers not involved in the fracas were also hiding under them. We only came in here for a quiet drink and now find ourselves in a war zone. What seemed like hours, but was probably only minutes, then a calm voice said, look this is not your fight so follow me and I will show you a way out. Who is this rescuer? Am I still in this endless dream? The voice said keep as low as possible and we will make for the off-licence door that leads to the car park. So with this brave knight in front, Pat following and me behind we took up a crouched position and attempted to make our way to the door as the brave knight managed to prize the door open, I was more than surprised, on turning my head to find a large Alsatian has also joined us, this was the pubs guard dog! Talk about "when the going gets tough, the tough get going!" Here was the perfect example this fighting breed, this protector of his master and property was now lined up in the queue. If you please! Waiting to get the hell out of there! This once vicious, snarling, growling, and teeth baring fighting machine that was called an Alsatian, was now reduced to a yellow bellied wimp dog, and shaking with fear, it was a disgrace to its breed. The coward dog was the first one out of the door (a very bad mannered dog) and now with the outer door open, Pat and I made our escape. The dog had disappeared within seconds, for some strange reason, the man who led us out went back into the pub. We quickly got into my car and drove out of the car park, passing us were police cars and riot vans. Phew, we were glad to get out of that hell hole, in once piece.

Poem

Making our way to the price regent for a beer
Was known as one of the better pubs there
And then the land lady was called a very nasty word
It suddenly all kicked off that's when the battle occurred
Two families at war with each other they really fought
It's always been a peaceful pub or so we thought
But were both in for a shock on that night
Have never seen a rumpus like it a terrible fight
The big man was hit with the beer pulling handle
It might as well been with a soft scented candle
Bottles glasses and everything else went flying through the air
And also sailing by was a huge wooden chair
Thank god we were rescued from this real bad scary night
Outside and safe the end of our ordeal and plight

I had now worked on the mobile with Peter for 3 years and had worked on some of the best known places in London. This included the London stock exchange New Scotland Yard, the Houses of Parliament, the Bank of England, St Paul's Cathedral and many more. Peter and I had already signed the official secrets act forms and had our clearance certificates. These enabled us to work on any military bases and all government buildings and offices. As usual, Peter picked me up one morning and said we have what should be an interesting Job starting next Monday. What's that then Peter I asked? It's at the bank of England, Peter proudly said. It's only for a few days, so it should prove to be different from our normal work. On arriving at the Bank BOE from the first hurdle that had to be overcome was the fact that no vehicles were allowed entry. So all tools had to be carried in by hand. Our job was to run some copper pipe around the basement area. So the few tools we needed were put through scanner and an x-ray machine and had to be left on site, until the job was completed. The security is what you would expect with a bank, which holds the nations wealth. It's what could be described as "total". No wonder it had never been robbed in its history. Armed guards and solders Patrol it permanently. The walls in the basement are probably 5ft (1.5m) thick and it was on one wall that we needed to get brackets on to support our pipe. Peter started to drill into the wall and was drilling away from about ten minutes when an excited voice bellowed " Stop drilling immediately you fool!" it was the clerk of the works. Don't you know that live cables run down the inside of these walls. If you had hit one, you wouldn't be here now. Someone had forgot to give us a elf 'n safety talk, so we were flung off site and told to return when we had been fully inducted. Just to think how lucky peter was to have missed these live cables that are there of course to deter anyone from trying to break in. For some reason we never returned back there.

It was now 1974 and I was still working on the mobile with Peter. The wages were very good but the downside was the long hours that we had to work. Peter would sometimes pick me up at 5:30am and say, today's job is near Portsmouth. So we would drive all the way down there, finish the job maybe at 8pm and then drive back. Getting home at say midnight, and then he wanted to be back on the road early the next morning. The outcome of all this is I wasn't getting home or a social life so was hardly seeing Pat as we worked every week-end. Pat was saying, you can't keep this up, and she was right of course. I had the appearance of a simpleton that was using massive doses of heroin and crack cocaine, with bulging eyes, that were nearly coming out of their sockets and grey pasty face and being completely knackered. Peter was used to it as he had been doing it for years and was a workaholic. On one of the rare days that we finished early, Pat and I went for a meal in our favourite Pub called the Crown, in St Johns Wood and the conversation turned to the fact that we both had separate flats and it seemed to be silly paying two rents and seeing we seemed to be a match made in heaven. By the end of the evening we decided that we should get a place together, but where? London was too expensive to buy a house even in them days, but, one of my friends, Brian had ten years earlier moved with his wife and kids to a new town that had been built which was 45 miles north of London, and this was in Bletchley, Milton Keynes, Buckinghamshire. So we both arranged to meet Brian and his wife Margaret on the following Saturday. Brian happened to work for the building firm Wimpey and he worked as a site surveyor for them. The site was just outside Bletchley town centre and Brian showed us around the houses. A two bedroom semi-detached house with a garage was selling for £8,500 and a three bedroom semi was £11,000. This may seem cheap now but this was 1974. Brian's words were, if you lay down a £50 deposit, you can have any one of the houses as easy as that. This seemed too good to be true, but true it was, because we did indeed put a

£50 deposit down on one of the two bed houses as we couldn't afford a 3 bed house and was told the house should be ready to move into in eight weeks. As all the houses were new-builds we had both visited Bletchley a few times over the years because we used to stay with Margaret and Brian for weekends and they added attraction for me was the train service to London was very good and even in them days it only used to take 50 minutes to get to Euston Station. And what made the move even more appealing on the weekend visit to Bletchley I got talking to the builders who were working on the new shopping arcade in Bletchley called the Brunel Centre and as luck would have it a new sprinkler system was being installed and the firm called Wormalds needed two more fitters. So after talking to the boss of Wormalds, and telling him of my experience in all forms of pipe-work, he agreed to take me on, when I finally moved to Bletchley. So after putting down a deposit on the house and staying the weekend with Brian and Margaret we drove home to London and both felt elated about our very first house! Fantastic. In 1974 ordinary working people like us were just starting to buy houses, as the wages started to improve, building societies were willing to lend you 3 times your salary, so house buying for working class people started to take off. At this time, it was now left for me to tell Peter about the purchase of our new house. I knew he wouldn't take it well because this successful partnership we had going, would break up as I would be leaving the firm. I was surprised how well he did take it, once I had told him; I think he thought we could still talk me round in staying together, even when I had moved! We worked together on a few more small jobs before I was due to leave. Pat and I used to drive up to Bletchley every week and see how the house was going and it was on one of these visits we were able to witness the completion of our house and the builders gave us a moving in date for two weeks time. This all worked out well as I was now able to give my notice in with Matthew Hall and to tell the Wormalds Boss I would taking up his offer of employment. On informing Peter I was give two weeks notice he snapped at me. You've been at the firm seven years John, where's your loyalty. Peter was such a firm's man and felt any man leaving was letting the firm down and to him it was an act of treason. I was due to leave on the Friday but there was no respite in the workload or hours Peter had me working. Peter had a rented mews garage just off the Portobello road in Notting Hill Gate, where all surplus materials that Peter had collected off previous sites were stored. He would drive to the lock-up garage on a Monday and load his van with the week's work he was scheduled to do. On the Tuesday night Pat had said to me don't forget you must be home early Wednesday as I have booked up for the show and we can't be late! On the Wednesday morning is ait to Peter, what ever happens I must not be late tonight as I'm going out. At the time we were driving down to Chatham in Kent to finish off a Job we had started a week earlier. By 1pm the water was put on the system and Peters next words hit me like a ton of bricks, seeing that its still early I think we will go down to Gillingham, it's not far away and do a small Job there. But Peter, I protested, I'm going out tonight and I need to be home early. You couldn't argue with Peter he was the one driving the van. As he went to get his work sheets signed, I thought to myself we will see about that! So quickly making my way to the van I found the sack of fittings marked "Gillingham" opened it up and proceeded to throw all the fittings into an adjoining field and then throw the bag away. I watched as Peter approached the van and I said, before we drive to Gillingham I think it would be a good ideal to check we have all the fittings on board. Don't be silly John I loaded them myself so I know they're on board. Well said, I've just been in the van and didn't seem them! They must be there he screamed, you're not looking properly. His face was blood red and the eyes were bulging, within the next half hour he had completely cleared out every fitting from the van shouting and swearing, I'm sure I put them fittings on, the pipework is on, so why aren't the fittings? Well Peter, it looks like we will have to return home! You haven't thrown them away have you John. Don't be silly peter, trying to suppress a smile, why would I do that? Peter finally agreed we would have to return home, but it was with a heavy heart that he did so. Peter it seemed was still trying to repay the firm for burning down the bakery, all those years back. (I wish I had been there). I got my early night all because of my devious deed. He drove me to my flat and I said, Peter seeing that I'm leaving, I won't be in tomorrow as I'm moving to the new house on Saturday and I have a lot to sort out. (Two suitcases in fact!) Facing me with tears in his eyes, he sobbed, I'm going to miss you so much, it's been great working with you and hugged me tightly. Thankfully a full blown kiss never followed. Although Peter had worked the balls off me but we built up a good rapport between ourselves and I would also miss him, but I won't be missing the long hours and having a social life!

"Buying our first home"

Pat worked at Woolworths head office, in Marylebone road just off the Edgeware road. She was employed as one of the many secretaries that worked there; she worked for the head toy buyer for the UK. Quite a responsible position and had worked in that office for 10 years. She had given in her notice a month previously and did so with a bit of soul-searching as she had spent a happy 10 years there. They offered to pay her fare to London, if that would keep her there but she decided a clean break would be the best, even though job wise it was going to be a step into the unknown. But she hoped to get employment in Bletchley. So we had now both left our jobs but I was due to start my new one on the Monday. It was now Saturday the 1st of November 1974 and I was now 35 years of age. This was the day of the move to Bletchley. A new life, a new dawn and the first home in my life I could truly call my own, after spending so many years in and out of other peoples places and children's homes. A friend of mine kindly gave me the use of his old battered white van to do the removals so with my worldly goods that consisted of two falling apart suitcases and Pats suitcases and some of her bric-a-brac collected over the years, we set off to our new life. We had already picked up the keys to our new house the previous week and so just over an hour later we were outside our brand new house. It was the only one of the semi-detached houses that was ready for occuPation as all the other ones were still in different stages of construction. Builders like to get one house occupied on a site as this helps deter the thieves. What a great feeling, opening the front door to your first house. We had arranged for a new bed to be delivered on this day and low and behold it turned up as we were looking around the house. We managed to buy a second hand three piece suite as money was very tight at this time. The mortgage was £79 a month, it may not seem like much now but in 1974 it was quite a big slice of your wages. I drove the borrowed van back to London and then drove my car back to our new house. A new life had started. As our house was situated right on the edge of the new estate it felt strange not having any neighbours as the rest of the plots were still only half completed. The back garden of our house had a fence but there were no fences on any of the unfinished houses. So on the Sunday of the move in I decided I would walk down the back gardens of all the unfinished houses and look in the houses and see if they had the same cupboards as our house. On noticing one of the houses had an extra cupboard. I thought this warranted investigating so seeing that I had my back door key on me I wondered if it might fit one of the back doors? On turning the key low and behold it unlocked! Unbelievable, surely this must be a one off? But I tried the next houses back door with the same key. It seemed the builders had brought the same locks and keys for of the housing estate which was totally unacceptable but my view was not one of the tenants will ever know so as long as I say nothing about it there will no problem. Pat decided that she would have a few weeks off before looking for work to get to know Bletchley and get used to this new way of life. The Monday had arrived and I was due to start for Wormalds. What the pleasing thing about this job it was only about 10 minutes walk from the house! I had been told at the Job interview that I would be taking over from the foreman pipefitter who will show you around for a day and then he would move on to another job. I had arranged to meet Dick on the job, an old work mate from London who was also starting with Wormald the same day. Arriving on the Job I was greeted by Dick who looked a bit glum. What's up Dick I asked? What's up, he said, I can't find anybody around and looking at the job it seems to be in a right state. What have we got ourselves into? Where was that foreman? Where was anybody? Asking one of the builders where were the pipefitters? Oh, them he signed, they travel up from London and don't get in before 10am, but I think they all got the sack last week. Both Dick and I waited in a cafe 'till 10, then went back on site and watched as two men put on their overalls. Are you the new starts I said to them, is one of you the foreman? No mate the meaner looking one growled. The foreman got sacked last week and both of us are only working till dinner time and then jacking it in. We only came in today to show you around and to pick up our tools. But why are you leaving and why did the foreman get sacked, I asked? Well he said we all had a row with the construction manager, Mr Packham last week and he's a nasty evil sod so three men left last week and we're leaving today. Having heard all of this Dick and I should have turned around and walked away. The two men disappeared for about 20 minutes and returned to say, we'll show you around the job now and once we have we will get doing and if that Packham bloke shows up tell him that we both said he can get stuffed. After showing us all over the job, they informed us that all the first fix pipe that had been installed was completed as was now ready for testing. Don't worry about putting an air test on as we have already air-tested it so it's ready for water testing and the water test needs to be completed today. As they departed was that a wry smile I noticed on both their faces. I turned to dick and said things just don't seem to stack up, they wouldn't tell us the reason they are leaving and why come in this morning for just one hour. It doesn't make sense. There's more questions than answers I'm afraid and we were about to find out the hard way the answers. Let's just make sure dick that they have left no open ends. The shopping mall had just about 10 shops in it, so all the pipework above the false ceilings had finished but the false ceiling pipe work had not been installed yet, everything looked in order so we both went to the valve-set and dick said, I think we should put the system on air, because I don't trust them tow-rags, they may have left an open end somewhere, it should be alright I said confidently, lets go for it. Right Dick, you crack the valve very slowly, and I will Patrol the shops if you hear me shouting shut the valve and drain down right away. OK Dick said, let's do it, so I walked into every shop and informed them the sprinkler system was going on test but there will be no problem with it, just letting you know folks. So I walked around the shops looking up at the ceilings making sure there were no water marks showing and twice going round to see dick at the valve set to tell him all was OK. I then returned to the shops and was talking to the shop assistant in the large cash and carry linen shop. It was then that I heard this dreaded whooshing sound from above the ceiling. Oh no I don't believe it that sound means only one thing, an open end somewhere! The shop was full of women and children as it was half term. What happened next was like something out of a comedy come horror movie. A torrent of black water tore out of the false ceiling bringing it down on the women and children. The screams of the terrified shoppers was ear piercing not only were they all drenched in black water they had bits of ceiling tiles all over them. Even though it was quite a serious situation it looked like a scene from a carry on film. By now blind panic took over, women grabbed their kids and ran screaming out the shop in terror. They were followed out by the water logged and bedraggled shop assistants who on their way out swore at me in a very unladylike manner. Charming. I myself was in total shock. I was in this cannot be happening syndrome. I stood there rooted to the spot. I had only just started on the firm two hours ago and now this comedy of errors was taking place. I was quickly brought out of my dream like state that I found myself in by a false ceiling tile falling on me followed by gallons of muddy water. Right, pull yourself together John! Immediate action is now needed and now, it was needed fast because I was now standing in water that was filling my army style boots. So running as fast as my water filled boots would let me, I ran hoping to see dick at the valve set station but horror of all horrors the valve set door was closed, and dick, who was supposed to be manning the valve was nowhere to be seen. I didn't have a key to the door but I could hear by the water flow rushing noise that he had turned the valve fully on. Please ground beneath me open up and swallow me up! Running up and down like a demented lunatic I spotted dick sitting in the cafe in conversations with one of the builders, completely oblivious to the drama that was taking place. Dick had now spotted my frantic gestures and arms waving and slowly got to his feet and calmly strolled out of the cafe. What's up John, you look a bit stressed. I wasn't stressed, I was near suicidal! Dick was a very laid back lad but quickly shut the main valve and got it drained down. As dick drained down I asked him why he had opened the valve full on? Well I hadn't heard from you so I thought everything was OK. We got the system drained and made our way back to the shops. What greeted us was not a pretty sight. Most of the cash and carry stores ceiling was laying on the floor and water were still pouring out from above. About half the stock was soaking wet and the owner was going ballistic. These things happen I boldly said. You two fools should be sacked on the spot. You've ruined most of my stock, he shouted and this is going to cost your firm a fortune. Lets get out of here dick, I said and see if there is any more shops damaged. We didn't have to look far because on the opposite side to cash and carry was a tobacconist that too was flooded out. My stock, the owner was shouting, it's ruined; I'll have to throw it all away. Well Dick, it looks like you have to be the man to phone head office, and inform the boss what's happened. You must be joking he said, you're the main man so it's up to you. What do I say to him I pleaded. Just tell him how it was. We're probably going to get sacked anyway so stuff him, dick said. Definitely. Mr Packham was a no nonsense Australian brought in my Wormalds to shake it up. He was the construction manager and he had a fearsome reputation. Any breech of the firm's rules or any misdemeanours and you were out on your neck. His nick name was sackham Peckham, so this was the man I now had to phone. The conversation went something like this, with a bit of tongue in cheek.

(Me) Can I speak to Mr Packham please?

(Mr P) Packham here, who are you and what do you want?

(Me) Well Mr Packham, my name is John Banfield and I started on the Brunel centre in Bletchley this morning and just to let you know we've had a bit of a mishap with the water and there's been a flood.

(Mr P) What you mean "a mishap and a flood", explain yourself man

(Me) Well Mr Packham, the cash & carry fabric shop we were water testing now has 3" inches of water on the floor that won't drain away and the false ceiling is now laying on the shop floor.

(Mr P) I can't believe what I'm hearing, explain to me why it has no false ceiling and how the shop got flooded

(Me) Well sir, the men we took over from told us it had been air tested so we went ahead and put the system on water but they left some open ends.

(Mr P) Are you both f**king idiots? You know you should have put it on air, just to make sure everything was OK"

(me) well Mr Packham, the managers of the cash and carry shop took it quite well under the circumstances because only 50% of her stock was water damaged so she will be claiming for that, plus the loss of trade for two days and also some of her customers were not too happy with the ceiling falling down on top of them and being drenched by the waterfall that followed so they are also claiming compensation for shock and trauma but fortunately the other shop that got flooded was a large tobacconist so his stock was stored in his back room.

(Mr P) You're now telling me there is another shop that was flooded?

(Me) Yes, and he's saying that half of his stock is ruined but the bad news Mr Packham, is that he reckons with the trauma of seeing his stock floating past him he thinks he will be needing the services of a solicitor and he points out his loss of stock is nothing to what he hopes the high court judge will award him eventually

(Mr P) don't go anywhere; I'll be up to see you both within two hours to sort this mess out.

(Me) Ok Mr P we await your arrival.

A Holden estate car pulled up and as this huge man alighted from it this was the first time Dick and myself had set eyes on this Aussie Mr Packham. He looked as people had described, mean, big and aggressive. We were both prepared to be given the sack there and then so were ready to face up to him and to tell him what he could do with himself (get stuffed). After introducing himself to us both he said, now run through if you would, exactly how you came to be in this position. After explaining how two fitters told us the system was ready to water test we went ahead with it. He looked quite shocked and uttered; I sacked the last foremen and two fitters on the Tuesday of last week and sacked the other two fitters on the Friday because I found them all in the pub on two occasions. These two men should not have been on site so it looks like they sabotaged the job. I would like you now to show me the damage done and see if we can find the open-ends that caused all the damage. As both the shops were now closed we were able to get a clearer picture how the flood occurred. Looking up to the pipework above sackham Packham shouted, strewth mate, they've taken a 4" inch (100mm) tee out, the bastards. No wonder there was so much damage. He sighed; I suppose we're getting the sack now? Dick chimed in, not caring one way or another. No, no sackham Packham replied, don't be silly, this was not your fault.

His whole demeanour had suddenly changed and we both realised why. When he said the insurance won't pay out for flood damage if they know that sacked workers sabotaged the installation. We will tell the insurance assessor that the rubber in a clamp holding the tee was split, this caused the water pressure to force the tee off the clamp and in the tobacconist shop we'll say a sprinkler head was faulty and it went off, so if you two can stick to that story they will pay out and if you can finish the job, I promise to give you both a good bonus. A week later, an insurance assessor turned up with sackham Packham and was satisfied with the load of old cobblers we gave him as to how it all happened. We received our promised bonus and finished the job and both left the firm. We were both asked if we wanted to start a job in Weymouth, but we both didn't want to work away and never wanted to see sackham Packham every again! Dick went back to London to work and I started with a firm called Mather & Platt.

Poem

We had just started a new firm on that day
We didn't know it wasn't going to be out day
Is that the dreaded sound of water I can hear?
Should have listened to dick and put system on air
Not very nice hearing women and kids screaming and shouting
A tide of water falling just like a gigantic fountain
The owner of the fabric shop was in deep shock
Watching as the black water was flooding all her stock
What's that sailing by is it them curtains and drapes
All in amazing pretty colours most sizes and different shapes
Hope they sue our firm in a court of law
Deserve every penny they get and that's for sure

It was now November 1975 and I was now 36 years old. We had now lived in our new house for a year now but Pat still missed the bright lights of London and also the shopping trips to Oxford Street. We used to frequently visit Jean my sister who lived in Bermondsey, south London and stay the weekend. On this particular weekend Jean had invited us down because it was the lord mayor's show on the Saturday. The Lord Mayors show is a colourful parade of people from all walks of life from dancers, to fire-eaters and a big part of the show is a march past by the three armed services a spectacular sight with the massed bands and pipers from the regiments, plus the lord Mayor. The journey time by car to Bermondsey from Bletchley was about an hour and a half, so we set off about nine o'clock intending to park at Jeans house in good time, to be able to walk to the show which only takes about 15 minutes. My normal way to Jeans house was to get to Victoria Station then up Victoria Street and then go over Westminster Bridge then 10 minutes later, you would arrive at Jeans. On this day I got to the traffic lights at Westminster Bridge, hoping as usual to cross over Westminster Bridge but there were signs everywhere saying Victoria Embankment closed, all Bridges up till Tower Bridge are closed, please follow diversion signs to Whitehall. I said to Pat, I'm not going all the way round there, it will take ages, so spotting a gap in the metal barriers that was probably there to let police cars and mounted police through I drove through the narrow gap, then realised why the barriers were in place because to my dismay I was now on the Victoria Embankment and this was the route for the Lord Mayors show! Both sides of the embankment were lined with thousands of spectators. You can imaging how surprised both Pat and I were and equally excited crowds seeing this 1960 something dilapidated green ford corsair coming towards them. They all must have thought that I was the first one starting the parade because a huge roar went up and all the flags stated to wave. I noticed that Pat had now slumped down in her seat in sheer embarrassment and she cried out Oh My God! I on the other hand was loving it, with my arm sticking out of the window and giving a regal wave and I noticed people taking photos which made it even more fun. However I had now covered about one hundred metres when I noticed a police sergeant gesturing with his arms for me to stop. As I brought the car to a halt, the sergeant gave me a military type salute and with a wry smile said, good morning sir, I think sir has taken the wrong road and does sir realise that he is on the route that the Lord Mayors show is just about to start. Err, um, I muttered, I'm sorry sergeant, but I got confused with all the signs. Well sir, he said, if your good self would drive further up this road you will see a police officer standing at a slip road and he will direct you where you should turn off and good-day to you sir he said as he once again saluted me. (They certainly don't make them like that anymore.) The crowd got into the spirit of things and good humorously started to boo and with shouts of let him carry on, and I'm sure I heard three cheers for the old banger! I have often wondered how many people in that crowd have still got photos of me driving along that route that day.

Poem

To the lord Mayors show we were going that day
Then made to do a detour and go another way
Look there's a gap ahead I will drive up there
Just where the road takes me I know not where
But hey, why are all them people waving at me
So many thousands as far as the eye could see
Why are they cheering me in my ancient green car?
Surely the cannot be mistaking me for a star
My euphoria was abruptly ended by this man in blue
With a salute saying this road you cannot go through
Everyone in their life deserves just a moment of glory
This comical saga that happened to be a true story

Seeing that Dick and myself had left sackham Packham and his crazy firm I needed to get work, so decided to phone my old firm, Matthew Hall and see if they would restart me. Matthew Hall was one of those firms that if you had a good work record with them and if they had work they had no hesitation in taking you back. No problem came back he reply but we only have a vacancy for away work in Liverpool and Manchester at the moment and seeing I needed to work, I accepted the offer. The firm gave me the address of Alex a fitter who had worked for them for many years and it was arranged for me to make my way to Northampton where he lived and he would drive us both up to Liverpool where the job was. Pat wasn't too pleased about it but knew it was only short term. Early on the Monday morning I drove up to Northampton introduced myself to Alex who was a huge Scotsman and was nearing retirement age. I parked my car outside his house and we set off to Liverpool in his car. On the journey, Alex told me all about himself and his work history. Alex had worked most of his life working away and loved it. So as this was my first time I was pleased that I was with someone who knew the ropes but he did admit that he struggled a bit with the work as his joints were now stiffening up. I put him at ease by saying don't worry Alex; I'll do the donkey work. Just before we left his house, his wife was telling me she had been nagging him to retire, as she said, he's not up to it anymore, so can you look after him and make sure he doesn't work too hard. And as Alex was a gentle giant and had a nice demeanour about him it would be a poor show if I couldn't help him in every way. We managed to find the job after driving around Liverpool for a couple of hours. It was in the dock area named Seaforth docks and the job was a nearly completed grain silo. As with all city docks by the seventies, Liverpool's warehouses were deserted and shipping hardly existed. The foreman on the job greeted both Alex and myself warmly and showed us around the huge site. As we climbed to the very top of the tall building he said well gentleman over there is a Job every one has refused to do! As we got nearer I could see why. In the middle of a round shaped building was handrail that surrounded an open floor that went all the way down to the ground floor. Above was a large glass dome, this is where the problem lay. The dome needed sprinkler protection but there was nowhere a tower or ladder could be used. Have a look at it lads and see what you think, but before you start the job, I suggest you both look for digs as they are hard to get around here. Alex and I walked the Streets knocking on doors asking for digs but nothing doing. Alex then said, I've been digging for forty years and if stuck for digs go to a police station, they always have bed and breakfast lists, given to them by landlords. So armed with the only address they had we made our way to the lodging house. It looked really tatty from the outside but it was getting late so we knocked at the door. Opening the door was a really rough looking man, yep, what do you want? Have you any vacancies asked Alex. You have to share he snapped, OK Alex said. Right follow me, the rough hard looking man grunted. He led us into a room that had seen better days. There were three beds either side of the room and it seemed it would be a struggle to walk between the beds. I noticed there were no wardrobes in the room, but hooks on wall above each bed where clothes were hanging. If you want the room it will be £2.50 (50p would have been too much) a night. We'll take it Alex said before I could say I'm out of here. Why did you say we would have this dump-hole? And worse still share it with four other men? His reply to that was John, if you could have seen some of the rat-infested dumps I have lodged in you would say this was a palace. Well I can tell you now Alex, I chimed in, I'm only staying here one night and if I can't find something better tomorrow I'm going back home! We got back to the site and looked at the job again, with the foreman and he said If you say you cannot do the job, fair enough, I'll give you another Job, but if you agree to do it and complete it, then I'll let you both have a day off with pay! Phew what a carrot to dangle in front of someone! They must be desperate to get it done. We both looked at it from all angles, it can't be done I sighed. I've just had an idea, Alex beamed proudly, we get an extension ladder and I will hold the ladder with my arms as far up the ladder as I can. Always up for a challenge, I said to Alex, let's do a dummy run on this, away from the handrail and just see if you can hold me on the ladder at the height needed to do the job. So with me now at the required height I shouted down. How long do you think you can hold me, for ever he replied. And I was convinced he could. OK, you've proved you can support me even without the hand rail so we will do it. So we made all the pipe up and was ready to attempt the task. Trust me wee John, Alex said, as I climbed up the ladder with the pipe. I slowly got to the rung on the ladder I needed to be and was able to screw the pipe in. I have never been so terrified in my life, my legs were shaking in an uncontrollable manner and that was the only one I was going to do that day. When I got down I had to sit for quite a while to get over the shock of it all. I knew we could do it, Alex shouted triumphantly, only another five to go! I felt physically sick, what was I doing up there, I must be had! Just one mistake and I could have been brown bread. The foreman came to see how were getting on and was highly delighted to find we had managed to get one of the pipes in position. His words were, I know it's very awkward so take as long as it takes (you bet we will) and you can go home now and I'll see you in the morning. Let's go for a pint Alex suggested and I was certainly up for that because I was dreading spending the night in that six bed room doss house. My view on it was if I had a few drinks inside me I wouldn't notice the bleak surroundings. We both returned to the dump about eleven that night and made our way to the bedroom and on entering were pleased we were the only people there. Alex said, give me all your money and your watch and I will put it in my money belt that I always wear around my waist when I stay in these dodgy places (my god was his last job on a pirate ship?) and don't worry laddie, I'll look after you! (What was he expecting, all his old crew mates!!) We both settled down for the night and with the amount of alcohol I had consumed was quickly into a deep sleep. This sleep was rudely interrupted by this yelling and shouting and looking across the room, watched as two near naked men were laying into each other on top of their beds a frightening sight I was witnessing, in between the head butting, kicking and swearing they were both dishing out to each other. One of them was accusing the other of stealing money out of his trousers. It was ended by the owner who burst in through the door and managed to separate them and on hearing their story grabbed hold of the accused rogue and made him repay the money he had nicked and physically picked him up with his bag of clothes and flung him out of the door and telling him never to return back there. Alex was proved right to be on his guard! Very little sleep I got after all that what with the burping, the gasses being exploded and worse the thunder like snoring, even with the pillow over my head, it hardly made any difference. The morning couldn't come quickly enough. With Alex so used to such noises he slept through it all! Unbelievable, that certainly had been a hard day's night!

Arriving on site the next morning the foreman on seeing me remarked, My God John, look at the state of you, it looks like you have been up all night! After telling him all about the night's saga and saying if I don't get better digs for tonight I'm off home. Leave it with me he said, you start work and I'll get something sorted! Alex and myself managed to install two more pipes that day. I've sorted what seems like good digs for you both the foreman greeted us at lunch break. One of the canteen girl's mother-in-laws house and you'll like it there. The address was in Bootle not to far from where we were working, it was in a run down part of town so knocking on the door we were most surprised to find a warm and welcoming lady with an immaculately tidy house. Her name was Mary and till recently had been a nurse in a local hospital for many years but had decided that being a landlady was easier than nursing. She had only two other lodgers as she had only started taking people in two weeks previously. With a full breakfast and an evening meal thrown in, all the food home made, it was the answer to every lodger's prayer. Alex and myself had finally completed all the pipework around the glass dome and true to his word the foreman gave us the day off as promised the following week so we were able to go home for the weekend on the Thursday. Can you imagine trying to attempt this dangerous ladder stunt these days? It makes my blood run cold just thinking about it!

Alex and I made good friends with one of the fitters on site. He was a local man named Frank and being a single man used to drive us both to pubs or clubs all around Liverpool. On one of these nights out, we went to the city centre as he wanted to show us his favourite pub where a jazz band played. Like most city centres parking is at a premium so you have to park in adjoining Streets and walk to your venue. What surprised us both as Frank parked his car, a young man came over and Frank handed over some money. As we set off to walk I asked Frank why he gave the man the money. Oh that he replied with a shrug of his shoulders is how it works here in Liverpool. These scallies as they are called divide up the Streets leading into the city so a selected Street is agreed between themselves and this becomes their territory so any cars that park for the night have to pay a fee and as Frank pointed out, if you refuse to pay, you are told, well mister, I can't guarantee your car will be in one piece when you return. So it is wiser and prudent to pay up. They Patrol their Street and you return to a vandalised free car. Frank was telling us one of his friends did not like the idea of paying this money so parked in one of these Streets with his large Alsatian in the back seat. When one of the lads asked for a payment to look after your car mister, he said to him, that snarling beast I have in the back seat is quite capable of looking after my car thank you very much. To which the lad replied, yes but can your snarling beast extinguish a car fire? His friend duly paid up! I suppose you can look at this in two ways, on the one hand, you could call it blatant extortion, on the other hand they are proving a service, without them, you could come back to a stolen or vandalised car. I call it free enterprise, car insurance companies should employ these lads nationwide and car premiums for motorists would drop dramatically! I believe this Street practice still carries on in

Liverpool to this day. After working on the site for a few more weeks we were both asked if we would work in Manchester seeing that we were already working up north.

POEM

Alex was one of those good guys and a Scot
An old and wise man affectionately known as jock
The job we're going to is right on the docks
With Alex who came from that school of hard knocks
Working off a ladder like that hanging in mid air
Shouldn't be working like this you know have a care
Its what he wants done and he is the foreman
And such a manly name and its Norman
With a two hundred foot drop working off a ladder
Not prudent at that height to have a full bladder
Looking down at that drop far below was sheer hell
The task was completed and lived to tell the tale
But what about them awful lodgings they called them digs
Like living in a pigsty with a herd of pigs
The last thing you expect when sleeping through the night
Two down and outs punching away in an almighty fight
From a hovel to a palace we have now found
After sampling that hell hole to the finest lodgings around

Pat still found it hard to settle down in Bletchley, and the main reason being she couldn't get a job that paid decent money compared to London. The wages were half of what they paid in the capital. When Pat went for interviews they offered her Jobs, but she couldn't bring herself to work for such low pay! But in the end she accepted a job in the offices working for the co-op in Bletchley high Street. For half the salary she used to earn in London but realised beggars can't be choosers and it helped her settle down much better, but I remember on one occasion it was a Sunday and Pat had cooked a lovely roast dinner for both of us and she took the well done and mouth watering golden chicken out the oven ready for the big carve up. We had a little tiff that just grew into a major row, with the kitchen window wide open at the time, all I could see was this beautiful well cooked fowl flying through the window. There's your dinner if you want it Pat yelled. I stood back, completely flabbergasted, but what made it more comical just as the chicken flew through the air my next door neighbour Simon who had opened the back gate and was level with the kitchen and watched the well cooked chicken fly past his head onto the dug up earth. As he looked in the window he said, don't you want that then? To which I replied, No not now. Well he smiled, here's your spade back and seeing that you don't want the chicken, I'll have it and give it a good wash and have it for my dinner tomorrow and tucked it under his arm and promptly walked off with it. When I met Simon a few days later his first words to me where, I took your chicken home, washed it thoroughly and we ate it the following day for our dinner. The best free chicken I have every tasted. Are you due for any more rows, he smiled?

Poem

Had one of those silly rows like most couples do

But on this Sunday morning into a temper Pat flew

That cooked succulent chicken should have been on my plate

Instead it landed on the earth near the back gate

As it flew through the air and hit the ground

That foul now flying cost me a hard earned pound

Simon must have thought this was his lucky day

Seeing a well cooked chicken as in the earth it lay

Then gleefully picking it up saying that's my dinner you know

His swift response that Sunday was pick up and go

The moral of this tale is eat before you fight

Because its all to late once your foul has taken flight

Goodbye to Liverpool

The foreman on the Liverpool job was so pleased we managed to complete the glass dome on the Wednesday he beamed after work tonight lads you can go home and I'll pay you up till Friday, thanks for what you've achieved on the job, and here's the address of the job in Manchester that you will be starting on Monday. As we drove home from Liverpool, I said to Alex, when we start the job in Manchester and if we find the digs are no good we will travel to Liverpool every day to Mary's digs in Liverpool, it's about 25 miles but it will be worth it. The four days off soon came round and I once again packed my bag and drove to Alex's house and we again set off but this time to Manchester. We soon found the Job and it was in the city centre and called the Arndale Centre. As soon as we met the new foreman he said, don't worry lads, I heard all about your last bad digs so I've sorted you out some good ones. I have booked you both into a pub in Salford called the Black Horse and two other lads working for me lodge there and they tell me it is a great pub! (I was soon to find out why!) Compared to the job in Liverpool this was a doddle, just erecting, first and second pipe work in shop units we finished our first days work and headed for our digs, which was only a ten minute walk away. As we entered the pub two of the lads from our firm were already sitting at the bar drinking, have a drink lads they shouted. Were having our first blacken (a blacken means having a drink straight from work without washing). You'll like it here, one of them said, every night the pub serves "afters" so you can drink as long as you want to. And boy could these northern lads drink! Compared to them I was a lightweight. They seemed to have a completely different culture to the southerner as they used to say, you're all southern softies, sod tomorrow lived for today was their motto. One of there observations was, if a northerner goes on holiday and comes back completely skint then he knows he's had a good holiday. If a southerner comes back from holiday, still with money left, then they've had an even better holiday! The pub used to stay open as long as customers were buying, by 12 o'clock I used to get to bed, but the other lads would stay there until 3am or later and then have to get up for work at 7 o'clock. How they managed it I never knew but they were all hardened drinkers and could all drink like fish. Once a week we used to visit Bernard Manning's night club. There was always a stag do or a hen night going on and Bernard Manning at that time was an excellent comedian. The atmosphere was terrific and I was now starting to embrace this out every night on the town culture. When I used to come here on weekends Pat used to ask if I was enjoying myself up there, well, we have the odd drink now and again I used to tell her, then why have you never any money left out of your wages? Good question, my dear, I have to admit I got so used to going out every night while I was up there and when I got home at weekends, I wouldn't wait for the Monday to come round so I could carry on clubbing and boozing. One of the nights in the pub we did stay up later than 12 o'clock was and that night we were all being entertained by a group of police officers. They seemed to be hell bent on drinking the pub dry they had been lodging in the pub for a few days. They were all members of the Fraud Squad from the met police in London. They were celebrating a conviction in a Major fraud trial in Manchester and by 2am that night were all completely legless and were due at the old bailey in London at nine that morning. They were all high ranking officers and the head man said, I need to make a phone call to a colleague. He returned five minutes later and said to me, that's been taken care of, I've told him we have some loose ends to tie up, so we can't make it, it will have to be the following day. But like all good things, they all come to an end and my spell in Manchester finished and it was with sadness that Alex and I said our farewells to everyone. It had certainly been an experience. As we drove home, Alex remarked that he had lodged away man years but this stint away had been his best ever! We reached home and I shook his hand and hoped we would meet again on another Job. Alex had been transferred to a local Job and I was transferred to a London one.

Poem

Those men of the north my god they could drink
My monthly quota in just a day they could sink
These lads we worked with the salt of the earth
Take people for what they are not what their worth
Work hard and play hard that is their simple motto
Getting all that drink down their throats until completely blotto
Between the north and south there's this culture divide
But working and drinking together proved we can all abide.
It's always a sad day leaving your buddies and friends
Another final page in the book and so it ends

On returning home from Manchester I worked on a few more London jobs and on one of these jobs I got talking to a fitter who told me his old firm had a large job starting up shortly near to where I lived. I phoned them up and was offered a job with them and they agreed I could start once I had got married.

GETTING MARRIED

It was now the summer of 1977 and I was 38 years old and Pat and I had never thought about getting married. It was a thing to do in the distant future but that all changed when I observed the bump on Pat's stomach getting bigger by the day. So we decided this would be a good time to wed, as we had very little money at that time, and Pat, was good at dress making she was able to make her own wedding dress and was able to design it in such a way that her extra large girth was not showing. Just before the wedding Pat said to me why don't you have a word with the Bank Manager and see if he will give us a loan to help pay for the wedding.

Poem

Am I really getting married at thirty eight years old?
Is this where it all starts of doing what I'm told
Now had come that crucial time when you will bring
Onto her finger you must slip a gold wedding ring
Now look at me I am looking so much bigger
Used to be so thin now have lost my figure
Hoping it has got some give in it my wedding dress
That's why I have designed it that more looks less
A single man no more now starting a new life
The wedding ring was slipped on now man and wife
You're getting bigger by the day that's such a girth
I'm not thinking it won't be long before the birth
Please do not ask me Pat now we are married
Now over the threshold now you want to be carried
My backs not up to it you're quite a weight
Lets not go down that road and try tempting fate

I made an appointment on the following Monday and duly arrived outside the Managers door and knocked and was told to come in. As I entered his office I noticed a very stern looking man sitting at his desk. He was in his late fifties and had the appearance of a retired army officer.

(BankM) Sit down Mr Banfield, what is it you want? And the conversation went something like this:

(Me) well sir I started off, in a most Pathetic grovelling voice, I am getting married shortly and wondered if your good self would let me have a loan?

(BankM) You're getting married, and you want me to give you a loan?

(Me) That's right sir, and it would be very much appreciated.

(BankM) How much is it that you're after?

(Me) five hundred pounds would be fine.

(BankM) You want me to give you five hundred pounds.

(Me) Yes please sir

(BankM) Tell me, Mr Banfield, have you heard of that word saving?

(Me) err, I mumbled, yes I have sir

(BankM) How dare you come in here wanting a loan to get married. I had to save up before I could marry so I suggest you do the same.

(Me) but there are special circumstances why I need a loan

(BankM) then you had better tell me what these are then

(Me) well sir, my future wife is in the family way.

(BankM) lets get this straight, you're saying your future wife is in the family way. What on earth do you mean?

(me) no sir, I don't mean my future wife's in my families way, but she's in the family way, she's up the duff, actually that is what I was trying to get across to you.

(BankM) (Looking bewildered) what are you talking about, I cannot understand a word you are saying!

(Me) well sir, it's like this. My future wife is expecting

(BankM) I've ran out of Patience with you, who the hell is she expecting?

(Me) No sir, she is not expecting anybody, she's pregnant and with child.

(BankM) Do you mean to tell me your girlfriend is having a baby and you're not married, this is outrageous behaviour. Couldn't you control your urges man!

(Me) well sir, these things happen.

(BankM) These things may happen, as you put it, but I'm a part-time churchwarden and this behaviour is all alien to me and my answer to your loan request is a resounding NO, now get out of my office and try and lead a more Christian way of life!

(Me) (Observing) how silly of me, I thought banks were there to help and advise people with money problems.

I knew the first time I set eyes on this bank manger that he was a pompous twit with his Home Counties accent that made you want to spit teeth and with a major attitude problem, I had no chance of getting a loan! Even though I'm a Christian, I probably would have got a better result going to a synagogue and asking the chief rabbi for a loan!

Poem

Surely the bank manger is the man for a loan
How wrong could I be if only I had known
I told him that Pat was in the family way
The baby is due soon it could arrive any day
The attitude of the man and such a terrible prude
And such a middle class twat and oh so rude
What do you have to do to get a loan?
Was like trying to get blood out of a stone
It didn't go down well asking for sausage and mash
And having to explain to him it only meant cash
Just get out of my office with not a care
Saying it with such malice and an icy cold stare

Mather and Platt

With the wedding over with I phoned up Mather's and Platt and told I could start when ready. So once again giving my notice to Matthew Hall, I started with this new firm the following week. Mather and Platt was a northern based firm and had it's headquarters in Manchester were it started trading in the early part of the twentieth century, mainly making all types of industrial machinery. They also became the largest manufacturer of cast iron fittings for the plumbing and fire protection industries and about 1910 formed a sprinkler company. I was told to start on the Monday morning at John Lewes shopping centre at Milton Keynes which was handy for me as it was only about 5 miles from home! As I approached the site hut I noticed a man who looked to be in his middle fifties and who looked as if he was down on his luck in appearance, hammering a sign on the side of the hut which read "Mather and Platt". Hello I said my names John and I'm starting on the firm today! A hand came out to greet me, my names Ray, I was told you were coming, what made you want to start on this disorganised chaotic and run down firm is beyond me! (Oh dear this sounds a bit worrying). How long have you been on the Job I asked? I came last week, with my brother-in-law and we're setting up the site. How long is the job due to run I enquired? Over a year ray said, but tell me, why did you leave a highly efficient with high standards and a well run company to work for us? It's local, I replied. I had just met the infamous Ray Tulley who not only was he a wag, but had a great sense of humour. Ray and his brother-in-law Frank had worked for the company for the past 25 years and for 7 years of that time had put sprinklers in stores up and down Oxford Street in London. One of these jobs he had was in Luton, near the airport and liking the area, moved to Dunstable in the eighties from their homes in London. Chatting with Ray, on my first day I was very surprised to learn that Ray was the firms top foreman with his laid back ways and his shabby looking appearance, you would have taken him as the labourer. Ray was telling me before he joined Mather & Matt, himself and Frank worked as window cleaners on tall buildings in London, the method for cleaning the windows was done with a wooden cradle lifting the cradle up was done by the means of a rope and pulley which went to the top of the building attached on each side of the cradle each man would in turn pull on the rope and tie it off lifting it up about 3 feet (1 metre) the other man on the other rope would also pull it up to 2 feet and when level and tie off, repeating this until they reached the top. They had been doing this work for about 10 years but what made them realise that this was a dangerous profession when they had pulled them selves up to about half way up the building when Frank didn't tie off properly and they found themselves clinging on to the cradle which was now in an upright position supported by only one rope. Being fit and strong at the time they managed to grab the swinging rope and attached it back to the cradle and slowly eased themselves down they both jacked in the Job there and then and decided they had cheated death this time but may not be so lucky next time! They then both joined Mather & Platt. The John Lewis store was massive so Ray had to take on about 20 fitters because all their tools and equipment were out of the ark, all the bigger pipes on the job were screwed by hand which took at least 4 men and took ages to do. My old firm would have screwed it on a machine with just one man, the firm was living in the past and eventually it was the downfall of them. They had a London branch but all the paperwork for jobs was dealt by the Manchester office, so lots of mistakes were made. One day Ray took me to the back of the hut and pointed out to me all the pipe and valve sets that were laying in a field that were for the Job had been delivered a total of 3 times and a large shed was filled up with over ordered valves and fittings. What are you going to do with it all I asked ray? Throw it away came his reply! If you find a buyer that would be great, I'll let you deal with it then, he said. It was fortunately that I knew Jim who had his own pipe fitting business and he was as bent as a butchers hook and as soon as I told him about the over order of materials, and the amount involved he come on the site the same day. When he inspected it all, he couldn't believe his luck. After a bit of bargaining with him we agreed a price of £400, this was to be split between 4 of us, but when we were only taking home about £60 a week at that time, you can see it was a tidy sum. It took Jim about a month to take most of it away. We kept some back in case it came in handy. When I told Ray about the deal, he was delighted seeing that he was ready to throw all of it away. His words were, I think that was a most agreeable outcome! Ray had that way with words.

Stuart Arrives

We all broke up for the Christmas holidays and the New Year came in which was the year 1978. I won't be back to work for 10 days of the New Year and on the 11th January Stuart was born. In them days, Milton Keynes didn't have a hospital so Pat had to go to Aylesbury's Stoke Mandeville Hospital for the birth. All in all, I have to admit it was a traumatic time being at the birth, there was shouting and swearing with screaming and crying and also there was blood sweat and tears and as everyone knows, childbirth can be a painful and emotional time so who was it that was acting out all of this drama? Why it was me of course! Pat seemed to take the birth in her stride. What a bonnie boy Stuart was but all parents say that about their children don't they? And me being two months short of being 38 years old, I was getting on a bit! Like all new parents, you have to learn to adapt to this new welcome addition to the family. What a joy to behold, cradling your own child for the first time, a magical and awe-inspiring moment that you remember for ever!

Poem

Sitting on that hospital chair you just have to wait
What will be will be it's all down to fate
The mystery of life will it be a girl or boy
This long awaited child will give us so much joy
The first light appears it's the beginning of the dawn
Into this world he arrives a new boy is born
The first sight of the baby is just pure elation
There cannot be a prouder parents around anywhere in this nation
It's one of god's true miracles a mother giving birth
Just one more new life starting out on this earth
Them words have that ring about them father and son
When growing up together we're going to have such fun.

It made bringing up a child that little bit harder as both Pat's and my parents departed this earth many years previously. The one thing that was quite a high priority now that a baby was on the scene was to see about getting central heating installed in the house. But how were we going to pay for it? We still didn't have any sausage and mash (cash). The only person I thought may be able to help me out was Tony, the Abbey National manager whose building society branch that was one of the shops not affected by the flooding disaster, as Dick and myself installed the pipework. I had a mortgage with the abbey and had got to know Tony, so I thought I had a good chance of a loan! Flooded out any more shops, Tony asked as I met him in a prearranged meeting at his Bletchley branch. I understand you want some money, he said with a smile. That's right I replied, as much as you can spare, I joked but five hundred pounds will do for now. And what do you want the money for John he asked? Explaining about the new baby, and needing central heating, Tony then said there is no way I could let you have any money unless there were exceptional circumstances involved. Now let me see, your baby needs a warm environment, for health reasons isn't that so? Um, yes that's right, Tony I replied. Right that's it, then, I'm recommending your loan is approved on the grounds that this is a health issue and these loans are very rarely refused, so call in next week and I should be able to write you out a cheque. How things have changed! In the late seventies, a building society manager had to get approval from his head office before he could give you a loan. A week later I duly arrived at the branch and the cheque was waiting for me. The central cost £400 to install and with the £100 left over we felt very rich as this was nearly two weeks wages for me! Because the loan was added on to the existing mortgage it went from £79 a month to £83 a month.

We finally finished the John Lewis store in Milton Keynes and moved on to their warehouse in Blakelands, Milton Keynes. It was always a pleasure to work with Ray as he had a great personality with a good sense of humour. Our firm also had a job near by in Wolverton. It was called the Angora Centre, one of the builders who was working on the John Lewis warehouse was also doing the shop fitting in a shop unit in the Angora Centre and asked Ray, if he would be prepared to install sprinklers in the shop unit but not to get it done through our firm, but to do it privately on the side! Ray and I went to look around the unit and ray left it to me to negotiate a price to do the job. We agreed a price which was £700 and seeing we didn't have to buy any materials it was going to be a good earner. The plan was Ray and his brother-in-law Frank would work on the warehouse Job and I work on the shop unit and both of them could join me at the weekends. I had worked on the unit all the week and Ray and Frank came in on the Saturday, I was drilling away and happened to look out of the window and noticed a figure bent over and looking through the shutters of the unit. I stopped drilling and froze because I recognized it to be our senior contracts Manager Ken Wiseman. I signalled to Ray and Frank not to move, Ken was now shaking the door, trying to gain entry, I was shaking even more, because I knew if we were caught it would have been instant dismissal but when someone is in a light area and looking into a dark area it's hard to see anything. With a few more shakes of the shutters Ken moved on, looking at other units. We watched as he got into his car. We worked late into the night to finish the job, we all realised that was a lucky escape. But why, we all wondered was he looking at the shop in the first place? About a week later, Ken the contracts Manager turned up at the warehouse and had a rather angry tone to his voice and he went on to tell us, he had a telephone call from the manager of the toy shop in the Angora Centre who wanted to know, why was it that the identical shop next to his only paid £700 for their sprinklers when his had cost £3,000 (OUCH) The sprinklers were fitted by other Mather & Platt fitters legally, Ken went on, I wondered why our firm was not getting to do these shop units so I went up there on the Saturday to find out why. Yes we know Ken! I think he had his suspicions it was us that had installed the pipework but he could not prove it. When he left, Ray said no more private jobs until this all dies down. Just before Ken left, he said to me, John, I've been looking at your fares travelling to Milton Keynes from Bletchley and the right fare is 50p a day return, not £1 a day you are getting. So from next week that's what you will get! And as quick as a flash I replied, I'm moving to Dunstable in two weeks time, so what are you going to do about that then? Well he said, just let me know your new address and we'll pay the appropriate fares and travel time. The fare and travelling time from Dunstable to Milton Keynes worked out at about £30 per week. For Ken, who was trying to save the firm £2.50 a week, it turned out to be a very costly exercise. I gave Ken an address in Dunstable with the householder's permission and for the next four years used that address. I worked it out; it probably cost the firm in extra fares and travel time about £4,000, all for the sake of £2.50p and to think I was quite happy with the fares I was getting in the first place. We finished off the John Lewis warehouse in Milton Keynes and Ken the manager told us our next Job would be in London, at Prescott Street at the headquarters office of the Co-oP a five minute walk from Tower Bridge. We started on the Monday and Pat had told me over the weekend that she was once again with child. Still life in the old boy then! (Ahem) On our lunch break Ray Frank and myself used to explore all the different areas walking to Tower Bridge, the Tower of London, and other places of interest. There was a park near the Job and we would sit in it sometimes having our lunch. Sitting on the park bench every day was a tramp with a full mop of grey hair that was level with his shoulders. One day we sat year to him and ray asked him if he would like one of his sandwiches, oh that's awfully nice of you old boy, he said in an accent that wouldn't have seemed out of place at Eton College. After a small talk between us, I said to him, down on your luck then? Well yes, you could say that, he replied. If you lads are interested, I'll tell you how I came to be in this position. We all said we would like to hear his story so this is what he told us.

My name is Clive, and I was brought up in Dorset. I was an only child and my parents were quite wealthy, so they sent me to one of the best boarding schools in the area. From there I went on to university and gained a masters degree in Physics, it was while studying, I was told that my beloved parents have both been killed in a road accident in France. Their loss had a profound effect on me and I took comfort in drinking, this was the start of my problems. Just as I finished my degree the war started so I joined the RAF as an officer. I met up my wife who was also an RAF officer and we had two children together. I rose through the ranks and by the time the war ended I was wing commander. I left the service and set up a factory in Oxford making car parts for British Leyland, the factory was dong well so I was able to send my two boys to boarding school. They grew up and left home and I started to take up the drink once more and also started to bet very heavily. My wife decided she could take no more and divorced me and in the settlement my ex-wife lived in the family home and I lived in our other house we had in Kent. I couldn't pay the bills so the firm went in to liquidation and I went bankrupt. The house I lived in was mortgage free as was ex wife's one but one night I got so drunk I slept on the sofa and the next thing I remember is being dragged out the house by a neighbour and in my drunken state was not sure why! It transpired that the coal fire I had alight, coal had somehow fallen onto the carpet and this in turn spread to the curtains. By the time the fire brigade arrived the house was just a heap of bricks. Unfortunately the household insurance policy had run out so I had no house, nowhere to live and completely broke. Being in my late fifties I knew I couldn't start up again with anything so I made the decision to hit the road and have now been sleeping rough. And occasionally begging for the past 10 years! On hearing such a sad story it brought a lump to my throat the amazing thing about Clive, there was not a trace of bitterness in him. I have never met such a positive person in my life, even though his circumstances were so dire. There was a seaman's mission building in Leman Street near the car park and after talking to the manager, about Clive, he agreed to make a room available to him when needed. Ray, Frank and myself were in the various stages of losing our hair. We had gaps in our gums where teeth used to be, but our friend Clive who was in his late fifties who had been sleeping rough for the past 10 years had a full mop of hair and a full set of sparkling white teeth! Amazing! My own observations on Clive's situation were here was a man who once had everything in life and had lost it all, but hadn't lost his pride or principles.

Poem

Walk on by he looks like a down and out
Probably a lazy sponging scoundrel that there is no doubt
Don't we all have that view let's be quite Frank
Wouldn't we all say look at that smelly tramp
No cosy bed to sleep in must be very tough
What an awful position to be in sleeping rough
But he's just an old drifter a man of the road
And just a nowhere man and of no fixed abode
It all started off for him with his excessive drinking
Into a never ending spiral pit he found himself sinking
Surely this couldn't happen to me but I can be sure
One never knows what life has for you in store

When Pat first told me she was pregnant again we knew we needed to get a bigger house and it had to have three bedrooms so once again I went along to see Tony the Abbey National Manager. Hope you haven't come to see me for more money again? He said in a jocular manner, well yes I have actually. We need a three bedroom house and it's going to cost about £5,000 so we need to borrow that amount. Tony went to his desk and pulled out some forms, right John, your wife is having twins right? No no, I answered, she's only expecting on child, Tony gave me a quizzical look. John, holding one of these forms up, on this form it's a request for a straight forward loan and if I fill it in you have no chance of getting it. On the other hand, if I fill this one in, it's a compassionate and special needs form and I can near enough guarantee you'll get it, so John, he asked, "Is your wife having twins"? Yes, Tony, my wife is having twins. Right I shall fill this form in, and within two weeks you should have secured it. Right on cue, two weeks later the money came through, and we managed to find a nice three bed semi-detached house five minutes from our old house and paid £23,000 for it. It may sound a small amount but this was 1980, things worked out fine, because two months after moving in our daughter Judy was born.

Judy is born

Once again, Pat had to go to the Royal Bucks Hospital in Aylesbury, for the birth and Judy was born on the 12th April 1980 and I had reached the grand old age of 41 years. Just holding my little bundle of Joy, for the first time I had that feeling that most dads must have, this little girl will always be my princess and so it proved to be.

Poem

Such a joy to behold our family is now complete
Looking at this new born child so beautiful and sweet
Is it not every fathers wish to want a girl
Now staring back at me like a rare exotic pearl
It's said that little girls are made of sugar and spice
And my heart has just melted like that thawing ice
Will always remember this moment till my last day
Just one of those memories that will always stay
We named our child Judy such a dear little thing
So much fun and happiness she is going to bring.

We finished the job at John Lewis Warehouse and were told by Ken, our construction manager that our next job was at Thomas del-la-rue in Luton. That should suit you fine John, seeing that you live there! (Did he know something?) Beside Ray, Frank and myself, that were at the de-la-rue premises there were four fitters from the north London branch of Mather and Platt. These four men were a right motley crew; rough diamonds would be a more accurate description of them. Between them they had served a few years inside. Thomas del-la-rue was a printing company but with a difference. They printed bank notes for nearly every country in the world but not the pound note or the American dollar, French franc or the German mark. The first two days on site were spent getting security passes, but on of the most interesting talks was from the manager and it went something like this:

Good morning gentlemen, I am the manager of this printing plant and we print money here for seventy five countries. In the past gentlemen we have had contractors working here who thought they could get through our security system and steal our foreign bank notes. Well let me tell you gents, these men are now serving time, so don't even think about it. He then went on to make an amazing admission. As we speak, we are checking you all out on the police database and this will take about three days so if any of you have a police record, you'll be thrown out of the building immediately. And he added you will be escorted at all times by members of our security team and you will be searched on entering and leaving the premises. These are our strict rules and if any you don't agree with them, then we cannot let you work here. Of course everyone agreed to the terms and conditions of employment. We were all shown around the building and to see millions of bank notes being printed and stacked up in cages was an eye opener. An area was set up outside the printing press building for our site huts. The four ex-cons were discussing amongst themselves the best way of getting the bank notes out. Unbelievable the rule on the job was that no pipe or fittings were to be left in the building overnight. So it all had to be returned to the compound at the end of the shift. Returning from the first days work inside the building the four lads had worked out a method of getting the bank notes out, the plan was to stuff the notes into a 6" (150mm) pipe that had been brought into the work area and into the off cuts of that pipe would go the notes. The pipe was sealed both ends by two plastic caps, smaller pipes were loaded on top of the 6" pipe and then wheeled out of the building into the compound! Two of the men kept the guards talking just far enough away from the money cages while the other two rammed the notes down the pipe. Ingenious but very simple. They then wheeled the pipe to the compound and put the bounty into sacks and threw the sacks over the perimeter fence. On leaving the premises all cars were searched. They then drove to where the bags of loot were and went happily on their way. They worked on the job 'till Friday, filling the pipe up with all different kinds of currency and then told our project manager it was too far from London to be travelling daily. Then knew that if they stayed working there the police check would reveal their past criminal records. But unfortunately for these likeable rogues when they tried to dispose of these foreign bank notes to a shady unscrupulous dealer, they were only offered a tiny sum for them as the dealers knew no other selling outlets were available to them. So they accepted a pittance for them. They were just glad to be rid of them. They were given £500 for them all. The notes were worth thousands so they were really stitched up. Ray Tulley, our foreman was not only a very amusing man; he also was very much into spiritualism and went to mediums for reading. When I first met him he explained to me how much he believed in the spirit world. I used to tell him it was not really my thing, but he kept on about it for so long. I agreed to sit in on one of his meetings that took place in his house one night. He had invited along a physic artist who was going to draw rays spirit guild. Ray was convinced that everyone on this planet is given a spirit guide when they are born and there guide acts as your guardian throughout your life. Ray claimed that this artist was one of the best in the country so I was looking forward to it. Ray introduced me to him and I was quite surprised to find he was quite a normal looking man with a great sense of humour not quite what I was expecting. I thought he would be a right nerd. I sat in the background as the artist began drawing an outline of Ray on a large sheet. He was using all different crayons coloured and slowly the picture started to come alive. By the time he had finished I was amazed to see the head of a read Indian chief with a full feathered head dress a truly outstanding portrait. Ray was thrilled with it. They physic artist explained to ray that this Indian chief had died fighting the American cavalry in the Indian wars. He made it sound so very convincing. He didn't do it for the money because when ray asked him how much he owed him he said, just give me what you think its worth. Ray offered him £10 but the man said, just give me five pounds, I'm quite happy with that. As the artist was leaving he turned to me and said by the way you may be interested to know that your spirit guild on this earth is an ancient Egyptian pharaoh and I can draw him if you want. I never took up his offer thinking its a load of rubbish, but it makes you think doesn't it. I used to work most weekends, I always made sure I got home in time on the Saturday and Sunday to take kids to local events or country shows, and on this particular Sunday we were all going to Thornton College which lies between Bletchley and Buckingham. This day was going to be a special one because not only was their going to be the usual side shows and attractions associated with these fates but the starts of the show that day was the band and marching display team of the RAF. Judy was still in her pushchair and Stuart was just over three years old. A large roped off area had been set aside on the large lawn for the display. As this was to be the main event a large crowd had gathered to watch this eagerly awaited show. As like anything that's to do with the military I made sure we had a bird's eye view of the proceedings. The band and the display team were lined up just outside the roped off area. I watched as the band master lifted his baton and the air was filled with expectation as everyone was eagerly awaiting the spectacle. As I looked round to tell Stuart that his should be a good show to my shock and horror I watched as he ran under the perimeter rope and proceeded to sprint to the middle of the field where he promptly sat down, much to the merriment of the thousands of spectators. I looked over to Pat and said, I think you had better go and get him as he will come to you rather than come to me. You must be joking, I'm not going to get him she cried I'm looking after Judy, you've got to go and get him Pat had won the argument with that dreaded icy stare that only women are capable of giving and so feeling very embarrassed I ducked under the rope. I had taken only a few steps when the crowd in unison gave me a huge round of applause, my face was properly as red as a letter box. No wonder Pat refused to do it. Stuart was now sitting down crossed legged with a big smile on his face. As I approached him he had that look on him as if to say, this is the start of play time daddy. As I bent down to pick him up, he sprang up and with a look of catch me if you can you unfit middle age daddy and with the crowd shouting hooray, to his every twist and turn I felt like a right twit. It must have been quite comical for the crowd this man trying to catch this little boy, who was giving him the runabout. At last I managed to grab hold of him with the good humoured crowd now giving me chorus of booing and jeering. Picking Stuart up and firmly holding him under one arm, I quickly made my way back to the spectator's area. The RAF band and drill team duly marched on and gave an impeccable performance but also one of the stars of that day was Stuart. Looking back at it now, I think how funny it all was but at the time it was all so very embarrassing and I wish this wasn't really happening to me.

Poem

Happy family day out it's all off to the fete

The royal air force are marching it should be great

No doubt they will be the stars of the show

But the saga that followed how was I to know

Within just a few seconds Stuart was now firmly seated

And with the cheering and clapping he was warmly greeted

Now go and fetch him Pat said you're his dad

His still only just a baby my poor frightened lad

Watching me chase after him the large crowd started booing

Obeying orders from the wife my duty I was doing

Just who this young lad is holding up the band

And me with the brightest red face in the land

Now firmly under my arm he only wanted to play

Just magical family memories at the end of the day

The job at del-la-rue had been completed and we were told our next job was to be at British Leyland, Oxford. Ray had been going back and forth from there for years so he knew the buildings very well. In the eighties British Leyland went into partnership and they sold their soul to the Japanese car company Honda but without their expertise they would have folded many years previously. The Cowley plant in Oxford summed up everything that was wrong with British industry, out of date, living off past glories, inefficient and a disillusioned work-force with bad management putting all these together, it was a shambles. Joining Ray, Frank and myself at the plant was the lads who managed to nick all the banknotes from the del-la-rue job. Within minutes of us all having had our health and safety talk they were already talking about what would be the best way to get one of the newly built cars out of the plant; this should prove to be interesting. For the Oxford job we agreed that we would car share, so I used to drive to Ray and Franks houses in Dunstable, which was twelve miles from Bletchley and as well used to each get full fares paid. We were on a winner doing it this way. We worked most weekends at Oxford and this involved coming in on the Saturday working all day and carry on through the night and finish Sunday at 12 pm. It was tiring but we got used to it. The security on the entrances and exits of the Oxford plant were a joke anyone could just walk in and out at will as usual we completed a weekend and came in again the following weekend and noticed a long queue waiting to get in. As we got to the security post a plant manager said we must have our photos taken and these were to be put on a security pass and worn at all times, we later found out the reason why, it transpired that a painting contractor was working early on the Sunday morning. He was painting the roof support girders, lost his balance and plunged to the floor below. Unfortunately the door man died. As in these cases the police were called in and on searching the pockets found his name and address. They then relayed this information to the met police who promptly went to the mans address. Knocking on the front door a woman answered are you Mrs Murphy, they asked her, yes I am she said, well Mrs Murphy, we have some bad news for you, your husband Shaun fell while painting today and unfortunately last his life. We were told the lady recoiled back in total shock. That's impossible she cried, he's upstairs in bed, sleeping off a hangover. Well madam if that is the case may we go upstairs and have a word with him? The wife led them into the bedroom and sure enough her husband was in the bed. He wife then woke him up, Shaun; these police officers would like a word with you. They then asked him are you Mr Shaun Murphy, the husband replied, Yes I am, what are you doing here? And what do you want? Well Mr Murphy, we are here because this morning a man had a fall at British Leyland in Oxford and as a result of his severe injuries was found dead. Can you now explain to us why your documents were found on him? The man then had to admit why his name and address and documents were found on his friend. He had sold his exemption certificate book to his friend telling the tax office it had been stolen and was himself using a stolen one; this was a massive fiddle that was going on at this time. The police weren't interested in the fiddle; they just wanted to know who the man was found dead. The man gave the name and address of his friend to the police and they left to tell some other poor family the sad news. A sad but strange story. We were all issued with our photo identification cards because of this accident we couldn't help notice that when we used to wash our hands in the washroom a group of Indians were sometimes stripped down to the waist shaving and using the showers, but none of them had the ID cards on them. This was promptly reported to security who wanted to know why they had no ID cards on them. When they asked them why they had no ID cards, the Indians stared back at them with blank looks. They rounded them all up and took them all to the office and it became clear that these men could not speak any English. An interpreter was brought in and the full story was unravelled. These men were crew members of a merchant navy cargo ships that had docked in the pool of London. In those days some ships took up to two weeks to unload and then to put a new cargo on board. When the ship was ready to sail again they would rejoin their ship. At the Oxford plant they had set up beds in a long cupboard behind the car production lines that were no longer in use and as there wasn't a night shift working no-one was the wiser. They even managed to get hold of company overalls so the blended in as production workers. Some crew members were signed off ships they would wait for a new ship in their rent free home at British Leyland. IT all came to an end for them after the accident, evidently they had been using the facilities at the plant for years and as they were thousands of workers with no checks carried out on them they were able to get lost in the crowd once again, a story, hard to believe but true.

Stoke Mandeville Hospital

Pat had not been feeling well with stomach pains so she went to the doctors and he referred her to a specialist and he diagnosed the problem. It turned out she needed to have a hysterectomy. This needed to be done quite quickly so within two months she was admitted to stoke Mandeville. Pats biggest worry was how well the kids were going to be looked after by me in her absence, but I was able to reassure her that they are only children after all, have no worries. I took the week off from work and on the Monday dropped Pat off at the hospital, making sure she got settled in alright. Her last words to me were make sure you give the kids decent meals reassuring her that they were in capable hands with the lecture on child care I was given by her, I got the impression she didn't trust me. I left the hospital that first day with a list as long as my arm, with all the do's and don'ts of looking after children. As we pulled away from the hospital car park I turned to the kids and said, right kids for the next seven days, you'll be eating MacDonald's and fish and chips and at home I'll make you beans on toast. Yippy they both shouted in unison. Kids know what's good for them don't they! The next day we visited Pat in the ward, her first words were you haven't even washed their faces or combed their hair (are you supposed to do that?) and look at them they are still wearing the same clothes that they had on yesterday. Well it certainly saves the washing and ironing. And what did your dad give you to eat kids? Well mummy Judy said excitedly when we left here yesterday Daddy took us straight to MacDonald's and we all had a burger and fries, followed by a yummy ice cream and daddy said if we are good children we can go to MacDonald's every day (me thinks, Judy sweetie daddy loves you but don't you realise that daddy is now in that big cold dog house) Pat exploded, is it your intention to feed my children junk food for the rest of the week? No of course not dear I think Judy must have heard me wrong. Pat of course didn't believe a word I said from then on, on every visit after that the kids were immediately cross-examined by Pat as to what they had eaten and how I was looking after them! Before Pat entered hospital I was told I must wash up the dishes every day and also Hoover the house every day, of course I will I lied. Pat was due to be in hospital for seven days, so my plan was after the sixth visit I would get the kids to bed and wash all the dirty dishes that had piled up in the kitchen and give the house it's first Hoover, that was the master plan. Once again we visited Pat and she seemed to be in a very happy mood as the operation went very well and she was due to be discharged the next day. Let's go to the canteen Pat suggested, as she was now allowed to walk about. Sitting in the canteen were a mix of Patients and nurses. Stuart was sitting with us and Judy was running up and down between the tables we were sitting next to two nurses and one of them said in a sympathetic manner, Oh look at that poor little girl, she's got her tights on back to front. On hearing this Pats neck managed to swivel around making almost a complete turn, my God she shouted, you've put Judy's tights on the wrong way round. That's it; I've seen enough, I'm going home today, she said sharply. No, no I pleaded you need your rest; you were booked in for seven days so you must stay. How can I let her see all the dirty plates piled up in the sink and the house looking like a tip. Pat had a word with the ward sister and she said there was no problem with her going home that day as long as she didn't lift a finger and had complete rest. Oh Dear me, I'm in the trouble now, I hope everything is spick and span in the house Pat demanded. Err erm, I found my self stuttering. As we left the hospital, I said to Pat, don't expect the house to be at its best because I was going to clean it from top to bottom tonight when I got in, but you coming home has all changed that. Well at least I warned you before you entered the house. But she did agree with me, that the best place for her when she arrived home was straight to bed. This was for her health and the other reason was for the sake of her mind. She agreed she would crack up if she saw the state of the place, phew that was close, got out of that one.

Poem

It was to the doctors that Pat went that day
And one week in hospital that she needed to stay
You have no idea of childcare you haven't a clue
And I'm supposed to be handing them over to you
You will feed them only junk food that's for sure
Grub that's not properly cooked still frozen and raw
Laying in that hospital bed hooked up to a drip
Knowing when she got home it will resemble a tip
Handing them both over to you was done with regret
And knowing their in for a week of total neglect

It was while I was working in London for Mather & Platt that I met Phillip again. I was sitting on a wall having a tea break and a man approached me and looked up at me in a strange way, he was wearing a London electricity board uniform and said in a puzzled voice, what the hell are you doing Phillip sitting here? I'm not Phillip I replied, what do you mean you're not Phillip, don't muck about. I realised he had mistook me for my twin brother Phillip. It took a while to convince the man my name was John and I was his brother. It transpired that Phillip had been working for the electricity board for years when I explained that I had not seen him for twenty years; he gave me his address in Balham, south London. After a handshake, the man walked off, shaking his head in disbelief, his words were "two peas in a pod". On one of the few Saturdays I had off I drove down to the address I was given, to a small block of flats and ringing the door bell I was quite surprised to be greeted by a woman with the words, Phillip, fancy seeing you here, come in for a cup of tea. Well it's obvious we must look alike, but I'm not Phillip, I'm his twin brother, John I said. Harry she called out, come and have a look out here, just as he approached the door, she teasingly said, guess who this is? With an outstretched hand he shook my hand, hello Phil, how are you? I quickly corrected his mistake and told him I was given this address and was told Phillip lived here. He used to live here he answered but moved about two years ago, I will give you his new address and telephone number. Well, well he went on; Phillip never once mentioned anything about his family, anyway good luck with your meeting with him. As soon as I got home I phoned Phillips telephone number, he answered the phone and it was like my voice echoing back at me. After all them years we still both had exactly the same accent, it seemed so bizarre. We arranged to meet at his house the following Sunday which was situated in Surrey. Pat and the kids were with me. When we knocked at Phillips door his wife opened the door and ushered us all in. Phillips children were quite a bit older than mine, but as kids do they quickly made friends with them. On chatting to Phillip it soon became obvious that we had very little in common. After twenty years it felt more like talking to a stranger than a brother. I was quite surprised to hear that he was now a Jehovah's Witness but his wife and three children were not. This I would imagine would make it quite difficult for all his family, as witnesses have strongly held views that not everyone agrees with. When I thought about it, the Jehovah witnesses were the family he never had, a brother and sisterhood looking after the welfare of every member, but as I made it clear, not something I could or want to get involved in. After a few hours chatting we said our goodbyes and promised to keep in touch, but it was to be quite a while before we made contact with each other.

Poem

After all these years was finally meeting my twin brother
The question was how we would take to each other
Would expect us to be close seeing we were twins
It's all down to fate it's funny what life brings
With such a traumatic childhood and them tears and fears
All now a distant memory in those far off years
It affected him so very much being such a young lad
Phillip became a Jehovah witness it's the family he never had
No more pain and worry now that he has found
With his friends and Christians with there love all around

I was still with Mather & Platt and had been now working at British Leyland for quite some time and because it was such a large contract. Delivery lorries were arriving daily. On one particular day a large open backed lorry arrived on site. It had its own built in crane. On board the driver asked the lads on site, where he should the two large crates off. Drop them off next to the site hut they told him, we can use them to sit on while we have our tea breaks! The two crates were duly unloaded with the driver saying I don't know what you have in them? But my jib just about managed to take the weight the two crates were signed for and the driver departed. There were still about twenty other wooden crates that had been delivered but still unopened everyone wondered what fittings were in them both, these heavy crates but could not be bothered to open them. They had laid unopened for about four weeks and it was the men's dinner break. Some men were laying on them sunbathing, others just sitting on them eating their grub. It was a surprise to us all to see a police car pull up, outside the site hut with a lorry behind it. Four policemen got out the police car and once of them said to the foreman, where are the two large crates that were delivered to you about four weeks ago? Oh, them two crates there over here, and we haven't even opened them up yet. But why, the foreman asked are you so interested in them two crates? Well the policeman mockingly replied, because you haven't opened them up, its good news for us, but bad news for all of you! The policeman and the driver then produced two crowbars and started to wrench one of the boxes open. After quite a struggle they managed to get the lid off and now what was exposed was thick silver paper. As this was torn open and we all witnessed an amazing sight, for in front of us all was thousands of new 50 pence pieces, stacked neatly in rows. We all could not believe what we were seeing. It was like looking into Aladdin's cave. These shining silver coins were glistening in the morning sun. The comments from the men were something like this! Gosh lads, look at that treasure trove, and oh bother, why didn't we open the crates, the other comments were unprintable. And to think we had been sitting on a goldmine for four weeks, the police then opened the other crate and once again that was full of 50p pieces! It transpired that these two crates had been loaded with the 50p pieces at the royal mint and had somehow got mixed up in the delivery chain and got dropped off at British Leyland by mistake. If only someone had bothered to look at the labels on the crates they would have seen Royal Mint written on them and they would have stripped the crates completely of the silver coins, they would have removed them quicker than South American piranha fish devour their prey! The police reckoned there were thousands of pounds worth of coins in each box. The crates were promptly loaded back onto the lorry and returned to where they were meant for in the first place. Grown men were walking around with tears in their eyes and were physically sick for days after this episode.

Poem

Oh no not another lorry unloading more boxes of gear
Once again more crates and fittings double ordered I fear
Put them over there with them waiting to be unpacked
Just so many of them now are double stacked
The police came and opened them boy what a sight
These newly minted lovely coins all shining and bright
Staring at those rows of coins in the first crate
Would I have taken some well that's open to debate
Loaded up into the lorry they took the bounty away
Without doubt it proved not to be our lucky day.

The Job at British Leyland had finally finished and Frank, Ray and myself were transferred to the Barbican in London. This consists of quite a large area dominated by luxury flats and penthouses and lies between barbican station and Moorgate station. You have to be well wedged to live in these apartments and flats. The whole of the ground floor area is taken up by the flats car park so every tenant has their own parking space. Because the car park has no windows the whole sprinkler system is put on air in the winter to stop it freezing up and when the spring arrives it is put back on water. We had to change some old pipe in the lift area and replace it with a larger diameter pipe and seeing it was the summer, the system was on water. We drained most of the water from the main valve but there is always water in the pipes that have to be drained out by smaller drain valves. The one we needed to get at was directly above an old but a very sought after valuable Bentley. As I put my bucket underneath the valve ready to open it, one of the car park attendants came rushing towards me shouting before you open that valve you must make sure that not one drop of water falls on that car. He then went on to explain that last October, two fitters from your firm changed the system from water to air and while draining down from that valve that you want to drain down from, a few drops of water fell on that Bentley and the owner immediately phoned your firm up and insisted that they be sacked on the spot. Your firm had to take the men off the job and to keep them quiet said they had both been sacked! But who is this man I asked? He is, he went on to say, a senior high court judge and he is one of the most detestable and miserable old sods you will ever encounter. The day after your fitters spilled water on his car he started a new trial at the old bailey and I pity the poor defendant in that case because the judge was not a happy man that day. Ray and Frank were draining other parts of the car park while it was left to me to open the valve above the Bentley. I wonder why? So with the bucket under the valve I gingerly opened the valve handle and to me relief found there was only a few drops of water came out. So I was able to tie the bucket handle onto the main pipe directly below the valve so it would catch any drips that may come out. Ray came over and was pleased that very little water had come out. Let's have a tea break now and then start work after it. We had only sat down for about ten minutes when the car park attendant came rushing into our site hut in a very agitated state. You've ruined his lordships car, it is completely covered in black water, there's going to be merry hell because of this he shouted. We all abandoned our cups of tea and raced to the area and shock of all horrors the judges immaculate what used to be white Bentley was now completely covered in black gunge, and what made matters worse the ladder was missing and it was still pouring out, surely I'm dreaming all this? I'll wake up in a minute won't I? Ray woke me up from the hypnotic state I found myself in by shouting that's it we're all be down the road for this. After about five minutes searching for the ladder I found an electrician working off it, with not a care in the world. Can I have my ladder back please mate I asked, or words to that effect? I quickly ran back with the steps I don't know why I was still panicking because the damage was now done and it couldn't get any worse. I then closed the valve and came to the conclusion that this valve had not been opened for years and stagnant water had built up and over the years turned into a think back smelling gunge, so when I opened the valve, nothing came out as there was an airlock holding the water back. The air lock then evaporated and forced the gunge through! We all stood around the more black than white car, in total shock, but all of the other trades were in fits of laughter, but you couldn't blame them, we also, would have been in hysterics if it had happened to someone else! The car park attendant said to us, well lads there is some good news, the judge went on holiday last week and won't be back for a fortnight and I wash his car once a month and hopefully if that black stuff has not penetrated the paintwork, he will never know! The quicker I get clean water on it the better it should be! As we watched him hose the car down we were relieved to see all of the black gunge washed away but more importantly it had not stained the white paintwork. Relief all round, we dipped into our pockets and between us gave this good Samaritan five pounds for his trouble.

Poem

Winter was approaching time to put the system on air
It was always done at this time of year
Bu these flats were luxurious mainly for the very rich
Also a nasty geriatric judge a son of a bitch
The worst kind of snob and from the old school
From a wealthy gentry family such a silly old fool
And there stood this Bentley the colour a brilliant white
But after my little water mishap not a pretty sight
What if he had witnessed this gungy water so black
No doubt about it we would be facing the sack
But the parking attendant had managed to put it right
With washing and polishing left it so sparkling and bright

Mary

In the war years when I was evacuated to Culham court, I remembered a young girl pushing me on a swing, I was about 4 years old and she was slightly older. It was the first and last time I saw her but I remember her telling me on that visit that she was my sister and over the years the memory of that day always stayed with me. I had told my other two sisters about this sister but they knew nothing about her. So it came as quite a surprise when out of the blue I had a phone call from Jean my sister to say a woman had knocked on her flat door in Bermondsey, London and introduced herself as Mary, your long lost sister. Of course, Jean was taken aback but not too shocked as I had told Jean of her existence years earlier, but I don't think she ever believed me! I phoned Mary up and we arranged to all meet up, for a family reunion. It was agreed that we should all meet up at our house in Bletchley. Two weeks after we made contact it was on the Sunday that everyone came up for the reunion. It was April 1983 and I was now 44 years old. Jean and Irene were the first to arrive; they both came up by train. Mary and her husband then John then arrived by car. Pat and I and Stuart & Judy made up the gathering. Phillip, the brother had still not been traced. Of course Mary was very keen to know all about her family and where we all grew up. I started first and went on to explain to her how Phillip and myself were evacuated at six months old to Culham Court and after many homes later finally arrived in London aged 11 years old. Jean and Irene then told her all about their growing up with mother in London, but were never told they had another sister! Mary then told us about her upbringing, Mary went on to tell us that she remembered being up at Culham Court with Phillip and myself, having to move away when reaching five years old, she remembered ending up in a children's home in Banbury in Oxfordshire, where she stayed for three years and at the age of eight was adopted by a middle class family who had a son, but Mary was the daughter that they had always wanted. She went on to tell us she had quite a privileged lifestyle with very good schools and this showed by the impeccable pronunciations she had with words. Mary always knew she had siblings and wondered if they too had been adopted? And at this reunion Mary told us although she was happy with her adopted parents, she always felt because of the adoption that she was not wanted or loved by her biological mother and as none of us were adopted, she wondered why me? I was quick to put her mind at rest and to assure her as far as I and brother Phillip was concerned she got the better deal. Because although some of the homes Phillip and I were in were quite good, others were truly awful and it seems Mary was adopted just after the death of our father. So it was circumstances at that time that dictated Mary's fate and I'm sure it was done with her welfare at heart. It was a lovely day and a great deal of reminiscing took place, but all good things come to an end and our farewells were said and promised that the next reunion would involve more family members.

Poem

That first meeting with Mary pushing me on that swing

She was my big sister such a sweet young thing

It was at Culham court the Thames flowed near by

Did not see her again and I never knew why

But those were hard times the country was at war

Families were split up and everyone was so very poor

The reunion came was it really thirty nine lost years

Our journeys had taken different directions and many were tears

The day went very well we got to know each other

Mary had now met her sisters and her long lost brother

The Service Man

The barbican job had finished and seeing our firm didn't have much work on, I was asked if I would like to take one of their vans on and be a service engineer. The work involved servicing and maintaining old and new systems. I accepted the position with the view, better any job than no job. Accompanying me was an old fitter names Mons. The reason he acquired this name was on account of his father who fought in the First World War in France and was wounded in the town called Mons. Old Mons only had 6 months left before he retired and had been on the firm for years. I picked up the service van on the Monday and was given a list of all the jobs that had to be done for that week and with Mons in tow, set off for our first Job. It was in Islington, North London. The work sheet stated that a valve set needed servicing. As we approached the large council block, I noticed that there were no lights on in the car park of the flats and saw that glass was scattered around the entrance. I said to Mons, I think it's best if we park outside and carry out tools inside we don't want to be getting a puncture. As we stepped into the darkened car park I shone my torch around and located the valve set and said to Mons, let's go back to the van and fetch our large searchlight type torch as it is pitch black in there and all the lights have been smashed. As we neared the van, we both turned our heads towards the car park because the sound of an engine had just started up in there and the next moment to our amazement we saw a white car exiting. As the car came more into view, we noticed the long red stripe on the side of the car which was written Metropolitan Police, but what made this episode more surreal was the sight of a policewoman sitting in the front passenger seat in a state of undress. She was desperately trying to get her white blouse back on and her hair looked a mess. The male officer driving was trying to steer the car and at the same time attempting to get his shirt on. We could not believe what we were witnessing and with a screech of tyres the car had disappeared up the ramp. It just left us both to contemplate just what these guardians of the law might have been up to!

Poem

This was my first day with my white service van
With Mons as my mate I was a happy man
Our first job that day was a bleak council block
What we were to witness came quite as a shock
All of a sudden like a bat out of hell
Two near naked bodies appeared with their faces so pale
Wait a minute aren't' they supposed to be the law
Don't we expect from them just that little bit more
It seemed they might have been doing some love making
And at tax payers expense a liberty they were talking
But maybe they were doing a bit of cross-dressing
Permission from their chief constable with his approval and blessing

Meeting Brian Again

Mons and I had now been working on servicing and the maintenance side of the company for a few months and as jobs never took longer than a week to finish, we got to work in many locations and all types of buildings so it was on a Monday morning that we arrived at the head quarters of one of the biggest oil companies in the UK, which was shell. It was in the city of London and one of the tallest buildings in the city. We parked the van in the buildings car-park and made our way to the receptionist area and asked for the service manager after a short wait a very pleasant and well dressed man approached us. Hello John, he said it's been a long time since we last met! I was taken by surprise he seems to know me but I haven't a clue who he is. You don't know who I am do you John he said with a smile? Um, not really, I replied, I'm terrible with faces and names I sheepishly answered. Well John you will remember all them years ago at Heathrow airport, I worked with you as a fitter and at the time I didn't know one end of a pipe from another but you very generously gave your time and knowledge to teach me the game! Oh, yes I remember I said, its Brian isn't it? As he warmly shook my hand, well, well Brian, you seem to have done well for yourself, fancy meeting you again after all this time. Come into my office and we'll have a chat he said. So Mons and myself followed Brian into this enormous plush penthouse style office with a secretary busily working away at a typewriter. Go for a coffee break he told her, I have some catching up to do with this man. Brian was keen to find out what I had been up to but I was more interested him finding out how he had fared in his life. Where do I begin with my story he said! Well John, you will remember I worked with you at the Heathrow airport and left you to work on the oil rigs. My wife had typed me a made-up C.V. and I started to work on a north sea oil rig off the coast of Scotland as an experienced engineer and hoped I could get by using the knowledge of the fitters that had also been taken on to install the pipework and the large amount of equipment that was needed to transfer the oil flowing out from the seabed to massive pipes taking the oil to the storage tanks on the mainland, but unfortunately for me, these so called fitters I soon discovered had also made up phoney C.V. At least John I had knowledge of pipework but these men had none. There was ten men in my workforce and I later learnt the trades they were qualified in ranged from a pastry chef, a gardener, and one of them proudly admitting to being a dustman, but the one job that stood out for me Brian said, was one of them was a ships waiter, on a large cruise ship. He was so skinny and slightly built. He looked like he would have trouble lifting a full tray of food! Of course they had all been drawn to the big money being paid to oil rig workers at that time, and as Brian put it, even if they had been found out that they were impostors. Rig workers were air lifted off every four weeks so they would have four weeks of very good wages! Brian went on, here I was stuck with these men who had never seen a pipe before let alone fix one and myself who had never installed anything as complicated as this before. I'll just have to bluff it, and hope it all works out well. So I read all the manuals of the different complicated values and followed the instructions on how the set-up should be installed. Even though all these men were inexperienced and useless I couldn't let on about my own shortcomings! But things went better than I thought and three days before we were due a weeks leave we finally completed the installation and my biggest worry was will it work? What surprised me was how well this motley crew and total misfits had pulled together and managed to finish the job! And the pastry chef even pulled me aside and pointed out that the massive two ton main valve we had installed could have been erected upside down and to my horror he was absolutely right, he had noticed that the identification marking arrows on the valve were pointing down when they should have been pointing up, to enable the oil to flow up and discharge to the outlet pipes. I then had to inform the senior manager of the rig that the valve needed to be taken out so the only thing I could think of was that I had found in the crate the vital locking bolt that secured the non-return clack in position was missing and guess what, he swallowed this blatant lie and even thanked me for being so observant and made the comment, if you had not discovered that bolt Brian, that valve would have been useless and with the pressure of oil flowing up the pipe it could have blown half the rig away! I will be informing the bosses at head office of your skill and expertise in this matter. It took two days to put the valve the right side up and no one ever knew it was a major cock up and believe it or not the day we opened the main valve to start pumping the oil, everything worked as it should have with no one more surprised than me. Brian then went on to say for the next five years he worked on many more rigs both gas and oil all over the world and became an expert in them. He went on, one day I was on leave in London and he was called into the head office and there they made me an offer I couldn't refuse, the bosses asked me if he would be willing to study at university and gain a degree in Mechanical Engineering and they would sponsor me and also pay me a decent salary while I was studying, as they thought I would make a good project manager, in the future of course. I accepted this once in a lifetime offer. I gained my degree and never looked back and John you are now talking to the director of all UK and European and North American operations dealing with anything that involves mechanical engineering on rigs or building in these parts of the world! And John, it's all down to you, how can I ever thank you? My reply to that was Brian, it couldn't have happened to a nicer man. Mons and I completed the Job we came to do that day and with handshakes all round left Brian that day thinking how well he had done in his life and maybe I had helped in a small way and in Brian's extraordinary story for him to achieved such success. It proves that good guys do win sometimes.

Poem

What a shock to meet Brian after all these years
Did I detect his moist eyes surely they're not tears
Am quite astounded he seemed to remember me right away
Like meeting a long lost friend on a reunion day
He had really hit the jackpot since working for shell
I was so pleased he had done so very well
But with a great personality just how could he fail
Brian from that run down estate what a great tale
It would all change for him they day he got his degree
I wonder in his twilight years does he still remember me?

Judy in Hospital

The year was now 1984 and I had reached the aged of 45 years and Judy our daughter had for the past year been suffering from asthma and on this particular evening had suffered a very bad asthma attack and as Pat was working at her part time job cleaning the office of the local co-op I called the doctor who fortunately arrived soon after. He took one look at Judy and said to me, your daughter needs to be admitted to hospital straight away so I'm phoning for an ambulance and it arrived at the house within minutes and the paramedics quickly fitted a plastic mask over her head which attached to a box called a nebuliser. Capsules are then inserted into the compartment of the mask once the machine is switched on, these capsules convert into liquid which produces a mist which turns into a fine spray within two minutes of this treatment Judy was rosy checked again. The doctor said Judy will have to be admitted to hospital for a few days for treatment and observation and as Pat took Stuart to work with her I went with Judy in the ambulance to hospital. I had phoned Pat at her work and told her all about it, what had taken place and agreed to keep her updated on any news. Both Judy and I arrived at Milton Keynes Hospital and by this time Judy didn't need the nebuliser anymore which was great news. It was now time to get Judy booked in so a rather stern nurse sat Judy and me down and proceeded to start filling in a questionnaire form that are needed to admit a Patient in hospital and the conversation and dialogue went something like this:

(Nurse) can I have the child's full name please

(Me) Yes, nurse, it is Judy Banfield

(Nurse) Does Judy have a middle name?

(Me) erm, I'm not sure

(Nurse) you're not sure if she has a middle name?

(Me) I believe she has, but it escapes me at the moment

(Nurse) Ok we'll leave that then and carry on, now what is her date of birth

(Me) Err now let me see, I always get mixed up with Judy and her brothers dates

(Nurse) What do you mean, you get mixed up?

(Me) Well I know Judy is four years old and was born in April but it's either the eleventh of that month or the twelfth as there's only one day difference between he two of them

(Nurse) shaking here head, you don't know if she has a middle name and don't seem to know what her birthday date is? Ok we will move on again, has she been inoculated against measles?

(Me) I'm not sure

(Nurse) well has she had a whooping cough?

(Me) Not sure about that either nurse

(Nurse) now getting rather agitated. You don't seem to know much about her do you?

(Me) I'm not doing too well with all this am I nurse?

(Nurse) You can say that again, she squawked in a sort of I give up tone of voice

(Nurse) Tell me something Mr Banfield, is Judy your daughter?

(Me) Oh yes nurse, very much so.

(Nurse) –In a raised voice and rolling her eyes in despair – if you are the father of this child how come you know so little about her?

(Me) ah, it's probably because I'm always at work and leave all of these matters to the wife, as you do.

(Nurse) by the way, where is your wife? She snapped

(Me) oh she's at work right now and should be along later

(Nurse) good because this is all a complete waste of my time, I have never met a parent who knows so little about their child than you. I will get the information of your child's medical history off your wife – with that she stormed out of the room.

(Me thinking) She started off the interview with me in quite a calm and professional manner but ended it as a mad she-devil and a stressed demented snap dragon, I wonder why?

(Judy) Daddy that nurse seemed to be a bit angry!

(Me) Yes Judy, I got asked more questions than I could answer I'm afraid

(Me thinking) She seemed such a nice nurse when she started off doing the questionnaire but seemed to get angrier as the interview went on. She probably got out of her bed the wrong side this morning. The nurse eventually was able to get all the correct information off of Pat and thankfully Judy only spent three days in hospital and was then discharged.

Poem

Oh my poor little Judy struggling to breath air
Looking at her white face just to hard to bare
The doctor then said this child is not very well
Was a sickly look about her so very pale?
She must have medical care and needs it right away
Every second counts you see we cannot afford a delay
But these nebulisers save lives a wonder drug I feel
Such a remarkable recovery for someone so ill
Listening to my dumb answers the nurse was not impressed
All too much for her poor thing became so stressed
But I'm only a man and what do we know
We just pay the bills and go with the flow

After working on a few more small jobs with my van partner Mons, they day of his retirement was here. It was on a Friday and I was told to bring Mons down to head office in the van. Mather & Platt's office at the time was in Balham South London, and we duly arrived there about 10am, on entering the office with Mons I was expecting there to be a presentation ceremony with drinks laid out and maybe a thank you present for the thirty years Mons had worked for the company. Instead of that the construction manager shook Mons hand and thanked him for all his service to the company. But more telling was the wages clerk who wished him well and told him I will send your P45 to you and the money for your week in hand that you have worked! I could not believe it! Here was a man who had worked hard for the firm for all those years and it was all ended with a thank you and a handshake. We left the head office and I drove Mons back home to Milton Keynes which we had moved to a couple of years earlier. He had been used to good wages all his life as he worked for most weekends and his retirement pension was about £50 a week and he found it very hard to manage on that small sum. So to supplement his income he did gardening for elderly people throughout the year and it was in the winter of his second year of retirement that he collapsed digging a frozen garden and unfortunately his heart couldn't take the strain and he passed away the next day. Such a sad end, as he only lived two years into his retirement, a quiet and an unassuming man, a true gentleman. Once Mons had gone I no longer wanted to carry doing service work so went back to site work, but at the time, the hours were being cut for all staff so when I heard that the firm were offering voluntary redundancy to all staff but it had to be taken by the end of that week. Before I volunteered to be made redundant I once again phoned Matthew Hall to see if they would take me back on again, the answer was yes so I accepted redundancy. I had been on Mather's & Platt's for five years so I was given £1,000 pounds in redundancy payments which was quite a tidy sum in those days and left Mather & Platt at the end of that week. Matthew Hall said I could start with them in about a months time and as I knew a local builder who offered me a job labouring for him in a new school that was being built, I thought it would make a nice stop gap and a change to my usual work.

The school building project

I met the builder on site where the new school was going to be built and he agreed to pay me cash-in-hand, but warned me it would be hard work. Have you ever assisted brick-layers he asked? No I replied, I can't see there being any problem as I'm very fit. That's good he said, because this morning I have three brickies starting who are very fast and are doing all the brickwork up to the footings so I suggest you stack bricks in piles six feet apart so when they get here they'll have a good start, oh and I'll show you now the exact mix that's needed, it is vital you get every mix exactly looking the same, if not, you will be getting different coloured cement on the courses and it will be condemned by the building inspector. No worries I assured him, just show me once and every mix after that will be exactly the same. He then proceeded to show me the make-up of the mix and how he wanted it, you put eight shovels of sand in the mixer followed by two even shovels of cement and one even shovel of lime. If you follow that procedure you'll have the perfect mix every time! I don't know where the brickies have got to he sighed, they all like a drink and probably they have hangovers, but I keep them on because they do a good job and there fast and make me money. As he was speaking they all alighted from a rusty white van and staggered towards the mixer. It looked like they had been sleeping rough all night, a motley and scruffier trio you could ever meet in your life! After being introduced to me, I found out that Ted was a Geordie, Brian was a Scot and Kevin was a scouser a combustible mixture of men that could ever be assembled. They started work and even though they had major hang-over's they were still able to lay bricks at speed. As soon as I made a mix up for them, they would be ready for another one. After two hours of back braking work I was absolutely knackered. As I had never done this type of work before. The brickies saw that I was struggling and insisted the boss brought in another man to help me. The boss agreed so this extra man said he would sort the bricks and I was to make up the mix for them. This working relationship went very well but what I didn't do anymore was to put exactly the right mix in the mixer, just got it near enough, thinking that would do. As the days went on the walls went flying up and everyone was pleased and so pleased was the boss, he took his holidays knowing things were gong so well or so he thought, because as the cement on the walls started to dry after about a week, it was obvious all was not well because the cement on different levels of the wall were not the same colour and even for a non-builder like myself it looked terrible. As the three brickies were now staring at the wall in amazement, and just at that time would you believe it, the building inspector arrived, with the words I'm sorry but I cannot pass any of those walls, I'm condemning them all, knock them all down and start again, and this time get your mixtures right. I'll be back in a couple of days to check up on your progress. Oh dear me, what have I done!!! I don't think the boss is going to be pleased! One of the brickies had phoned the boss while he was on holiday and so he abandoned his holiday immediately and was on site the next day. On inspecting the walls, he turned to me and uttered, you are a useless incompetent idiot, amongst other things, I showed you how to make to a mix, but you totally ignored what I told you. You've cost me a fortune, you are a (about twenty swear words) idiot. Now get off the job, you're sacked and seeing how angry he looked with his eyes popping out of his eye sockets and his fists clenched I thought this may be the right time to retreat in a hasty manner as I don't like seeing blood (even my blood!).

Poem

It was my first full day arriving on that site
Will make a good impression and get everything just right
Working here will be a doddle it's only a school
This task should prove easy and no problem at all
It's just a matter of getting that mix spot on
How was I to know I would get it so wrong
Whoever made this mixture up is obviously a damn fool
So said the building inspector and promptly condemned it all
Then showing up on site came this very angry boss
His demeanour did show he was more than just cross
Such offensive language I'm hearing show me a little respect
Try calming down a lot of frustration I do detect

STARTED MY OWN BUSINESS

Getting the sack didn't make much difference to me, because I was due to start back with Matthew Hall the following week, but that plan fell by the wayside because an old pipe-fitting friend phoned me and asked if I would be interested in starting up our own firm together. Brian, was a very experienced engineer and had worked for quite a few firms and thought I would make the ideal man to go into business with and after telling me of all the work he could get hold of I decided I had nothing to lose so we formed a company called J & B installations and our main work would be to sub-contract off of pipe-fitting companies. We had been warned that there were a few firms that once you worked for them they would turn you over, either by holding payment for work done or denying had done a certain job! Brian knew the owner of a company called Firefight, based in Watford, so our very first job together was working in a shop unit in Acton, West London. We were able to get all our equipment such as screwing machines, 6"x4" dies, workbench, stilsons, chain tongs and all other gear needed to complete any pipe fitting job from friends we knew in the game so we purchased them very cheaply. The only downside we both realised being partners was I lived in Bletchley and Brian lived in Romford in Essex. So we were about fifty miles apart from each other. So we were using two cars to get to jobs, not a very economical situation. We finished the shop unit quite quickly because when working for yourself you tend to speed up because time is "money". As we completed the unit, the owner of Firefight paid us in cash there and then, so we thought, we've hit the jackpot working for this guy. So the next small job we did we were once again paid straight away but on the next job we completed he said, sorry lads, I'm a bit short of the readies at the moment, so I'll send you a cheque, you'll get it in a few days. So we did a few more jobs for him and he would pay a bit from one job and half the agreed price of another one. We had finished and by this time we had fallen into the trap, when we asked for a payment of a curtain job he would say, don't be silly, I've already paid you for that one so by now you had been really sucked into his web of lies. We had been warned about these conmen, but this one you thought butter wouldn't melt in his mouth. But what saved us from this unscrupulous tow-rag was we happened to be working in a factory that we knew sub-contract labour was not allowed because before we started the Job he told us, under no circumstances must you tell anyone in this factory you are sub-contractors because the works union is very strong and I've told the management you are both on the cards and if this job goes well I could get more work in the other factories, and with this knowledge this was the tool we could beat him over the head with. He came in on this factory job and I knew we had to be as cunning and ruthless as he was to stand any chance of getting the £700 he owed us. I had it all worked out, so we showed him the work we completed and made sure we stopped and talked outside the factory bosses office. I then said to him, if you don't pay us the money you owe us, I'm going into that office and telling the owner that we are sub-contractors so what's it to be then. Err, um; don't be like that John, can we discuss this outside. No I shouted, we either settle this here and now or I'm in that office. A look of horror swept across his face, OK, he quietly mumbled. I'll settle up what I owe you but let's talk about it outside. We knew we now had him by the short and curlies. As we walked to the back of the factory, he said, that was bang out of order what you did in there, so tomorrow I'll square up with you, everything I owe you, but you're never to do any more work for me again. Brian quickly interjected; you must be joking mate, why would we want to work with a lying, cheating scumbag like you. With that he quickly made off to the car park and drove off. Sure enough he turned up the next day with all the money he owed us, plus the money for work we had completed in the factory. He just wanted us off the job as quick as possible in case we said anything to the factory bosses. We were delighted, we got what we were owed and wondered just how many others had been conned by him? We now had to find someone else to work for and fortunately Brian knew of a firm that was based in Southampton, but had work all over the UK. We started a job with them in a large warehouse in Hemel Hampstead and we found them to be an excellent firm to be subbing to and they had given us a very good price to do the work. We had been working in the warehouse for about eight weeks and had about a weeks work left before we completed the job. It was Friday and Brian was repairing a leak that had broken out on a job we had finished in Acton. We were duty bound to repair this leak as it was in the contract we had signed. All the roof work in the warehouse was done off two high towers. One of the towers was nearly as high as the apex of the roof and the other one two meters shorter. This allowed us to make up a full range pipe and with a man on each tower, fix and install the pipe in one go. Seeing that Brian was away, I installed half of the pipe on the small tower and pulled the other half of the pipe onto the larger tower. I then screwed the pipe into the first pipe and was pleased that now, all the high level work was completed and it just left a weeks work of ground level pipework to finish off the job. My normal way of getting down off the tower was to open a trap door on the standing part of the platform and walk down the metal steps that led down to floor level but for some reason I decided to climb down the outside of the tower. Big mistake, the next thing I knew I heard this loud clanging sound and the whole tower vibrated and as I had a pair of stilsons in one hand I was virtually climbing down the tower with one hand. I then found myself flying through the air backwards, a most unpleasant and terrifying experience. As I was flying through the air I felt so disorientated and helpless and my one thought was there is no-one that can help me now, I'm on my own. As I was falling to earth, I'm sure I must have done two backwards summersaults and even managed a pike manoeuvre on my traumatic way down. Then there was total blackness. As I opened my eyes I found myself laying on my back on a concrete floor. What am I doing laying down here I wondered? It was then that I remembered flying through the air. As I lay there, I could feel sticky blood on my face. Quickly gathering my thoughts together I wondered what damage I might have done to myself. So I did a quick spot check, first of all I'll try wiggling my toes, ah, that's good news, they're all moving fine and I can feel movement in my legs, so far so good. I can life both my arms slightly up, and clench both my fists that's a good sign but my biggest fear was what damage I had done to my back. As I lay there my workmates were gathered around me and I could see shock and sadness in their eyes, I must look in a right state I thought to myself. It was then that I heard a voice, my names Bob, and I'm the safety officer, how are you feeling mate? Not good I replied, am I dreaming? I have just fallen from that height and he's asking me how I'm feeling? The next thing a voice shouted, get me a chair boys then bent me over and said, you've been so lucky, I don't think you have broken any bones so what I'm going to do now is sit you down on a chair and wait till the ambulance arrives. You'll be fine, he said (hold on a minute bob, aren't you supposed to examining a casualty before making a snap judgement?) One two three, lift, is the next thing I heard as bob and three other men gently sat me down on a plastic chair. Sitting there feeling like I had been hit by a steam roller and feeling very groggy, and not knowing much about what was taking place. One of my eyes was completely covered over with congealed blood but from my other eye I noticed two ambulance men approaching me, hello John, my names George and this is Fred, he said in a kindly manner. Now what we are going to do John is put a neck brace on you and lay you onto a stretcher trolley so with the help of workmates they gently laid me on the stretcher. George then asked the onlookers did any one see John fall. A carpenter stepped forward and said, yes, I saw everything. He was climbing down the outside of that tower and I watched as he went tumbling down and was he was falling he hit his head on an electrical power box attached to the wall. By the time he hit the floor he was already unconscious. And how long was he unconscious for George asked, about ten minutes he replied and then he slowly came round. Thanks very much, that information is very helpful to us. After they both checked me over completely, they asked me how far did I fall. When I told them it was about 30 feet (10 metres) they were amazed my injuries were not too bad. Right George demanded, who was responsible for putting John on that chair? I was, a voice shouted, I'm Bob, and I'm the safety officer, well Tim, George firmly said, as a safety officer you should know better than to life somebody up whose had a fall. After giving him a bollocking and telling him he needs to retrain again in health and safety I was wheeled off to the waiting ambulance.

Poem

Climbing down the outside of that tower a risky undertaking
I remembered it so well as I slowly began awakening
I'm twisting and turning oh now in a right state
Will it be an endless sleep its down to fate
Not very good for you when landing on your head
And oh so very lucky not to be pronounced dead
Managed two somersaults and a pike flying through the air
The next thing I recall is sitting on a chair
It's all down to the lord above looking after me
The best person at your side that you will agree

HEMEL HEMPSTEAD GENERAL HOSPITAL

As the ambulance made its way to hospital, George said to me to survive that fall and have none life threatening injuries is a miracle but I still cannot get over that so called safety officer picking you up and putting you on that chair. His stupid actions could have seriously disabled you for life! I think someone up there was looking after you. Both George and Fred my ambulance knights wheeled me into casualty and after explaining to the waiting crash team the details of the accident and my present state of health, they left, promising to return the next day and see how I was doing. With the doctors and nurses poking and prodding me they could not find any visible injuries so they asked me what area of my body did I feel most pain? Well I said, my neck seems to be really painful so gentle removing the neck collar and feeling around my neck asked me to identify where it hurt the most. When they touched certain spot I squealed like a piglet. Looking a bit concerned they said a neck ex-ray would be needed and it revealed that I had fractured my neck. The surgeon told me that I had to wear a neck collar until the fracture healed, but went on to tell me how lucky I was because when I was picked up after the fall and placed on the chair, if I had fractured the vertebrae below the one I fractured I would have been paralyzed for life! Not a thought worth thinking about! Pat came to visit me that evening, with the kids in tow and her first words to me were what have you been up to you silly sod and she added you haven't done too badly with you think about it, you've had sixteen stitches in your head and fractured your neck, never a truer word was spoken. Pat never stayed long, the first visit as I felt groggy, I didn't feel well enough to talk too much that evening although Hemel Hampstead is only about half an hour away from Bletchley by train, she decided to head home with the kids as it was better than staying and communicating with a dummy. After Pat left I got talking to the man in the next bed to mine. It turned out that he was in to have his wisdom tooth removed, when he told me this I said you're having a laugh, but it turned out it was the case as some wisdom teeth need to be extracted using anaesthetic. His operation was during the next day. His wife came to visit him and after about ten minutes of her arriving there conversation seemed to get rather heated. The next thing I know his wife had appeared at my bedside. Hello, you poor wounded soldier, what happened to you then? After explaining I had a fall at work she said, oh you poor thing and started to fuss around me, who is this woman? Eventually she returned to her husband and after some more raised voices from them both, she left the ward looking a bit tight lipped. Once she had gone he turned to me and said I must be a sucker for punishment, why is that I asked, well he replied I was married to my first wife for ten years and I got shot of her because of her constant moaning and nagging and her aggressive attitude towards me, I let her have the house because of the kids and we got separated then got divorced and would you believe it, I married again and she is even worse than the first one, at least with the first one I had money, but this one spends every penny I earn and nags and moans constantly and wants kids with me but I don't want any more. I might as well kept the first one at least I'd have money to spend! The poor man, I felt so sorry for him. The doctors wouldn't give me any pain relief tablets as they thought falling from that height there could be hidden injuries and their reasoning proved to be correct because after the third day in hospital the pain in my neck was slightly better but now I started to feel pain in my left knee so once again I was wheeled into x-ray and it was discovered I had fractured my left knee, but I still think I got off lightly. My partner Brian came to visit me and told me the full story about the accident, he told me one of the carpenters was on the roof of the show house that was being built in the warehouse and saw a small tower slam up against your tower, he watched as you were knocked off backwards, you did at least two summersaults while falling then hitting your head on an electrical box. He said he felt quite sick as he thought you had been killed and rushing down to help you was amazed to see you regain consciousness after a while, but thought you would never be able to work again! I told Brian it was best if he found another partner as I didn't know how long I would be off. Pat came to visit me on the third evening without the kids this time and was quite taken back to see me with my left leg in plaster and slightly raised on a pulley. After ten days in Hospital I was discharged and told to take things easy, to let my physical injuries heal and also the shock and trauma to my system of such a fall.

Poem

There was I in the ambulance and in so much pain
Where did that silly saying come from no pain no gain
But I'm a man you know we just grin and bear it
We just put on a brave face and show courage and grit
With them twists and turns and falling onto the deck
And with all my other injuries only fracturing my neck
How come I got off so lightly no one will know

Maybe it was just written I was not ready to go
Why was I so mercifully spared I know not why
Not deemed ready for that meeting place in the sky

A friend of Pats picked me up from Hemel Hospital but it was hard going getting into her car, with one leg in plaster and a neck collar clamped around my neck I was not in a very fit state. I could not turn my neck either way, the hospital told me I needed extensive physiotherapy to get it turning again. As it was September and the weather was very warm I was able to recuperate sitting down in my back garden taking in the warm sunshine a tonic in itself. Pat had already been to see the abbey national manager and explained I wouldn't be able to pay the mortgage because I didn't get paid when off work. I managed to walk the ten minutes it took to get to the Red Cross in Bletchley where I had daily sessions of physiotherapy but unfortunately there seemed to be a barrier stopping my neck moving in any direction. This was a bit worrying to say the least. I had now been out of hospital for four weeks and the x-rays on my neck showed that the fracture had healed but what was stopping movement taking place? Ray Tulley my old foreman from Matter & Platt had heard about my accident and on hearing physio was not working suggested to me that I should consider meeting a very good friend of his, who was a clairvoyant and a healer. I had nothing to lose so he arranged a meeting with her around Ray's house in Dunstable. Ray said I won't tell her anything about your accident I will just tell her you require healing on your neck area. As I entered Ray's house and went into the front room I was introduced to a woman in her early forties. This is Margaret, Ray said, you must be John she beamed, don't tell me anything about why you need healing because I will try and pick up the reasons. I understand from Ray it's your neck that needs some healing so I will start right away. She sat me down on the dining room chair and explained what was about to take place and who was helping here with this healing. She told me I have two people I call up who help me in healing, one is a man, who was a surgeon in the ninetieth century and the other one is a red-Indian chief who died about a hundred years ago. I must have had a bemused look on my face because Margaret softly smiled and said I sense John that you're not sure about all this but trust me, it does work in most cases! Now what I'm going to do now is stand behind you and then call up my helpers to assist me. I could hear her taking deep breaths and then she gently placed her two hands around my neck and with her fingers slowly massaged the neck area. I noticed within a short time how incredibly warm her fingers had become, she suddenly let out a shout and withdrew her hands from my neck, oh dear, she cried I've just felt your pain, and had this image of you falling in a large building it seems to be a building within a building (she must have picked up on the show house in the warehouse) how incredible. She carried on with this finger touching with her finger tips. By now they seemed to be quite hot, something unexplained was taking place. After a few minutes she whispered, now John, try and gently turn your head, one way and then the other. I must admit I wasn't too optimistic; I was going to get back any movement as my neck felt like I had two metal bars either side of my neck stopping me turning it. Well I'll give it a try but I don't hold out much hope. I tried very gingerly to first turn my neck left but all I could feel and hear was a grating and crunching type sound, I then repeated the same thing on my right side and low and behold I felt a slight movement. Eureka, Margaret had also noticed the very small turn that I had made and you could see the joy in her face. That's enough for now John, she said don't over do it. I'll give you a little more healing now and as from tomorrow night I want you to read this passage from the bible. She then handed me a written quotation from one of the scriptures. Please read the passage out loud and try slowly turning your head from side to side at the same time. I and my two spirit guilds will send you absence healing at exactly nine o clock and hopefully within seven days you should be getting much better movement. After the healing session she told me as she started administering healing to me the pain that I had suffered hitting the ground was transferred to her and she had an image of me actually falling. When I offered Margaret a payment for her time and effort she mildly scolded me saying, I do not do healing for payments of any kind, it's a god given gift to help people in their lives. So that was me told then!

It was now the first night at home and the time was now nine o'clock and with me sitting in my favourite chair I started to read the lines that Margaret requested. Trying slowly to move my head each way and unbelievably the grating and crunching had almost disappeared and I had much more free movement in my neck and amazingly by the seventh night as predicted by Margaret I was able to move it in all directions. Fantastic, there was I thinking the worse and seven days later my neck was getting better by the day. What are my thoughts about healing? Well you cannot help being impressed how a two hour session with healing helped me to regain full use of my neck where many hours of physio were of no use! Does Margaret have magical powers? Or is it in the mind? After what she achieved with my neck I have to say I found the experience quite moving and even uplifting and the best result of all was that it was very successful.

Poem

Arrived at the Red Cross to sort out my neck

No movement whatsoever after making contact with the deck

They tried physio and massaging but it just wouldn't turn

Believe they became rather worried I was later to learn
A call from Ray saying healing could be for you
Much better than the pain you are now going through
Then met Margaret who gave me a lovely Christian greeting
Getting straight down to work with fingertips which began heating
With love and belief at ease did I feel
And her truly amazing fingers she then started to heal
I was doubting Thomas before she worked on me
It's a god given gift you would have to agree

I had now been off work for five weeks with my neck still a bit sore but moving nicely. My left leg was still in plaster but that was due to be removed at the end of the week. My method for getting up stairs was to put the leg in plaster first and then follow up with the other one. Coming down it was done in reverse with the unplastered leg leading. A day before the plaster was due to be removed I was ready to come down from on top of the stairs and instead of leading with my unplastered leg I put my plastered leg first, big mistake because as soon as the leg touched the staircase I became completely off balanced and I went flying head first down the stairs. As I was sliding down I though to myself I hope my head does not make contact with that solid front door looming straight ahead but once again someone was watching over me because my head ended up about an inch (25mm) from the front door. I managed to get myself up and was very relieved to find that no further injuries had taken place. The plaster was removed and thankfully the fracture had healed in spite of the torpedo like velocity I had achieved on the stairs. As every day was nice and warm I used to sit out in the back garden soaking up the sun. I noticed a head appearing from our back garden fence, hello John a voice said, why you aren't at work you lazy sod? The voice belonged to a heating supervisor I had worked with on Matthew Hall a few years earlier and what are you doing in your back garden of that house I asked/ I'm working on the ladies central heating he replied and I couldn't believe my eyes seeing you lazing in that garden! He then asked cheekily have you got a hose I could borrow, because I have an air lock in the system. Come round I said and we can have a chat. On entering my house he noticed me slightly hobbling, what you been up to he asked? I then told him the story of the accident and my short time having my own company. I asked him are you working for yourself now? Oh no, he said, I'm a site supervisor and when these private jobs come up I just book off sick! He then said I hear Matthew Hall have a new job starting up shortly, in High Wycombe, why don't you give them a ring? I did indeed phone and was offered a Job with them at the RAF bunkers Naphill, which was starting the following week. Although I wasn't fully fit I accepted the job as it was due to last four years and the bonuses perks and the wage rates were excellent.

Bomb Bunkers High Wycombe

It was about a forty minute drive to the bunkers and on arriving the entire new workforce was shown around the inside of the structure from top to bottom. It was about a hundred feet (33m) with four feet (3m) thick walls. An enormous structure with three ton brackets holding the pipework it was estimated that even if the bunker took a direct hit by a nuclear bomb it would still be able to operate. The top half would have not survived but the bottom half would have been able to operate. As the job progressed we started to get regular visits from the air force officers from the NATO countries and on one of these visits a high ranking Dutch officer had left all his junior officers to look around a section whilst he wanted to see the men at work. He was chatting to the pipe fitters in perfect English and seemed very interested on the construction side of things. On all sites there will always be a prankster and this site was no exception. As this high ranking officer was chatting to us all the prankster was working on a bracket directly above the officer and delicately placed a used white paper tea cup on his hard hat. It was able to stay on the hard hat because he had attached sticky tin foil tape to the bottom of the cup. And on the cup he had drawn with a parker pen a nude lady with her bits highlighted. We all found it so very difficult to keep a straight face. This was sometimes done to visiting site engineers and that was funny enough but to have it done to the highest man in the Dutch air force made it even funnier. With handshakes all round he wished us well and set off to find his fellow officers. We all just had to see what the reaction would be of them seeing this cup on his hard hat so we all kept a discreet distance and followed him through the maze of passages. He finally caught up with them all as they were inspecting one of the many valve stations that had been installed. The look on their faces on seeing him was mixed, some looked astonished, others looked quite bemused while a couple had to turn away to hide their chuckles but what amazed us all not one of them pointed out to him about the cup, probably felt so embarrassed by it all. One of our engineers who was showing the party around said to him, sir I think you should look what's stuck one your hard hat. With that he took his hard hat off, took one look and much to the surprise of everyone I should think, burst out in a fit of laughter, much to the relief of everyone I should think. This very senior officer had a good sense of humour. If he had been a British high rank, heads would have rolled. There were seven more bomb bunkers built at the same time all around the UK. This was because the cold war was still very much alive at that time but now I should imagine school children are shown around them. As things have moved on so much in the world and the Soviet Union no longer poses a threat. I spent two happy and very rewarding years at the bunkers but one day I was called into the site office and told I was being transferred back to the fire engineering division for a job in London.

The year was 1986 and I was 47 years old and I had always been interested in all kinds of music but since 1974 when Abba first hit the must world I was smitten and amazed by what unbelievable musical talent they all had and what makes their story even more amazing, English was their second language and with that in mind how were they able to write such wonderful and clever lyrics and melodies and in my mind they were master tune smiths of the highest order and I believe their music will be played for many generations to come. It was a sad day in 1984 when they told the press that they were splitting up, the music world had lost one if the greatest groups of all time. I think you may have guessed that I am a huge fan! So my personal tribute to them is a combination of some of their songs in a poem form.

Poem

Winning the Eurovision song contest made Abba "money, money, money"
And how about that wonderfully catchy tune "honey, honey"
It all took off for them with that classic "waterloo"
And how could you ever forget "knowing me knowing you"
Such a haunting melody that Benny composed "I had a dream"
Then of course one of their greatest hits "dancing queen"
Just listen to them lyrics "the day before you came"
Also that more upbeat song "the name of the game"
What a beautiful but sad balled "I've been waiting for you"
Followed by that delightful gem "the way old friends do"
Thank you for the music Abba "when all is said and done"
You have brought so much joy into the lives of everyone

I had a farewell drink with all the lads from the bomb bunker on the Friday and we all said our farewells. After working with men for two years with the highs and lows of site life you get to know and respect your fellow workers and such farewells are always quite sad. I arrived at Matthew

Halls head office in Tottenham Court road on the Monday morning and was quite surprised to see Peter Beesworth sitting in the reception area. What are you doing here I asked him? I didn't know, he said, you're back with me on the mobile. That's news to me I replied. I've been waiting for you to arrive he smiled. So let's go upstairs now because the project manager wants to go through the job with both of us. Rumour has it that it's quite an important job. We both walked into the manager's office and were greeted warmly by him. Gentlemen take a seat and I'll explain about the job you will be doing. Firstly gents you will be working in Government buildings, some will belong to the war office and others are with the ministry of defence. For some reason they wanted men to carry out the work who had served in the forces and it has taken 12 weeks for you two to get clearances to undertake the job. He went on, here is the address of the first job and there you will meet a Colonel Jackson who is clerk of the works. For all ministry buildings in London in spite of the bad traffic we were outside the building that was on our work sheet it was a stones throw from the bank of England, on the other side of the Street were modern office blocks but the address we had been given here was fine Georgian terraced houses surely there's some mistake. As we got out of the van we were approached by a smartly dressed man with a handle bar moustache gentlemen he said, I am Colonel Jackson and we have been expecting you both if you would like to follow me inside I will get you signed in then you will have photographs taken, I.D. cards issued talks on security and the task we require you both to carry out while you're working here in government offices and after all that's taken care of you will be required to both sign the official secrets act and all this will take up most of the day. In these talks we were told exactly what they wanted us to do, what they were worried about was if a pipe above the false ceiling burst, or a sprinkler somehow got damaged all our sensitive work on each desk would be rendered unusable. Their reasoning was a burst pipe or damaged sprinkler was more likely to occur than a fire breaking out so our brief was to drain the whole system down and take every sprinkler head out and drain off every drop of water left in the pipe. When we pointed out this would take forever as in the building was hundreds of drops to drain out we were told we are the clients and that's what we require. After filling in all the forms and given a guided tour of all the areas we would be working in and knowing what was required of us. We again met Colonel Jackson who handed us a large printed card he said, your need this for parking outside on the road, place it on the drivers side and you will not get a parking ticket. On the card was written "this vehicle has permission to park outside these premises on a permanent basis, any queries please contact Mr Jackson clerk of works, ministry of building and works on this telephone number" Just as we were leaving the building colonel Jackson said because of the sensitive nature and highly secretive work we do here you will both be accompanied by two of our security team at all times. That's OK Peter said we have no problems with that. We dove off that evening thinking this should turnout to be an interesting job. We duly arrived at the job the next day and parked the van with the printed exemption card clearly displayed. Once inside the building we were introduced to the minders who were to be our constant companions wherever we worked. Both these men were in their forties with shaven heads and their manner suggested that they had been in the forces. We had been working for about two hours and Peter asked me to go to the van and get another pair of stilsons. On getting the stilsons and locking the van doors I noticed that a parking ticket had been stuck on the windscreen. Oh dear me, Mr Jackson will not be very pleased when he sees this. I handed Peter the ticket and he said, this should be fun, as he showed Mr Jackson the ticket who in turn went into a rage saying every swear word ever known to man was uttered by him, he shouted heads will roll for this, you mark my words! Within seconds he was on the phone and whoever he was speaking to seemed to have a high ranking position, when he had finished the phone call he was a much calmer man and he said to us that won't happen again gentlemen. Both peter and I realised Mr Jackson without doubt was also a very important person in the security service and not a clerk of works as he claimed! When we first started to work in some of the offices the staff would cover up their work in front of them but as they got used to us walking back and forward they didn't bother and just carried on working even our two minders who were supposed to be with us at all times got fed up just standing around watching us work and one of them said I know you two have been vetted and have security clearance so it is silly us following you around all day so we will let you get on with your job without us in attendance. In some offices the mainly woman staff were studying what looked like aerial photos, they were using a microscope that was mounted on a frame, all very hush, hush. We did hear that most of the staff working there were head-hunted while still at university and had posh accents on them that cut right through you very "too to much" all home counties educated gals. We had now been working there for some time and it was a very time consuming job and we had just one more area to work on and this was at the top floor of the building. The two minders said they now had to be with us at all times and we realised why because electronic codes had to be programmed into the main door for it to open. This door was the same type used in banks to keep all the deposits in. As we reached the top of the stairs, yet another vault type door had to be opened in the same way. Once this one was opened we stopped inside a large circular room with a highly polished rounded table in the centre of the room. The chairs around the table were high backed ones, a bit like the ones used in those gentlemen clubs around the table were all different coloured telephones but what was the big eye opener was the amount of open metal cabinets that were packed with files that were marked with crosses with many colours. These files had written on them words like top secret, most secret etc. Being in that room was like being on the set of a James bond movie. When I asked on of the minders, what occurs in here then? He growled back at me, just do your work and don't be asking questions. Peter and I spent two days in the room and when we had finished the job could not stop talking about it. We realised not many people get to see the inside of that room. We were both impressed. What was this highly secret room for we wondered? Unfortunately we never got to find out as of course no-one would tell us. We had now completed all that had to be done and so it was time for us to leave. Colonel Jackson came and thanked us for, as he put it, a splendid effort chaps and it's been a pleasure to meet you both. What a nice man. On our way home I said to peter, we will never in our lives get such an interesting job like that again.

Poem

Meeting up with Peter again I should have walked on by

Working with him last time we never saw eye to eye

He could and would work every single hour that god made

The workaholic robot is what he got called in the trade

A leopard doesn't normally change its spots but you never know

But this job sounds just great I'll give it a go

These people working in these offices are they all spies

Is James bond about to appear with them piercing eyes

All those coloured phones and files is this for real

This room had the nations secrets stored there I feel

We completed the contract the job was all finished and done

It's in these kind of places where wars are often won

After Peter and I had finished the government jobs, the office wanted me to carry on working on the mobile but I didn't fancy the long drives to get to jobs and the long hours that had to be worked, so they reluctantly let me go back on site. The year was 1989 and I was 50 years old and the new job was at:

Oldham's Press Watford

London was where all the daily papers were printed but in 1990 newspapers started to relocate from Fleet Street. The daily mirror moved all their printing to Watford, in a huge building that used to print magazines. All the old printing presses were stripped out and nine new state of the art machines from Germany were installed, they were massive. They erected them on the ground floor and they reached to the third floor and at one million pounds a machine they were not cheap. The building took over a year to refurbish and to get up and running. The total cost of all the works was about £30 million and where did all this money come from? It came from a man called Robert Maxwell, who owned the Daily Mirror, Oldham's press and hundreds of other companies. The trouble was he was a big crook and robbed the pension funds of most of his companies to pay for all this work and for his millionaire life style but the biggest losers were the Mirror Group Pensioners, who numbered about 30,000 in all. He had cleaned them out of everything they had build up in their pension pot. Maxwell used to come on site occasionally to check up on the progress of the work. He would arrive in the style of a visiting statesman with all his flunkies following up behind him, a ruder arrogant and nasty man you could not meet. He ruled his staff with an iron fist and they were all terrified of him, but as the saying goes, every dog has his day and Maxwell realising that everyone was now on to him, sailed his luxury yacht to the med and jumped overboard, a fitting end for him. He was such a despicable man; he doesn't even merit a poem about him. It was still 1989 and the Oldham's press job came to an end. I was then transferred to a job opposite Victoria station. The building was being refurbished for a major American investment bank called Soloman brothers and no expense was spared in the design or materials used. The reason I enjoyed working on the job was because all my old work mates were working there and there was a great atmosphere about the job, plus we worked every week-end so it became a good paying fun job. What more could a man want? Nine months into the contract the job was now taking shape and the builders were due to hand the completed building over to the clients. This was going to be a grand affair and Soloman Brothers had agreed to foot the bill for the entire evening's entertainment. Soloman Brothers had agreed that all workers and their partners who had worked on the contract could attend the bash but the builders had other ideas. They didn't like the idea that lowly pipe fitters, plumbers, electricians and god forbid labourers should mix with them, so they decreed that all the firms working on site could only send men who had the status of Supervisor or above so this eliminated all us underlings and there was no chance of us getting into the do because you had to have an invitation card. All the trades from the different firms were outraged at this decision and decided to do something about it and as Soloman Brothers had their own printing press one of the plumbers managed to obtain the names of all the men who wanted to attend the function and while the printing staff were at their lunch break boldly over five days printed off over a hundred perfect invitations in each mans name! It was now Friday and after the working day, the function was due to be held. The day went quickly and we watched as the senior managers, site engineers and the like accompanied by their dressed to kill partners made their way into the large hall. We couldn't wait to see the look on all their faces as this rabble made their entrance. We all lined up the main door and on opening it were confronted by a burly security guard. You may have invitation cards, he snapped, but I can't let you all in dressed like that. One of the lads shouted at him, listen you knobhead, there's nothing on that invitation card about a dress code so let us in, or else. At that moment we watched as a very smartly dressed man approached us. He had officiously come over to see what all the commotion was about. Gentleman, what seems to be the problem, he said in a thick New York accent. One of the men replied we have invitations but this guard won't let us in because he reckons we're not dressed properly. But who are you all he demanded to know? We're the workers who built this place a voice shouted. Well in that case men you're more than welcome to come in, I'm not worried what clothes you have on. As we entered the area set aside for the bash, we couldn't believe our eyes, there were rows of tables crammed with all kinds of exotic foods from around the world. Other tables had the finest wines and spirits available there were even stalls laden down with beautifully made wedding style cakes and magnificent gateaux's that looked so tempting. They seemed to be looking up at me and saying "eat me" and being a man with a very sweet tooth, I obeyed them! When the managers and site engineers spotted us, you could see the shock on their faces. The man, who had issued the invitations out, shouted at us, where the hell did you get them invitations cards from, this function is for the office staff and senior managers only. One of the ceiling fitters mockingly told him we know people if high places mate so get stuffed. On hearing raised voices the well dressed American came over to our site manager and asked him what the problem was. The manager explained to him that he had not issued these men with tickets and therefore they should not be allowed in here. The American man then laid into him, how dare you refuse these men entry, I am the vice president of this company, and I have given them permission to enter, as workers, they have more right to be in here than you, so let that be an end to this matter! The manager just stood there opened mouthed and looked like he was about to cry like a baby! His humiliation was completed, when the men laid into him, with words like, you plonker, you're a knobhead, and other unprintable words! He then said, right men, enjoy yourselves, eat as much food and drink as you like, you all deserve it.

One of the fitters we had been working for the company was a guy called Craig Johnstone, who it must be said liked a drink. On observing all the drinks that were available and free, he was delighted to see that some of the scotch whiskey on display was the finest on the market and well matured. My man, he said to the barman, I would like a large glass of your finest scotch, if I may. Certainly sir answered the barman, you're my first customer and you seem to know your whiskeys!

In the middle of the hall, a man with a cream jacket and a bow tie was playing melodies on a grand piano all very soothing. As the evening were on, I was drinking quite moderately even though it was a free bar, I just wanted to sample the delights of the food mountain on display. On one of the stalls there was a complete roasted pig, a whole goose, and a goose with its wings and webbed feet still attached, with a chef in attendance, ready to carve up as much as anyone wanted. Most of the workers were congregated around the free bar, and as the evening wore on the free drink started to take effect. The banter started to get much louder and a few swear words were hurled in the direction of the senior managers and there wives. Craig Johnstone, the whiskey lover, had tasted everyone one of the whiskeys displayed and was now very unsteady on his feet, so unsteady in fact, it was one step forward, and two back with him, normally a quite chap he went up to the piano player and told him to stop playing all that rubbish and play something more lively. From playing background music, he started to belt out loud rock and roll rhythm and blues. The managers looked on in shock, but realised they couldn't say anything as they were totally out numbered by the manual workforce, especially now comments were being directed at their wives and to the fact they were all so ugly. Craig called them a load of ponces; you could see how uneasy they now were. The mood of the men was still a happy one, but most of them were very drunk, one of the plumbers was standing by the cake stall, he then bent over and for some reason known only to himself, head butted this virgin gateau, and not content with that, also head butted a large bowl of jelly, and then proceeded to head butt a beautifully prepared trifle, he stood up proudly, with all the contents running down his clothes, the place erupted in hysterical laughter. He stood there, with a drink in his hand, chatting away to people, as if this was a perfectly normal occurrence, was this to be his dinner the following night? What made the scene even more comical, was one of the sparks, had stuffed the goose in his jacket and all you could see was webbed feet dangling out of his top. It was one of the funniest sights I have ever witnessed; it looked like a sketch from a comedy film. In the meantime, Craig had cornered the vice president and was laying into and saying he should be shot for making vast profits, but he took this outburst with amazing good humour and charm. That's probably why he got to become a vice president in the first place also knowing how to deal with people, especially very drunk ones. The managers and their wives decided this was now not a good place to still be, so they all quickly departed and as the do was coming to an end, and there was still so much drink left over, each man was given a full bottle of his choice on departure. This pacified the more unruly among the men! I have to say this was one of the best and funniest gatherings I have ever attended.

Poem

Behind Victoria Station, Soloman brothers is where I was transferred,
Where one of them never to be forgotten evenings occurred.
Workers were barred it was just for the chosen few,
Probably it was because we were such a motley crew.
Lots of tickets were forged on the firm's printing press,
It must have been about a hundred more or less.
Because of all the free beer, there was so much drinking,
And pints of beer mixed with neat whiskey, men were sinking.
A feast fit for a King it was very grand,
Until it all went pear shaped and got out of hand.
The plumber became very drunk and was on the loose,
And hanging out from his jacket was that unfortunate goose.
The jelly and gateau then received a full head butt,
By one of the sparks who was a complete nut.
It was one of those nights, a pity was never recorded,
Had it been a BAFTA would have been awarded.

I worked on a few more smaller jobs in the London area, and the year was now 1992, and Stuart had reached the age of 14, he was doing well it school, and one day he brought home a school project that all the schools in the area were taking part in. This was to see which pupil could write the best poetry about Milton Keynes, and the best effort would win quite a decent prize. I asked Stuart if he wanted any help with it, if you want to was his reply. I don't really like poetry so I set about writing how children viewed the world in general, so I came up with the title "through he eyes of a child", and tried to write it as I thought a child would see things. I made it short and sweet, so only wrote 20 lines, and handed it to Stuart, who upon reading it grunted as fourteen year olds do, and he said it's not very good but it will do. He handed into his English teacher the next day. About three weeks passed and Stuart came home from school and told us his English teacher was very pleased with him because his entry was judged to have been the best one, and therefore it had won first prize. The English teacher said to Stuart the school and myself are very proud of your achievement and I am pleased to tell you, that you and your family will be invited to the award ceremony in Central Milton Keynes, where you will be presented to the mayor, who will award you with your prize. About two weeks later we all made our way up to the presentation ceremony and were greeted by Stuart's English teacher, who proudly remarked, whoever thought Stuart could write poetry like that? I am amazed, I never thought he had it in him, I am so proud of him as you all must be? Before the ceremony got started I was taking to the teacher, and noticed she had a Yorkshire accent, and how nice it sounded, and as she was quite an attractive young lady, with a lovely sense of humour and great personality, I said to her, "you look younger than springtime, and could I not compare you to a summer rose", she smiled sweetly and said "you're a bit of a flatterer aren't you Mr.Banfield". I then noticed a look in her eye, and said she "do you write at all?" oh no I replied, I'm far too busy at work, but I realised she had guessed who might have had a lot to do with Stuart's poetry effort! After a few speeches by various dignitaries, the mayor stood up and announced Stuart as the winner of the poetry competition and to come up and collect his prize, which consisted of a large sized Collings English dictionary, a comprehensive encyclopaedia, and some gift vouchers, and to much applause, Stuart returned to his seat, I must say, I did feel a bit guilty about my part in Stuart's winning, but I had no idea he would win anything, to me it was just like helping him with his homework! As we went to leave, I said to his teacher "that's a feather in your cap", she replied "I think that's a feather in all our caps, don't you!" what an earth did she mean?

Poem

Can you help me with this poetry Stuart begged me,
There's a good prize in it if I win, please agree.
Thought it best if I kept it down to twenty lines,
Hoped I could do it justice with some riddles and rhymes.
Through the eyes of a child, that was the theme,

Children sometimes live in a fantasy world when they dream.
And to think of it we entered it for fun,
It became the winning entry first prize it had won.
Getting poetry to sound right and making sure it flows,
Not always quite as easy as that, as everyone knows.

Most of my work was in the London area and for the next two years, I worked in various locations throughout the capital, one day, I was asked to report to head office, the next day, I wondered what they wanted? As I entered the office, the construction manager said "how would you like to fill your lungs up with sea air?" "What do you mean?" I asked, "Well John, I know you have worked away for us in the past and there's a job starting in a couple of weeks time, and it's in Plymouth, and it's at the naval dockyard. One of the reasons we want you to go, is because you already have clearance to work in military establishments because of the work you did at the war office in London. It will last for about three months, and every other week, you can come home for a long weekend, do you fancy it?" "I'll give it a go" I replied. So it was mid summer and the year was 1994, and I was 55 years old.

Plymouth Navy Base

As I set off that day to Bletchley train station, I was looking forward to something different in my working life. Plymouth is nearly as far south as you can get and with such beautiful scenery on offer, it will hopefully feel like a holiday! Having arrived at Euston, I made my way to Paddington main line station and as the ticket has already been paid for by head office, I boarded the intercity for the long haul to Plymouth. As I sat on my seat awaiting the departure of the train, a very polite young man asked me if he and his two friends could sit on the three vacant seats, please do I gestured. We made small talk at first as you do, and I discovered they were off on a two week cycling holiday, and picking up the bikes in Plymouth. When I told them I was off to Plymouth, one of them asked me would you join us for a drink? Oh yes I replied, that would be nice. They had come well prepared because from their backpacks came an assortment of beers, spirits and lagers. I was now thinking to myself I don't think I'll now be getting the nap I was looking forward to! It transpired that my new friends were on leave, and were German army officers, who had liked Britain so much when training over here, decided to see more of it when on leave! I started off drinking lagers, then vodka and in the end anything, that they pulled out of there booze bag. There master of the English language was amazing, as were their manners, and with the drink flowing, and the very interesting conversation between us, by the time we reached Swindon, which was the second of five stops, I was feeling a bit merry, but hey, who cares, as I wasn't due to start work until the next day, so lets party. It takes about five hours to reach Plymouth, and as the train pulled into Plymouth station, we were all completely wrecked and all nearly fell onto the platform. With hugs all round from my German friends, who had been great companions, it was now left for me, to try and drag my heavy suitcase out of the station, and try and find the naval base. I had been told be the office that I was report to the main gate that day, and once I had been cleared and given my security pass, the site engineer of our firm, would show me around the place I would be working at, and then take me to my digs, that had been booked up for me. It was too far to walk to the base, so I hailed a taxi and ten minutes later, I was outside the base. As I approached the main gate, I noticed two armed MOD police officers standing guard, "yes sir, what can we do for you?" one of them said, "I've just come to sign in as I'll be starting work here". "Right then sir, go through that door over there, the duty officer will check your paperwork out". I knocked at the door marked base security officer, and a sharp voice cried out, "Come in". As I entered the room, I noticed a stern looking naval officer sitting at a desk, right he shouted, let's have a look at your papers. On showing him my clearance security papers, he asked who I would be working for, and had I read the rules and regulations regarding the working practises at this base. Yes I have I lied, well mister, let me tell you something, you have just broken one of them, now would you like to tell me which one you think it is? Um, ah, I don't really know I meekly said, then let me enlighten you he angrily snapped, it is a no drinking allowed on the base rule, and as you smell like a brewery, you haven't obeyed the drinking rule have you? Eh, sorry about that sir, but it was a long journey down here! Well Mister he carried on, you will not be allowed on the base today because of your drinking, you'll have to apply again tomorrow for your ID card, but completely sober you understand. Now Mister would you lift your suitcase on to the desk, as I would like to search it and before I do, have you any think in suitcase that contravenes the rules and regulations of this base! All I have in my suitcase is two weeks supply of clothes and that's it, I answered defiantly. As the rummaged through the clothes he suddenly spun around and shouted, what's this? Erm, that's my camera I said proudly and with his other hand, shouted and what are these then (is this man an idiot? He doesn't even know what binoculars look like!), get in that detention room now he shouted at me angrily, sit on that chair and don't move an inch. Guards he shouted get in there and watch that man. With that, two pistol packing MOD policemen came in the room and stood either side of the closed door. What's going on I asked? I've only come here to get my ID card, so I can start work, shut up, the mean looking one of the guards shouted, speak only when spoken to, your now in custody. In custody I protested your having a laugh, I told you to shut up you'll be able to have your say at the interview your about to get! Although I was still feeling the effects of the heavy drinking earlier that day, I was sobering up remarkably quickly, and I still didn't have a clue why they wanted to interview me! Moments later, I heard raised voices coming from the corridor, and seconds later, the door opened and in walked the duty officer, who had searched my suitcase, followed by a high ranking naval officer. Oh dear, I seem to be in some sort of trouble here, but what could it be! The duty officer said "right then Mr. Banfield, this is commander McNulty, the base security officer. They then sat down opposite me, the duty officer then said, Mr. Banfield you are being interviewed for bringing a camera and binoculars into this naval base, and the interview that followed went something like this!

Duty Officer: Firstly what was the purpose of bringing a camera and binoculars into this naval base?

Me: Well, I was hoping to watch some ships through the binoculars when walking on the cliffs after work, but with the camera, I was hoping to take a few snapshots of warships while on my tea breaks!

Commander: Am I hearing this right? You wanted to take photos of royal navy ships of this base?

Me: Eh, yes that's right sir, but they wouldn't be very good photos, because as you can see, the camera, is only a cheap old Kodak instamatic!

Duty Officer: Now Mr. Banfield, we would like to know the reason why you want to take photos of navy ships?

Me: Oh that's simple, I just love the look of warships, and it was a disappointment to me that I never got to join the royal navy.

Commander: Getting rather agitated, let's get this straight; you wanted to take photos of the ships on this base, because you like ships? Did you know some of the ships we have here are classified?

Me: That's interesting, I've never heard of these new classified ships, are there new warships acquired by the royal navy?

Duty Officer: Who now seemed to be getting hot under the collar, and started oozing his tie, we have the latest submarines based here Mr. Banfield , would you be interested in taking photos of them?

Me: No, no, subs are boring, as most of the sub is below water, so it's not at all interesting.

It was at this point it dawned on me, they thought I was up to no good with my camera, so a grovelling apology now had to be made.

Me: I am so sorry if I have given you cause to panic, because of my stupid actions, in bringing a camera onto the base, it was stupid of me, and I hope you will accept my apology.

Commander: Okay, Mr. Banfield, sit there, whilst we discuss this in the next room.

About ten minutes later, they both returned to the room. The effects of the drink had worn off and by now I was feeling quite sober.

Commander: We have discussed your case, and have come to the conclusion that there was nothing sinister in your action, and we have taken the view that you are naïve and a bit of an idiot, but didn't intend to breach security on this base, so we will issue you with your ID card and you may commence work here tomorrow, but please leave that camera at your residence.

Devonport naval base was one of the most interesting jobs I had ever worked on, it goes back to the reign of Henry the eighth, and the first dry dock ever built which was constructed all in oak, and its still there today. As we got to know the civilian workers, who were employed by the navy they told us stories about the history of the base, and one of the many tales happened round 1775. It's said a drunkard sailor returned to the base having spent the night drinking and bumped into a naval officer and told him what he thought of him, and then swore at him. He was immediately arrested and the next day faced a court martial, and was found guilty of swearing at an officer and duly hung. This sailors ghost has been seen many times roaming about the base, still dressed in the navy uniform of that time! How spooky!   Also on the base is a lone building where they used to make all different size ropes for the old wooden warships. Captured French sailors were made to make the ropes, from the Napoleonic wars, and if they refused to make theses ropes, they found there own necks firmly placed into the rope with a loop at one end, a noose in fact. Then the trap door was opened beneath them and they were duly dispatched.

The job at the base was coming to an end, and the project engineer told me, this will be your last week here, because as from next week, you are being transferred back to London.

Poem

I was off to Plymouth and was catching the train,
Letting that big beast of an engine take the strain.
Meeting these very nice Germans, my God could they drink,
There own weight in a drinking session they could sink.
And on this drinking journey met these new found friends,
Its great meeting new people but sad when its ends.
Arriving at the naval base still a little drunk,
A large variety of potent drinks we all had sunk.
Sitting at his desk the duty officer looked quite mean,
With a bulldog type head a sight to be seen.
He began opening up my suitcase shouting what have we here,
You're in big trouble as he gave me an icy stare.
Then he started shouting at me I know not why,

Surely he can't be thinking I'm some sort of spy.
In them bygone days I would have walked the plank,
With many gallons of sea water I would have drank.
Or tied to the mast and then forcible stripped,
Now knowing what's to come being brutally whipped.
But good job it's just a dream I'll be alright,
Knowing that this officer's bark is worse than his bite.
But it all ended well I'm very pleased to say,
It all finally got sorted out on that crazy day.

I worked on a few more jobs in the London area for the next year or so, and of course was still taking a keen interest in both Stuart's and Judy's welfare, as they were both now entering the uncharted waters that involves young people leaving school. Stuart had stayed on at school and was 18 by the time he left, and gained good A levels, and then went on to college to study for a HND in mechanical engineering. Judy on the other hand left school at 16, and trained at both college and in a hairdressing salon to be a hair stylist. The year now was 1996, and I was 57 years old, and was called into the office to be told myself, and a few workmates would be starting a job at Kings Cross underground station, and all the work would be done on nights. The whole tube network was to be covered by fire protection, this was because a few years earlier, there was a major fire at Kings Cross, with the loss of many lives, and there was a public outcry over the lack of fire safety equipment, so AMEC as my firm was now known, had the contract to supply and install the sprinkler systems and all other fire fighting equipment. It was a huge undertaking, but with the hourly rate at time and a half, plus a good bonus, everyone was up for the job, in spite of the nightshift working Pattern.

Kings Cross Underground Station

I used to start work at eight in the evening at our stores near Borough station on the northern line, load all the pipe work onto a lorry, and drive to Kings Cross station, where it was unloaded in an unused part of the station, away from passengers. The last train of the night left at 12:30am, so work couldn't start until then, unless it was in the storerooms or away from the general public. Once I had delivered the pipe, I drove the lorry back to the stores and then caught the tube back to Kings Cross to start work! Before any work could proceed, every night, there was a health and safety talk that could last for an hour or more. Kings Cross had never had such extensive work carried out on it, and some of the large wooden oak doors far below ground had not been opened for years. After days of searching around for keys for these doors, when opened inside were old workshops, with still old tools in them. On entering one door, I noticed an old newspaper on a bench, as I picked it up it just disintegrated in my hands, but I was able to pick out the date, showing 1917, so that door hadn't been opened for 79 years, so it was a room frozen in time. Once we got started working installing pipe work in rooms and tunnels, we had to put up with thick layers of dirt and grease that had built up over the years, and we could only work five hours a night, as the first train of the morning was at 5:30am. Working in this environment could prove to be quite hazardous, so extreme caution had to be taken it all times whilst working underground, so safety talks were quite important, and on this particular night before work commenced, every contractor working on the station was assembled in the canteen for what was to be a major health and safety talk by senior bosses from London underground, insurance chiefs and construction managers, from all different firms working on the tube network. Before the talk started, our construction manager said to as all I hope you men have read all the leaflets and health and safety rules, including the booklet of the working practices on the underground system, because you may be asked questions on it! Oh dear, I hope it's not me he picks out because like all the other men, I was given the paperwork and I promptly threw it all in the bin. All of us AMEC men were sitting in the front seats, with the men from other firms sitting behind us, opposite us were seats where the managers sat. Our resident site supervisor who was running the job was sat in the back row. As we sat there waiting for the main man to arrive, we all had the same thought, is this going to be another one of them boring, trying to keep your eyes open talks. The big chief then boldly walked in, followed by this army of flunkeys, who all sat down in the front seats opposite us, with the main man standing. He then opened up his speech, praising the workforce and saying how well all the firms had pulled together, with hardly any accidents being reported. After talking for about twenty minutes, with the most boring talk that had ever been given throughout the history of man, complete numbness had now set in, my body and brain had shut down, and I was in a paralysed state. What brought me round from this deep slumber I found myself in, was an elbow being dug into my ribs, the elbow came from Portsmouth John sitting next to me, wake up you prat or words to that effect, as I awoke, the head man was starring at me, "you've heard every word I been talking about haven't you?" he said in a mocking tone. Eh, I may have missed a few words I replied my eyes still felt very heavy; well in that case, you may like to tell me that you fully understand the rules that appertain to the function of the working practices of the London transport underground system? What was I suppose to answer to that, I didn't have a clue what he was on about, he might as well talked to me in Mongolian! One of the lads sitting behind me whispered, I think he's just come from the pub and he's pissed, tell him to get a life and f—k off, after hearing that comment, I know had to try and keep a straight face, as I knew all the lads were really enjoying the discomfort they knew I was feeling. "Well he snapped, what's your answer?" I starred back at him blankly and was completely tongue tied. I couldn't ask him to repeat the question, as I never understood it in the first place, um and erm is all that I could say, then he turned to a senior manager sitting next to him and said, I give up, I have asked the man a question and he just stares at me a silly blank expression on his face. I then noticed Arni, our site manager was waving his arms about to catch my attention, and with the first finger from both hands, proceeded to point to both of his eyes, what the hell is he doing I thought? It looks like he's been down the pub and he's in another world, has he completely lost it? The main man once again said, I'm still waiting for an answer from you, and again, looking at Arni, who was still frantically pointing at both his eyes, that's it I thought, Arni is trying to show me the word the man wants me to say, so I blurted out "eyes" the boss looked at me in utter astonishment, eyes he shouted, what do you mean eyes? Yes eyes I once again said. Arni quickly came to my rescue, what he means is that he has read all the paperwork relating to the contract and fully understands them! The main man shock his head from side to side in bewilderment and said, I hope the next man I ask a question to won't be as a stupid as this man! Of course the lads sitting behind me couldn't contain their laughter at the answer I gave, and for years after, I was never allowed to forget it. Once that meeting was over, I approached Arni, and asked him why he was pointing at his eyes, he said, I thought you would have realised that pointing to my eyes meant that you had read all the paperwork is it me I said? How was I supposed to work that out? It was funny at the time, and gave everyone a good laugh!

Poem

This was something completely different our very first tube station,
And is one of the busiest networks throughout this nation.
Must be done on nightshift, not such a good thing,
But with higher hourly rates good rewards it will bring.
We then started work at the world renowned Kings Cross,
And with me saying "eyes" just didn't impress the boss.
No doubt was thinking we have a right one here,
As he proceeded to give me an icy cold stare.
Arni came to my rescue trying to help me out,
And hearing eyes the boss wandered what I was talking about.

We worked at Kings Cross for about six months, and then moved on to Baker Street, which was a much bigger station. It was the world's first tube station and ran above ground to Great Portland Street in about 1864. As it was a larger station, more men were required to work on it, so they needed a first aider, and I was told, I was to do the first aid course, but I pointed out, I would faint if I saw blood pouring out of a wound and even watching operations being performed in hospitals that are shown on television, makes me feel queasy and ill, so I'm the last man you want to be a first aider. However they got there way, so I did a five day course at St Johns ambulance centre based in Harrow, and somehow managed to pass it. So all you out there, I'm more likely to run, than treat, you have been warned! Before we can start working anywhere on the station, we had to wait for the last train to depart, this was about 12:30am and Friday nights were always busier, because being at the end of the working week, people spent Friday nights in the pubs. I didn't have to wait long to put my first aid training into operation, because on the first Friday night after I passed the course, the last train was due to depart in five minutes, so there was a big scramble by the usual Friday night drunks, dopeheads and low life's to be on it. Most of the rabble didn't have a ticket, and just climbed over the ticket barrier, but this burly, bare chested, shaven headed, tattooed bull of a man, decided that climbing over the barrier was for wimps or men displaying there feminine side, and as he had a girlfriend in tow, and was probably trying to impress her, he thought he would jump the barrier in one leap just like a high jumper. He managed to nearly clear the barrier, but unfortunately for him, his right foot just clipped the top of the barrier, and he did a mid air summersault, resulting in his head hitting the tiled floor with a sickening thud, within seconds, there was blood everywhere, which made me feel quite ill, and I was feeling sick myself, it was me needing the treatment. The raging bull had a deep gash on his forehead, and I quickly ran to help him, don't move I told him, we need to keep you still, saying it in a very professional manner, his words back to me were not what I was expecting, f—k off mate, your not touching me you poof, if you lay one finger on me I'll nut you, I'm getting up right now! I was then surrounded by all his drunkard mates, shouting at me, leave him alone, we'll look after him and promptly picked him up, and carried him onto the train. I stood there dumbfounded. It didn't say things like this happened in the first aid manual, you're supposed to take control of the situation, apply first aid, and call an ambulance if necessary, but in this case, I ended up with egg on my face, not a good start to my first aid career with a Patient your trying to attend to threatening to nut you. If the big bull had been sober and jumped the barrier he would have probably sustained a major injury, but with him being very drunk, he got away wit it!

Baker Street has five different lines running through it, and is the biggest of all the tube stations, so we worked on nights for months in offices, storerooms and tunnels. One of the offices we installed pipework in was where the men from the emergency crew were quartered. This eight man crew were mainly responsible for lifting up the tube trains, with large heavy jacks when a person jumps in front of a moving train. They went by the name of the "one under crew" not a very pleasant job for anyone, but most of them used to be ex firemen so were used to seeing gruesome sights, they would tell us some of the stories. They said they were always puzzled that when they had to attend a "one under", is that the person in most cases would jump under a train when they finished work, but not on there way to work! It just seems so sad, they couldn't confide in a friend, before taking such drastic action! Our first tea break of the shift was at 1am, and we all used to sit outside the station forecourt, and on this particular night, we all watched in amazement as a man in his early twenties with only a pair of boxer shorts on, was running at full speed against the traffic, down Marylebone Road dodging in and out of the traffic, is this man on a suicide mission? He managed to avoid getting smashed to pulp and then promptly ran into the station forecourt, and proceeded to climb one of the flagpoles that are near the entrance to the station, within seconds he had nearly reached the top of the seven metre pole, when suddenly the pole snapped and he came tumbling down. He fell on the paving slabs surrounding the poles, I said to the lads, this man won't be requiring first aid, he will be needing a body bag, but amazingly he picked himself up, and ran in a gap in the closed shuttered station doors, and with the night station manager and all of us contractors running after him, he had the speed of a cheetah, and by the time we caught up with him, we spotted him jumping off the station platform and onto the track, and disappearing into the tunnel. Fortunately for him, the current had been switched off to allow repair work to be carried in the tunnel. By now the transport police had arrived and they were just about to go down the tunnel after him, when all of a sudden he reappeared, covered from head to toe in soot, he looked like one of the black and white minstrels. The cops managed to grab hold of him, and detained him in a cell overnight. When we asked them the following night how the man was, they told us his mates had been in to see them and admitted that they had spiked his drinks at a party; this explained his superhuman strength and energy. They all realised it was a silly thing to do, as he could have easily been killed! And I was still waiting to give first aid to my first Patient!

The Baker Street contract was coming to an end, so the firm asked me if I would take charge of two underground stations, one was Wanstead on the central line, which was a nice little station, and only a two man job. My old mate Bob Burns worked with me until we completed it in six weeks. We then went to Brixton station on the northern line. You can imagine that we were a bit apprehensive about working there, because on our first night of starting there, a large notice board had been placed outside the station asking people if they had witnessed a fatal stabbing that had occurred two days earlier. I said to Bob, are we expected to work in a war zone? But our fears proved to be unfounded, as the job went very well, all the staff were very helpful, and chatting to local people. Outside the station on our tea breaks, we found them all to be so very friendly! But one of our engineers was a bit silly one night, when paying us a visit, he left his keys in the ignition on his company car, right outside the station. He had to get a taxi home as the car was never found again, what a silly billy! I worked on many other stations on the tube network, it was always interesting to hear the stories that station managers has to tell, and it was at Highgate station, on the Northern line, the manager was telling us about the lady in a Victorian dress, who he and many others have seen walk along the platform and then just disappear through the station wall. He said when he first saw it he found it quite spooky, but then got used to it, it only seemed to happen late at night, I would have thought it would have been quite eerie. The few nights we worked there, we never caught sight of the lady! After working for about a year on the underground, all the stations that needed fire protection were finally completed.

Poem

I was sent to Baker Street situated on Marylebone Road,
The oldest of all the stations and it certainly showed.
Was now a first aider fully trained ready to go,
Treat any injuries someone might have from head to toe.
But please don't bleed near me, that's my biggest fear,
Just one drop of blood and I'm out of here.
The first casualty I attended just wanted to nut me,
That's not a very good start you'll have to agree.
One year a first aider not one person I attended,
My career as a medical man never started or ended.
The stations at last were all now complete on time,
The end of the journey, the end of the line.

The year was 1998, and I was asked by head office if I would work away in Edinburgh for a few weeks at the Scottish library. The job up there had fallen behind schedule, I willingly agreed, as I fancied a change of scenery. On the Monday I flew Easyjet from Luton; I arrived on the job at midday, and was shown around this very old and historic building. The earliest books that were printed are kept there, you could taste the history of the place, I'm going to enjoy working here I thought, as I'm into history. The only trouble was they couldn't fix me up with digs, as the Edinburgh festival was on, but I managed to charm the receptionist who fixed me up in her mother's house in the centre of town, "how lucky was that"?! One of the parts of the library we worked in was the ancient and modern bible section. This part held the rarest and most valuable collection assembled anywhere in the world, we were told, it was in safe hands, as it was Patrolled and watched over on a regular basis, not by the libraries security guards, but a monk who was in spirit form. He was often seen in his brown cassock and around his waist a knotted tassel and standard monks bald plate, we were told, a guard, new to the job, started his first night shift in the bible section, and they decided not to tell him about the regular occurrence, he was about two hours into his shift, when he burst into the head guards office, with a white face, bulging eyes, and incoherently mumbling that he had seen a ghost, dressed in a monks gown, walking up and down the aisles where the bibles were stored, and then just disappeared through the glass fronted cabinets. He threw his uniform on the floor and resigned on the spot, never to return. I would have loved to have seen this monk Patrolling the aisles, but I never caught sight of him. I feel, there is more to the afterlife, that can't be explained and I'm a firm believer of that! We used to work on Saturday's until 1pm, and the rest of the weekend, explore the lovely city of Edinburgh, from the castle to its fine buildings and I found the Scots to be very hospitable and friendly, and with there long history, a proud nation. It was on a Saturday, that we had just finished work, and I was walking towards my lodgings when a coach pulled up alongside me and the driver asked me, can you tell me where the nearest garage is? Sorry I replied I'm new to these parts, what's the problem? The heating won't switch off and my passengers are on the verge of fainting! Where are you taking your passengers to I enquired? To the military tattoo at the castle he said, but I'll have to drop them off here and try and find a garage! Have they all got tickets I asked, yes he answered glumly, I have a ticket too but by the time I find a garage and get the repair fixed, the show will have finished. As quick as a flash, I said seeing that you won't be using the ticket, can I have it? Eh, I suppose so he said, it's no good to me now, but you're have to sit with my coach load of female Chinese students! That's ok, I don't mind I said, so he handed me his ticket. These tickets were like gold dust to get hold of, what a result! I made my way up to the castle, and was directed to my seat, and sat amongst the happy and smiling students. I had always wanted to see the tattoo, but who would have thought it would have been this way. I completed the section of the job I have been sent up to do, and after a heavy drinking night with my new found friends, I returned home the next day.

Poem

Arriving at the library steeped in the pages of history,
That holy man looking after his bibles, that's some mystery.
The guard running out crying I've just seen a ghost,
Only a monk doing his duty, Patrolling by his post.
If you had the time and was prepared to wait,
You would have seen this spirit with the bald plate.
Then all of a sudden he just flew off in flight,
Just disappearing through the cabinets and then put of sight.
What a good stroke of luck with that coach overheating,
The tattoo I attended, an event that takes some beating,
Was time to leave auld Scotland birthplace of the clan,
Those past generations of brave hearts fighting for there beloved land.

Returning from the job in Scotland, I worked at the British museum which is to be found between Euston Road and Oxford circus. Millions of pounds were spent with the help of lottery money, giving this fine building a major revamp, for the 2000 millennium. A week before the grand opening, I was pressure testing the system with water in the main area. This test had to be on for four hours and if there were no leaks on the pipework, it would be passed off then signed as a successful test. This was the day that Nelson Mandela the then president of South Africa and all his entourage were viewing the new African section of the museum. As I glanced out from one of the windows, I noticed five sleek black cars parked in the back service road of the museum, with men, all dressed in black suits, white shirts, and black ties, with earpieces talking on walkie talkies. They looked and were acting like FBI agents. It all looked over the top as I Patrolled the area under test. The door suddenly burst open, and standing there were two other black suited men, who are you and what are you doing in this building? Shouted the older of the two, in what sounded like an Eton accent. Testing I replied, testing what? He demanded to know. The sprinkler system I said, just leave the testing and get out of this building now, he went on, this is a secure area, and no one is allowed in it. The younger of the two then shouted, get out now, and you won't be allowed back in for two hours, sorry I can't do that I said defiantly, they had both really got my back up, with their arrogant attitudes, the system is now on ten bars of pressure, and if I was to leave and a head broke, this place would be flooded. I noticed that the upper chest area inside there jacket pockets were both bulging, were these two idiots carrying side arms? Ok, if you say I have to leave, then I will, but if anything happens, and there's a flood, it's all down to you! They then walked to the door, and conferred between themselves, and walked back and the older one said, we are going to allow you to stay, but you can't leave the area, understood? I interjected, what happens if a pipe bursts, I'll have to leave to drain down the system. They didn't answer me, but both glared at me and walked out, ten minutes later I decided to inspect the other room that was on test, but the door was locked from the outside, I then tried the main door, and that was also locked, would you believe it them idiots, had locked me in, fortunately, there were no leaks, but if there had been, I would have been in big trouble! I watched from the window as Nelson Mandela was bundled into one of the cars and the convoy of cars sped out the museum at speed. It was only then that the door was unlocked! I later found out, that men from the special branch and MI6 were there that day, and my observations that day were if this is the calibre of the people being employed by the security services, then we are all doomed, as they were cocky, pompous, big headed and full of their own importance.

Poem

It was to the British museum I was sent to work,
Being amongst the worlds treasures is that not a perk?
But who were these toffee nosed gits wearing black ties,
Scanning every face in sight with their ever shifting eyes.
They were there to protect this great man Nelson Mandela,
A true hero of his people such a splendid fellow.
Was still testing the system while he was on his tour,
They then decided I wouldn't get out by locking the door.
But what do you expect these idiots had attended public school,
And I must say there's no fool like a posh fool.

Warburgs – Moorgate

The year was now 1999, and I was 60 years old. I was transferred to Warburgs in Moorgate. It is one of the capitals largest stocks and shares, buying and selling financial houses. It was having a major refurbishment, so a complete floor was closed, and then refurbished, and then the floor above it would be closed while they occupied the newly refurbished floor. This method carried on all the way up the building, to the tenth floor. The last floor to be completed was the ground floor, as they couldn't close this off, it was decided half the floor would be closed off and done on days, and I was informed that I was the person that will be working nights to complete a small section at a time so that the public and staff could go about their business in the day! Each of the floors above took about six weeks to complete, and the ground floor was expected to take about the same time, things went well for the first month with the day shift men marking up the drop pipes in red paint that were under water pressure and all the pipes with no water in them were marked with green paint. Both the red painted pipes and the green ones had plugs inserted in them so my job on night shift was to take the plugs out of the green painted pipes with no water in them and install the pipework with a false ceiling sprinkler head. It was on the Thursday night shift of the fourth night that all went pear shaped, the firm deemed I was quite capable of working on my own on nights, as they thought only one man was needed but of course it was to save money, never a good policy to work single-handed when working with water. That's good I thought only four heads to do tonight, I'll be able to get away early, as I slowly unscrewed the plug on the first green painted pipe, I noticed more water than usual was dribbling out and it seemed to have a bit of pressure behind it, surely they couldn't have painted the wrong colour on the pipe, and I am now taking out the plug on a live pipe, but I should not give away to such thoughts and carried on unscrewing the plug, I had about two more turns to go, before the plug was fully removed when all of a sudden water jets were shooting out from all sides of the plug, oh no, them idiots on days have painted the live pipe green, but no worries, I'll screw the plug back up, but my worst nightmare was about to happen, the pressure was so great, it blew the plug right off, and the force of the water, knocked me off my steps, I was like a drowned rat, as I laid on the floor, I thought this is my worst nightmare, this cannot be happening, I'll wake up in a minute, but this was no dream, and within seconds, the water level was up to the first rung of my steps, the moment came when I just wanted to die when I looked over to where the lifts were situated and looked up in horror as the water started to pour down the lift shaft surely things can't get any worse than this? Oh yes they can Johnny boy, because once the lift shaft was full of water then it started to enter the ground floor offices. Now the fire bell was ringing, the builders face was white, what the hell happened John he asked, I think he was in a state of shock like I was, he quickly organised his labourers to manoeuvre huge rubbish skips under the pipe which was in full flow now, the security people were quickly on the scene but they couldn't find the key to the valve set so I couldn't drain it down as now the electric pump had now cut in. A large skip was filled with water within one minute, but what a star Steve the builder was, as each skip became full it was replaced by an empty one and the full one was wheeled out onto the road and emptied, Steve's prompt action saved the day, the key was found and I rushed round to the valve set, shut down the main stop valve and drained down, but once all the water was completely drained, I returned back to the affected area and Steve the builder had set up a pump, and it was pumping out water from the lift shaft, he also had a team of men sucking up the water with a Hoover type machine from the carpets, and had in place drying machines once the carpets were nearly dry. I found my steps which have floated to the other side of the reception desk, and went back to the pipe that caused all the trouble, I wanted to know why this painted green pipe was on the live system, as I climbed the steps and examined the pipe to my horror I saw that the pipe was painted red, not green, and this cock up was completely down to me. Once my boss had been informed of this episode I had visions of me that being hung drawn and quartered or nailed to a cross and crucified! Six in the morning was the finishing time for the nightshift and by four that morning Steve and his men had dried out all the lobby area and the office carpets in spite of all the water, the lifts were still in working order and nobody would have known that major flood taken place! When I thanked Steve for all that he had done and said his actions probably saved my job he said, John, we're all a team here and it would be a poor show if we couldn't help out each other, what a very nice and wise and generous man. As my boss started work at the office at nine in the morning I had three hours before I had to inform him of the night's fiasco, I drove home, which normally took 90 minutes, and waited till nine and phoned the boss! The boss was a right miserable git, and had a serious attitude problem, and the dialogue between us when something like this, with tongue in cheek.

Me: good morning Les, John here.

Les: good morning John here

Me: thinking to myself, that is not even remotely funny you overweight and overpaid idiot

Les: what can I do for you?

Me: well Les, last night I had a small leak at work

Les: I don't wish to know your toilet habits thank you very much

Me: no, no, not that kind of leak, this was a pipe related leak

Les: so why are you phoning to tell me about small leak?

Me: to be honest with you, it was a bit more than a small leak

Les: then how big was the small leak?

Me: I have to admit, it was more like a flood.

Les: a flood, what do you mean a flood, he shouted?

Me: well, I unscrewed the plug on the drop line, and the force of the water knocked me off my steps

Les: how could there be water in a drained down system you stupid idiot?

Me: unfortunately, it wasn't the drained system the plug came out of, but the live one

Les: you're supposed to be one of our top engineers, what's the matter with you have you lost it?

Me: it was a genuine mistake on my part I have to say

Les: you took the plug out of a live system; I can't believe it, the next thing you're telling me, is the main pump activated.

Me: Um, yes it did actually, and it was like watching the outlet pipe of the Hoover Dam discharging its water but there's one good thing at least we know the pump works.

Les: who now sounded a bit hysterical; just tell me what damage you have caused.

Me: well firstly, within minutes the lift shaft was filled the water, and once that was full, the water rushed into the offices and soaked all the carpets, but it's not all doom and gloom, the builders were outstanding and saved the day, so the only bill your be receiving is one from him, for all his men's time and effort spent mopping up.

Les: tell me now why I shouldn't dismiss you here and now?

Me: well for a start we all make mistakes and the other thing, I should have had someone else working with me, you broke all the health and safety rules making me work on my own.

Les: after a long pause I think you have a valid point there John, I'll phone the builder, and see if we can come up with a story that will exonerate you of all blame, and sweep this episode under the carpet so to speak, and forget that hasty mark I made about you being dismissed.

Thankfully I never heard another word about the episode!

Poem

You did not have much say where you were sent,
It was to Warburgs at Moorgate was where I went.
Not a good idea to be working on your own,
Against health and safety rules if only I had known.
Then taking out the wrong plug, not a very good move,
Like something from a disaster movie so it was to prove.
The water under pressure sent me crashing to the ground,
It was now a waist high deep with chaos all around.
And because of my silly blunder, the area was nearly destroyed,
With quick reactions from the builder, meant I was still employed.

One of the back entrances of Warburgs was only used in the daytime for goods coming in and out, at night it was permanently locked, it was double doors and set back into the building, this gave Dave the old vagrant plenty of room for his sleeping bag and his worldly possessions, the building security people turned a blind eye to him sleeping there, and the unwritten rule was he could come at night and be gone with all his gear by 7 am, it must of been like a hotel room because on the wall it had an extract fan that blew warm air out in the winter! It turned out that Dave had been sleeping there the past six years! Every morning an armoured security truck would pull up outside Dave's door and throw sealed bags in the doorway, these bags contained receipts and documents to be signed and other unimportant material which is of no value or use to anyone except Warburgs, but it was on a Monday morning that once again the truck pulled up and threw the bags in the usual doorway and then drove off but on this visit they threw the bag that had been collected from a high Street bank, and it contained thousands of pounds in used banknotes from all denominations. At the end of their shift they realised they were missing their money and came back and drove back to Dave's doorway hoping to retrieve the lost bag, pulling up outside the door, they must have been very relieved to see the bags were still there, but searching through the bags, there was no sign of the bag containing the cash it was missing and so was Dave, his sleeping bag and worldly goods were still there, and lucky Dave was never seen again, a story that lifts the heart, because some people in life really deserve a stroke of good fortune!

Poem

He slept that night in a doorway that became his home,

With hardly any possessions not even a toothbrush or comb.

He had reached rock bottom and was called a vagrant,

With no fixed abode and not smelling sweet or fragrant.

Some people would look at Dave and call him a tramp,

But just imagine walking the Streets in winter so cold and damp.

This will never happen to me but don't be so sure,

Dave never thought he would be sleeping in an office door.

Probably reckoned his lifestyle would lead to an early grave,

But life is full of surprises and one happened to Dave.

Now no longer and nowhere man, and having a great life,

More likely has a large mansion with a lovely looking wife.

Skin Cancer

With many jobs completed in around the London area the year had now moved on to 2001, as I always had worked in false ceilings, and confined spaces, I often bumped my head, and I always ended up with a sore head and the more often than not I tended to hit the same part my head which started off as a cut and then became a scab and as my daughter Judy, used to trim my hair, what I still had left, she noticed a scab I had, the last time she cut my hair had now turned into a mole type raised spot. Go and see a doctor about that she ordered, but being a man I took no notice, so the next time Judy cut my hair she remarked how this spot had changed its colour and shape and should be looked at quickly as that spots that change colour are sometimes not good news, I took her advice, and took myself down to the doctors, and on examining the raised spot he said, oh dear, that looks nasty I don't like the look at that, I will refer you to a skin specialist (not very encouraging words doctors, you could have been a bit more diplomatic and considerate in your choice of words, why didn't you just inform me, I was doomed, and about to die?) I duly reported to the skin specialist who was examining the raised spot and said that in his opinion it looks like sun damage, and looks like melanoma, and he would now give me a local anaesthetic? And cut it out to do a biopsy to see if it's malignant or non malignant! On hearing these words from him I suddenly had the urge to visit the little boy's bathroom! As he poked and prodded at my head it felt like he had removed most of the contents inside it! That's it he finally said, all done, your get the result of the biopsy in about three weeks, I understand your going on a cruise, just enjoy yourself and don't worry, you must be joking by the time the results arrive I could be brown bread and be 6 feet under!

Pat and I got away on our western Mediterranean cruise, and like all cruises, a good time was had by all, but although I'm quite a positive kind of bloke, at the back of my mind while on the cruise, my thoughts sometimes drifted on the melanoma that had been diagnosed and wondered what the outcome might be? But three days into the cruise, I thought worrying about it was silly, and decided not to give away to such reports! We returned from the cruise and the next day I made my way to see the surgeon who had the results of the biopsy. I was ushered into his office by the nurse, sit down Mr Banfield, he said in a sympathetic manner, oh dear I thought he's feeling sorry for me and is he about to deliver me some bad news? Without looking up from his notes he started turning the pages over and then back again, then followed a deadly silence about two minutes (not a good time to be using the word deadly), at last he spoke, you had a biopsy done on your sun damage melanoma, three weeks ago and I'm just going over your notes, then another long pause, I'm thinking to myself come on man am I about to die or not? He then looked up from his notes and said Mr Banfield you'll be pleased to hear that the findings of the biopsy on your melanoma was that it was non-malignant, so that's put your mind at rest no doubt, and you may be surprised to learn the test showed that this melanoma first started off when you worked in Africa all those years ago. I left his office feeling really good about things and made a promise to myself from this day on, I would never even think about things in a negative light, and I've kept to my promise.

Poem

A mole like you have can prove dangerous so Judy said,
So say those magazines and medical books that she had read.
It must be attended to very quickly and without delay,
Sit back and do nothing and you will surely pay.
I think it's more of a mole than a scab,
Will soon when the results return,
The test came back negative I will now be surviving,
To live life to the full I will now be striving.
Gloom and doom kind of thoughts I shall have none,
Now every day on this earth will be a positive one.

Cruise to Norway

The year had now moved on to 2002, and I had reached 63 years old, and I said to Pat, we have sailed to the Western and Eastern Mediterranean a few times now let's try somewhere different next year, so with a little persuading, I convinced Pat that sailing up the Fjords would be the ideal holiday cruise. She was a bit reluctant as she thought it would be cold even in July, I was able to put her mind at rest and we duly boarded the cruise, not only did we want to savour the breathtaking scenery of the Fjords, I wanted to visit the home and resting place of my favourite Norwegian composer Edward Grieg. The ship sailed from Newcastle and it was called the Black Prince, as we took our first steps on to the gangplank I noticed that people in front of me appeared to be quite elderly, as a least four of them were being supported by carers, and the people in front of them were being pushed up the gangplank in wheelchairs and what was more worrying these people were the crew! Have we boarded the wrong ship surely this is a saga geriatric cruise? We made our way to our cabins and freshened up and changed, then made our way to the top deck where we had been told drinks and snacks would be served, so everyone could mingle and get to know one another and at 6 p.m. the ship was due to set sail, the entertainments manager said he had a special treat for everyone because on the quayside there was assembled a band that would be playing all the old favourite tunes that most of you should know. As he finished his little speech the band started to play and they were playing the latest hits, but these latest hits were not from the year 2002, a century earlier in the year 1902 and what was really astonishing most of the old passengers assembled on deck knew all the words to these tunes being played. I realised this cruise is for the very elderly when a lovely old lady hobbled up to me supported by her walking sticks and said excuse me son can you direct me to the nearest bar? Here I was 63 years old being called son, how old was she? On board the Black Prince I was not surprised to learn was a doctor, and two nurses and a very good carpenter who was probably a dab hand at making pine boxes for obvious reasons. Was it a coincidence that it appeared that the lifeboats on board had the look and shape of coffins.

As we sailed up the fjords, the weather was brilliant with clear blue skies and endless sunshine; Pat's worries about the weather were unfounded. Meeting some of these fellow passengers was a joy to behold with their stories about life before the Second World War and even their wartime stories. I used to chat with Ben, who was aged 90, who needed the help of a walking frame to get about, but was a very positive and resilient man, with a very good sense of humour. As Pat wasn't interested in seeing Edward Grieg's house and his resting place I took the trip myself, as a house came into sight I could see that it was perched on top of a hill this should be a pleasant climb I thought to myself, on reaching the top I could see a group of people huddled around a man laying on the ground, as I got closer, I recognized that man on the ground was Ben, How the hell did he manage to get up here because I couldn't see his walking frame just two walking sticks. On one of my earlier chats to Ben he told me he had suffered three previous heart attacks and also had high blood pressure, and had managed to walk up the steep hill, what a trooper! Some people were bending down tending to Ben and were talking to him in Norwegian, no wonder he looked a bit confused, he is a passenger from the Black Prince cruise liner I told them and I think an ambulance should be called as he has had heart trouble in the past, poor Ben looked so pale and was not able to move or talk, an ambulance quickly arrived and I told the paramedics about Ben's heart problems and that he was a passenger on the Black Prince. We never heard what happened to Ben after that! It was a wonderful experience looking around Edward Grieg's house and seeing his small summerhouse in his garden where he composed most of his classical masterpieces and then walking to a large lake in the grounds, and looking up to rock face overlooking the lake, seeing where the great man is entombed just looking at the outstanding scenery around there must have gave him so much inspiration for his composing. The cruise was coming to an end and every day brought a fine sunny day, Pat had to admit it was one of the best cruises she had ever been on, our fellow passengers were an inspiration to us all, the very elderly people had helped to put the Great into Britain, and with most of them having health issues, not once did I hear a moan or groan from them they just wanted to have a good time and enjoy themselves. You will not see scenery or outstanding landscape sailing up the fjords anywhere on this planet.

Poem

The Black Prince berthed securely at the quayside and moored,
Both walked up the gangplank ready to step on board.
Most of the passengers were elderly, thats what we found,
Some of the world's oldest people seem to be around.
And with them old-fashioned manners and their bygone ways,
With such dignity and fortitude seeing out their last days.

Recalling forgotten stories and tales in their once useful for years,
Remembering such lovely distant memories trying to hold back tears.
Soon we'll be reminiscing with my stories retirement is nearing,
What will I do without work, that's what I'm fearing.
Just look at that magnificent scenery it changes at every bend,
We'll be sorry when this cruise finally comes to an end.
Wished it could last forever but that's always the way,
Hoping I will be returning to these fjords one day.

The year had reached 2003 and its only one year off my retirement, in one way I was looking forward to it, but also feeling a bit apprehensive knowing it be such a big change in my lifestyle, for the past year I've been working in McLaren Mercedes new state-of-the-art building where there new SLR sports car was due to be made this is what made my job so interesting, such a different variety of locations and workplaces we got to work at, sometimes you could be working on a new build office block, and then find yourself working in an occupied factory.

The job at McLarens was coming to an end so I got transferred to what would be my last job working for AMEC, it was near Heathrow airport, and it was the immigration and Asylum holding building, people from all parts of the world were detained there, but in most cases the asylum requests had been turned down and they were waiting to be deported. I thought it was quite ironic that I started with my firm at Heathrow airport in 1967 now 37 years later and my last job with them ended up back at Heathrow, I have completed the full circle so to speak! Working in the immigration building carried some risk to all us contractors, because we had to pass through the occupied parts of the building to get to the extended new build. These rejected asylum seekers were due to be returned to their country of origin at any day so they really had nothing to lose by starting trouble, on every occasion before we entered the occupied section 2 security guards had to accompany us, and on this day there was only one female officer present I can't let you enter she said, there has to be two security officers for safety reasons, she phoned for back up and after a wait of five minutes, we could see in the distance, a slightly built young lady. As she approached us we could plainly see that this protector of men was pint sized, even I towered above her, and I'm on the short side. There were about 20 builders along with my crew waiting to go in and most of them were big, hairy and mean and here was a slip of a girl sent to protect us! You can imagine the builder's reaction on seeing her, they all fell about in fits of laughter, a 10-year-old schoolgirl would tower over her. While we were working we got chatting to the mini size guard and she proudly told me, she had been through the selection course of the Met police and had been accepted to join the training. We found out from other guards she was bonkers and a complete nutcase, but somehow managed to get into the Met, that tells you all you need to know about the Metropolitan police force, God help the people of London! The last few weeks before I retired went flying by, and before I knew it them weeks now became my very last day, going to work that day it seemed so surreal and I felt a bit excited, but also a bit sad knowing that I wouldn't be working in the trade any more, as I passed a room in the building I heard two men talking to each other, they were talking about the new job that was starting up shortly at terminal five at Heathrow and my heart sank, as I thought I won't be part of that, I'll be gone, and that really saddened me. I had worked in the pipefitting trade 37 years, and loved every minute of it, millions of people go to work every day and it's just a job to them is just an end to means. The site engineer had told me I was allowed to pack up work at dinner time so in a building where I was working all the trades gathered around me to watch me make my last pipe, as I took the stilsons off the pipe they all gave me a round of applause and I had to admit I had to hold back the tears as it was really now all coming to an end, and I thought to myself I'm just not ready to retire! I was then handed an envelope by the lads who had been very generous in the amount they collected for me, as a going away gift. As I shook each man's hand I managed to keep the tears at bay, but it was hard, because I had known some of these men over 20 years. After many jobs working together they had become more like brothers than workmates! As I walked to my car I was in a trance like state and thinking surely it cannot be 50 years ago that I set off on my first day at work. I sat in my car in the tears just streaming down my cheeks, it was like the times when I had to leave some of the many children's homes that I grew up in and then had to leave with the staff and children waving me goodbye. I knew I should be rejoicing at this time, a lifetime of working had come to an end, I drove home with a heavy heart, and now my whole life would now change forever! Over the years in your working life many people you know retire but you can never visualise yourself retiring, that always happens to somebody else, but then you become that somebody else!

Poem

My work all started at Heathrow in the far distant past,
And that's where it all ended time whizzed by so fast.
I never thought it possible I had reached my 65th year,
And it was my last day at work, retirement begins here.

A different outlook on life I will now have to face,
Maybe I'll find a new challenge I can grasp and embrace.
With hair so white I'm now officially an old grey,
What's great about it, I can either work, rest or play.
I will now climb that mountain and ford that stream,
And nothing has to be such an impossible dream.

The Parrot

I had now been retired six months and remembered Pat telling me that when she was much younger she used to have a cockatoo bird, so I decided I was going to surprise her and buy a parrot. We had never kept a pet, and I thought this would keep her company. I phoned a man who sold parrots and arranged to meet him, so he could show me what he had in stock, he showed me a three-month-old parrot and told me this bird would be the ideal present for your wife, as its young, so she can teach it to talk and also because it's a male parrot they tend to like female owners as they can sometimes be aggressive towards male owners. It's an African Grey he said proudly and because I like you and you seem interested in buying it I can let you have it at a special price (this man sounds like a Jewish parrot breeder me), how much is it then I asked? £550 a parrot, and £250 for the extra large deluxe cage, (surely he must be talking in Israeli shekels and not in pound notes), 500 quid for a non-talking baby parrot, I protested, your having a laugh. No, no, sir at that price it's a steal. I sold his brother last week £600. I bet this bloke used to be an East End barrow boy, and could sell snow to Eskimos. After about half an hour of bartering he wouldn't go lower than £500 for the bird and for the £200 cage, I had previously made enquiries into the price of a parrot and I knew they were expensive, okay I said, £700 for the parrot and the cage, and shock his hand, the deal was done, it grieves me somewhat to be parting with £700 and to use that old saying, I felt sick as a parrot! Sorry about that! As I drove away from his house with the parrot squawking its head off in its supersize cage, I couldn't help but think it would have been cheaper for me to fly to South America, climb a tree and just grab a parrot off a branch, and cut out the middle man. I knew Pat would still be out shopping as a pulled up outside the house, so I quickly brought the still squawking bird indoors, placed it on the dining room table and covered the cage with a large sheet, the parrot stopped squawking immediately, peace at last! It wasn't very long before the front door opened and Pat then walked into the front room, close your eyes I said, I have a surprise for you, Pat stood there with her eyes closed, as I whipped the sheet off the cage, right you can open your eyes now I proudly shouted, Pat opened her eyes and screeched what's that? It's a surprise present for you I proudly remarked, it's a parrot she said, I hate parrots, their messy and can be very aggressive and they take a lot of looking after and she went, not only that, they sharpen their beaks by pulling out chunks of the furniture, if you had brought me a cockatoo I would have been happy, but I'm not happy with that thing! It's not what I want, you can take it back. But apart from all that you like it I said with a grin, let's compromise I retorted, if after three months you and the parrot don't get on I will sell him. Okay Pat replied, that's a deal. That's excellent news I thought to myself, in three months, I have it swearing like a trooper! The parrot had now been in the house for about three hours, and observing him from my chair, I noticed that he hadn't moved from its perch, and his eyes were firmly fixed on Pat, that's good I thought, he's even bonding with Pat from his cage, I recalled the breeder had said that male parrots prefer women than men. As the evening drew in, I said that, I'll open the cage so that the parrot can fly out, and get to know us. Before I open the cage I said, seeing that it is now your parrot I'll leave it up to you to give him a name, I've been thinking about name for it Pay said, and Bart sounds a good name for him, so that's what we're call him, that's good I thought, Pat is taking an interest in the parrot. As I opened the cage door, Bart shot out his cage and letting out a loud squawk, proceeded to fly round the front room at great speed, as he got near to Pat, he dive bombed at her and pulled out of his dive just before he reached her head. What's it doing she yelled, he is using my head as target practice, no, no, I said that his way of bonding with you! But he soon got fed up with circumnavigating the front room, and promptly landed on my shoulder, he then lightly pecked at my ear, he then hopped on my other shoulder and did the same on my other ear, Pat then made the comment that male parrots are not supposed to like blokes, but he seems to have taken to you! This is not going to plan me thinks, so I put my finger near Bart's feet and he hopped onto it, I then walked over to where Pat was sitting, and placed Bart on Pat shoulder, but Bart just stood there staring at Pat's face, totally transfixed, after about 10 minutes Pat spoke, and said hello Bart, you deciding if you want to be my friend? But he then sidestepped up Pat's shoulder until he had reached her ear and with his mouth wide open, lunged at her ear, and gave her a nasty bite, Pat gave out an almighty scream, and probably could be heard half a mile away, what did he do that for she demanded to know? I don't know, I answered; he's properly only playing with you! Playing with me? If he does anything like that again, he's going Pat shouted. Bart had a mischievous streak, and would refuse to get back in his cage, if he saw I was about to grab him he would fly away, in the end I had to resort to get a large bath towel and throw it over him and then bundling him into his cage. He would then make ear shattering squawks until I covered him up!

For the next month or so, things were looking up, Bart would sometimes stay on Pat shoulder but mainly it was mine, it was a Sunday evening, Bart sitting on my shoulder as usual, he then lifted off, and flew round the room a few times and then landed on Pat's shoulder, have you come to say hello to me, Pat asked Bart? But within seconds, Bart had firmly clamped on the same ear as in his last attack on Pat. She cried out in pain, and shouted that's it parrot, your days are numbered around here, he had made Pat's ear bleed, I realised Bart had to go, but I thought you're a male parrot and you're supposed to like women, but you seem to prefer my company, why? And then it dawned on me, Bart must be a homosexual parrot, that's why it prefers my company; I've paid £500 for a woman hating poof parrot. I put an advert in a local pet shop stating I had a friendly young African grey parrot the sale, for the bargain price of £500 including the big deluxe cage and to my surprise the next day I received a phone call a man, who was interested in buying the parrot and cage. I arranged for him to view the parrot and cage the same day. A car drew up outside my house, and out stepped two very smart men in there early twenties. My names Simon and I've come to look at your parrot your selling, this is my partner Adam. He seemed to know a lot about parrots, and said, your parrot is in good condition, but I can only give you £450 for the parrot and cage, I didn't want to muck around bartering, so I agreed on that sum, and he duly handed over the money. Before he left, he asked why are you selling your parrot? Oh I said, my wife seems to be allergic to it for some reason, (how could I tell him that Bart enjoyed taking lumps out of Pat's ears and that they both had this mutual hate for each other). But on the other hand, I probably could have told him how Bart liked men rather than women, as these two obviously preferred men rather than women!

Poem

Hope this will please Pat, an African grey parrot and a cage,
Cost me a fortune for a bird just twelve weeks of age.
Pulling away the sheet, told Pat to open her eyes,
Seeing a parrot sitting there gave her such a surprise.
Surely you could have brought me a much smaller bird,
Something like a cockatoo that's what I would of preferred.
Because for the last half hour all its done is squawk,
It's cost an arm and a leg and it doesn't even talk.
You can get rid of it if we do not gel,
At a car boot market or a bring and buy sell.
Bart finally plucked up some courage and perched on Pat,
Just planning his next move, just staring as he sat.
The next thing that happened it then opened his menacing beak,

And as quick as lightning firmly bit into Pat's right cheek.
His peck caused blood to flow, it happened at speed,
Maybe it thought some fresh blood would supplement his feed.
It's between me or him leaving she shouted out in pain,
That stupid parrot is not only demented, I'm sure he's insane.
It must have major gender issues; I guessed it was gay,
This crazy mixed up lady hater, known as an African grey.
Should have got my money back under the trade descriptions act,
Was sold the worlds first gay parrot, and that's a fact.

My Metal Detector

I knew I had to get myself a hobby, so with the money gift the men at work collected for me, I brought myself a metal detector. On a Sunday I tried it out at the nearby playing fields, I thought I would try using it on a bank next to a river, so switching it on, I made sweeping movements, and within five minutes, got a very loud signal through my earphones, what could it be? Bending down to see if there was anything on the spot where the signal came from, I picked a damp moth eaten wallet and opened it up, and low and behold, inside one of the compartments was a very damp £10 note, and also a £5 note, the signal came from three 20p coins tucked away in a zipped compartment of the wallet, eureka, I have only being detecting for 5 minutes, and already have found £15.60, this could be the start of something big? I carried on sweeping along the bank, and once again got a loud signal so started digging away, when out from nowhere a man appeared and asked me in a hostile tone, what do you think your doing? Digging I replied, what does it look like I'm doing? Well you shouldn't be digging here, this is council property and I'm a councillor, you people think you have the right to dig anywhere you please! Me thinks I had better come up with a good answer quickly, so I thought of that army saying "the best form of defence is attack", you idiot I said, the council have built thousands of houses and factories on green fields, and the place is covered in concrete, and every things buried there is now lost forever, and you're your worried about a small hole I'm digging here! My aggressive attitude seemed to have paid off, because he meekly said, yes I suppose you're right, you have a point there, and just walked away, not saying another word. Phew, I thought, he could have reported me and I could have been in trouble, so I'll have to be careful where I go detecting from now on.

After contacting a few farmers I managed to persuade one of them, that it was possible there could be buried treasure on his land, I then signed an agreement with him to split half of anything that might be found! The farmer had many acres of land, so was this the place I was going to find a pot of gold? I think I'll start detecting around the farm buildings and work away from them. One hour had passed and as yet, no signal bleeps were heard, but moving the detector near a dip in the field, a strong signal came up, this is it, I though, I'm in the middle of a field, that's never had buildings on it, and virgin land, I've hit the jackpot, so digging frantically, I was soon down to an arms length and was still getting a signal, could this be a treasure trove? So digging even further down, I finally found the source of the bleeping, pulling a lump of clay apart, I was astonished to find in front of me, the unbelievable sight of a ring pull. How in heavens name did a ring pull get to be buried in about a metre of earth in the middle of nowhere? For the next few weeks, I walked many a mile, in all the farmers different fields, searching for that hidden treasure, and what was my reward for all this searching in all weathers? Five old horse shoes, a rusted gate, and five more ring pulls. I decided to give metal detecting a rest for a while, and locked the machine in the shed!

Poem

Brought the latest metal detector now lets find some treasure,
Searching for that pot of gold should give me pleasure.
Having this agreement with the farmer anything I might find,
Would be divided equally between us a contract we signed.
A metal object was detected quickly dug up the ground,
Just bits of old tat, is all that I found.
I was hoping to find some Viking treasure or maybe Roman,
But digging up them dreaded ring pulls was this an omen?
I've been searching for weeks just finding bits of old junk,
Rusted metal that over the years, into the ground had sunk.
Back to the shed, the detector went under lock and key,
A complete waste of my time, I think you'll all agree.

Table Tennis

When Stuart was fourteen he joined a table tennis club and became a very good player, he came home after one session and asked me why you don't join the club. I'm too old for that I told him, no your not he said, there's blokes much older than you playing there, so at the age of 53 years I also joined this table tennis club. After a couple of months, we decided to form a team, with Stuart, myself, Alf who was even older than me at sixty, and making up the fourth member was a younger friend of mine named Dave who was forty years old. I thought the Wombats would be a good name for the team, and it was agreed that's what the team name would be. There were seven divisions in the league, and we were placed in division 4, we became quite a good team, and soon made our way up the division, because we all had completely different styles, other teams found us hard to beat. There were about a hundred teams in the league, and the first ten of them teams were in the premier league. We entered the cup competition and with skilful play and lots of luck, we found ourselves in the final, and our opponents happened to be one of the top teams in the premier league, these guys were not far short of being professionals, they could probably play with one hand tied behind there backs and blindfolded one eye and still would have gave us a good thrashing, but seeing they could have eaten is for breakfast, they were severely handicapped, so we only had to get 5 points, in a 21 point game, and if everyone of our team got the five points or more in there games, the cup was ours. It wasn't going to be easy to get even one point off these players. We sent Stuart on first as he was our best player, he was up against a player I had watched in training, he was so good, he could serve a ball to his opponent, the spin his body around in a full circle and return back his opponents ball, he was built like a tank, and his name was Igor, he was Russian, and looked like a mafia hit man. Before the game started I said to Stuart, if you manage to get five points or more off him, and win the match, don't dare shake his hand, just run for your life! Stuart was narrowly defeated by Igor, but thanks to the handicap system, has gained vital extra points for our team, Igor was very generous in his praise for Stuart's performance and greeted him at the end of the game with a bear hug. I should have known you can't tell a book by its cover, Igor was a gentleman! Myself and the rest of the team managed to get over the five points needed per game, and halfway into the match, we had built up so many points, we couldn't be beaten, so the premier league team conceded defeat, and we were duly crowned challenge cup champions, not bad for a newly formed team. Instead of a poem at the end of this tale, I decided an anecdote would be appropriate.

Pat and myself were going through a bit of a sticky Patch in our marriage as most couples do occasionally. So we both decided to go to a marriage counsellor. He sat us both down, and asked us what the problem was, Pat then went into a tirade telling him every issue we have had since we've been married, she went on for so long, the counsellor got up, went over to Pat, embraced and kissed her passionately, he then rips off her clothes, and makes passionate love to her. Afterwards, Pat sits down in a satisfied daze. The counsellor then turned to me and said John, that's what Pat needs three times a week, can you do that? I thought for a while and said, well, I can get her here on a Monday and Wednesday, but not Friday's as I play table tennis that day.

The Asda interview

The year had moved on to 2005, and now aged 66, I had been retired for a year. I was quite happily working on the inside and outside of Stuart's home, when my eye caught an advert in the local paper for staff wanted for a new local Asda store that was opening shortly. I phoned the number given, and asked if they were taking old greys? Old greys the young lady said, what is an old grey? Your speaking to one I replied, I don't understand what you're talking about, please explain. I use that term I said, because I'm 66 years old and I have retired, oh I see she said with a giggle, of course we do, as long as you are fit and healthy, we employ the older person, full or part time. Would you like an appointment to be interviewed by one of our managers this coming week? she asked. So an interview was arranged on the Thursday at 2pm, and I dressed for the interview in what is called smart casual. The manager conducting the interview was called Mr. Cole, and after being introduced to him, I sat in his office, and the interview went something like this:

Mr Cole: Here at Asda's John we like to be informal, so even though I'm a senior manager, you can call me Terry.

Me: Hey Tel, that sounds good to me.

Terry: I see that your 66 years of age John, why do you want to work for Asda's?

Me: Well Tel, I've still got a few years left in me and as Asda's are the new kid on the block, as far as supermarkets are concerned in this country, and have a very good reputation with the public, I would like to be part of it. I didn't want to go too overboard with the bullshit!

Terry: Good answers John, now don't be put off by me ticking boxes with my pen, because every question I ask you, I put a tick in one of the boxes depending on the reply I get from you.

Me: That's cool by me Tel

Terry: After asking me many more questions, he said if we offered you a position, what sort of job would you like in the new store?

Me: Well Tel, I like mixing and working with people, so anything that lets me do that.

Terry: Yes, I think that you're probably a people person!

Me: Tell me Tel, how long have you worked for Asda's?

Terry: Oh, getting on for twenty years now John

Me: You're a senior manager now, are you hoping to go higher in the company

Terry: For the next five minutes, he went on to tell me about his hopes and dreams within the company

Me: Are you married Tel?

Terry: Yes John, and I have two lovely children, and then went on to explain how old they were and all about them.

Me: That's good Tel, a happy family man, and because of that, I hope you belong to Asda's pension scheme?

Terry: I would be a fool not to belong to it, as is a very good one.

Me: That's good Tel, are you...

Terry: John sorry, can I stop you there, there's something not quite right with this interview.

Me: what's that then Tel?

Terry: I don't know how it happened but you are interviewing me! You are asking the questions, and I am giving you the answers, and it should be the other way around!

Me: I'm sorry about that Tel, but I'm interested in other people and their lives.

Terry: No need to apologise John, I've enjoyed our one-way chat (he said with a grin).

Me: Have I got the job then Tel?

Terry: Just a few more questions to ask you, and then we are done, but please let me ask questions.

Me: Ok.

Terry: After a few more questions he said, that it, all done this interview is finished.

Me: What happens now? Am I going to be taken on?

Terry: I'm not allowed to tell you right now, but you have ticks in all right boxes, so I don't think you have anything to worry about.

Me: I've enjoyed our interview.

Terry: Shaking my hand, yes so have I John, I have never had an interview like that, and I probably never will again.

Me: what did he mean, is he being kind or flippant?

I was phoned up by Terry a couple of weeks later, and offered a job as a meeter and greeter, this is someone who stands in front of the entrance of the store, and welcomes customers with a welcoming smile and greeting. I thought about it, but I turned it down as I didn't want to be tied down in a permanent job I only wanted to work when I wanted to!

Poem

That sounds like this may suit me, working for Asda,

Has a good reputation like the ride in a Mazda.

It would really be completely different working in a large store,

I'll probably regret it if I don't apply that's for sure.

With an outstretched hand, Terry the manager beckoned, do sit down please,

Just relax and make yourself comfortable and feel completely at ease.

Please stop there John you seem to be interviewing me,

That's not how it is done as I'm sure you'll agree,

I ask the questions, the answers should come from you,

But the opposite happened, but how I haven't a clue.

That's the first time I've been interviewed by somebody seeking work,

But I just knew you processed this unusual funny quirk.

Ben Nevis

It was now 2006, I was now aged 67 years and since retiring I had been working on Stuart's house, but when I wasn't working around there, I would work for a neighbour and friend called Don, who was a master builder, and a mere slip of a lad at the grand old age of 75. Seeing that our combined age was 144 years, I told Don it would be prudent to have written in there building contracts that while we were doing work for them, that a special hotline number to the accident and emergency response team at the local hospital, in the case of us having heart attacks, a stroke, or fainting, due to overwork or falling unconscious! It was now September, and Pat and I decided, a holiday would be nice, so we booked a coach holiday to Fort William in Scotland for six days, staying in a nice hotel overlooking a Loch for three of the days. There were organised coach trips to places of interest, it was on one of these three days and I said to Pat "I think I will walk to Ben Nevis and back today it, should be a nice walk". So after breakfast I set off for the walk, as it was such a warm day, I thought better that I travel light, so I had on a light pair of trousers, a T-shirt and trainers, and a baseball cap. It took about two hours to walk 5 miles to Ben Nevis, I stopped off at a newsagent on the way and brought two Mars bars and two cold drinks, my thinking was that I would keep a cold drink and a Mars bar for the return journey back to the hotel. I quickly tucked into the Mars bar and drank the cold drink, I then put the other drink and Mars bar into a holdall I was carrying, and walked to the base of the mountain. I looked up to see this wonder of nature towering majestically into the clear blue sky; it was standing there proudly like a medieval cathedral in all its glory. I approached the main Path that snaked its way up the mountain, and noticed a large display board detailing all the do's and don'ts about climbing, some of the do's were to wear appropriate clothing for the climb, sturdy footwear, and a rucksack with enough food and drink for the climb. The notice stated that these items were essential, as the weather can change very quickly throughout the year; well I thought none of this concerns me; as I'm only going to climb for about 10 minutes or so, and then make my way down. As I started to climb the well worn Path that countless multitudes had trodden before me, I thought to myself this is child's play, with a slight breeze and a warm September sun beating down the 10 minutes climbing I was planning to undertake had now stretched to an hour and I was making steady progress, looking at my watch, it showed 1:30 p.m., and by talking to a descending climber, I was told I was about a quarter of the way up, with that in mind I figured that by 2:30 p.m. I should be halfway up and then I'll call it a day. Although the terrain was much more rugged now it was all relatively easy. On reaching the near enough halfway point I sat down on a flat slated service and opened my cold drink, taking in the magnificent panoramic scenery that lay around me, now John, what do you do now? Do you make your way back down or carry on this enjoyable climb? It always seems in life when you have to make a quite important decision a little voice in your head seems to butt in, this little voice was saying if you go back now, you're probably regret it the rest your life, and you may never get the opportunity ever again, and I'm sure it also said, don't forget he who dares wins! Ok voice you win, I shall carry on up. I like to think that little voice I heard was in fact the positive side of me coming from the engine room of my mind! So up and onwards I ventured, and I noticed the higher I'd climbed, it started to feel chilly, as the sun had now disappeared, and I was starting to climb through the cloud base, time to sit down me thinks, and eat my welcoming Mars bar, and finish the rest of my drink. As I sat there, I was told by a descending climber that just around the next ridge was the three-quarter way mark, this lifted my spirits enormously he also told me it wasn't a good idea to climb at this height in just a T-shirt, as the weather can close in very quickly. I thanked this kind soul for his prudent advice, and made it to the three-quarter way mark. What do I do now? The climber had told me to reach the top would take about 45 minutes, and as I now above the cloud base and could see clearly above me, I decided to press on, in for a penny in for a pound I thought. The going was much harder now, as underfoot, there were rocks and boulders, and with only trainers on, my feet were now starting to hurt, but never mind I must carry on regardless, climbing ever higher, I spotted a sign which read to the summit 1 mile, this gladdened my heart immensely, and it gave me an extra spurt, and before I knew it I was standing on the summit of the tallest mountain in the British Isles. Around me were the remains of an old weather station, which had been abandoned years earlier. As the weather had closed in, the view around was restricted, as I turned around to start making my way down, I felt quite emotional, but the same time, quite proud of myself, because here I was an elderly old grey at 67 years of age achieving a lifelong dream. It had taken about four hours to complete the climb and as the mountain was over 4000 feet not bad going. I was the only one on the summit at the time, so I would be on my own on the descent, and as it was quite chilly now, I decided not to hang about any longer, climbing down is so much easier than climbing up, and two a half hours later, I found myself at the same spot where it started off on the climb. As I had only started off that morning to go for a walk with no intention of climbing the mountain, I never took the camera with me, and the regret is, I have no photos of the occasion. I now faced a 5 mile journey back to the hotel, as it was not on a bus route. So with aching feet, starving hungry, and very thirsty, after what seemed like a lifetime, I finally made it back to the hotel. It was now dark and it had taken me so long to walk to the hotel the time was now 10 p.m., Pat's first words to me were, "where have you been? We have all been worried about you. We're just about to send a search party to look for you, I explained to Pat, I got carried away and just had to climb that mountain. She soon brought me back down to earth saying "well the kitchen staff said they couldn't save your dinner, so the only thing I could get you for dinner was a banana, and a cold drink". Welcome home to the returning hero!

Poem

A coach holiday to Scotland we booked for a week,
It was lots of miles of walking I did seek.
Firstly I'd hike to Ben Nevis and decide when I'm there,
If climbing that mountain was an option, but would I dare?
Arriving at its base I started to climb a short way,
Will take things slowly remembering that I'm an old grey.
Getting to the halfway point was like climbing a steep hill,
Even your average schoolboy would find it wasn't a big deal.
With only a T-shirt on I started to feel the cold,
Was this because I was an ancient wrinkly and so old.
I made it to the top in spite of my age,
Another stage in my life, to be added to that page.
Just taking part in the climb had given me such pleasure,
One of them moments in life I will keep and treasure.

Returned to London to work

It was a week before Christmas, and it was the year 2006, and my old work mates invited me down to the Cross Keys pub in Moorgate for a get together, it was so nice to see old faces, they talked about jobs and events, that I had been part of with them, and I began to feel quite nostalgic for the great working days of the past, after a while, the conversation then centred around me, how was I keeping? Was I enjoying retirement etc, when I told them I still worked on various jobs, one of the office managers boldly said, I've have a new contract starting in the New Year, that may suit you John, as I see that you're still fit and active, think about it, and if you're interested, give me a ring. That's something worth thinking about I thought, I'll see how I feel about it in the New Year. As time seems to flyby when you're older, the New Year had started and it was a February 2007, I had a telephone call from the same engineer, who had offered me a job at the Christmas get together. What are your thoughts about me returning to work for my old firm I asked Pat? If you think you're capable of it, go for it she said, on the other hand you must be quite mad to even be considering it at your age. As it was still wintertime and there's not much to do that time of year, I phoned the engineer and said I would start work with him on the Monday, the job was at Chancery Lane in Central London. The job was an office block and fire protection was required on the upper floors from the 16th to the 25th floor. There were no windows yet installed, and a cold winter's wind came gusting in through the floors, you couldn't feel your fingers most of the time, so I did have doubts about being there? No not a bit of it, I loved it, I was back to the work that I had been doing for all those years! It's your birthday tomorrow John said Chris the fitter I was working with, I had worked with him for many years. How old will you be then he asked, only 68 I said, that is so old he said, you must be the oldest man ever to work full-time on a building site! He was probably right. I worked on the site until May, then packed it in I had really enjoyed the experience and was pleased I was still capable of doing the work!

AGE CONCERN

It was now a month since I had worked on the London job, and I started to get a bit restless, as luck would have it, I spotted an advert in the local paper for gardeners required for age concern, that sounds like the job to me for, even though I couldn't tell difference between a weed and a plant!

I went for the interview and was asked a few questions about pruning and general garden maintenance; I answered the best I could, as my knowledge of gardens was non-existent. The man and woman interviewing me looked in total bewilderment at the answers I gave them, there were probably thinking, has this man never seen a garden before and yet he wants to be a gardener! Just one more question to ask you John, can you explain to us, the meaning of the word cultivate? Cultivate, I said, in a confident manner, but thinking to myself this sounds like a new hand cream that has come onto the market, I said yes, it's where you prepare the ground for planting and the growth of plants and crops, I wonder what they make of that answer? Just one more thing John, why do you want to work for age concern? Well I answered, I like old people, because I am one myself, and I get on well with people. Thanks John, the man said, please wait outside, while we talk over things, 10 minutes later I was called back into the office, and once again sat down opposite them, the lady smiled and said you'll be pleased to know will be offering you a job as a gardener, when can you start? All I can say, is the ridiculous answers I gave to their questions they must be desperate for a gardener or no one else had applied! After a couple of induction courses, and the obligatory health and safety course, I duly picked up from a warehouse all my garden equipment, and was ready to be let loose on all those grannies. Age concern would supply me with all the details of what the householders wanted done to their gardens, so I would turn up to do what is required and then move onto the next house. Most of the ladies were in their middle eighties or older but were young ladies when the Second World War was on, so they all had wartime stories to tell. What made all these gardening jobs more interesting was the different houses I went to, some were in upmarket areas but others in not too well off parts of town, one such house was in a shabby part of town and the worksheet for the house stated that all that was needed was a general tidy up, but on arriving at the bungalow I had to fight my way to get to the front door, because the garden was so overgrown with trees, brambles and bushes that it was like hacking your way through a jungle. I managed to locate the front door and was not a surprised to find the doorbell hanging off, I couldn't knock on the letterbox as there was only a hole where it used to be, why was that voice inside my head telling me to turn around and run? So banging on the door three or four times I got no reply, that's good I thought to myself he's not in, I was just about to leave when I heard this voice shout out okay, okay you don't have to bang the door down. I must have waited a couple of minutes while locks unbolted, padlocks opened the door bolts pulled across, Is this a drugs factory I'm thinking? The last bolt was pulled across and the door slowly opened and sitting in a wheelchair with only one leg was a hunched up old man, but about time you showed up he snapped, I been waiting two months for someone to call round, and glad to see they have sent a man around at last, because the last three they have sent have been birds and they've taken one look at the work to be done and scarpered, I keep telling your people its too much for a woman to handle? I'm John I said, I'm from age concern, I know who you are idiot, you have an identity badge dangling from your neck, this was my polite welcome from Mr Jones, not only did Mr Jones have an attitude problem but he was a cantankerous old sod. You had better see the back garden before making up your mind if you want the job, because to be honest with you, as soon as your people see the back garden they make excuses and flee. You'll have to come through the front room to get to the back garden at the entrance at the side is blocked, and you won't get through, he said with a smirk. The front room was very dark and no wonder, next to the Patio doors, were two large trees, I managed to partly squeeze the doors open and facing me was a mass of vegetation, it was so dense and tangled it was impenetrable, a jungle in fact, no wonder others had observed it and quickly done a runner. I made my way back to the front room, and he must have seen the shock on my face, it's a bit of a mess isn't it? he said, I told your people in the office that I haven't touched a garden in seven years, I lost my leg 17 years ago and that's the last time I was out there? So what do you reckon? Do you want to take it on? I don't mind taking it on, but it will take some time to do it and at £10 an hour, can you afford it I asked? I have money put aside, so start it and we'll see how it goes. It took a month to finish his jungle and the garden was cleaner and tidier than the inside of his house. When you had finished a gardening job for a client, they had to fill in a form to say they were satisfied with the work done, and on the same form my comments I had about the client and their garden, so the following words are what I wrote in the comment section. "As I walked up the Path to access the work to be carried out at Mr Jones garden, I thought I'd stumbled on a film set remake of a Carry on up the Jungle, on making an inspection of both front and back gardens, I realised I had indeed discovered the lost jungle here in Milton Keynes. It is not a green bin Mr Jones requires to clear all his garden waste, but the largest skip ever made in this kingdom! Even the ground force team would have took one look at this overgrown jungle, and made their excuses and made a quick about turn. Mr Jones admitted to me he had not touched garden the past 17 years, but it looks like it could have been 70 years. On his worksheet for the work to be carried out on his garden, it stated that it would just require general tidy up of both gardens, this has to be the biggest understatement of the century! But being a man who relishes a challenge, I have made a start on the front garden, when I start working on the back garden I will need a chainsaw, and a long curved sharp jungle knife, as a hedge trimmer and the tree cutters won't touch it, this back garden will be a major project, but my jungle army training will come in handy. I'm hoping I will not discover a fully grown Congolese gorilla lurking in the undergrowth, thumping his chest, and defending his territory, Mr Jones had made the comment, I think you'll find my gardens are in a bit of a mess! I think he said that with tongue in cheek as I'm sure I detected a chuckle".

I worked for age concern that the rest of the summer of 2007, and then left them, as some more building work came up working with Don.

Peter Pan's Pipe Confession

Just were does time go, before I knew it, the year had moved onto 2008, and it was the month of May, and I was 69 years old, ever since retiring I had been meaning to go down to London, and hopefully see someone from the Royal Parks in Kensington Gardens, to confess to my part in the disappearance of Peter Pan's pipes, which is covered a few chapters back in the book. It was a warm May morning and I took the train from Bletchley to Euston, by going after nine old grey's get the cheap rate and getting a travel card entitles you to use all the London transport system. Arriving at Euston station I made my way to Lancaster Gate Underground station, which across the road from the station is one of the entrances to Kensington Park. I crossed the Bayswater Road, and after 10 minutes leisurely stroll, I found myself at Peter Pan's statue, the memories come flooding back it, was really 52 years ago when we were all hanging on Peter Pan's pipe when it suddenly came away in our hands. I made my way across the Serpentine Bridge and in front of me was an imposing Georgian building which is called the Magazine, from this building maintenance and running of the park is organised, I noticed a sign saying Park manager and knocked on the door, and a female voice said to come in, what can I do for you a young lady sweetly asked? It's a long story I said, but I'll come straight to the point, 52 years ago myself and some friends were swinging on Peter Pan's pipes, when suddenly they broke away from the statue, and the heavy bronze pipes fell to the floor, so we panicked and threw the pipe into the Serpentine, so I was just wondering, if this is of any interest to you? She replied, to be honest with you, I know nothing about these pipes, that was way before my time, but it's an interesting story, and yes, with them being the original pipes, it would be nice to get the recovered, oh my name is Theresa Short and I'm the assistant park manager, and your name is? Sorry I said, my name is John Banfield, well John, we don't have the facilities to recover the pipes, but every now and again, the police divers have training sessions, to the next time they have one, I can get in touch with you, and you can show them the area in the water you threw them. I said to Theresa, I know it was a long time ago, and I always have felt a bit guilty about the pipes, and would be delighted if they were restored back to the statue. I wished Theresa well, and with a handshake said with your charm and grace your days as an assistant manager will soon be over and you will be installed in your rightful place as a manager. She smiled sweetly; I am still waiting the developments to occur in retrieving them!

WHO WAS MY FATHER?

When I first came up to London from Bournemouth one of my first questions I asked my mother was what was my father like, and where, before I could say another word she shouted I don't want to talk about him, and I don't want you ever to mention his name again, as I grew up, I often wondered about him, as I only remembered seeing him once, when I was about four years old. The only thing known about him was his commendation certificate, that my sister Irene had managed to get hold of, stating that he gave his life to king and country in the Second World War! None of the other members of the family who lived in the Midlands knew anything about him, and what made the task even harder, he was not registered on the United Kingdom census. My three sisters Mary, Irene, and Jean and myself were keen to find out about our father, who was he? Where did it come from? And as I was writing my autobiography it would make the perfect ending to find out all about him. As he was not on the UK Census, there was a possibility he would have shown up on the Republic of Ireland Census, so with that in mind, we all decided we would embark on a search mission to Dublin, where we found out that all of the Republic of Ireland Census records are housed. My three sisters and I all made our way to Dublin, from our nearest airport, and thanks to Terry Bigley, a cousin who lives in the Midlands, who kindly put as in touch with a Dublin man known as PJ, who we all met up with on our second day there. He came with us to the census building in the centre of Dublin, this is where we were going to trace our father, I said confidently to my sisters, although the name Banfield doesn't sound an Irish name, but my thinking was, because he is not on the UK Census, he must be on the Irish one! We all signed in the census building went up to the first floor, there were hundreds of large books stacked on the shelves, there were five books with the initials B wrote on them so I eagerly scanned pages and were delighted to come across a page of Banfield's. As we didn't know his date of birth up, we assumed it was somewhere between 1905 to 1908 we quickly looked down the page for a match. There were about 15 Banfield recorded in the book, but unfortunately our nowhere man father was not amongst them, how can this be? He's not on the UK Census, and neither on the Irish one the mystery deepens. We spent a day looking round the lovely city of Dublin, and the next day we all returned home, very puzzled and none the wiser on his birthplace! It was in the beginning of March 2008 we all went to Dublin and the month had now moved on to June, I practically given up all hope of ever tracing the whereabouts of his place of birth!

For a few years now on most Sundays, Judy and I would meet up and spend a few hours on our bikes, taking in the local villages and places of interest, I called round to her house as usual to go for a bike ride and said to her where'd you fancy going today Judy? She's replied since it's the 15th of June and it's Father's Day, I thought it would be nice for us all to go to Bletchley Park (the old wartime code breaking place) because they're holding a genealogies themed open day there, and you never know you may be able to trace your father somehow! She said it more in hope than expectation! Judy's husband Lee, sometimes cycled with us, and he joined us this day. It's only about 3 miles from Lee and Judy's house to Bletchley Park, on entering the building we found a large hall had been set up with many stalls showing the best ways of finding your family tree, and how to go about it! By talking to some stallholders they would be willing to help search for your family tree, but it could be a costly undertaking, people react in all different ways when told a certain thing is going to cost them quiet a lot of money, some go away a say I'll think about it, some will say, oh I will ask my partner, and see what they think, and then would make a quick exit, but with me on hearing how much the cost was for all the research, my reaction was to go weak at the knees, sweaty, develop a dry mouth, and start feeling sick, but before I nearly collapsed in a heap from shock I heard Judy calling me, dad, come over here quickly, there is an exhibit over here and it's to do with the Commonwealth War graves commission, it is worth giving it a try you never know! A lady was just thanking a man for his help who had helped her with an enquiry, what can I do for you a kindly voice asked, looking up from his computer screen, I wonder if you can help me I started off, I'm trying to trace my father, the only thing we know about him, was that he was in the British Army, and it was probably in the war years when he was serving, his name was Philip Matthew Banfield, that's all we know! The man then typed in the name I'd given, sorry he sighed nothing has come off my screen with that name, that didn't surprise me, because up to now, I had a fruitless quest for him! Let's see what happens if I eliminate Philip from the name, the kind man said. There was a large screen behind where the man was sitting, so we were able to watch as he typed in just Matthew Banfield, there were about 10 second pause and then the screen came to life and what we all had wanted to know, after many years was now in front of us and the citation that came up on screen read "in memory of private Matthew Banfield, army number 1544577 Royal Pioneer Corps, who died aged 40, on the 23rd of February 1947, son of James and Christine Banfield, husband of Josephine Banfield of Paddington, remembered with honour in Kensal green cemetery. Commemorated in Perpetuity at the Commonwealth War Graves commission." I just couldn't believe what I was seeing, and I felt quite emotional and I could hear Judy's excited voice saying that we've finally found your dad, and my granddad, which made it more poignant, as both Stuart and Judy never knew their grandparents on both sides of the family, which was quite sad really. I thanked the man and lady from the War Graves commission for their help in tracing my father, and we left Bletchley Park in an elated mood, and we carried on with the bike ride to a village pub where we had a nice meal and drinks. I said to Judy it's all down to you, us finding my father, if you hadn't suggested that we went to Bletchley Park today, we would have never found out about my father, and it isn't it ironic it happened to be on Father's Day!

Now that I had his army number, all that was left for me to do was once again write to the historical disclosures section in Glasgow, and hope for the best, that they had records on him. After writing to them with all his details, I received three weeks later a large brown envelope with his complete army service history, and just as important, where he was born. I was over the moon with the information I received.

My Father's Army Service

As I gingerly removed his service records from the envelope I became quite excited, what was I about to discover about him? Looking through his army service records, it showed that his date of birth was the 5th September 1905, and he was 34 years old on enlistment to the army, it seems he signed on for service two months after war was declared which was on the 28th November 1939. The first surprise came when looking at the where were you born column, it stated in the parish of St John's in the county of Dublin, are you a British subject – yes. The surprising thing is two months ago we all went to Ireland to check the census and he was not on it! He joined up into the Royal Artillery as a gunner, but after six months service things started to go downhill somewhat because he was kicked out the Royal Artillery and for some reason, was transferred to the South Staffordshire regiment. It appears he was a bit of a lad, because things went even further downhill for him, and he was under close arrest from 20th December 1941 to 26th January 1942, awaiting trial by court-martial on the following charges, being concerned in the distribution of public property, and stealing the same. He was found guilty of the charge and sentenced to undergo detention for 42 days; after he was released from detention he was once again kicked out of a regiment and transferred to the Royal Pioneer Corps. It seems he mended his ways because he was not transferred again, maybe he thought if he carried on the way he was going he would run out regiments to go to! He stayed with the Royal Pioneer Corps was until the 10th January 1944, and was discharged as unfit for service because of a gastric ulcer of all things. At his court-martial my father was charged with distributing and stealing public property, but in his defence I would say, he was showing his entrepreneur skills being very enterprising and showing he had the initiative to succeed. To me, what remains a mystery is that he died two years after the war in 1947, with no war wounds, and yet my mother received a war widow's pension for the rest of her life, and father was listed as a casualty of war and buried in the military section of the graveyard, which is looked after by the Commonwealth War Graves commission! In his life as with his death there are more questions than answers!

Poem

Arriving at Judy's house that Sunday for our usual bike ride,
Let's try a different route she said one we haven't tried.
This Sunday at Bletchley Park they're holding their genealogy fair,
You never know you luck, possibly finding your father there.
These are the buildings where wartime coding people were based,
Wouldn't it just be great if somehow he could be traced.
The War Graves staff obliged and typed in the Banfield name,
Up on the screen behind him from the archives it came.
His army service record came up, even his date of birth,
Even to where he was born and raised on this earth.
Now no longer and nowhere man, he has been found,
To trace him was my mission I felt duty bound.
My search for him has finished its all over at last,
A new battle has started now it's to research his past.

The reader may be interested in the reason I decided to write my memoirs. The idea came about a few years ago while cycling with Judy, I used to tell her stories about things that happened in my life, and she would say why don't you put all them stories together and put them in a book, but when you're working full time you never have the time. I then retired and Judy once again mentioned about writing the book, by now I had reached 67 years of age, so I thought, why not, better late than never! The reader will also note that after every story or adventure that has taken place in my life, I sometimes finished it with a poem, although I know I cannot even think of myself as a poet, I do like poetry, and the reader can make there own mind up, as to how good or bad it is!

It is now September 2008 so the book has taken about 18 months to write, this was mainly written from about 11 p.m. to 2 a.m. each night, because I was still working by the day. I hope my family and friends or even if I am blessed with grandchildren, who read this book will have noticed that positivity runs through the book, as I've always tried to be in life, and that there has never been any room in my life for negativity.

Observations — Anecdotes — Poems

The Three Way Mirror

Looking in my bathroom mirror, I'm just a spotty youth,
Some would say rough around the edges and even uncouth.
Pretending that I am a grown-up man thinking I know it all,
Just only a dreamer thinking I am so cool.
Once again looking in that mirror middle age is now here,
Will I reach old age, so far and yet so near.
This body is now sagging my hair is falling out,
I'm gradually falling apart, that there is no doubt.
Now looking in that same bathroom mirror what do I see?
Who is that old man staring back at me?
It just seems overnight I have become an old grey,
And nothing can every keep them advancing years at bay.
Soon it will be a battle to get up the stairs,
Where has the time gone, bring back them youthful years.
You just cannot hold back time and that's for sure,
As you will never know just what's in store.

Double Trouble

Old is when your wife says, let's go upstairs and make love, and you reply, I can't do both!

You Just Can't Win

I was sitting at home quietly reading my newspaper when Pat the wife sneaked up on me and whacks me around the head with a frying pan, what did you do that for I asked? That was for the piece of paper I found in your pocket with the name Jane Briggs written on it. Don't be silly I said, a week ago, I went to the betting shop and that was the name one of the horses I bet on. She was satisfied with that answer and apologised.

A week later I'm sitting in my chair reading when once again she whacked me over the head with a frying pan this time knocking me out cold. When I woke up from this unprovoked assault, I ask her what was that for? She answered your f--king horse just phoned.

Food for thought

Scientists have discovered a food that his diminishes a woman's sex drive by 90%, is called a wedding cake!

Tiny feet but clean dishes

Why do women have smaller feet than men? It's one of them evolutionary things that allows them to stand closer to the kitchen sink!

Man's Best Friend

If your dog is barking at the back door, and your wife is yelling at the front door, who do you let in first? The dog of course, he'll shut up once you let him in!

This Body of Mine

How can I ever find the words to praise this fantastic, marvellous, unbelievable and complex state of the art creation, and one of nature's miracles, and what are all these things? It's the human body, and my own one in particular.

We started this partnership when we came into this world together all them years ago which was 1939. It is a partnership unique to us both, there were two of us, and yet we are one! We have experienced happiness, joy and laughter, but sometimes tears, sorrow and sadness, but together we have come through these emotions, it has bind our relationship.

When I have wanted to walk that extra mile, and worked those punishing hours, you have always given me the strength to carry on. We have an unbreakable bond that cannot be broken, and of course, you are my constant companion. We are both on the same side, and the premise, what's good for you is good for me holds true. I am expressing my gratitude and everlasting friendship, to my best friend this body of mine.

I have cared for you, as no one else can, as you have for me. I have given you a duty of care, which is your right and my responsibility, we came in this world together and we shall depart this world together, but I hope this partnership can go beyond three score years and ten, and we are able to live many more years with each other until of course, like everyone else, we reach that final judgement day, together of course.

I dedicate this book to my wife Pat, son Stuart, and daughter Judy. Without Pat's Patience and encouragement to push me on, my story would not have been told. It was Judy who persuaded me I should write my life story, after listening to some of my stories for the "tenth" time on our many weekend bike rides. I would like to thank Stuart making me the man I am today, a "pauper"! only joking son, and his help in getting my handwritten effort into type has been without question invaluable, and he should be mentioned in dispatches.

And how would I ever have managed without my spell master and my Collins English dictionary, if it hadn't been for these two friends, you would have been reading this book in broken English.

I end this book, to ask the reader, to fill in the missing day, month, and year of my departure from this Earth, as this will give people who read this book the amount of time I spent on this wonderful Earth!

John Anthony Banfield

                                      Born: 20th March 1939

                                      Departed:

Lightning Source UK Ltd.
Milton Keynes UK
22 July 2010

157351UK00001B/5/P